Igniting the Flame

William Merle Taylor

Arête West Publishing

Arête West Publishing
www.aretewest.us

Copyright © 2008 William Merle Taylor

ISBN: 978-0-6151-9917-7

Cover photo: Author at Mammoth Lakes in 1954 preparing for his senior cross-country season at USC.

IGNITING THE FLAME

CONTENTS

Acknowledgements

The editor, Cathy Fong, has shared with me every sentence, word, in conversation as well as in text. Her lasting support and dedication to this work is of lifetime worth. Dick Weston was a silent editor, Steve Emery of photographs/map. A life with such friends surpasses the word *acknowledge*. There were others whose interest and feedback came forth, especially Robert Griffith, Margaret Larrabee, Sheila Kaufler, Linda Gill, and Herb West.

The young people of Sir Francis Drake High School and Arête West formed with me a good deal of this book. Most importantly, however, have been my wife, Patricia, and our two sons, Jess and Cory. Patricia remains the goddess of travel that inspired those early trips to Greece, and who by marriage deepens and enriches life. Our two sons remain closely attached to everything I do. They are the companions of this work.

William M. Taylor
October 10, 2007
San Anselmo, California

PROLOGUE:
PROPERTY OF THE UNIVERSITY OF
SOUTHERN CALIFORNIA

A CHILL IN THE AIR told of fall. Shutters had been placed over the rustic cabin windows. It was going to be hard to leave the clean air of Mammoth Lakes, the high altitude, the smell of pine, and those afternoon thunderstorms. Compared with Los Angeles, Mammoth was paradise. I was preparing to return to Los Angeles for my senior year at the University of Southern California. I would later discover that there is life beyond sports, but in the summer of 1954 this was not evident to me.

The mountains were where I felt the most alive. I was there working at a resort for a camp run by the City of Los Angeles. I did not realize at the time just how much those six weeks at close to eight thousand feet were going to assist my distance running. Each afternoon I would go on a fairly easy run. Just a few miles each time, but daily. I would run from the resort down to Mammoth Creek, then eastward toward the old town. This route took me through sage and offered a view of the Sierra range that I felt belonged to me. On the way back to camp, I wove up through a forest of tall, green pine. I could smell the needles, bark, sap. A jeep road brought me through the woods to the resort. I would sprint the final hundred or so yards into the guest parking area.

The lettering on the back of my college warm-up top read: "Property of the University of Southern California." It could not have been said any better. I am afraid to say that, at the time, I measured my human worth by my half-mile clockings. After mediocre high school marks and two years at a junior college, I developed into a top collegiate runner, earning a full athletic scholarship to a national championship team. The letter I received from the head USC track coach put it directly: "We are looking forward to your becoming a national champion for the University of Southern California." This was incredible. My boyhood dreams had suddenly become reality. I was so proud. So fulfilled. And I had my senior year waiting for me in Los Angeles.

I believe my running identity began in the Los Angeles Coliseum one night when I was five or six years old. This intense memory only emerged later in my life. That night, no one was in the vast Olympic Stadium (which could seat 100,000 people), except my father and I. My dad sent me running, waiting for me in front of the Greek columns at the open end of the great stadium as I ran around the huge track. Above him was a flameless caldron that had received, by torch, the fire from Olympia, Greece, for the 1932 Olympic Games.

Some of you will be able to picture where the USC football team comes out of the tunnel at the closed end of the Coliseum. But on my run around the track that night, all I can remember is a lonely light above the dark, threatening tunnel. I was scared as I ran down the track toward my father. Surely, monsters were within the tunnel and coming after me. I remember looking down and wanting my short legs to go faster and faster. I just had to hope that I could escape whatever might be after me.

It was from that tunnel that my track hero emerged in 1947. I was thirteen. The feature race of the meet was Mel Patton of USC against Herb McKenley of Illinois. I can still hear the sharp, piercing noise of the starting pistol that whined out of the tunnel. There was suspense as a large track crowd of some ten thousand waited to see which great sprinter would emerge. Then I saw him. Tall, thin Mel Patton with the SC aegis on his running top came out alone. The partisan crowd gasped. Where was the great Jamaican, Herb McKenley? As they say in the sport, he was "left in the blocks." Patton finished just one tenth of a second over Jesse Owens's 220-yard world record. Mel Patton became my track hero not only because he ran for USC. I liked him because he was quiet, humble, and on his way to becoming the fastest man in the world.

Years later, at age nineteen, I came around the final turn by the tunnel and heard the Coliseum announcer say, in an excited voice, "Here comes Taylor!" I was closing fast on two great half milers on the anchor leg of a featured sprint medley relay, before the eyes of over forty thousand people. I had the fastest time that night and it earned me a full athletic scholarship to the University of Southern California. The little boy who had run down the same track toward his father was not on my mind that day.

One of my high school classmates wrote in my yearbook, "See you running for USC." Another wrote, "See you in the Olympics." Their enthusiasm for me came from my strong attachment to the sport and the university. Not my potential collegiate ability. Two years before the "Here comes Taylor!" in the Coliseum Relays, I had run dead last in my trial heat for the Los Angeles City finals.

I remember being seven years old and watching my father listening to USC football games on the radio at his father's home in Altadena. At the dining room table, he marked down on a piece of paper where the football teams were positioned on the field at a particular time. This was the same table where my grandfather made me eat my oatmeal. And threatened to whack me with a folded up newspaper when I got into trouble.

There was no television back then, just the radio and the wonder of imagination. Late in the game, with the radio moved to a windowsill for me because I was playing outside, I heard the USC fight song for the first time. It was the familiar, "Fight on for old 'SC / Our men fight on to victory." It became a kind of family hymn.

One afternoon my father took me down to the Trojan campus to watch a football practice. There were only a few spectators within the training compound. I was right there by the great USC athletes. I identified with two of the backfield stars, Robertson and Peoples, as they threw the football to one another in a mini-scrimmage.

Later I watched the USC track team working out. They practiced on the same athletic field that the football team used. There was not enough room for a circular track but there was a long straightaway. One of the runners was executing a particular stride for a coach. Long spikes made a noise as they sank into the dirt track. The USC coach, Dean Cromwell, perhaps the most famous track mentor in America at the time, was there that afternoon. My boyhood fantasies were real. In an intimate way.

In 1948, Dean Cromwell became the head coach of the U.S. Olympic Team. My hero, Mel Patton, after a disappointing fifth place finish in the Olympic 100 meters, won the 200 meters and anchored the 4 x 100 meters relay team to victory. Dean Cromwell led the USC track and field program to twelve national titles. He would tell me in 1955 after seeing me race against UCLA that I could "break the world record in the half mile" if I got my hips "loose."

Gulp!

Part I: Proximity is Destiny

M<small>Y EARLIEST MEMORIES</small> are of the city. We lived all over Los Angeles when I was growing up—in houses, apartments, duplexes, and for a little while, in a flat above the streetcar track at Highland and Santa Monica Boulevard. My neighborhoods were filled with movie stars, radio shows, trapdoor spiders to dig up, a hitching post on Hollywood Boulevard, football games and track meets at the Los Angeles Coliseum—it was an exciting place to be a young boy.

A world with horrible-looking maggots

We lived in a real house in Culver City. It was painted white and had a fenced-in backyard and a large walnut tree. My mother brought avocado sandwiches and corn on the cob out to the backyard there on my birthday. The date was likely about 1937, as the records tell of an enormous flood in Los Angeles that year. I can still see the powerful river flowing curb to curb past our home. It took my red wagon down the street. When I located it under some trees, I smelled a dead animal. It was a dog with maggots crawling all over it. I learned at that moment that I lived in a world with horrible-looking maggots.

"Why did a little boy have to die?"

My mother took me with her when she went out to see a woman friend who lived in the country. In the late 1930s you did not have to drive very far from Los Angeles to be out in the country. We came upon an accident. I can still see the tall sycamore trees alongside the road. We were told that a little boy had been hit by a car and killed. When I told my mother's friend about the little boy, I could not stop crying. I kept asking, "Why did a little boy have to die?" That afternoon, I saw the woman's breasts as she walked out into a hall nursing her baby. She was an attractive woman. I thought her breasts were beautiful. She covered herself when she noticed me, but I did not feel that I had done anything wrong.

We lived in a feeble gray duplex on Waring Avenue, about a mile south of Hollywood and Vine. Some of the radio shows were broadcast only a block or so down the street. When my mother had tickets for the *The Lone Ranger* broadcast, we received a free loaf of white Langendorf bread for attending.

Mrs. Dewey's orphanage was right across the street. I just missed living next door to Marilyn Monroe. Yes, the sex goddess was in this Hollywood orphanage until 1937. Little did I know that I would be living there in less than two years!

I had a big treat every Saturday morning because I was able to walk by myself to the Hitching Post to see cowboy movies. It was located just off Hollywood and Vine. There was an actual hitching post out in front of the theatre so that you could tie up your horse. And one was required to check in one's toy guns and holsters at the box office when purchasing a ticket. The "weapons" were hung up on pegs inside the booth. When you went up the aisle for candy at the Hitching Post, you walked slightly bow-legged.

Tim Holt and Wild Bill Elliott came across as real cowboys. Hopalong Cassidy was too old to identify with, and I did not like the way he tucked his pants into the top of his high black boots. But I liked him. The singing cowboys, Roy Rogers and Gene Autry, seemed phony. Artificial. I did not know then that, within months, I would be living in the country and having contact with real horses, corrals, ranch life.

I had my father to myself

We were living in Hollywood when my father took me with him one day to work on a house he was building in Bakersfield. Just the two of us. I had my father to myself. Bakersfield is about one hundred miles north of Hollywood. A contractor, my father let me swim in the water along the side of the new pool he had just completed. I was not ready to go out into the deeper end yet; I stayed right next to the edge. On the drive back that night, I stood behind the cabin of his flatbed truck, letting the warm summer wind sweep back my hair. It tickled. Unfortunately, my dad got a ticket. The cement mixer attached to his truck did not have a taillight.

One day I swiped a pigeon from a loft on a garage roof. My first pigeon. When my mother came home she made me take the bird right back. And I had to confess to the owner that I had stolen the bird. The same thing happened when I took some animal crackers from a nearby grocery store in that neighborhood. My mother made me take them back and confess to the owner. Good for Mom!

The Hollywood YMCA had summer camps up at Green Valley, near Lake Arrowhead. It did not register on me that the "C" in YMCA stood for "Christian." As a young boy, I spent a week up at the Green Valley camp one summer. We sang fun camp songs, even a hymn: "The Little Brown Church in the Wildwood." I believe there were a few prayers that recognized God. The YMCA, with its emphasis on sports and good values, remained a positive influence on me throughout my pre-college years.

I sold my raincoat for four cents in order to buy a creamy Mary Ann candy bar. Do you remember the peanut butter inside? America needed rubber for the war. So I received four pennies for my raincoat and bought the candy bar. I think my mother was upset.

I was roller skating in front of the duplex on December 7, 1941, when I heard that the Japanese had just bombed Pearl Harbor. I was eight years old. Japanese gardeners were disappearing from our neighborhood. We covered our windows at night to block out any light in case of an air attack. At this time, my mother decided to take us to live in the country, while my father went back into the Army Air Force as a flight instructor.

My earliest memories are of Los Angeles, but my life did not begin there. I was born in Seattle during the depression. We did not live there very long. When my parents returned to Los Angeles, my dad built that new home for us in Beverly Hills. Although we lived there only briefly, my mother did give him credit for having foretold that, someday, very expensive real estate would fill the whole area surrounding Beverly Hills. But she would also say with a certain sarcasm—even bitterness—that my father could not hold on to money. She said that it slipped through his pockets "as fast as he made it." Relatives told me that my dad was very innovative, talented. As a landscaper, he created narrow canals surrounded by lush green ferns and garnished with unusual bridges for the wealthy people of Beverly Hills.

My father loved to fly. He had lied about his age in order to join up and become a pilot in World War I. My mother would brag about how Bill flew with the popular aviator, Billy Mitchell, over Washington, D. C. after the war. She also enjoyed telling about how playful he could be. When they were courting, he once flew a private plane down close to the classroom in Claremont where she was teaching. This led to his license being suspended for a while.

Shortly after Pearl Harbor, my father began accumulating flight hours so that he could return to the Army Air Force as an instructor. Around that time, in 1942, he stopped living with us. We were not together as a family. The duplex was the last place we lived where my dad slept at our home. One time we went to see him in a hotel. He had a terrible case of poison oak. My mother said that was why was he was staying there, something about him being more comfortable? I believe they were separating at this time.

We needed money. My mother was able to locate a teaching position way out in the country in a place called Newhall. The cowboy town was on the other side of the hills, to the north of the San Fernando Valley.

We moved into a red cabin-like shack that was squeezed in between a couple of other ones. Right across the street was the only school in Newhall, with kindergarten through the twelfth grade all on one campus. There was one main street in "downtown" and it had a drug store, a five-and-dime and a motion picture theatre. The movie theatre was called the "All American." That was about it. Perfect!

I was very happy in Newhall. The "Huck Finn" life offered me many adventures. One day, after a heavy rain, we took some wooden planks and made a raft. Another time we hitchhiked out to Saugus and caught some baby chipmunks at a pig farm. When I got home, one bit me. I had to worry about rabies. We used sheets of tin to slide down steep hills on top of dry oak leaves. One can really pick up speed that way. The milkshakes at the drugstore were thick, creamy, and very cheap. And you got to drink the whole milkshake: what was left in the tin container, too.

I fell in love with my fourth or fifth grade teacher, Mrs. Bishop, in Newhall. I thought she was beautiful. One Saturday morning she had me come out to her house on Lyons Avenue to do some yard work. I am sure my feelings about her were obvious. Mrs. Bishop gave me

My dad holding me

oatmeal cookies and hot chocolate after I had raked up some leaves in the front of her house. She had poise, wore glasses with thin silver rims that made her appear intellectual. Mrs. Bishop would often wear a white silk blouse; she always looked neat and clean.

At a Saturday morning school event, I told someone, "I wish Mrs. Bishop was my mother." I did not realize that my mother was within hearing distance. If looks could kill... But it was true. I did not always like her. Or better, my mother frequently made me feel uncomfortable that she was my mother.

Two of my friends, the Donaldson brothers, had two horses. R. E. Prather and John Burkert actually lived on small ranches. These four were my closest grammar school pals.

The Donaldsons lived at the southern end of the town. Their father was the manager of the Newhall electric plant. While walking home one afternoon, I made up a cowboy song—"I'm a singing cowhand just a-singing away / just a singing cowhand, riding all day / I'm a singing cowhand, just a-moving along / I'm a-singing, / for I want to ride on the prairie, where I sleep out every night," etc. It concluded with, "I'm a-singing." I was nine years old.

One day, I was coming back from a ride on a big Donaldson horse when it suddenly took off and began racing at full speed toward the stables, which were still quite some distance away. Yes, I was riding bareback! And it was a long way down to the street below. I kept hoping that my "wide-body" horse would not suddenly shy and throw me off.

My father called one night and told my mother that he had picked out a horse for me. A tall one. Fifteen hands. But my mother said no, that we could not afford to feed it.

My mother, my younger brother Harold, and I spent a lot of time out at the Burkert ranch. They had a large corral. The rest of the property extended up over a hill toward Highway Ninety-nine. It is known as Highway Five today. I rode their buckskin bareback. Sometimes we climbed up on the donkeys. One of them would run up to a water trough and abruptly halt and lower its head. While I never plunged into the water, it was not because the donkey did not give it a good try.

Just before the Donaldson's, as you dropped down into Newhall on the old road from San Fernando, you could see the Prather ranch off to the right. My little friend, R. E. Prather, wanted to be a jockey. One day he rode the school principal around the cafeteria after the man tried to force us to eat something that we found distasteful. With a war going on, Americans were supposed to eat everything on their plates. When the principal demanded that we eat the food, R. E. suddenly leaped up to the top of the lunch table and jumped on his back. The little guy got him in a headlock. It was exciting, threatening, and hilarious. After a short ride, the principal leaned forward, grabbed R. E. by the heels, and flipped my friend over his head and onto the floor. R. E. was suspended for a few days. His mother blamed me. I was not invited out to their ranch anymore.

Doesn't it itch?

Johnny Barnhill told me, as we stood in front of the drugstore in Newhall, that his younger sister and her boyfriend had sex. I did not know about sexual intercourse yet. The girl and her boyfriend were only sixth or seventh graders. I asked him what that meant. How did they do it? Johnny told me "the boy puts his thing in the hole of the girl." I asked, "Doesn't it itch?"

There was no humor in what came next. This exciting information led to shame. I shared this fascinating discovery with someone else. Next thing I knew, there was a special assembly at the school library. Just for the boys. I had no idea what was up when I sat down at one of the tables. Then I was singled out as one of three or four who where spreading rumors about the Barnhill girl having sex. I felt humiliated, ashamed. Great introduction to sex, huh?

I felt even more humiliated because I was the teacher's boy. My mother did not discuss the matter with me. I do not recall her ever using the word "sex." At the same time, Mom could be quite natural. Natural? When she discovered that someone had put a snake in her classroom desk drawer, she remained expressionless. Picked it up, went over to the door and tossed it out into the schoolyard. Nothing said. Just poise. Cool!

I was very happy when my mother moved us from the row of red shacks to a small beach-like cottage with screen porches at the front and back. It was neat. And it had a small backyard with a large shed. I found myself some pigeons. I named my first bird Tuffy. He had a white head and white, creamy colored feathers extending out from his legs. Tumblers, or rollers, are the gymnasts of the sky. They can do multiple back flips—sometimes three, even six in a row. It is very important that they stop tumbling before they hit the ground, however. I really liked tumblers with feathers on their legs. Tuffy appeared to be wearing white shorts. His body, and most of each wing, was black with a bluish tinge. The wings had white feathers at their tips. Tuffy became my All-Time Favorite Pigeon.

I never did get my own horse. But one morning, almost magically, I discovered two small donkeys grazing in the small lot next to our cottage. A friend and I rode them out toward the Newhall ranch without a bit or hack-a-more. We were only a few blocks from the west end of town when I did a funny, awful thing. I took a broom handle from a refuge pile and stuck it up the ass of the donkey my friend was riding. The donkey took off full speed down a dirt road toward town. As my friend screamed, it became funnier and funnier. Fortunately, the donkey eased up before my friend and the animal reached any streets with traffic.

In Newhall, I had my first "sort-of" date with a Donna Jewel. She was to meet me at the motion picture theatre for the afternoon film. It turned out that we were a ceremonial date, a trial performance for the other girls at my expense. Tall, dark-haired, freckle-faced Miss Jewel stayed with her girl friends and never came over to sit by me.

In addition to teaching all day, my mother took a night job out at a war factory. I worried about her because she would have to walk in the dark from a bus stop to the plant. We did not have a car. She would return home close to midnight or later. I remember hearing her come in, feeling happy that she was back.

I only saw my dad once after we moved to Newhall. I can remember running up to him as he walked toward our cottage across the dirt parking area in front. My brother, Harold, ran with me. My father was wearing his tan Army Air Corps officer's uniform. He looked really handsome. It was 1943. He had flown into Newhall to see us. I had a dad!

I saw the smoke

I saw the smoke, heard the sirens. Something had happened out on the Newhall ranch out toward Highway Ninety-nine. I was sitting on my bike at the time. I even thought of riding out there. I would have discovered my father lying dead in the cockpit of the double winged Army trainer. The cadet that he was training had flown them into the power lines. A newspaper account said that the wires fell across Highway Ninety-nine, blocking traffic until the California Highway Patrol arrived at the scene. The plane, once entangled in the power lines, flipped over. A wing crushed my father's skull. My mother later told me that, to avoid such a fate, my father never sat in the cockpit that was directly under the wing. His body was not removed for hours, because the Highway Patrol had to wait for the Air Force officials to arrive at the crash scene. My dad had been coming to see us.

That night my little brother and I were sleeping outside behind the cottage. That was fun. We had a large roll-away bed. All of a sudden, the parking area lit up with bright white lights. The Highway Patrol officers had arrived with the news that my father was killed that afternoon. I felt bewildered, confused, strange. I can still see the smoke. I almost rode my bike out there. It was August 1943. I had just turned ten in July.

It had only been weeks since my father told my mother on the phone that my summer job bagging potatoes was good for me. Four cents a sack. Nine dollars for a full week of work. The flatbed truck picked us up at 6:00 a.m. You crawl on all fours, dragging a gunny sack between your legs and digging the potatoes from the loose, recently plowed soil. The peanut butter and jam sandwiches tasted oh so good at lunch time.

The papers told of how the student pilot had crawled away safely from the crash. The funeral for my father was held in Pasadena. An American flag covered the casket; it was presented to me at the conclusion of the service. It seemed heavy. Some woman, who meant well, said that I was now "the man of the family."

Both of my grandfathers were clergymen. Thinkers. Highly committed men. My dad's father, The Reverend William Frank Taylor, was a Methodist minister. He was born in 1862, during the Civil War. A graduate of Boston University, he moved his family from Massachusetts to Ohio, Kentucky, Indiana, and eventually, California. He died the year before my father's death, at the age of eighty. Fortunately, he missed experiencing the death of a son.

My grandmother Christine gave birth to my father on September 6, 1899, in Springfield, Massachusetts. Dad was the seventh of eight children in the family, but he was raised as the youngest because the eighth child only lived for just over one year.

Growing up, my father must have been influenced by liberal values in the home. His brother, Marcus, told me that William Frank Taylor had become more of a Unitarian by the time he was the pastor of the First Methodist Church of Pasadena.

My mother told me that my dad was an atheist. This puzzled me because she also said that his favorite hymn was "Abide with Me." That is a pretty heavy Christian hymn. She said that my dad loved to sing and that they had had taken singing lessons together.

People seem to remember my father mostly for his playfulness. My cousin Bobby was the one who first told me that my dad had more fun than anyone he has ever known. I admired Bobby. Whatever he did, he seemed to do it carefully, thoughtfully. He told me that one day when they were driving by oil derricks in Long Beach, my dad stopped the car and spontaneously climbed up to the top of one of them. Then he waved down to Bobby.

Can you believe what I missed—a father who loved to sing, who could be so fun loving? And what he missed—seeing me running in a USC uniform in the Los Angeles Coliseum? Instead, after the plane crash, I was alone, frightened, and put in an orphanage. I was taken from the countryside, separated from my pigeons, friends, horses, and placed in a terrifying environment. What if something happened to my mother?

My mother needed time to locate a higher-paying teaching job and then a place to live. This explained the orphanage. Well, not to a ten-year-old boy. I felt so lonely that first night in the infirmary at Mrs. Dewey's Home. Why in the hell did they isolate a frightened kid the first night that he was separated from his only remaining parent? I remember the clinic vividly: it was a small, white infirmary on the north side of the orphanage grounds. A nurse forced me to swallow thick castor oil. Mrs. Dewey only let visitors come and see the orphans on Sundays. I remember really wanting to see my mother more frequently. I am quite sure she did not come every week.

We slept in a large dormitory on the second floor of a large, red brick building. The girls were in the southern section, immediately across from the gray duplex. My brother Harold's cot was five or six beds away from me down the aisle. Suddenly my brother and I were just two of many boys sleeping in a large, impersonal dormitory. No roll-away bed out in the backyard next to the pigeons.

It was easy being the sport hero at a small orphanage. I ran for touchdowns as I pleased. The other orphans encouraged my fantasy of becoming a great football player. I did have a sense of the field. And perhaps the most speed. One of the girls at the orphanage, Adeline, kissed me on the cheek one night. She was the one I liked. I did not wipe the lipstick off until the next day. It would have been more memorable if she had been Marilyn Monroe.

I was "called out" by a Vine Street Elementary School classmate while walking back to the orphanage one day. I took him. His mother reported the fight to the principal and I was called into the office, asked to explain my side of the story. I did. The principal congratulated me.

I wanted to get back to Newhall to see my pigeons. My friend John was taking care of them. One night I talked a friend into escaping with me. My friend and I climbed out the second floor window and hiked up Vine Street. This took us past Hollywood Boulevard, and then over to the Cahuenga Pass. We walked up the center of the divided freeway, past the Hollywood Bowl. It felt so strange being out there alone with the traffic of two major freeways sweeping by on each side of us. I had not thought about how long it would take just to reach the San Fernando Valley. It was late by the time we arrived in Studio City. As we approached Lankershim and Ventura, not that many yards from the entrance to Universal Studios today, I remembered that once my mother took us to visit a close friend just a hundred or so yards from that intersection. This woman and her family lived right across the parking area from our small cottage in Newhall before they moved to an apartment in Studio City. We were tired, and still maybe twenty to thirty miles from my pigeons.

I can still see that cream-colored apartment door. The entire family was up, even though it was about eleven. I told them that we had gone out for a haircut and gotten lost. I had first seen Keith Rescoe, the tall, good-looking son of the family, when he was in the twelfth grade at our Newhall school. I was surprised that night to find that he had joined the Navy, was married, and had a child. Keith told us to jump into the back of his pickup truck and drove us to the orphanage. He was wearing a Navy PT coat. Gave me a silver dollar. What a nice guy.

Around midnight, we climbed back through a window onto the second floor. My little brother, Harold, came right over. I think he slept with me the rest of the night. Poor kid. Now I realize that I left my seven-year-old brother at the orphanage. That must have been extremely frightening.

Adeline and the other girls would not even look at me the next morning. They were made to feel that I had been disloyal to Mrs. Dewey. Twenty years later a Freudian psychoanalyst would tell me that my running away from Mrs. Dewey's Home was the healthiest thing he had heard about me.

Pigeons, ducks, and movie stars

HAROLD AND I SPENT six months at the orphanage before my mother was settled enough to take us back. She located a two-bedroom apartment less than a block from the entrance to Warner Brothers in Burbank. It was only a couple of blocks from a neighborhood of movie stars in Toluca Lake. What a place to grow up! There were two lakes, a golf course, motion picture sets across the L. A. River and a gravel parking lot behind our garage that allowed for barefoot football games.

One of the first things I asked my mother to do was to retrieve my pigeons for me. I got my favorite bird, Tuffy, back. I loved being able to just go out to the pigeon cage and watch them. In a certain way, they were my family.

Two brothers, Alexander and Stanley, lived upstairs in our apartment building. They had recently moved to Toluca Lake from Philadelphia. Alex built a pigeon loft for me. Both brothers helped put up a basketball backboard with a rim toward the back of the driveway. Stanley, the younger brother, was playing "B" basketball for North Hollywood High School at the time. North Hollywood? Even though the apartment was in Burbank, just over the county line, we were able to attend a Los Angeles City school.

I increased my number of pigeons. Then I added ducks and banty chickens to my farmyard behind the garage. And I had a dog. And a cat, always a cat. I brought the country to Toluca Lake.

Saturday morning was a time to fish, catch ducks, or play football on the Lakeside golf course. The two lakes were alongside the clubhouse and fairways of the golf course. Expensive homes surrounded the upper lake. Immediately to the south was the meek Los Angeles River. Ugly cement flood-control walls channel the water today. Just beyond the river were motion picture sets. We would go and see a

Frankenstein movie at a theatre, then look across the river to the sets the next morning and see where the monsters were filmed. And when the full moon was out, Wolf Man was roaming around over there. He was the scary one for me. His hair began growing over his entire face under the light of a full moon; his savage-looking teeth were ready to rip into one's flesh.

I loved being able to walk just a couple of short blocks over to the lower lake on a Saturday morning. The smell remains with me. It was a kind of stench, like stagnant water, yet not repulsive. I remember the sound of the dragonflies, too. We mostly caught blue gill, but there were also bass patrolling back and forth just off the shore.

One morning I discovered a very large bass at the deepest portion of the lower lake. I ripped some blue gill meat off a fish I had just caught and placed it on a deep-sea hook. I did not have a fishing pole, so I used a kite string. I waited until it swam out of sight so the splash from the bait hitting the water would not change his route. My heart was pounding. He would be back. The big bass appeared right on schedule. He went immediately over and swallowed the bait. Within seconds, I was dragging a twenty-seven inch fish up the bank. Barefoot, I worried about climbing through nettles.

I walked the two blocks back to our apartment with my hand through the bass's mouth. The tail was touching the sidewalk. I filled the bathtub with water and was surprised that the bass was still very much alive. He could not even turn around. My mother was quite upset and she sold the fish to the neighbor upstairs for ninety cents.

I caught three baby ducks shortly after they had hatched in a nest alongside the lower lake. They, too, went into our bathtub. They were really cute paddling around in the water. But my mother blew up when she saw them. So out they went with the pigeons and banty chickens. I named the ducks Huey, Dewey, and Louie, of course. Louie was my favorite. He would turn his head sideways and look up at you with one eye. These were happy times.

NOTE: See Appendix, for a map of this Toluca Lake neighborhood.

I could see the advertisement for *The Outlaw* from my bedroom window. It was on top of the mountain above Warner Brothers that separates the San Fernando Valley from Hollywood. The "Hollywood" sign you see continuously on television and in motion pictures today is just below where *The Outlaw* banner was on display, but on the other side of the mountain. The notorious Howard Hughes produced this Western. I have no idea how I got into the theatre. I suppose my mother took us. In the movie, when Jane Russell leans over, displaying her breasts, this young boy found them attractive. No hesitation. I was ten years old.

Bing Crosby came walking down a fairway toward us one morning. We were searching for golf balls in the reeds along the riverbank. In his low, familiar voice, he said, "Hello men." Yes, he wore that hat and had a pipe in his mouth.

We played tackle football just off one of the main fairways at the country club. Or up at the North Hollywood Park with its large grass fields under eucalyptus trees. We considered the Lakeside Country Club pool our swimming pool. Even privately-owned rowboats that we found docked on the upper lake were ours to use. "Private property" did not apply to Huck Finn kids. It was our neighborhood. Today we would likely be shot. The country club is locked up. Members only!

You had to know that we were going to cross that river and sneak into Universal Studios to explore those motion picture sets. One day we did climb, hand over hand, over the river on a cable. It was very hard to let go and drop down on the far shore. Our hands ached, but we were frozen because of the distance that we had to fall.

It was not long before the security guards captured us over by a pond. The pond had been used in World War II movies to represent the ocean in military landing scenes. The security police pretended that they were going to keep us locked up for the night, but only for a moment did we worry; we knew that they were going to let us go.

My mother's initial teaching job was in Van Nuys, at the McKinley

Home for Boys. I had to wait before I could enter a public school, so I was back in an "orphanage" during the day. But this time I was an outsider and "the teacher's boy." Fortunately I could leave the Home every afternoon. My classmates had to stay and sleep in a large dorm. I became more acceptable when I showed my speed in a rugby match. I ran the length of the field before I got rid of the ball. In the touch football games, I was still able to pick off passes, score touchdowns.

A sixth-grade jerk let it be known that he did not like me. He kept harassing me. I wanted to impress my classmates with my courage, so I put my shoulder into him as we passed each other in the hallway. Later that day, he delivered a swift blow to my nose. As I bled profusely, an older guy who had become sort of my bodyguard kicked and pounded my enemy. I should have done something to stop my protector. This "Castle" had not started the fight. I believe I said that it was not his fault.

"Oh, Frankie!"

At this time, "bobbie sockers" were fainting over Frank Sinatra. It was the mid-1940s. While I thought their hysterical behavior stupid, their antics served us well when we saw Frank Sinatra approaching us in his new kayak on the upper lake. We had "borrowed" a rowboat from one of the mansions. He seemed unsure of himself, tentative, as he tried to turn it around in the narrow lake. We were unmerciful. Standing on one side of the rowboat, we fell over backwards and screamed, "Oh, Frankie!" The man with the singing voice that would be dominant over the next fifty years was not amused. No wave, no smile. He just paddled away. We were just kids. Sinatra always was a jerk!

In those days, we walked a lot. Sometimes we went down the full length of the Lakeside golf course to Lankershim Boulevard. Then we crossed over the river, going past the entrance to Universal Studios to the intersection of Lankershim and Ventura. From there we would catch the trolley to Hollywood, or all the way to the Los Angeles Coliseum. Sometimes on Saturday mornings we would walk through the Toluca Lake neighborhood listening to football games on the radio, then up to the Lakeside Pharmacy on Riverside Drive. One time

John Wayne came out of the drug store. His face looked red and he did walk with a tilt. But this was no big deal. We were used to seeing movie stars. They were a natural part of life in Toluca Lake.

"Thanks for the memory"

My neighbor, Stanley Klein, was with me when we said, "trick-or-treat" to Bob Hope. We were surprised when he answered the door and invited us into his living room. There he was, the most popular comedian in America, seated in a chair across from us. Hope looked at Stanley and exclaimed, "Eek what a beak! Is that a hose or a nose?" I felt defensive for my Jewish friend, but Stanley thought it was very funny.

It was during this time that I came to love the scent of freshly cut grass from the lawns of the mansions. We moved our way through the Toluca Lake neighborhood with a portable radio in order to hear the football games being played in the East. In the mid-1940s, Bill Stern and Harry Wismer were the best-known national football announcers. In certain ways, the radio was more exciting than television would be. Wismer, with great anticipation, would say, "Army kicks off. It's a high end-over-end kick going down to the five-yard line." Imagination is a wonderful treasure. Glenn Davis and Doc Blanchard were the two great Army running backs. I liked Davis the best.

At night, Harold and I played basketball games out in the driveway. I hung a light bulb out of my bedroom window. The neighbors could hear the bouncing of the ball well into many an evening. These make-believe games between my brother and I were intense. We imitated the great teams and players of the day. I would be the Whiz Kids of Illinois, and Harold would be Kentucky with their two great players, Groza and Beard. Or we would pretend to be USC and UCLA stars. I would take Bill Sharman of USC; Harold would be Don Barksdale of UCLA. I even imitated the noise of the crowd after one of us made a shot.

Harold, who was three years younger than I, would become a much better basketball player. But during those early years, I controlled the score. I was able to make the games dramatic, suspenseful, by keeping them close. One time he accused me of cheating. This was so absurd that I cracked him across the jaw with a hard right. When I saw my little brother reach for a hammer in the garage, I took off for the corner of the apartment. Just as I was making the turn it came twirling about five or six feet over my head.

My earliest track meets were down the driveway between the apartments. My brother and I would place bamboo poles on cardboard boxes, creating flights of hurdles. The shot put? Out back behind the garage. A large rock would do for the iron bulb. We had the pole vault back there, too. No landing pad or sawdust, just a stick for a vaulting pole and the ground. I clearly was not going to be a thrower. Or a pole vaulter.

Tuffy was missing. I remember seeing the man who owned the parking lot next to mine walking around with an air rifle. Tuffy and his mate often landed on the telephone pole that separated the parking lots. The man could have shot my favorite bird! I began a search for my missing pigeon. I wanted to believe that I saw Tuffy in a cage up on Riverside Drive. The loft was set on a vacant lot one block from Bob Hope's estate. This pigeon had a white head, long white feathers extending from its legs. So I pretended that it was Tuffy. Swiped it. It was not Tuffy. I had taken someone else's pigeon. Frank Clark tracked down his bird. I had to give it back. Frank was my age. There were red birthmarks on his face. His dad was a big, overweight lawyer who always had cigar juice dripping from his mouth. I heard later that Frank's mother was institutionalized for mental illness. Frank was a good guy, a kind, sensitive person. Even though we never attended the same school, we became close friends. Frank Clark taught me some things about character, friendship.

When I needed to move my pigeons and ducks, Frank Clark came through for me. The vacant lot next to his apartment had available space for my loft and pens. The eviction of my animals came about after a neighbor's complaint to the police about the number of them I had in my farmyard. Frank's lot was over a mile away, but I had a bike, the kind with those wide handlebars.

A junior high school friend, Buddy Beatty, brought me into his Studio City pigeon-racing club. His father had birds with pedigrees from European countries. Pigeon racing is big over there. Roy Rogers was a member of the club. It had only been a few years since I had seen his movies at the Hitching Post theatre in Hollywood. Roy Rogers came one of the nights that we were delivering our birds for a weekend race. I met the singing cowboy in the driveway of the club secretary in Studio City. He was wearing a creamy colored western suit and expensive-looking cowboy boots. Roy Rogers seemed gentle, shy, like a nice man. He did have those thin slits for his eyes.

I can think of three people whom I measured by their cowboy boots. In addition to Roy Rogers, one will be a handsome Gregory Peck-type packer in the High Sierras, the other the most publicized American track athlete of the mid-1950s.

Roy Rogers surely stocked his loft with pedigree birds. A pigeon I entered in the race that night was a young offspring from two pigeons I had trapped in the McKinley Home barn. Yes, from a barn on the acreage of the Home for Boys where I had gone to school for a brief period. It was an old, run down place. I spotted the birds up in the rafters. How did I catch them? I used an orange crate from a grocery store. You hang thin wires down from an opening, so that the pigeon can push its way in to reach the grain. But the bird cannot come out because the wires come up against a ridge when being pushed the opposite way.

On race day, I saw the McKinley Home barn bird come in low. It folded its wings back and landed on the telephone pole across Riverside Drive. Exciting! It had just flown 200 miles, from Madera or one of those San Joaquin Valley towns, to me. Later in the day, when the club members gathered with their sealed pigeon clocks that recorded the time of arrival for their birds, I learned that my little hen that lacked a pedigree had beaten all of the ones that Roy Rogers had entered in the race.

I was usually self conscious of the
spread between my teeth.

My early USC hero football hero was Ted Tannahill. He would break free on long runs for touchdowns. In 1946, on the gravel parking lot by Warner Brothers we would play football, barefooted. I would pretend that I was Ted Tannahill.

My mother drove us to sporting events all over Los Angeles. I do not remember any other mothers or fathers taking us all the way down to the Coliseum or over to Gilmore Field. One time she actually fit seventeen of us into her Club Coupe. We were headed for a football game at McKinley Home. My teammates were hanging out of the trunk. This game took me back to the field where, a couple of years earlier, I had broken free on a long run in a rugby game. Now I was up against some of those same grammar school classmates with my unofficial North Hollywood Junior High sandlot football team. We did not have any uniforms. Each kid had to provide his own pads and helmet. Early in the game, playing defensive halfback, I perfectly timed a pass thrown out in the flat by a familiar quarterback and ran untouched into the end zone for the first touchdown. I knew that Emerson was going to float one out there. My teammates were all over me. I was fulfilling my boyhood football image.

In the second quarter, Richie Morse made a clean, beautiful tackle on one of the McKinley Home players. Unfortunately, Richie broke the guy's leg. The superintendent of the school was so upset that he called the game. Richie—the most talented athlete in our class—and I were good friends throughout high school. At times, we came into direct competition with one another. I respected his ability, and the way he carried himself. Richie was not a painful rival.

Unlike Richie Morse, Bert Convy became a difficult friend. He lived across the street from me in Toluca Lake. The first time we met, we wrestled and fell into a ditch, and he won. Over the years, Bert always seemed to find a way to torment me with his teasing remarks and put-downs. He twisted things just enough to make me feel defensive.

There was an indication that I had middle-distance running ability when we were having a decathlon. When we simulated the 1500-meter event by racing around the block from my apartment in Toluca Lake, I left my friends way behind. I flew past the entrance to Warner Brothers and then by Lanes pool hall, uncontested. When I arrived at the apartment driveway, I was all alone. I was only competing against three or four of my friends, but two of them were outstanding athletes. I ignored this early evidence. I had good lungs and decent speed, but I wanted to be a sprinter or hurdler.

A Patti let it be known that she liked me. She was one of the best-looking girls in our junior high. One day I was asked to stand next to this tall, beautiful seventh-grade girl for a photograph. That was it! End of contact. I remained attracted to Patti. Later, at USC, Patti will be chosen as one of the "Helen of Troy" coeds for the 1954 Homecoming Game.

In the 8th grade we advanced from photographs to "spin the bottle." A Toluca Lake girl, Kay, enjoyed kissing. Me too. Kay became my girlfriend for awhile.

Being a student was not on par with being an athlete for me. Nor did my mother encourage us to do any serious reading at home. I had

no sense of the value of an education. Our intellectual life on Toluca
Lake Avenue was zilch. This surprised me, because Mom was a music
teacher, and her parents made great contributions to education in China for over twenty years. She was very proud of having graduated from
Pomona, where she had been the lead soprano of the college choir.
Mom did work crossword puzzles. Endlessly. She was always asking
me, "What is a five letter word that begins with...?" I did enjoy reading *The Tattooed Man* by Howard Pease. In the adventure novel, a boy
steals his way on a freighter bound for the Far East and the ship is out
to sea before the captain discovers him aboard.

Every now and then, my mother would sing a few verses of the Pomona alma mater for us—just a few. The soprano did not sing anymore.
This seems so strange. An education at Pomona—one of the most respected colleges in America. A beautiful voice. Yet what I remember
most about my mother in the home was her endless cigarette smoke.

Who was Mary Elizabeth Hager Taylor? She was a Hager. The
Hagers were proud, intelligent people with a strong family identity.
My mother was born in Hong Kong in 1901. Her parents, Charles
and Maria Hager, were two brave, committed Christians who sailed to
China in 1883 as missionaries. She lived high above the wharves of the
Hong Kong Harbor until she was nine years of age.

Every year the Hagers would gather on Christmas Eve. Each year
at this gathering, there was a serious moment after dinner when
Uncle Harold would read from the Gospel according to Luke about
a child being born in a manger. I did not think about why my uncle
would suddenly become so emotional, why he choked up as he read a
few Bible verses. "Unc" was not given to sharing sentimental feelings.
Later, I realized that he was thinking of his parents, my grandfather
and grandmother, who died less than ten years after returning to Claremont from China.

For these Christmas Eve gatherings, we drove to Huntington Beach,
then to Fullerton, finally Claremont. On one occasion, the Hager evening was held above the streetcar tracks, then later at the Toluca Lake
apartment. I remember the long drive through orange groves on the
way to Fullerton. The ground fog and the lack of street light made it

Hong Kong, c. 1905.
My mother, *left,* with her dad, Charles Hager

difficult for my mother. My family insisted on my singing a couple of
Christian hymns in Fullerton. I knew the verses to *We Three Kings,*
and *It Came Upon The Midnight Clear.* As I do not remember going
to church or Sunday school with any frequency, I likely learned the
words from the radio and in school. Mary Elizabeth was not religious
about these traditional Christmas Eve readings. She tolerated them.
My mother told me many times that she was not religious. That growing up as the daughter of missionaries did it (she was very firm about
this). And that my father, whose dad was also a clergyman, was not a
believer, either.

Sun Yat-sen, Sun Yat-sen, Pearl Buck, Pearl Buck—this was the annual chant at our Christmas Eve gatherings. Again and again it was
repeated that Pearl Buck had written about my grandfather's relation-

ship with Sun Yat-sen. It was as though we were important because of his importance. Dr. Charles Hager was a highly respected missionary, educator, and medical doctor who lived in Hong Kong from 1883 until 1910. Ms. Buck, who later won a Pulitzer Prize for literature, wrote in *The Man Who Changed China* that Charles Hager was very helpful to a lonely young man, and befriended Sun Yat-sen. The future "founder of modern China" lived in the Mission House in 1884-1885 and was baptized there by my grandfather. Maria Hager was not mentioned at these gatherings, but I learned from my cousin Bobby that she started the first kindergarten in China.

The Hagers were not comfortable sharing personal feelings. Words of tenderness were not expressed. They felt them, even deeply, but expressing them was verboten. Instead, they expressed themselves through competition. I saw this as their way of avoiding personal conversation. There were always games on Christmas Eve, and the intensity to win and to have fun. I later learned, by reading eulogies written by his college friends, that Dr. Hager "played games to win." But they added, "He never made excuses when he lost."

My mother (or, Mary Elizabeth, as we called her) had shrewd eyes. She was frequently not far off the mark when she went after one of my friends. Ironically, most of my friends really liked her. This was because she could tease, be down to earth, speak her mind. But, still, why so critical? I did not like my mother being this way.

Unfortunately, my mother could be anti-Semitic. She would never be cruel to a Jewish person, but she expressed anti-Jewish feelings in our home. Later I became aware that Auschwitz was operating its gas chambers at the time we moved into the Toluca Lake apartment.

Nor did Mom have anything good to say about the Catholic religion. Surely she developed this opinion in China during her early years as the daughter of Protestant missionaries. But I doubt that her father would have approved of her attitude. She also had it in for Notre Dame and UCLA. She claimed that the Notre Dame football teams cheated by taping their fists and hitting USC players under the pile ups. Further, she claimed that the players would then go to a priest on Sunday to be automatically forgiven. When the great Hugh McElhenny was about to take his turn in the California state high school long jump finals in the Los Angeles Coliseum in 1947, my mother criticized him for spitting after he crossed himself. Come on, Mom. McElhenny went on to become one of the greatest halfbacks in the history of football. He also won three events that night in the state track and field finals in the Coliseum.

They ate my favorite duck

When I went up to see my birds on an Easter Sunday, I came upon yellow feathers scattered all around the duck cage. That fat lawyer, Mr. Clark, had instructed his sons to kill Louie for their dinner. They ate my favorite duck.

The annual junior high football game was a contest between the Winter and Spring graduating classes. The entire school was let out to watch the battle. I scored the only touchdown for the younger guys, and then threw the winning conversion pass. We won by a score of 7 to 6. My "All-American" football image was sustained. Richie Morse and I alternated as the two quarterbacks. A classmate, Betsy, who was tall and beautiful with a great figure, announced before the game that she would reward the boy who scored the winning touchdown for our team with a kiss. Betsy approached me while I was standing by my hall locker after the game and I was so rewarded.

Boyhood hero sets record

The announcer made it suspenseful. I was in the Coliseum on a Saturday afternoon, watching the Los Angeles City high school track prelims. The year was 1948, and in just a month I would graduate from the ninth grade at North Hollywood Junior High. The high school finals were to be held the following Friday night as part of the famous Coliseum Relays. The meet regularly drew a crowd of some forty thousand people since it always featured many of the best collegiate and Olympic stars in America.

Dick Nash was the announcer at the high school city prelims. That same day USC was up in the San Joaquin Valley at the Fresno Relays where my hero, Mel Patton, was to race Lloyd LaBeach of Panama over 100 yards. It was thought that one of them could set a new world record on the fast Fresno dirt track.

Nash was dramatic. He first announced, "We have the results from Fresno." The crowd grew quiet. Nash held his pause, then reported, "The time," pause, "9.3 seconds." This meant that Jesse Owens's world record of 9.4 seconds was broken. Then, after another pause, "The winner," pause, "Patton." My boyhood hero had just set the world 100-yard dash record. It was an incredible thrill. I felt personally connected to Patton.

Wonderful timidity

Darlene was more suitable for me than Patti or Betsy. And she liked me. Darlene was more cute than beautiful. She was not a lanky model type like Patti and Betsy, but she had a good figure, and she was one of those special girls who could really make a boy feel special. Important. She was very sweet. On our way home from the Coliseum Relays at night we were sitting close together in the backseat of a station wagon. Each time the car made a turn, we edged closer and closer together. Finally our lips met. What wonderful timidity. I blew a chance to be with Darlene on junior high grad night because initially I asked Patti. Patti had a date. I was provided with a girl within our circle of friends who was going steady with an older guy. I do not remember either of us enjoying the evening. And I lost Darlene.

Sports, innocence, and pimples

S UDDENLY I WAS ON a large campus with some twenty-four hundred students. The tame junior high days were over. Walking
across campus was intimidating. I was a nobody, a squirt. Some of the
linemen on the football team looked like college players. And some of
the girls, women. One classmate who was very well developed for her
age was the actress, Susan Ball. She was already receiving movie roles
at Universal Studios. During some of my years at North Hollywood
High School, we were literally locked in during the day. *Life* magazine
had ranked us one of the worst drug campuses in the nation. I was
not aware of the dealers, nor did I notice any of my close friends using
drugs. I was told after graduating that the 4-H club had actually been
caught growing pot on campus. And that a member of a social club I
belonged to, as well as a basketball star who went on to play at UCLA,
were both on heroin.

Most of the tenth grade guys did not date. It was as though the girls
placed us on hold, as if we were not ready for the likes of Patti or Betsy
yet. Our clique of girls would gather us together for parties, but they
did not encourage any romantic attachments at that time. We did not
come of age in their eyes until we became seniors. One exception was
Jack Bylin, a new friend from Chicago. He and Darlene began going
steady.

Fear of the unfaithful female stayed with me when I saw Gregory
Peck play an immoral cowboy in *Duel in the Sun*. While Peck would
normally be a quiet, reflective man of high integrity in his other movie
roles, in this film he was downright nasty. Jennifer Jones played Pearl,
a "half-breed" who tried to resist giving herself to Peck. She was going
to marry the "nice guy" played by Joseph Cotton. She tries very hard
to be loyal, but she fails. I will have occasion to suffer such a fate as the

"nice guy" shortly.

My positive role models were the serious actors who played major Hollywood movie parts. Gary Cooper, Gregory Peck, Glenn Ford, Alan Ladd, and Jimmy Stewart replaced those early Hitching Post cowboy heroes. It was their Stoic values in the parts they played that formed my self-identity. Cooper had the most continuous influence on me. Not that I liked him the best. But the roles he played were of courage, humility, an engaging shyness, and most of all, uncompromising integrity. He could be ill at ease, hesitant, vulnerable, and of unusual strength.

The Western heroes spoke few words, were tall in the saddle, and looked people in the eyes when speaking to them. And, it was their inner strength and moral stature that captured the girl. John Wayne, when questioned about whether he was telling the truth or not in *The Searchers*, replied, "I said it. Didn't I?" While I did not especially like John Wayne, this example of natural, built-in honesty is exactly what I admired about my Western heroes.

When it came time to choose a sport in high school, football was not a realistic option because North Hollywood was still using an ancient football formation called the single wing. I was too small for what was required from those backfield positions. Because of the school rules, you had to choose football or basketball. One or the other. So it was basketball for me. My Toluca Lake neighbor and friend, Stanley Klein, had told the "C" basketball coach about me. When practices began, Coach Xanthos placed me on the first string team. I stayed there all season. We never lost a game. Our undefeated team was led by Richie Morse. I had the third highest point total for our league championship team.

I had to give up my pigeons when Frank Clark moved. There was no one to watch out for them. And I also had to give up my dog, Candy. That really hurt. She slept under my bed at night. But with my mother, brother, and I being gone all day, the apartment was not the place for a cocker spaniel. Once again, the Burkerts came to the rescue and Candy went to their Newhall ranch. It was very harsh to learn that Candy had to be put to sleep because of foxtails in her ears.

Spring meant track. I still wanted to be Mel Patton. Or maybe to hurdle like the USC world record holder, Dick Attlesey. I was the fastest boy at 180 yards for the North Hollywood "C" team, but my speed was only good enough to earn me sixth place in the league final.

Jim Smith and Jack Bylin became my closest friends in high school. Jim, especially. Although both of them lived a good distance away, we would meet at various parks on Saturday mornings to play over-the-line, football, or basketball, or we'd go to a motion picture theatre to see a film. During the summer months, we would set up the deck furniture for still yet another contest: we'd run across the yard and long jump over the chairs into a pool.

Santa Monica was our beach. We always played football along the shore. Patti and the other girls would be down there. They put their blankets down maybe fifty yards from us. I wanted them to see me completing passes to Jim, or running for touchdowns. They seemed to be far more interested in getting a tan.

Patton breaks another world record

Jim Smith and I saw Mel Patton break the 220-yard world record on May 7, 1949. We were there to see the USC vs. UCLA track meet. The 100-yard dash came first and the time that Patton ran was quite possibly the swiftest ever run. Some of the watches clocked him in 8.9, four-tenths of a second under his 100-yard world record. The meet officials decided the time was two-tenths of a second below his world record mark of 9.3, then they qualified it as wind aided. Later in the meet, it seemed almost anti-climatic when Patton broke Jesse Owens's 220-yard world record. My boyhood hero had, on the same day, likely run the two fastest sprint times in the history of the sport.

I was growing up in Los Angeles, where world records happened. My entire orientation to sport (and especially track and field) was enriched, deepened by this proximity. Los Angeles, at that time, was the

track capital of the world. It was the Golden Age of the sport. Patton
was known to always throw up after he raced over 220 yards. I was not
training hard enough yet to know what it felt like to dry heave after a
difficult workout. Give me time.

A week or two after Patton raced to record times at UCLA, I made
a humiliating mistake in the Los Angeles Coliseum. Our "C" sprint relay team was seeking to qualify for the L.A. City final. We thought we
had a chance. I handled the third 100-yard relay leg. But when some
of the fastest young sprinters in Los Angeles came racing down the
track toward my exchange zone, I took off too early. And by doing so,
I disqualified my relay team. I do not remember anyone trying to help
me feel okay about it, either. Sport can be unforgiving!

I was not chosen, as a tenth grader, to be in either of the two prestigious social clubs. Nor were Jim or Jack. Morse made it into one of
them. I did not really care which one selected me; I just wanted the
recognition. I felt rejected. I was rejected.

I did have our YMCA club, however. Almost all of the Sabers were
friends before we formed the club. We were a clean-cut group of guys.
Jack and Jim were in the club. We did not drink or throw wild parties.
Not only were we on the high school athletic teams, but we played flag
football and softball at night. Some of us attended the YMCA summer camps up in Green Valley as youth counselors. Most of the Sabers
were good academic students. I, on the other hand, favored sports and

Bill Taylor and Lefty Tamblyn as high school juniors in 1950.

did not take homework seriously. I received A's in journalism, and at times in English, but no other subjects held my interest—certainly not the frogs we dissected. All that one of my science teachers could do in class was talk about the value of yeast.

My mother gave up on a personal life to raise her two boys. She lived for and through us. She even moved out onto the front room couch to sleep so that she could watch television late at night, and give my brother and I separate bedrooms. Mom was a good cook, but the kitchen would not be cleaned for weeks. Grease stuck to the stove, pans, the sink, and counter. No, I did not help. Frank Clark tore into me for not helping at home.

When I returned to high school as a junior, I had added about four inches to my height. The basketball coach even put me at center for a game or two. I was on the "B" team. While I started some of the games, I was not one of the top players. And it was pimple time. One morning, while running late for school, I rushed into the bathroom to brush my teeth. The taste was terrible. What had I put in my mouth? There was zinc oxide on my toothbrush: the medicine for zits.

Bert Convy arrived on campus. My nemesis from across the street in Toluca Lake transferred in from Notre Dame High School to be with girls and to play on more competitive sport teams. Notre Dame was a new high school at which only boys could enroll. So, Bert continued to enjoy finding my weak spots, although I am fairly sure that he saw me as a close friend. I did not appreciate his presence.

I became the sports editor of the school newspaper as a junior. This gave me a certain status on campus. When the track season began, I gave the hurdles a final chance for a few meets. But North Hollywood had the best "B" hurdler in L.A. City. And my close friend, Jack Bylin, was faster than I over "the sticks." So, one afternoon, I asked the best distance runner on the "B" team if I could run along with him over his race distance. This Tyler said okay. We had some nice coaches, but they knew little to nothing about training track athletes. We frequently ran our actual event distance in practice. That is not how you do it today.

These days, your event distance is usually broken up into shorter segments. You run multiple times over reduced yardage at various speeds. Tyler's race distance would take us three times around the track. When we came off the final turn, I was able to pass him rather easily. Suddenly, I was the number one man in a middle-distance event. He quit the team.

While I won four league 1320-yard races, I did not really lower my time much and I only placed fifth in the league final. High school friends told me that I was going to be "a great middle-distance runner." Ridiculous! I didn't buy it. Great runners train for their event. They run longer distances over the summer, and join the school cross-country team. Hell, I was going out for football.

It was not too late for me to try football because Johnny Sanders came to North Hollywood as the new backfield coach. We switched to the T-formation for the 1950 football season and this gave me the opportunity to play out my quarterback dream. Harvey Nelson was still the head coach, but the Swede was finally ready to make the adjustment to this modern formation. However, Nelson was dead set against seniors coming out for the first time and taking the place of those who had been playing for the two prior years, so even with Sanders my chances were slim. I had thrown a lot of touchdown passes to Jim Smith in the YMCA league. And I still had that kiss from Betsy to remember how I scored that touchdown, passed for the winning conversion, to win the "big game" in junior high (and that was against many of the same guys who would make up the 1950 North Hollywood varsity team). At just under six feet, I was considerably faster than the other fellows going out for quarterback. And I thought I knew more about how to play quarterback from the T-formation than any of the others who were being considered for the position.

During the summer, four of the quarterback candidates were invited to go over to Van Nuys High School to spend a morning with the Los Angeles Rams All-Pro football star, Bob Waterfield. The former All-American at UCLA was not only a famous quarterback, he was the husband of the Hollywood sex goddess, Jane Russell (the woman who shared her breasts in *The Outlaw*). This mini-clinic was set up by the new backfield coach, Johnny Sanders. Sanders had been a "little" All-American halfback at Occidental College. Waterfield showed us how to make some hand-offs from the T-formation. When we ran a few pass routes for the Rams quarterback, he delivered the ball softly. It just hung there, suspended, inviting you to reach out and collect the gift. I had watched Waterfield throw passes to his All-Pro receivers in the Los Angeles Coliseum many times and there I was catching his passes.

Due to being the sports editor, I had the opportunity to be employed as a copyboy for the *Valley Times* newspaper that summer. I liked the feel of the newsroom. It looked like journalism might become my profession. At the time, I loved writing about sports. Why not have a job writing about my prime interest?

When I was not sure how to spell "Joseph," the city editor told me to look it up, for then I would remember it. The newsroom was empty when I took a phone call from a person who wanted to report that a baby had just been refused medical treatment at St. Joseph Hospital because the family did not have insurance. I was told that the baby died on the way to another hospital. The city editor is still in my head. To this day, he directs me to "look it up." Major track results came through on the Linotype at the *Valley Times*. It was my job to file the pictures in the morgue. I still have some of them. I took a few of Patton, one of Herb McKenley, another of Bob Mathias.

The sports editor at the *Valley Times* gave me a field pass to a pro football game at the Coliseum between the Los Angeles Rams and the Green Bay Packers. I was able to stand on the sideline next to the Rams bench. On one of the plays, the former Army All-American Glenn Davis almost ran into me when he was forced out of bounds. The players talked, taunted, swore at one another all through the game. When Bob Boyd, the NCAA champion over 100 yards, was knocked unconscious by a Green Bay player I witnessed a phone call come down to the Rams bench from a coach stationed high up in the Coliseum. Two All-Pro linemen were sent into the game to retaliate. After the following play, a Green Bay Packer was lying flat on his back. They had "taken him out." Instant justice!

At the end of the season, the sports editor gave me tickets for the championship game between the Rams and the Cleveland Browns. Otto Graham of Cleveland at that time was considered by many to be the best quarterback to ever play the game. He led his team to the NFL title that afternoon in the Coliseum.

My left leg folded under me

My senior year was packed with surprises. Mostly pleasant ones. One that would stay with me the rest of my life happened at the very beginning of the football season, and it was not pleasant. When I was relegated to an inconsequential scrimmage of reserves, chaos resulted. I was at the quarterback position; a pass play was called, but nobody knew where to go—pass patterns had not been practiced. And I did not have my familiar receiver, Jim Smith, to catch my throws. Jim had already quit. The new coach, Johnny Sanders, had encouraged me to stay out.

I decided to take off and run with the football when I could not locate an open receiver in that fateful scrimmage. I headed left, but I preferred running to the right or straight up the field. I made the turn okay, and I was picking up some yardage when suddenly I was hit from the front and back at the same time. My left leg folded under me. It felt like it was broken. Teammates helped me to the locker room. I had torn ligaments in my left knee. Thus ended my football dream. I did not realize then that my knee was going to cause me trouble over the following forty years; even now I have to be careful about what kind of pressure or twist I place on it. In 1951 when it happened, I just assumed that I would go on to other things. There was no deep reflection or fear.

When we became seniors the girls discovered us. Or, at least I was identified. The pimples were gone, I made it into one of the two prominent social clubs, and my confidence increased. As seniors everywhere likely know, it became our campus. I had identity and I felt good about myself.

We detoured the freeway traffic

The clean-cut, non-drinking Sabers did something awful on Halloween night. It brought police cars screaming. The heavy evening commute traffic from Los Angeles to the San Fernando Valley is congested even when it is not slowed down by a construction project. Full of tricks, we rearranged some barricades where the freeway ended, detouring the freeway traffic back into itself. Not nice. Sirens wailed. I fell face down on the far side of a dirt mound. Squad cars were pulling up just thirty or so yards away. Jim Smith and I escaped the initial roundup of Sabers. Hidden, flat up against a dirt mound, we observed our buddies being driven away in police cars before we felt that it was safe to walk away from the scene and over to Ventura Boulevard. It was not too long, however, before a squad car pulled up and the officers began to question us. Jim was flippant, even antagonistic. That did it.

"Get in." When Jim and I walked into the police station, we found all of the Sabers assembled. The YMCA song goes this way: "We are a bunch of Y boys from the old YMCA, / we have a word to say / about the building of our future nation." Well, not that night.

No one could leave the police station until one of their parents showed up. My mother arrived in full form. It was close to midnight. Unruffled, she teased my friends; no wonder they liked her. The police station scene was obviously no big deal for her. However, as we drove home, it bothered me that she made a big deal of how the "minister's kid" had been picked up by his mother, not his father. My mother always seemed to find someone to degrade. Yet, maybe she was right on. This time.

My classmate, "Speed" Vogel, a future president of the California State Bar, was picked up by his father that night. Al Glickman, the class clown, was at the police station. He thought it was really funny. Al will become a lawyer, too, and very, very wealthy. Some of you will be familiar with the Hamburger Hamlet restaurant chain that he played a part in forming. A really nice guy, Leonard Denti, was picked up that night, too. Leonard was probably the most-liked guy in the Sabers. He will join the army in the next few months and end up in Korea. We were not home free; an appearance before a judge was to be scheduled. But it never happened. A lawyer, Mr. Vogel was the adult advisor for the Sabers. He sat in on our club meetings. Somebody spoke to the judge.

I was able to switch over to basketball from football because I had not played in an actual football game. I was the second string behind a player who was one season away from becoming the L. A. City Player of the Year. Do you have any idea how vast and competitive Los Angeles City high school basketball was back then? Major college, even pro basketball players came out of the San Fernando Valley, San Pedro, West Los Angeles, Watts. Richie Morse captained our 1950-51 basketball team into the Los Angeles City tournament at the end of the season. I had to drop out early. My knee kept giving way in practice. Then in a game against Marshall, my teammates had to carry me off the court.

Patti, Bert, Speed, and my closest female friend, Joan Denny were in my speech class. And that class clown, Glickman. This led to fun moments. When I discovered a sound effects record in one of the school closets with the endless sound of a lawnmower, I put it out over the speaker system during a lunch break. No introduction, just the lawnmower noise. I observed from a window how students began looking around. They were not sure where the sound was coming from. One by one, they would glance about. I saw one or two of them try to see if it came from the front of the school. It was difficult to control my laughter. I bit my finger.

When I was hurt in that basketball game, Patti used this same sound system to announce my basketball injury to the student body. She expressed her wishes for my "quick recovery." I had identity. It was my school.

Rusty Tamblyn, of *Payton Place* and *West Side Story*, would entertain us at parties. You most likely remember him for his tumbling in *Seven Brides for Seven Brothers*. His older brother, Lefty, was one of my closest friends.

Jack Bylin ran for student body president. So did Bert Convy. It puzzled me that a humble guy like Jack wanted that role. It seemed egotistical to me. Gary Cooper would not have run for student body president in high school. They would have needed to draft him. Bert fit. I was surprised when he asked me if I would be his campaign manager. I am afraid I did not do much for him except lend my name. Jack won.

I would sit on a wall in the arcade with this lush female hanging on me

If you were a teenager living in the San Fernando Valley or in Glendale in the 1950s, you knew about Bob's drive-in. The one I frequented was on Riverside Drive, just up from our apartment on Toluca Lake Avenue. It is where we hung out after a night football game, dance, or a club meeting. You ordered the famous Big Boy hamburger and a milkshake or malt from the window of your car. People got out of their cars to go over and talk to someone they knew in another vehicle.

On a Saturday morning halfway through my senior year, four or five of us were stretched out in Lefty's old car. Someone posed the question, "Out of all the girls at North Hollywood High School, which one would you like to..." I chose this Mary, a sexy, sandy haired blonde from the class ahead of us. She had the best body on campus in my opinion. I liked the way her skirts came over her butt. And she filled out her sweaters very well. I did not know her. It was just Saturday morning fantasy time with my buddies at Bob's.

Within a couple of weeks, I was told that Mary wanted to go out with me. Did someone mention me to her? I do not think that the conversation at Bob's had anything to do with it. While I knew nothing of Greek mythology at the time, I had been chosen by Aphrodite.

I told you my senior year really picked up. Mary had actually just graduated with the Winter class at North Hollywood; she was attending Valley Junior College. At the nutrition or lunch breaks she would come by to see me on days that she was through with her classes. I would sit on a wall in the arcade with this lush female hanging onto me. Wild.

Mary came to some of my track meets. She would stand near the finish line when it became time for my event. I would have preferred that she not be there. Mary was never alone for long; guys always gathered around her. She had not belonged to either one of the two prestigious social clubs at North Hollywood. Unlike Patti, Darlene, and Betsy, Mary missed out. I think this is partly why she would return to the campus to claim me at the breaks.

Nobody spoke to me

In track I won four times over 880 yards in the varsity league meets, but my times were mediocre when compared with the better middle-distance runners in Los Angeles. Still my buddies kept pumping me up as a track star. I was not a star.

Track was big, big, big in the Los Angeles area in the fifties. The *Valley Times* gave the sport considerable space. A Pete Kokon covered high school track as though he were handicapping race horses. Each week the "What's Cookin' with Kokon" column would forecast the results for the high school meets, event by event. You got your name in the paper a lot even if you were only an average athlete. Pete had it right when he wrote, "North Hollywood's best" after my name, predicting that I would place fifth in the league half-mile final. Un-

Mary was the most attractive girl on the large
North Hollywood campus.

cle Harold came all the way over to Van Nuys from Pomona on public transportation to see me run in the league meet. My mother's brother never had a car. Strange, he took off and went to Berlin to see the 1936 Olympics alone. Bright and to the point, Uncle Harold chose to work the $2.00 ticket windows at the horse racing tracks for his employment. His comment to me after the race was, "You ran for fifth place." Not incidentally, the national high school half-mile record was thirteen seconds faster than my best time.

In the Los Angeles City half-mile trial, I did not even try to stay up with the pace. I had no confidence that I could survive at that speed. I was last out of the Coliseum tunnel and last at the finish. When I walked up to where my coaches and teammates were sitting, nobody spoke to me.

"You can become an outstanding college runner"

Just three or so weeks later everything changed. I doubt anybody thought I would win the school decathlon. But something happened to me. I was different. My speed, endurance, and confidence led to an upset victory over the best all-around track athletes at a very large high school.

Richie Morse won the award for being the top athlete of our graduating class. But I was nominated for Athlete of the Year, too. So was Bert. And Jack. (Jim Smith had dropped out of high school sports.) I was surprised when they called me up to the stage on awards night and presented me with a plaque for winning the school decathlon. Speed, who had set up the competition, informed me that the plaque would be placed in the trophy case in the main lobby. I was leaving high school as an outstanding athlete. Someone else saw the change in my running during the decathlon. Jim Slosson, a college coach and former USC half miler, was there when I took off and left the 440 field at the end of the first day of the two-day competition. He was the young track coach at Valley College. On the infield of my high school track, I heard Mr. Slosson say to me, "You can become an outstanding college runner."

Part II: Half Miler

On to the State

I WAS PROUD, POSSESSIVE. I expected loyalty. Mary and I had to be together constantly. It bothered me when I placed my friends second to my relationship with her. I felt that I had to be with Mary or I might lose her. That is not a sign of strength. My role models on the screen were the tall, lean, independent cowboys. And they were loved by beautiful, faithful women. Forever! But the scripts never explored the longer term relationship. What would life be like after the guy wins the girl? After I was eight years old, my home did not provide me with an example of a marriage relationship.

The summer after I graduated, Mary went to Catalina Island with her sorority. I was miserable without her. Nat King Cole was singing on the radio: "Hello, young lovers wherever you are, I hope your troubles are few." I was counting on Mary being loyal that week. I would learn later that she was not, that she let some guy kiss her.

I knew that my fear of the unfaithful woman was going to continue to threaten me if I remained with Mary. But I was not ready to give up this lush beauty yet. Mary was in her second year at Valley College. She wanted more time for the social life she missed in high school. Trying to possess her on campus all of the time would have been torture for me. I had my track season to protect. Worrying about who she was talking to, or watching a guy making a play for her, would have made me extremely jealous. So I blocked her out. I wasn't about to go snooping around corners to check up on her. My pride was too important to me. Learning to block things out is a necessary mental capability and this was certainly one of my early challenges.

Mary kept telling me that I was the one she wanted permanently. She asked that I wait for her.

Would Gary Cooper have joined a fraternity?

Coach Slosson wanted me to run cross country. I had never run farther than a mile. That sounds so strange today. Our training for the fall and winter combined easy runs with fast grass strides; we also played touch football. We ran three miles in the league cross-country races. My coach used the sport for conditioning and mental relaxation. Coach Slosson will prove to be a very good sport psychologist.

One of two nationally ranked junior college runners that Jim Slosson coached during my senior year was a graduate of North Hollywood High School. I remember watching this Don Hoover run in the L. A. City half-mile final. His fluid half-mile form was more impressive than where he finished that night. At Valley College under Slosson, Don lowered his time to some eight seconds faster than I had run over the distance. I remember seeing Don walking around Bob's Big Boy with his teammate after they both had placed in the 1951 junior college state meet. They made their way around the parked cars of the popular drive-in restaurant for some deserved recognition.

Lefty Tamblyn was my teammate at Valley College. He had missed his senior track season at North Hollywood because of grades. Jack Bylin went to USC and joined the fraternity that sang "The Sweetheart of Sigma Chi." He invited me down to see him at his house. Would Gary Cooper have joined a fraternity?

My career direction seemed obvious. I would be either a sports announcer, sports writer, or coach. When I had a clash with the school newspaper instructor, it led to my dropping the course. This journalism professor had censored me; she took me off football coverage because I had referred to the Valley College football team as inept. (Help was on the way for the next season, however, when UCLA farmed out two future All-Americans so that they could qualify for admission into the four-year school. Hardiman Cureton and Rommie Loudd, besides playing football for Valley, became a part of the 1953 Valley College track and field team.) That was the second time in three years that I dropped out of a class because of a conflict with a female teacher. As a junior in high school, I quit attending a history class because of my clash with a Mrs. Franco. I thought she was being unfair about something. The school made me repeat the class—with Mrs. Franco, of course. I did not like an authoritarian female telling me what to do.

When I entered junior college, my mother moved us into a small duplex on the western edge of the Toluca Lake community. My brother was attending Hollywood High School. This meant traveling over the Cahuenga Pass each day. Something about school districting required this route, but it turned out well in light of his interest in basketball. The Hollywood High School basketball coach, Guy Wrinkle, was one of the best in the L. A. City. And Harold was a very good basketball player.

I discovered a flicker of academic life in me. It arrived during my first semester at Valley in a Western Civilization course taught by a Dr. Dodson. This professor was a short, ugly German. Bald, he had a face as red as a beet. But he loved teaching Western Civilization and I responded to his expertise and enthusiasm. I even typed my notes when I returned home each day. When I received a B mark for the course, I felt good because I had worked for it. The grade slipped to a C in the spring, due to my life being consumed by track.

We had a poor cross-country team (no, I did not write this for the school paper). I became the lead runner, but nothing exceptional happened until the Metropolitan Conference finals at UCLA. Early on, a runner from Santa Monica who was superior to the rest of the field took off and left us. But as I worked my way with others along the ridge above the UCLA athletic fields, I found myself running near the front of the rest of the field. I had no particular finishing place in mind. I did not feel any fatigue. I can still see the narrow path winding through the sage toward Sunset Boulevard. Suddenly I felt a surge of energy and I left the other runners. I kept letting it out as I flew down the hill alongside Sunset and toward the very track where Patton had set the 200-yard world record only two and a-half years before.

Nobody was near me at the finish. I felt fantastic coming in second in a college conference final. Phil Clarke, a math teacher at Valley College who ran with us sometimes, named me the "Monarch Express." The Valley nickname was the Monarchs, of course. Coach Slosson was twenty-nine. While Jim had run at USC just a few years before, he never tried to compete with us in the practices. I was not aware how good a runner he had been in high school, before World War II delayed his college running. Decades later, I learned that in 1941 he won the L. A. City 880 final and recorded the second-fastest time in the nation for high school half milers.

Richie Morse was playing basketball for Valley. We were always friendly when we ran into one another. Jim Smith had joined the Army. Jack Bylin flunked out of USC. Quite a surprise. Jack seemed "perfect" in every way in high school. When he joined the Navy, he was sent to the Philippines. Darlene was the faithful girlfriend who waited. Jack and I exchanged letters during this time. Bert Convy tried professional baseball in the minor leagues. I believe he only played one season. He ended up back with Richie, Lefty, and I at Valley. Drama became his thing!

It worked

Okay, take a stopwatch out. It is February 1952. Let's find out if I have improved. Let's see if Slosson was right about my becoming a great college runner. He scheduled an 880 time trial. I was really nervous. A very good high school miler from Burbank, now a teammate, Ralph Smith, would run against me. And so would Lefty who, in high school, was clearly better than I in the middle distances. We called our track the "weed patch oval" because it had small rocks and weeds on it. Smith set a fast pace. I stayed right behind him until the final turn. My finishing kick was there. I sprinted away from the two of them with a time that was some four seconds faster than I had run in high school.

When I heard the time I said, "It worked." I had put myself into the sport and it was paying off. This work ethic became part of my character. When I began racing for Valley in 1952, I was close to six feet tall and only carrying 150 pounds.

Our first meet was over at Glendale Junior College. It was cold. I held back, off a very slow pace, then flew away from the other runners and won the two-lap event. There was a standout half miler from Glendale in the field, but I had no trouble leaving him.

Four of us scored the points that led this new junior college to an undefeated league track season. The newspapers called us the Big Four. Who were we? Phil Serrins will be fast enough to place in the state finals that year in the 100 and 220-yard sprints. Clarence Lewis will place second in the state finals for discus. I will finish just two-tenths out of first to claim second place in the California 880 final. And Ernie Shelton will become the leading high jumper in the world two years later. World? Yes. Ernie was shy, lanky, and with freckles. A nice person. Ernie had a high-jump bar up on the wall in his room at home at seven feet. Nobody in world history had cleared that height yet. He was very determined to be the first one to do so.

During the Easter break, Ernie, Lefty, Frank Clark, and I drove up to the Kern River. We camped about a mile upstream from a village that had some cabins, a Western style bar, and a red barn. We heard there was going to be a dance on Saturday night and decided to see if we could find any girls. None of us drank, but that night we found ourselves drinking a considerable amount of beer. Ernie was literally an alcoholic virgin. Our athletic hero put down beer after beer before two gals came into the bar. One of them was wearing a white silk blouse over nice breasts. She was very sexy. That is, until she opened her mouth. The girl was missing a row of her front teeth. A little later, I heard Ernie attempting to convince Ms. Toothless that he was a great high jumper. With five or six beers in him, his shyness had vanished. Next I observed Ernie escorting Ms. Toothless out onto the lodge porch. Where were they going? What was...it hit me. Ernie was going to demonstrate how high he could jump. I raced outside just in time to see Ernie rolling over a wooden rail. He cleared it easily, crashing down into the bushes below the elevated porch. Ernie was fine. And happy, one could add.

Real trouble emerged after he escorted Ms. Toothless into the red barn for the dance. The two of them were having a good time when her boyfriend arrived. And his friends. They were local guys, and we were on their turf. Ernie was six feet three inches in height, so that slowed things down. But it was likely Frank Clark's cool behavior that kept the moment from turning into a brawl. That nice guy who had once watched over my pigeons at that vacant lot in Toluca Lake had chosen to stay sober. Frank talked Ernie into letting go of the girl. And he talked the local boys out of teaching us a lesson. When we decided to leave around midnight, we could not find Ernie. Our search ended in the parking lot. The soon-to-be world leader in the high jump was sitting down on the ground, whimpering, "Some son-of-a-bitch stole my gal."

My Valley College transcript shows that I dropped out of journalism on March 25, 1952. That was just about the time we drove up to the Kern River during the Easter break. This meant an "incomplete" on my transcript. I do not remember worrying about it. I was not focused on what it might take to transfer to a four-year college. I continued to lower my times and was undefeated going into the conference final. Pete Kokon continued to tell of Shelton, Taylor, Serrins, and Lewis as the Big Four in his "What's Cookin'..." column. My high school friends who followed sports had to know that I was a different runner in college. I was so proud.

I became the conference champion

The conference final was in Bakersfield, some hundred miles north of the San Fernando Valley. I do not remember thinking about my father's plane crash when we drove past Newhall on Highway Ninety-nine. We stopped for lunch just over the summit where you can see a nice western scene with a lake to the east. I was nervous. The captions under my pictures in the newspapers continued to make mention that

I was undefeated. One year before, I had placed fifth in the high school conference final. Now I was the favorite against college runners from El Camino, Harbor, Santa Monica, Bakersfield, East Los Angeles, and Long Beach. Bob Timson, a teammate from San Fernando High, was improving rapidly. In high school, he was a star in the mile; now he was finding the half mile to his liking. Bob had muscle elasticity. Beware of half milers with elasticity: such muscles tell of fluidity.

Timson and I moved up to the front of the field with about 100 yards to go. The two of us were at that moment when you have to reach way down if you are going to prevail. This is what defines the half miler—the capacity to "reach down" and run into the athletic abyss. I became the conference champion. When I received my gold medal, I requested a kiss on the lips from the beautiful queen. She responded nicely. Then my mile relay leg in the final event of the night was easily my fastest ever clocking. Valley won the conference title. All was well.

The Fresno Relays featured some of the nation's great athletes and

Winning the 1952 conference
title in Bakersfield.

teams. Large crowds of up to thirteen thousand would squeeze into the bleachers for an evening of exciting relay races and sometimes a world record. I was to anchor the distance medley relay on Saturday afternoon. On Friday night, Ernie, Lefty, and I were restlessly awaiting the next day's action in a downtown hotel. One of us filled a wastepaper basket with water and waited for an appropriate target below. We were on the fifth or sixth floor.

A target emerged when this convertible with four guys pulled up to the signal. I let it go. We would have dumped it on white dudes. It just so happened that they were black. Racial stereotypes made the prank seem even more threatening to us. I could see the neon streetlights reflected in the water as it fell. Direct hit. They came into the hotel looking for us. We had to remain very quiet in order to escape being located. We succeeded. The night was young. We yelled down to some girls and were surprised when they responded to our invitation to come up to our room. When our discus throwers realized that we had girls in the room, they demanded that we open the door. Our female guests became very frightened. Especially when they heard that the throwers were going to break the door down. They did. It came flying off its hinges.

The girls fled, running frantically down the hall. I filled a wastepaper basket with a good amount of water and headed for the discus throwers' room. As I rounded a corner, I had already begun swinging the basket of water forward when Coach Slosson appeared directly in front of me. He was wearing a dark blue coat and tie. He had just returned from a coaches meeting. It was too late to change the direction of the water. I can still see the water dripping from his face. He picked me up and carried me into my room. When he threw me down it broke the bed. Then this quiet, soft-spoken man screamed, "Taylor, you are NOT running tomorrow!"

I ran, of course, anchoring the relay team to victory before a large afternoon crowd. Only one team was ahead of us when I received the baton for the final leg of the distance medley. I was surprised when I had to work to out-kick this fellow at the end of the mile. That was a long time to wait for the finishing stretch. The mile never felt right to me. When I went up into the bleachers after the race, I walked past the head USC coach, Jesse Mortensen. He said, "Nice going, Bill." Wow—recognition from the USC track coach! My time was not impressive, partly due to my having waited for almost four laps before taking off. But still, *wow*.

That night, Occidental College, with the great John Barnes and Bob McMillen running the last two legs of the distance medley, set a new American record. A few months later in the 1952 Olympic Games in Helsinki, Finland, McMillen will just miss winning the gold medal over 1500 meters. Famous names like Bannister and Landy will finish behind the Oxy star. John Barnes, who would win his second straight national collegiate half-mile title a month after the Fresno Relays was on that Olympic Team, too. I mention this because in only two years I am going to become part of a USC school-record setting distance-medley team with a time almost as fast as this great Oxy team ran that night.

An athletic theft

Three conferences fed athletes into the Southern California junior college championship meet. Due to the number of entries in the half mile, we were separated into two packed sections. I was careless and found myself trying to fight my way up through a mob of runners just as we entered the final turn. I remember being bumped onto the in-field. This led to a very disappointing fourth-place finish in my section. So much for being "undefeated" my freshman year at Valley College! To make matters even worse, my teammate, Bob Timson, ran faster than my best time in the other heat. Just like that, an athletic theft. My season was stolen.

My tactical mistake at Riverside, combined with the shock of having a teammate run faster than I, focused me. I was not going to hang way back in the state finals the next weekend. We drove up on a chartered Greyhound bus to a town called Santa Rosa just north of San Francisco. Some of the other junior college teams from the Los Angeles area joined Valley in sharing the cost of the transportation.

A quiet town dressed in red and pink adobe

I was happy, relaxed, upbeat, when we stopped for lunch at Fisherman's Wharf. This mood continued when we pulled into the quiet town dressed in red and pink adobe. I found Santa Rosa enchanting. A few of us walked around the downtown area the next morning, some eight hours before the prelims. The streets were quiet and virtually empty. I flirted with a pretty girl in a variety store. I liked her, the weather, the town. I was in a very positive mood. Where did this come from?

When we arrived at the motel, Mel Patton came over and visited with Coach Slosson. My track hero had put on a little weight since his USC world record days. But his runners at Long Beach City College said that their coach "could still run 9.6 for 100 yards."

I was assigned to the same heat as the state favorite, Dave Casper of Mt. San Antonio Junior College. He was four seconds faster than I was, based on his time the week before at Riverside. Casper was tall, skinny, known to be unpredictable. Only three runners would make it from each heat into the final. On Friday evening, the weather was perfect. Warm, no wind. I remained relaxed and confident. An old oak tree on the grass infield at the far north end of the track dominated the site, giving it a pastoral feeling. Okay, it was time. When I climbed into the starting blocks, I kept reminding myself, "Stay up, stay up; don't fall back." We used blocks in the state final that year. The initial 220 was on a straightaway, with the race being run around three turns. This made for a much longer finishing stretch. We ended up way down by that big oak tree. I remember that the pace felt fast. I had to work at staying with it. Only twelve months before, I had finished dead last in the L. A. City high school prelims. When we came off the final turn in Santa Rosa, Casper was leading. I came up alongside of him, gradually applying more and more pressure as we flowed down the final stretch on a comfortable summer evening. Near the end, I eased away from him. I won my state 880 trial heat and I beat the state favorite.

Timson did not make it to the finals. I reclaimed my event leadership just in time. Suddenly, I was viewed as the co-favorite to win a California half-mile title. Winning a state title brings recognition that remains with an athlete for the rest of their life.

Slosson was a good sport psychologist. He knew how to settle down his athletes. He took us to an afternoon movie. I believe it was a Western. When we arrived at the stadium that evening, a bit of the charm was gone. The weather had turned cold, and there was a wind. I was not as relaxed as I was the night before. I experienced something new: a tension headache. The only trainer available was from the powerful Mt. Sac track program, Casper's trainer. In the years ahead, I saw him again and again at the track meets; I always dropped by to say hello and to thank him for helping me out in 1952 at Santa Rosa.

"Final call, 880 yard run"

It was not very long before I heard those ominous words, "Final call, 880 yard run." Every serious runner knows how this makes them feel. That final moment of anxiety when you realize your moment has come. It was time to race. I began talking to myself again: "Stay up, don't fall back; stay up." Eight other college freshmen and sophomores wanted to be up with the lead pack, too. This was the state final. We raced down the 220-yard straightaway and even though I tried to stay right up there with the leaders, I found myself back in the pack on the first turn. I do not remember anything else until we swept around the final turn with 150 or so yards to go. I was well back. Those up front began to tire, and I began picking them off. One by one. Perhaps thirty yards from the finish I went by Casper. Then I passed another one of the favorites. As we reached the finish line by the oak tree, I was in second place. Only Ed Wilson from Sacramento Junior College was ahead of me. By two-tenths of a second. I had placed second in the California final. I was very, very happy. How could this have happened?

The Big Four finished off the 1952 season in the state finals with one first-place, three second-places, and fifth and sixth scoring places. Ernie, in winning the high jump, remained undefeated in the event, and he placed second in the high hurdles, too. Lewis was second in the discus; Serrins fifth and sixth in the sprints. Only Mt. Sac was ahead of

Valley College in team points. Not bad for a school with a track called "the weed patch oval."

This heroic moment asked to be shared. With a girl. My thoughts turned to Mary, the "girl back home." This need was so strong that I ignored what the discus thrower, Lewis, had told me at the motel. He was not aware of my feelings toward Mary when he mentioned that during the track season they had a date, and necked.

I called her as soon as I returned. It was Sunday night. I wanted her to see my silver medal. Maybe have her wear it. Girls back then would display their boyfriend's award on a necklace. Mary had "a terrible headache." I believed her. Later a fellow would tell me that he was there that night. And there was no headache.

Paradise

LEFTY ENCOURAGED ME to apply for a summer job in the High Sierras. The City of Los Angeles offered a family camp with a cluster of rustic cabins up in Mammoth, close to the lakes. Mammoth is some 300 miles north of Los Angeles, on the eastern side of the Sierras. Working with Lefty up in the mountains sounded like a good idea. I went in for my interview and was hired.

Before I left for the summer, Mary let me know that she was ready to be my girl again. For keeps! We actually had been attending a music appreciation course together that semester. The instructor was a jerk. When Mary passed me a note during the final, little did I know that the professor thought I was cheating. The note said that she wanted to see me after class, that she wanted to be my girl again. I felt confident that I earned a B in that silly course. The final went well. But when I received my grades up at Mammoth I was shocked to see a D for the semester. In September when I returned to campus, I went to see the teacher. He told me that he saw me cheating during the final, and that he could not consider changing the grade.

Why didn't I take this farther? Bring Mary into it? This grade, along with that incomplete in journalism, would make difficult my entrance into the major university that was about to recruit me.

One could not have asked for a better way to spend the summer. A staff of some ten college students ran the camp, served the meals, washed the dishes, cleaned the cabins. Lefty and I handled the dishes. Our washtubs were outside the dining hall on an open-air porch. We had fun tossing unbreakable plates and cups to one another as we sang songs from the popular musicals of the early fifties.

There was a good looking high school girl on our staff. Adrienne and I arranged to have our day off together a few times. Once we drove up to Lake Tahoe, slept in a campground by that incredible blue lake. Earlier that evening, we discovered Nat King Cole singing in a nightclub. At the nearby Cal/Neva, we saw an unfamiliar performer do impersonations of famous actors and singers. The impersonator was Sammy Davis Junior. Nice evening entertainment. Adrienne wore a pretty white dress. Good summer fun.

Another time we headed into the backcountry together. I remember waiting in the thin air for Adrienne at the top of Mono Pass. Up at 12,000 feet. There were a few little birds hopping around. Minor plant life struggling out from cracks in bleak rock formations. That night we placed our sleeping bags close together, kissed.

Bob Griffith, a very close friend to this day, slept across from me in the bunk house at Mammoth. I was impressed that he was pre-med at Stanford. I did not offer him any academic challenges, but we sure shared some competitive sport moments. Like the volleyball games, ping pong, half-court basketball, and hiking. I was surprised that he hiked up to the Rim over the Mammoth Lakes as quickly as I did. I had just taken second in the state junior college half-mile final. Bob's strong legs, pride, and determination were the prime factors.

"Young man, you could do that anywhere"

Mary Russell, the attractive camp social director, was from UCLA. Mary spilled over with personality, had one major smile, and a good figure. She could be feisty, too. We became lifetime friends.

We would have up to a hundred guests in camp each week. Skit night was a lot of fun. A Dean played the trumpet, Lefty the accordion, Mary the piano. I was a singing MC. Nobody ever asked for an encore.

However, when I impersonated the singer Johnny Ray I received quite a compliment. When the hit record, *Cry*, was played on the record player, I mouthed the words as I acted out the wild antics of this strange personality. "If your sweetheart writes a letter of goodbye, it's no secret you'll feel better, if you just cry..." Rosemary de Camp, a much loved Hollywood supporting actress, was a guest one week. Ms. de Camp was a warm, friendly, very natural celebrity. After seeing me perform my Johnny Ray impersonation she told me, "Young man, you could do that anywhere."

There was a second girl from UCLA on the staff and she could be a real bitch. I had no trouble finding support for a prank. Armed with maple syrup from the kitchen, a couple of pillows, and a knife, we ambushed her as she walked past the bunkhouse. Her Bermuda shorts and a sleeveless blouse were perfect for the plan. As a couple of guys held her down, I covered her arms and legs with syrup and pillow feathers. Once released, she screamed threats at us and waddled away with feathered arms and legs that made her look like a chicken. It was hilarious.

A day or so later, I urinated purple. Fortunately I quickly discovered that my bunkhouse friends were urinating unusual colors, too. We were being paid back, big time, by the female staff members. They had spiked the Kool-aid. Thank goodness my urine was not a red dosage!

A Lou came down from the Mammoth pack station for a couple of square dances that first summer. He appeared to be interested in our social director, Mary Russell. The cowboy was tall, lean, looked you in the eye when he spoke to you. Lou did wear peculiar-looking cowboy boots with laces that stretched over the top of the instep. They were unlike both the smooth Western boots that Roy Rogers wore when he showed up that night in Studio City with his racing pigeons and the ones I will see before the next summer worn by Wes Santee.

I especially liked the way Lou hesitated in speech. He and Mary made a very striking couple. But Mary was engaged to a UCLA fraternity guy, her high school boyfriend.

My Mary from back home sent me a postcard. In it she confessed to letting a guy kiss her goodnight. I ignored the card. When I returned home at the end of the summer, I went over to pick up my state track medal, which she had been wearing on a necklace. She had a puzzled look on her face when I left her standing in the driveway. Bewildered!

It was hard to leave Mammoth and come down to the smog, traffic, noise of Los Angeles. I had fallen in love with the mountains. Mammoth was in my blood. It would call me back for three more summers: the next two, in 1953 and in 1954; then, for a final time, in 1965.

Stanford wants me

S TANFORD NEEDED A HALF MILER for the 1953 track season and they wanted me. A major university with a strong track tradition was prepared to award me an athletic scholarship. This came about because Hilmer Lodge, Casper's coach, had alerted the Stanford coach to my half-mile potential. Lodge was a Stanford alum; he will be awarded a USA staff position for the 1956 Olympic Games.

I took an overnight train to Palo Alto to meet the Stanford coach, Jack Weiershauser. The poor guy had to be down at the station at six in the morning to meet me. I was seated next to a woman on the night train. She was a nice-looking woman, probably in her thirties. She seemed very interested in hearing about my college life, and why I was going up to meet with the Stanford coach. After midnight, with the train cars darkened, most everyone was sleeping. I let the sideways rocking motion move my head down onto her shoulder. It was all so innocent. And deliberate. She was wearing a white knit sweater. I gradually let my head slide down onto her breasts. She became excited; passionately, she began stroking the back of my head.

The woman got off the train in San Jose. When she rose from her seat, she looked down, gave me a warm, friendly smile, and said goodbye. Perhaps thirty minutes later, I found the Stanford coach waiting for me at the Palo Alto station. Two members of the Stanford track team showed me around Palo Alto that weekend. (Bob Mathias was not one of them. He had just won his second Olympic decathlon title a few months before my visit.) The campus is vast. I saw a lot of space for running. Stanford wanted me. All I needed were the entrance grades.

The cross-country season that followed that incredible 1952 track season and the summer at Mammoth started out with the press touting me as virtually invincible. On a two-mile course in Griffith Park against Los Angeles City College, I broke free from everyone at the start and enjoyed a solo run through the woods. I felt fluid, free, fast. It was special being out there alone, with no worry of anyone catching you. Late afternoon shadows reached across a fire road, the cooling air was pleasant as twilight approached.

Cross country was not to be taken seriously by half milers. Right? In my case, wrong. The press began saying that I was "unbeatable." I bought into this image. Most half milers cannot tolerate cross country. I was different. Ask my old USC teammates. To this very day, they will tell you how exceptional I was in cross country. Unfortunately, I went undefeated through the junior college league meets. Nobody even challenged me. My time over three miles dropped down a full minute below what I had run in the conference final the year before.

Electrocuting a movie star

Ernie Shelton did not begin attending classes at USC until February. During a portion of the fall semester, the two of us slept in the front room of Rusty Tamblyn's studio apartment. The actor was gone a lot on location. He had remodeled a place behind his parents' home in North Hollywood. This was really nice of Rusty. We never should have done what we did to him one night when we discovered a magic set in a closet. In the array of his show-biz props we came upon a transformer with wires. From the foldout mattress that Ernie and I slept on, we could see Rusty's bed. He was out on a date. We waited up for him because we had placed a wire from that transformer under his sheets.

When we heard his car pull up, the excitement began to build and I became afraid I would not be able to hold back my laughter any longer. When Rusty came in we pretended, of course, that we were asleep. I think the movie star brushed his teeth. I bit my fingers to prevent an outburst that would ruin our fun.

Ernie was prepared to send the electric charge as soon as Rusty settled down in his bed. He seemed to take awhile. Come on, Rusty. Finally, he climbed in between his sheets. It was now almost impossible to keep our fiendish emotions under control. I nodded to Ernie. He turned, pressed down on the lever, and sent the current on its way. Rusty's scream confirmed the electrocution. He came straight up from the prone position. The All-City tumbler was airborne. He landed off to the side of his bed. It was, perhaps, the funniest thing I have ever seen. Rusty was mad at us. Damn mad.

"Bill Taylor will have to break all records to lose the Metropolitan Conference cross-country finals. He has humbled every conference opponent this season." This is what the sports editor of the Valley College newspaper wrote just days before the league final in cross country. But I went out too fast. In my mind, I could run away from the field and do whatever I wanted to do. A steep hill near the middle of the course demanded some respect. I had not paced myself well. The climb took a lot out of me. At the top, two runners went by me, and I was not able to respond and stay with them. I was not aware that one of the runners had finished third in the California high school mile final just a few months before. I had to wait fifty years for this information! I might have run differently had I known. I quit. Walked all the way back to the finish. Ernie ran by me. He ran cross country for the conditioning. When he jogged by he said, "*Come on*, Bill." Coach Slosson did not speak to me for a couple of weeks. We have never discussed my giving up that day.

When I faced all of the best junior college cross-country runners in the Southern California championship meet the next week, I earned tenth place. This was my reality. I was a damn good cross-country runner for a half miler.

When I heard that a high school friend had been killed in Korea, I asked, "Why Leonard?" Remember the little boy who was run over by the sycamore trees when I was four or five? I kept asking, "Why did the little boy have to die?" I was not old enough to reflect on death at that age. But I was nineteen when Leonard was killed. He was one of the nicest guys I knew in high school. Everyone liked him. Easy going, Leonard was comfortable with himself, friendly, and supportive of others. He joined the Army before graduating from high school. On December 4, 1952, Leonard wrote to me from Korea what follows:

Leonard

I guess Mom told you I was hit for the second time. But it was just a small wound. I'm back with the company and right back with patrol work. Dec. 1 was the first big snow and it sure is getting cold. I guess that's it for over here. So long for now and say hello the boys for me.

Your buddy,

Len

The night that I heard that Leonard was killed, I walked by myself in darkness. There were no street lights on Agnes Avenue. My mother had moved into an apartment near Van Owen and Laurel Canyon. Under a carpet of glittering stars, I protested Leonard's death to the universe. Why, why did the one who was of humility and goodness have to die? I cried.

The Sabers carried Leonard's casket to a grave in a cemetery in San Fernando. Rifles fired Taps for our friend. Then the American flag was folded and presented to his mother. Just like when my dad was killed and I was given the flag off my father's casket. Leonard was a really nice guy!

I learned that my pigeon-racing friend, Buddy Beatty, was killed while training racehorses. It was Buddy who had brought me into the Studio City pigeon club. Like Rusty, he was a champion tumbler. Dying from a fall from a horse seemed incongruous for someone who could do rapid flips and always land on his feet.

Two friends had died.

I went to the zoology professor and told him that I needed to receive a B in his course if I was to be admitted to Stanford. He helped me and we went over what to study for the final. I applied myself and earned an A on the exam. Even though this professor pinpointed what to study, I had to retain the information. I regret now that I was not interested in the sciences. I think it reflects my kind of Gnostic view toward physical objects. The Stanford coach wrote: "I am very glad to hear that you will receive at least 12 units of B, and 3 units of C. I was very sure that if you approached your instructors in the proper way, you would be able to convince them of your sincerity and desire to attend Stanford." This was early January, 1953.

Coach Weiershauser let me know that I could not begin training with the team until the end of March, due to Stanford being on the quarter system. I was not ready for Stanford academically. Not even close. I was supposed to take an entrance exam on March 14 in Los Angeles. I did not go. The 1953 Valley College track season was underway by then. We were loaded with the kind of talent that could win the state title. And I was elected co-captain. You do not pick up and leave a team once the season has started. I doubt that I would have been eligible to run for Stanford that season with my college season at Valley having started. Dave Casper and I were considered the two best junior college half milers in the nation. There was talk of our breaking the national junior college record.

The two best junior college half milers in the nation

I T WAS EARLY into the 1953 track season when I received the baton some six yards behind my rival, Casper, of Mt. San Antonio Junior College. We were on the anchor legs of the sprint medley at the Santa Barbara Relays. Going into the final turn of the half-mile leg, I saw his left foot land off the track and onto the infield. He knew I was there. I flew past Casper down the finishing stretch with the best time in the state through that date. For the third straight time, I beat Casper. Twice at the '52 state meet—in the prelim and final—and then at Santa Barbara.

At age nineteen, I found myself about eight seconds over the world record, four seconds above the national junior college mark. In April of '53, there was still considerable separation between my 880 times and national times. I had a ways to go. Running, being in top condition, brought rewards beyond winning races.

An actor is a thief

One morning, I was running down the beach enjoying the freedom of my stride at Malibu, when I approached a lone figure ahead. I ran effortlessly. The morning sun was still soft, the day retaining some of the crispness of dawn. I had the company of the breakers as they snapped, broke, some ninety feet offshore. Crack! Then the sea, with unpolluted white foam, ran up onto a smooth, sandy beach.

He was sitting there, just out of the reach of the varied distances that each wave traveled. He seemed to be writing something in the sand. As I ran past him, I looked down into the face of Richard Widmark. He wore a familiar expression. The movies became real. He did not say anything. Just seemed to study me. For those who remember him from the movies, it was that curious look. Actors look right at you. They are not afraid to stare. They want to possess you, take you into themselves. An actor is a thief.

I received a B in philosophy at Valley College. No special help by the professor on that final. Philosophy seemed to come fairly easily to me. I did not study for the course, yet I felt in touch with the concepts. Still, I wonder if that instructor was being generous. Perhaps I had told him that Stanford wanted me?

My friends in the drama department at Valley told me to be sure and see the Western classic, *Shane*. Alan Ladd, while fast with a gun, was a man of conscience and courage in the film. He did not take advantage of a married woman who had fallen in love with him. She was a good woman, but Ladd could have stolen her. Shane came through for the little boy, too. He fought the villain, played by Jack Palance, and gave the lad a hero with bravery, honor. Palance was an unforgettable, sinister gun fighter.

A sprinter from Los Angeles High School via Menlo Junior College became my best friend during that second track season at Valley College. Bill McCormick was fun. Stanford had recruited him for football. Bill was more interested in good-looking girls than academic subjects. And he always had one. And one for me. Something within my character was important to him. Was it my serious side? Life wasn't just for fun for me. Bill was all fun! We were inseparable that season. McCormick was my best fan. He would be there at the start of the half-mile races offering words of encouragement, and later in the season he would hum "Conquest," a USC-adopted motion picture sound track.

On April 18, the *Los Angeles Times* ran the headline, "TAYLOR, KIRCHMANN HIGHLIGHT JAYSEES." I was sure that some of my old high school friends saw that headline. While my half-mile time was not national yet, it was the best in the state. And a headline in the *Los Angeles Times* was a supreme sport moment for me.

I completed my second straight league season undefeated. The conference finals were held at Santa Monica Junior College on a cool evening. The Valley team was undefeated, too. Shelton, Lewis, and Serrins were gone, but an Anderson, Leach, and three top JC vaulters, along with McCormick and I, contributed enough points to win the 1953 state championship.

Me and my close friend, Bill McCormick on the
number one JC mile relay team in the nation.

I came down with a sore throat and a fever the day of our conference finals. Coach Slosson did not hesitate in running me. I won the
half mile by a considerable distance, but immediately after I finished
it felt like a saber blade had slashed through my skull. In the locker
room, I had the chills and saw that my flesh was purple. I sent word to
Coach Slosson that I would not be able to run the mile relay. Valley
barely won the team title that night. By one point. And they lost the
mile relay. I did not think about it that night, but I had stopped and
walked in the conference cross-country final only six months before.
Did Slosson question my reason for not running the relay? I accepted
the championship trophy with the other two co-captains and went out
into the night with McCormick and two girls. While I was feeling bet-

ter by then, I do not think that I should have tried to run the relay. My entire track life might have been different if I had not recovered after this meet. Major races were coming up over the next three weekends.

Criticism

In the Fresno Relays, Slosson had me running in three relays. First up was a wasted three-lap effort in the distance medley. I received the baton in a twilight zone. The leaders were out of reach. It was as though I was running by myself. However, we did place third.

I felt nauseated, unprepared to jump right back on the track twenty-five minutes later to anchor the 4 x 880 relay. After discussing how off I felt with one of the two Stanford athletes who had shown me around Palo Alto on that recruiting trip, I sent word to Slosson that I was not going to be ready for the second relay.

I sat up in the stands with the Valley team until late in the meet. Then Slosson inquired if I felt well enough to run a leg in the mile relay. This was the only time in my two years at Valley College that Jim put me on the leadoff leg. The first half of the quarter mile was on a straightaway, which meant a long finishing stretch as well. I felt very strong as I passed the field, moving Valley into first place. The Compton JC leadoff runner was one of the best junior college quarter milers in the country, but I took him. We won the relay against the top junior college teams in the state. And each of us received a Fresno Relays wristwatch.

Just as I was going to bed at the hotel, Joe Leach threw his rolled up sweatsuit into my room and yelled, "Here, *you* run for us, Taylor!" I was puzzled. I wish I had just held up the wristwatch I had just won and taunted Leach with it instead of letting him bother me. But, back then, I took the hit. Felt sheepish. Later, the coach's wife, Nancy Slosson, told me that Leach and another teammate waited for me after arriving back at Valley because they wanted to beat me up. Why? Because I dropped out of that second relay.

The next week in the college newspaper there was a mini headline in the sports page that read: "Too Bad About Taylor." Oh? I was surprised to read, "It's too bad that Taylor felt he was unable to run his

880 leg of the two-mile relay last week in the Fresno Relays. He had an upset stomach following a 1320 yd. stint in an earlier race, but recovered in time to run on the four-man mile relay team that won in a record time. Had Taylor run in the two mile relay, probably the least Valley would have been is third, and the Monarchs would have won the JC crown instead of Los Angeles City College. Third place is six points; Valley lost the meet by a little more than one point."

I deliver two straight undefeated track seasons in my event in conference meets, run relay leg after relay leg for the Valley teams, then I am blamed for not running just one leg at Fresno. The quote does not sting today. Back then, it ate away at me. Also, I did not think that people paid any attention to the team scores at the Coliseum, Fresno, or Modesto Relays, which are made up of irregular events. The scores did not define the worth of the team; the relay races and some special feature events were what mattered.

An incredible week

On Tuesday, May 12, just three days after the Fresno Relays, a peculiar 880 race was set up on the "weed patch oval." An outstanding California high school half miler, Bert Purdue, was to run the half mile against me in a workout. I was told that his coach was looking for competition for the exceptional lad because private schools lacked the quality and quantity of meets that were available to the public school athletes. I did not know at the time that Purdue had placed third in the state half-mile final the year before.

This race on Tuesday did not make sense to me. The Southern California junior college finals were on Thursday of that week. Then, the next night, the great Coliseum Relays. What was going on? And what was Leach doing in the half mile that afternoon? I did not get it yet. Purdue was eighteen—just a year younger than I was. The cocky bantam rooster liked setting a fast pace. We lost Leach before the final turn. I worked my way gradually past Purdue coming down a familiar finishing stretch. The time was my fastest from a standing start. And on our lousy track. But it still was far from a good national college mark. I had the dry heaves after I finished. I can still see the patch of stickers that were on the track below me. I was down on my knees.

My legs felt rubbery

Two days later we drove out to Riverside for the Southern California junior college finals. The half mile was run at twilight. The air was warm, and still. The conditions were perfect for a fast time. Just before the start, a competitor from another school came over and wished me luck. He said the other runners were pulling for me over Casper.

The first lap was very, very fast. I was just trying to stay up, be relaxed. Down the backstretch of the second lap, I saw that Casper was way out in front. I went after him. According to the *Los Angeles Examiner* race commentary, my rival was "twenty yards ahead." But I closed and closed down a long finishing stretch. Just before we reached the tape, with Casper only a couple of yards up on me, my legs felt rubbery. This was a new sensation. There was considerable commotion around the finish line as the officials compared their watches. The place was buzzing. Something big had happened. Dave and I had just missed the national junior college record. Jerome Walters of Compton JC, who in 1956 would make the U.S. Olympic Team in the 1500 meters, held the mark. Casper was less than a second from it. I was only two-tenths of a second behind Dave. This was over a three-second drop in time from the Tuesday clash with Purdue. Casper deserves the credit for the fast time. He went out fast and made it possible. We both became national runners that night.

The *Los Angeles Times* featured the two of us the next morning. We became the story of the junior college season. Along with a shot putter from Santa Monica JC.

The Coliseum Relays were the night after the Riverside feat. It was a long drive back from Riverside to the San Fernando Valley. No freeway went past Pasadena yet. And, on top of that half mile, I ran a mile relay leg at the end of the meet. What would be left in my legs the next night?

"Here comes Taylor!"

The Coliseum Relays was the premier invitational in the country. Forty to fifty thousand people would be in the 1932 Olympic Stadium. When it was time to begin warming up on the Coliseum infield, I saw Payton Jordan. At that moment, he was going to be my coach at Occidental College the next track season. Oxy? When did this happen? The Los Angeles newspapers had just announced that Oxy had landed me. No, I had not notified Stanford yet. Things were moving swiftly. When Payton Jordan ran for USC, he made the front cover of *Life* magazine. The handsome blond sprinter looked like a Greek god. Just one year before, Jordan had coached two of his middle-distance runners to the Olympic Games. I was going to have that kind of a coach! McCormick and Ralph Avalon, a top California junior college pole vaulter on our Valley team, had accepted Oxy track scholarships, too. On the Coliseum infield that night, I went up to Mr. Jordan and asked, "How should I warm up?" A master psychologist, Mr. Jordan said, "Just jog easily. You will be fine, Billy."

I noticed Joe Leach running around the infield. This was strange; he was not entered in anything. I had not read the program yet. Later, I discovered that Slosson had listed the two of us as possible anchor runners in the sprint medley relay. I was the lead name, but why was Leach even mentioned? He could not approach my times in the half mile. This hurt.

The Coliseum Relays committee had set up a special relay because of the outstanding freshmen on the USC, Occidental, and UCLA frosh teams, as well as the speed and middle distance talent at Valley, Mt. San Antonio, and Santa Ana junior colleges. The relay order for a sprint medley was as follows: 440 yards, 220 yards, 220 yards, 880 yards. Fortunately, the Coliseum Relays committee picked my event for the anchor. The national high school record holder for the mile and state champion over that distance would anchor for the USC freshmen. The winner of the L. A. City half-mile final in the 880 when I was a senior at North Hollywood High School would run last for Oxy. The UCLA freshman team would anchor a runner who had finished only four-tenths of a second behind the state high school mile champion the year before. Talent. Talent. Talent. And there was Casper! This had already been the biggest week of my running life.

While anxious during my light warm up, once out on the track I settled down and was confident. The future Olympic 400-meter champion, Mike Larrabee, gave the USC freshmen a lead after the opening quarter-mile leg. The Trojans then thrilled the crowd with their speed on the second and third legs. When the batons began arriving for the final exchanges, I was some twelve yards behind the USC star, Fernando Ledesma, at least six behind Casper. Dave raced by Fernando too quickly. I heard the announcer say, "That is Dave Casper, who set a new Southern California junior college meet 880 record last night at Riverside." I stayed relaxed, let the race come to me. Casper ran a stupid first lap in 51 seconds. That was way too fast. On the final turn, as we approached my familiar tunnel, I heard the announcer say, "Here comes Taylor!" I was closing on Casper. And Ledesma. I kept reducing the distance. Casper was spent. I went by him some forty yards from the finish. I came up near Ledesma, but the great runner had enough reserve to hold me off. Not by much.

It did not matter. I had lowered my time by another two seconds. While an unofficial relay split, nonetheless, it was only three seconds above the world record. My teammates were ecstatic. We received tall Coliseum Relays trophies for our second place finish. Within twenty-four hours, I had tasted the national level, twice.

On Monday afternoon, Slosson told me that USC had called to say they wanted me on a full athletic scholarship. The college of my boyhood dreams, a national championship team, wanted me. No school came close to USC in number of Olympians, or national collegiate track titles. They were offering me the chance to become a part of the great Trojan tradition. The SC aegis on the front of their uniform was known throughout the track world. Great, surprise, upset places resulted at the nationals for those who wore it. How could I say no?

I drove over to Eagle Rock to tell Payton Jordan that I was backing out on my commitment to be on his track team the next season, that I was going to USC instead of Oxy. Mr. Jordan told me that I was making the right decision, that I would always wonder if I did not take the USC scholarship.

Remember, Payton was a famous USC great. Their 1938 sprint relay team still held the world 4 x 100 yard record. Was I making a mistake? From an educational standpoint, no question. I would have responded to the Oxy liberal arts curriculum. I think the smaller classes and the academic atmosphere with the Ivy League architecture would have encouraged me to take my courses more seriously. Especially in the humanities. Then there was the loss of a coach who had just developed two Olympians in my events. That was a lot to walk away from. What a gift Payton gave me that afternoon. There was absolutely no attempt to change my mind. No guilt. He did say, just as I was leaving, "You will miss being on a world record 4 x 880 yard relay team." In a way, this happened. Oxy ran under the listed world record in the Coliseum Relays the next year, but finished second.

I received a letter that week from the Stanford coach, Jack Weiershauser. He congratulated me on "a very fine half-mile race" at Riverside, and told me, "It certainly shows what we have known all along—that you can run a very fine half mile." Then he warned me about other recruiters: "Now that you have indicated your true ability on the track, I am sure the other universities will put pressure on you to have you enroll at their schools. However, you have stated that you are coming to Stanford and that should be sufficient reason for them not to keep the pressure on you." I was NOT going to Stanford.

I do not know whether he read about it in the paper that week or received my letter first. I did write to him; I did tell him that I was sorry. However, when he heard about my going to USC he wrote a letter that seemed to question my character. Yet he wanted me to know that he continued to hold me in good regard. He closed his letter by asking if there was any way that I could change my mind. I had never told him that I would not consider other schools. And, at one point, I was very sincere about my intention to go to Stanford.

One week after the Coliseum Relays anchor leg, I won my trial heat in the state finals for the second straight year. The definitive meet for California junior college track and field athletes was held in 1953 in Visalia. Visalia is between Bakersfield and Fresno, to the east of Highway Ninety-nine. The newspapers featured the 880 as the prime running event. It was anticipated that Casper and I would challenge the existing national record. Here is what the *Los Angeles Examiner* published: "The national 880 record of 1:53.7, set by Compton's Jerome Walters four or five years ago, is due to go. Dave Casper of Mt. San Antonio has run 1:54.5 and L. A. Valley's Bill Taylor 1:54.7. Casper set the pace in the race in which both top clockings were recorded, while Taylor lagged along about 20 yards behind until the last 220 yards. Taylor finished with plenty of reserve." Oh yeah, but my legs sure felt "rubbery."

A news release from Visalia read: "Mt. San Antonio's Dave Casper (1:54.5) and Los Angeles Valley's Bill Taylor (1:54.7) are bearing down on the national 880 standard." I was only nineteen. I did not think about it before the final, but Dave carried that bad memory of tossing the baton in the Coliseum Relays to motivate him. The year before, I had gone into the state meet with a disappointing finish at Riverside the week before. Adversity can contribute enormously to one's will and concentration.

I wanted to win that state title. But I had no plan. I relied more on hoping it would be there. That I would have light legs and the speed that carried me to that great time just a week before. On the backstretch of the second lap in the final, I reached down and went after Casper. However, he seemed to be gliding along—his long, skinny legs eating up the distance without their usual frantic effort. As we approached the last turn, I became excited. He was in range. I had reduced his sizable lead to a few yards. I could win. But this time he seemed to be waiting for me.

It was just the two of us. I came off the final turn expecting to work my way by him. But somewhere down that finishing stretch I realized that I wasn't going to be the state champion. The Hilmer Lodge tactics worked. Dave, by waiting, had just enough reserve to hold me off. Both of us were under the state meet record. However, our times were almost two seconds slower than they were at Riverside the week before. For the second straight year, I missed winning the state half-mile final by two-tenths of a second. I left Visalia happy. We won the state team title. And, in placing second, I had run under the state meet record. But when I read the newspaper accounts I felt left out. Our quarter miler, Clarence Anderson, had set a new meet record in winning his event. And Joe Leach won the mile. The time by Leach was not impressive, but he really had improved during the season and his ten points were a major contribution to our team victory. The fact that I had run under the prior state record in finishing two-tenths of a second out of first was not mentioned. Points, a first place finish, were given priority over the quality of the marks.

I will not see it in print for over forty years, but the official collegiate track and field pamphlet listed Dave and I as number one and number two in the nation for 1953 junior college half-mile times. And our Valley College mile relay team was number one, as was the sprint medley team that I anchored.

The next week, our mile relay team was invited to run in the Compton Invitational against USC, Oxy, UCLA, and a foursome with Olympic stars representing the Grand Street Boys. Just before I stepped on the track to run the second leg that night, I noticed Verle Sorgen of USC preparing to run third. A week or two later, Sorgen will place third in the national collegiate 440 yard final. The USC anchorman, Jimmy Lea, will win the event. In just a few months, I will join the Phi Psi house and Sorgen and Lea will be my fraternity brothers. My world was moving very fast. Our Valley relay team was not capable of matching the relay splits run by the Grand Street Boys team with three Olympic gold medalists on it, or USC because of the Sorgen and Lea clockings. Because we were far behind the lead teams, Anderson let up early and walked across the finish line. Clarence did not cost us the full 1.6-second difference that would have tied the national mark, but we could have come very close to breaking it.

The Kansas cowboy

A Kansas cowboy, Wes Santee, received the most attention that night at Compton. His ferocious kick brought an overflow crowd of some ten thousand to its feet when he sprinted away from a Finnish miler and just missed breaking the world record. This was the year before Roger Bannister ran his sub-four minute mile. After the competition that night at Compton, the coaches and athletes were invited to an outdoor barbecue. I spotted Santee, watched him. And I noticed that he was wearing cowboy boots. Third pair of cowboy boots—first Roy Rogers, then the cowboy at Mammoth, now Santee. In just two years, Santee will be my good friend and teammate at Quantico.

It was okay to pretend to be track stars in the driveway on Toluca Lake Avenue when I was a kid, but at Compton, I was there to compete. I can look back and see how I was both a runner and a sports enthusiast. The journalist was in me at the meets along with my fierce desire to succeed. Great athletes have the capacity to concentrate, block things out that will distract them. Most runners are potential victims of forgetting why they are on the track.

The Valley College track banquet was painful for me. I felt ignored. Perhaps it was payback time for my not running the relay leg at Fresno? Payton Jordan was the guest speaker. Jordan will leave Occidental in a few years to become the head track coach at Stanford. Then, in 1968, he will be named the head U.S. Olympic track and field coach.

The Most Outstanding Athlete award went to Clarence Anderson, the state champion and meet record holder over 440 yards. Okay. But the "Most Improved" went to Leach. I had dropped my 880 time by over seven seconds and come within a second of the national record, yet I was denied special recognition. Joe did come out of nowhere to win the state mile title, but his time was some ten seconds off the national mark. I felt a little better about the evening when, as co-captain of the state championship team, I had my picture taken with Payton Jordan for the newspapers. While some jealousy haunted the ending for me, it had been an incredible track season. Even, unbelievable!

The smells of Quantico

I SIGNED UP to become an officer in the United States Marine Corps. While the Korean War was just concluding, the college draft remained quite real. And the USMC was the only way for me to be deferred from the draft and to become an officer upon graduating from college. Four-year-university students had the opportunity to join the ROTC and to qualify for a commission in the Army, Navy, or Air Force. But ROTC was not available on a junior college campus. So it was the Marine Corps for me. The contract required that I attend two summer camps at a place called Quantico. Upon graduation from a four-year university, I would be commissioned a second lieutenant and serve two years of active duty. The officers who came through the ROTC program had to stay in the service for three years.

Heavy humidity and mosquito spray

I still remember the smells of Quantico, Virginia. The disinfectants in the latrines, the odor of the dungarees, boots, shrubs, tree limbs soaked by heavy humidity and mosquito spray. Late at night, we jumped out of a truck that had taken us out into the jungle of the vast Marine Corps base some twenty-five miles below Washington, D. C. A chorus of cicadas provided the welcoming band. The insects would perform their concert every night. I felt empty, unknown, depersonalized. What was I doing there?

I arrived wearing my California State Championship track jacket. Do you think this impressed my drill instructor, the one who had just returned from combat in Korea with freezing-cold weather and endless deaths? Our DIs were unmerciful. We were college boys, deferred from war. They had paid the price.

How could the Marines bill this a "summer camp"? It was USMC boot camp. The future officers of the United States Marine Corps were turned over to these sergeants and corporals just back from the abyss.

They only had us for six weeks, not the traditional twelve weeks that regular Marines experience. And we had from Saturday noon until Sunday evening off. Enlisted men had to spend the full twelve weeks without any liberty, but we could quit at any time. The image of being a Marine Corps officer was heroic. But war, combat, felt terrible. Again, what was I doing there?

My drill instructor, Sergeant Dawly, told me, "You will never make a Marine." I took his words personally. Mistake. Come on Bill, figure it out. Boot camp is sadism with a purpose. As soon as he heard that I was from North Hollywood, he began calling me "Ms. Hollywood." It was a lovely time.

One hilarious, yet demeaning moment, came during one of the endless marching drill sessions. The drill instructors marched us up and down the paved streets, on the parade ground, telling us again and again to dig in our heels. During one of the drills my knee wrap began to unwind. Remember my trick knee? My football injury from high school? It could still go out, even lock. It helped to have a wrap around it when marching. But this time it unwound and began coming out through my trousers. As the cotton wrap trailed behind me, that lovable drill sergeant yelled out so that all could hear, "Miss Taylor, your rag is showing!"

The drill instructors ran two guys to death that summer. When a Marine would faint, collapse, while running the obstacle course in ninety to a hundred degree heat, we were told to "leave that sissy alone." Again and again we would hear, "He'll never make a Marine."

The running, of course, did not faze me. I had placed second in the California state half-mile final only weeks before. At that time, the Marine Corps did not care one bit about my track legs (this will change when I represent them on the track).

Rommie Loudd, the future All-American football player who UCLA "farmed out" to Valley College, was in my Marine Corps summer camp. And on one of those five weekends at Quantico when we could disappear between Saturday noon and Sunday night, Rommie and I went on liberty together. All we wanted to do was sleep. We planned to get a room and sack out.

The town of Quantico had a colonial-style hotel down on the Potomac River. It looked quaint, traditional. When Rommie and I sought rooms, he was not allowed to register. Right, Rommie was a Negro. He could be a Marine and be killed in defense of his country in Korea or somewhere else, but he could not have a hotel bed in Virginia. The word "black" was not used back then. Rommie insisted that I take a room. He went off "to be with [his] people." I did not wake up until four or five in the afternoon *the next day*! I had slept for over twenty-four hours. After I came out of the deep sleep, I felt incredibly good.

I saw Rommie back at the camp, asked him where he had spent Saturday night. The tall, handsome football star said, "My people took care of me." He had gone to a Negro bar. Someone took him home. I hope she was real pretty. As the two of us walked out of the camp together several weeks later, Loudd put it very simply—"I am not coming back."

Sergeant Dawly wrote on the back of my platoon photograph that final day: "To my little boy." I felt squelched, put down one last time. It did not occur to me that he might have liked me. I recognize today that there was a part of me that did want to be the little boy. That I was pulled between wanting a father and being a man.

USC dream letter

WHEN I RETURNED HOME from Quantico, I was happy just to be able to sit down when I wanted to do so. And being away from home for six weeks made me more conscious of my immediate surroundings. The Marine Corps discipline had become a part of me. It will last a lifetime. The USC track coach, Jesse Mortensen, sent me a dream letter. On August 4, 1953, the head coach of the collegiate championship track team wrote: "We have high hopes of your being a national champion in the near future at the University of Southern California." *High hopes. National champion.* These were the words of a lifetime for me. Time froze. USC, whose icons of football and track had decorated my bedroom walls, was expecting me to become their national champion.

I had a few weeks before my classes began, so I drove up to Mammoth. For the second straight summer, I was intoxicated by the higher elevation, the pure air, the smell of pine replacing the Marine Corps disinfectants. The manager, Dave Gray, told me that it would be okay for me to sleep in the bunkhouse and eat with the staff if I just helped around the camp. No charge. Nice.

I was in poor shape when I reported for the USC cross-country team in September. The Quantico marching drills had been tough on my legs. And the coach, Jack Davis (who the prior summer had just missed winning the 110-meter high hurdles final in the Olympic Games) was difficult. USC did not hire a distance coach for cross country when I was there. The role was given to a graduate student, someone who had done exceedingly well on the track for USC.

I was going to become one of them

When I joined the Phi Psi fraternity, the house where Lea and Sorgen were members, Davis told me that I would come to regret it. Jack was a proud, jealous, opinionated Kappa Sig. I had not yet heard the history of why Jack hated the Phi Psi's.

I joined this fraternity because the guys seemed more down to earth than in other houses on the row and because of their array of USC athletic heroes. For example, note this list of "the brothers" when I joined: Parry O'Brien, world record holder in the shot put and Olympic champion; Jimmy Lea, soon-to-be an Olympian and world record holder; Des Koch, who will become the national collegiate discus champion and place third in the Olympic Games; Verle Sorgen, multi-sport star at USC and a collegiate All-American in track over 440 yards. These guys were genuine Trojan All-Time stars. And I had a letter from Coach Mortensen saying that I was going to become one of them.

The cross country workouts were hard. I was not used to the new kind of training sessions that were becoming popular. They featured fast efforts over various distances with a short rest. At Valley College, Coach Slosson had trained me in a different way. He gave me more recovery time and put an emphasis on greater speed.

I was quite disappointed when Davis did not award me a cross-country letter. I was fifth or sixth man on the team. Normally the top seven, at a minimum, receive such recognition. Maybe there was a point system based on places in meets that you had to reach in order to qualify. Or, maybe Davis was paying me back for not pledging his fraternity?

I had started out living in a two story boarding house just off Hoover Boulevard, a few blocks from the USC campus. Ron Morris, who, just months before, had set a new national high school pole vault record, lived there. So did Marv Gough. The former Marine was an absolute Trojan fanatic. Gough had been an outstanding linebacker on the USC football team. He was just beginning as an assistant football coach when I met him. Years later, he will be fired for "enthusiastic" recruiting. My roommate was Doug Maijala, a former Marine and javelin thrower who would later become co-captain of the USC track and field team along with Morris. Patti lived in the Delta Gamma sorority across the street from our Phi Psi house. Mary was a just a few houses down the row. An interesting coincidence.

My little brother developed into an outstanding high school basketball and baseball player. I was really proud of him. In the last few minutes of a close game between Hollywood and North Hollywood High School, I watched him calmly drop in three consecutive set shots from beyond the top of the key to win the game for the Sheiks. In my old North Hollywood High School gym. Remember, Harold was playing for Hollywood High School.

Swish, swish, swish. When Harold sank those three, long, late game shots, I was sitting with my former vice-principal, Norman McLeod. I had become a college sport hero back on my old high school campus. It felt great sitting with him and feeling such a sense of accomplishment in sports. And, hanging those light bulbs out of my bedroom window for night basketball paid off for my little brother.

I felt her body up against my arm as we were crowded together, waiting for the student gates to be opened for a USC football game in the Coliseum. Students were lined up, eager to locate a good seat. When I glanced down to see who was up against me, I discovered a darling dark-haired coed. She wore a white blouse, white being the required color for those seated in the rooting section. I personalized this innocent contact, felt that the touching might suggest fate. I am quite sure that she did not even notice me that morning.

"I'm afraid of falling in love with you again"

One night, Mary and I went to see a movie in downtown Los Angeles. A spontaneous date, it felt so natural when we held hands walking down the aisle to our seats. Just like it had been when we were in love a couple of years before. After returning from the movie, I pulled Mary into my arms and those incredible lips were mine once again. Lush, warm, wonderful. Then I saw her tears and asked what was wrong. She told me that she was afraid of falling in love with me again. Oh?

I thought about calling her for another date over the next couple of weeks, but decided not to get that relationship going again. I almost called her. Then someone told me that she had announced her engagement, just a couple of weeks after those tears in the parking lot. Did she know that night that she was going to be engaged? What conflicting feelings did I produce in her?

Mary invited me to a Christmas party. Not my Mary, but the beautiful one from Camp High Sierra. I was proud of my track image as I entered her family home in Eagle Rock. Within moments, Mary yanked me into the kitchen and held up her left hand. There was an engagement ring! The cowboy had won the girl. My Western script had come true. Mary was a real prize, and she had chosen Lou, the lean, handsome cowboy from Tucson with the broken speech.

During the winter break, USC football stars Des Koch and Landon Exley and I drove up to the eastern Sierras, almost as far north on Highway 395 as Mammoth. We were resting by the main stream that flows out of Convict Lake when I rolled over and my knee locked. If I gradually straightened my leg out, then relaxed, the cartilage would slip back to where it was supposed to be. This time it didn't. We drove down to Lone Pine to find a doctor. He held the knee in such a way that it went back into place quickly. No pain. I was grateful and told him so. In trying the knee out, I gingerly began to cross the main street in town. No cars. Then a convertible pulled up to the crosswalk with some local boys. It was clear that they wanted to start something, to test out their manhood at my expense. Just as one of them was beginning to leap out of the car, Des came around the corner of a building. The muscular Koch, who played a gladiator in the movie *Spartacus*, said in his deep voice, "Having trouble, Bill?" The convertible quickly drove away.

One morning on the SC campus, Patti and a few of her sorority sisters walked by me as I was raking leaves. She greeted me with a warm, "Hi Bill." I was raking leaves as part of the track scholarship deal. The university could not legally just pay you to run for them; you had some chores to do under a time clock. Sometimes I wound the ivy up and down the wire fence around the track. It felt great being identified as a Trojan athlete by someone like Patti. On another morning, Roland Sink, a former USC track great and 1948 Olympian, said "Hi Bill" as he walked past me on campus. Before that greeting, I did not know that he even knew who I was.

The USC publicity release for track affirmed my Trojan position as the lead half miler. The official track brochure announced my presence as a member of the 1954 Trojan team in this way: "SC will be fairly strong in the half mile for the first time in several years, due to the running of Bill Taylor." I couldn't believe it. I was expected to be the event leader on the team that had won the national title for five straight years.

My name was on the press release that introduced Ernie Shelton, Jimmy Lea, Jon Arnett, Des Koch, and Leon Patterson. Shelton and Lea would win the national collegiate title in their events that season; Koch and Arnett would place second, the sophomore, Patterson, third. Three other great Trojan names were on the 1954 team: a Joe Graffio would place second in the 100 in the nationals, Willard Wright second in the high hurdles, and a sophomore, Mike Larrabee, fourth in the quarter mile. "Fairly strong" did not mean that I was of national prominence. However, the brochure also said that I was "expected to drop my time considerably." The USC school record was less than three seconds from my time at Riverside against Casper, just seven-tenths of a second from my anchor leg the next night in the Coliseum Relays. I certainly was in range of the Trojan immortality. Everyone on scholarship on the USC track teams was expected to place in the nationals. That is why we were there.

My roommate at the nationals in Ann Arbor, Michigan that coming spring was Mike Larrabee. Nobody was counting on him placing. His past times and places did not warrant such an expectation. As mentioned, Mike finished fifth. Ten years later, he will become the Olympic champion over 400 meters.

A little Canadian half miler with outstanding leg speed was going to run on the USC freshman team in 1954. I would not have to worry about him my junior year because freshmen were not allowed to compete for the varsity back then. Outspoken Murray Cockburn was my age. I was unaware that he was the Canadian junior half-mile champion. When the little bugger out-kicked me in a half-mile time trial, the campus newspaper gave Murray this headline: "Freshman shines in time trials with 1:57.6 880." A different write-up on our early season trial gave him this credit: "Canada's contribution to Trojan track and field completely stole the spotlight from more experienced SC runners." It did not say that Murray was twenty, too. Or that he was the Canadian national junior champion.

So much for the pre-season track brochure. I was going to have to fight for my half-mile identity at USC. After a couple of weak years in my event, major recruiting resulted in Cockburn, along with another talented half miler, being brought in to bolster the Trojan image. In a 660 trial, which is 220 yards short of the 880, a brash Ernie Amador edged me out. Ernie was equipped with muscular elasticity; he finished second in the California high school finals two years earlier.

The script had been written

A beauty like Lasley was not hard to locate. She was in a sorority across the street from the Phi Psi house. Unfortunately, Lasley had a boyfriend. He was not attending USC, or any college. I still went after her. The script had been written. There was a certain fatalism in me. A destiny. The movies had encouraged it.

On one of the few dates I could pull off with this adorable girl, we drove out to North Hollywood and I introduced her to my mother. Then it was over to Beverly Hills so that Lasley could make an appearance at a sorority party. I parked my '41 Ford Club Coupe on a street lined with mansions. It was a typical USC neighborhood. Rain was pounding heavily on the roof. My fantasy became real as we enjoyed lengthy kisses. Ecstasy.

Lasley was my Audrey Hepburn

I thought I had landed the girl when we went into the party, but once in front of her sorority sisters, she distanced herself from me. There was no quit in me. Stubborn, I had not given any thought to the wealth difference. Most of the girls in the most coveted sororities came from rich families. "Home" meant a large house in San Marino, or Arcadia, or Beverly Hills, or Pacific Palisades, or Laguna Beach. Lasley? Where was her home? I had not inquired. My Stoic image would land the girl. Just like the cowboy won Mary in Mammoth. Wealth had nothing to do with it.

Jim Smith and I had seen *Roman Holiday* in 1953 at the Vogue Theatre on Hollywood Boulevard. We, along with the world, immediately fell in love with that absolutely darling new actress, Audrey Hepburn. Lasley was my Audrey Hepburn.

We flew to Tucson, Arizona for our initial dual meet. Three of my Valley College teammates were competing for the University of Arizona: McCormick, Anderson, and one of those three strong pole vaulters, Ed Lafferty. Bill and Clarence had just finished playing football for the Arizona Wildcats. I let the meet record holder from the prior year set the pace in the 880 and then, going into the final turn, I went by him. This was my first victory as a USC half miler. I had no trouble taking my teammate, Amador. My time set a new meet record. It felt fantastic when, the next morning in the *Los Angeles Times* I read, "1st Taylor SC 1:55.5 new meet record." The win felt natural.

McCormick wanted to drive me to the airport so that we could visit awhile longer. Bill took me to the wrong airport. After racing across Tucson to the correct one, McCormick literally drove out onto the runway where the Trojan charter was waiting. Coach Mortensen was waiting at the top of the steps. Nothing was said, but it probably was a good thing that I had won that day.

The Occidental coach, Payton Jordan, staged what was likely the most spectacular college dual meet ever. The pre-meet hype was enormous. A photograph of me wearing the famous USC uniform appeared in the *Valley Times*. Surely, my high school friends and their parents must have seen it. I had advanced to the major college level in sports and it was important to me that people saw evidence of this. The *Los Angeles Times* ran a large picture of Marty Montgomery, Amador, and me because the 880 was being advertised as the feature event.

Six of us had 880 times within one second of each other. When we arrived over in Eagle Rock I found a large photo of myself in a multi-page glossy program. The Oxy stadium was packed on both sides of the track. Coach Jordan even arranged for fireworks to explode before the competition began. The teams even ran single file out onto the field and stood facing the main bleachers while the national anthem was played. Just before running out, we waited in a corridor where the bleachers separated. People were looking down at us like we were a football team about to come out on the field. A USC track team was big time. Unbeatable. National champions year after year. I received the stares as yet more confirmation of my place on such a team.

When Oxy upset USC in the 4 x 110 yard relay, the Tiger fans went crazy. They had no business taking our sprinters. Then Jim Terrill won the mile for Oxy, setting a meet record. Was little Occidental College going to upset the great USC track team? I felt comfortable out on the track before the half-mile event. But I let the race favorite, Eddie Shinn, break free. In order to go after him, I had to slow up and go around some runners. I closed the gap to some extent on the back-stretch of the second lap, but Eddie was five yards up on me at the finish. The winning time was just over one second above the meet record set by the Olympian, John Barnes. Nice company. I did not feel badly about finishing second.

I should have been more disappointed in myself. That carelessness over the initial lap cost me any chance of beating Shinn. And when the announcer told the packed stadium that Eddie and I had run two of the fastest times in the nation for the young season, I felt proud of this national recognition. He was four-tenths of a second up on me at the finish. Why did I feel satisfied just to be running at such a high level? It would have been better for me as an athlete to be mad, angry that I had let him get too far in front of me earlier in the race. Oh, USC defeated Oxy that day. It was not even close by the finish.

I did not know at the time, but my father had attended Occidental College for three years. Again, with his love of sports, and USC, can you imagine how much my running in this meet would have meant to us both, if he had not been killed?

Over time, I heard more and more stories about my dad. My mother told me how cats would follow him home. And how he would check the size of the other fellow in a traffic dispute, and if the gent appeared too big he would drive away saying, "He who looks and runs away, lives to fight another day." A collage of images formed around my father. Bill was a maverick; Bill loved to sing; Bill was very creative, talented; Bill could do anything he wanted to do. And my favorite, "Bill was the most fun guy I ever knew." I could have gained so much by knowing him. And how would his life have turned out for him had he not lost his life at age forty-four? What would he have experienced if he had lived another forty years? His sister, Clara, will live to be over one hundred.

His younger brother Marcus told of how the two of them were on an ocean liner going up the coast to San Francisco when my dad became seasick. My father, a very strong swimmer, literally jumped overboard and swam to shore. My uncle told me that my dad tied his shoes around his neck with the laces and dove off the side saying, "I'll meet you in San Francisco."

Dreams can come true

The next week, Stanford had to face our powerful team in the Los Angeles Coliseum. Mal Whitfield, the two-time Olympic 800-meter champion, had been coming over to the USC practice track to train. He was co-holder of the world record at the time, too. As I came around the final turn in first place against Stanford—yes, by the tunnel—the Olympic champion leaned his head out over the track from the infield, and made a face. He wanted me to relax. Whitfield was the most fluid, relaxed 800-meter runner to ever grace the American tracks. And he had taken an interest in me.

I easily won the 880 that afternoon. When they put the results on the electronic scoreboard under the Olympic torch, it hit me. For up there, above where my father had stood one night when I was a little boy, was "1st Taylor USC 1:55.5". I said to myself, "Son of a bitch, dreams really can come true."

My cousin Bobby came out onto the infield of the Coliseum that afternoon, just like I had when he ran for USC against Stanford in the late 1940s. I recall him saying, "It wasn't much fun knowing that the highest you would ever place would be second." His teammate was the 100 and 220-yard world record holder, Mel Patton. The Hager side of the family kicked in my track genes. I did not have Bobby's speed, but I had outstanding range. My 440 times revealed good speed; my middle and long distance marks were outstanding.

Jim Terrill, that Oxy star who had broken the meet mile record against USC two weeks before, was alongside of me going into the final turn as we were anchoring our teams in the two mile relay at the Santa Barbara Relays. There were no bleachers on the Pacific Ocean side of Carter Field, just the dark, lonely beach on the other side of a road. As Terrill and I entered the final turn, I remember hearing his breathing, the sound of our spikes clawing into the dirt surface. For that brief moment, we were removed from the other athletes, the crowd. I was waiting for the finishing kick.

When we were right where I had seen Casper step off the track with his left foot the year before, Terrill and I suddenly had company. Mal Whitfield was anchoring the Los Angeles Athletic Club team. The world record holder suddenly pranced up alongside of us. And the son-of-a-bitch was humming. This time he did not make a funny face as I came off the turn. He just sprinted away from the two of us. Terrill held me off by a yard or two. That was okay. Jim was of national stature; just being able to run with the best was very affirming for me. Tilt. The wish to belong is an important human need. But it is not the ingredient that produces champions.

Whitfield was all over me after we finished. He let me know that I should have given him more of a battle when he hummed past us going around the final turn. I was running Terrill, not Mal Whitfield. However, this scolding by the world record holder in the 880 will contribute to the greatest victory of my track life.

"Where are you parked?"

I saw Rommie Loudd for the last time at a track meet between two all-black high school teams in Watts. I took a USC freshman track friend with me. Jefferson and Jordan were likely the two best prep track teams in the nation. I gave no thought to the racial differences; I probably believed that a track meet was not a confrontational setting. I did feel a little uneasy when I noticed during the meet that my friend and I were the only whites in the stands.

When Rommie and I spotted one another at the end of the meet, he called me over to meet a UCLA teammate, Milt Davis. Davis was an All-American defensive back. Rommie then asked, "Where are you parked?" He let me know that they would walk us to our car. Oh! So the fellow who could not sleep in the same hotel with me on the Potomac in Quantico because he was a Negro, thought it necessary to escort two white guys out of a black neighborhood. Sadly, I read in the *Los Angeles Times* years later that Rommie had been arrested in Florida for dealing in drugs. Big-time drug movements. Shortly before this, I read that Rommie had become the commissioner of a new professional football league. I heard no more about my Quantico friend, the All-American who was refused a room while we were on liberty together!

Puffy white clouds

WE FLEW OUT of the Burbank airport into an afternoon sky decorated with puffy white clouds. Until that flight to Tucson a few weeks before, the only plane I had ever flown in was a piper cub. My father took me up in it over Glendale.

Toluca Lake is only a couple of miles to the south of the runway; our charter banked over my old neighborhood. As we broke through the pure white thunderheads, a powder blue sky formed a dome over the earth. I was happy. I was flying north to race against Cal in a very positive mood. Remember the state meet in Santa Rosa when I was a freshman? I was in a similar positive frame of mind. Now I was flying north as a junior half miler on the NCAA championship team. The next afternoon in Berkeley I would face two nationally ranked half milers, Lon Spurrier and Ed Wilson. They were number two and number five in the nation. Again, number two and number five. This ranking included all of the U.S. 880 runners.

I flew up with a team that had Ernie Shelton, Jimmy Lea, Des Koch, Leon Patterson, Mike Larrabee, Joe Graffio, Jon Arnett, Willard Wright, and Howard Bugbee on its roster. Only Bugbee would miss winning or placing in the NCAA finals that season, and that was because of an injury.

I didn't fear the Cal co-captain, Lon Spurrier, or his teammate, Ed Wilson, even though Spurrier had run 2.5 seconds faster than I had at Oxy a couple of weeks before, Wilson 1.5 seconds faster. Remember Wilson? Not the evil gunslinger in *Shane*, but Ed Wilson, who, in Santa Rosa two years before, edged me by two-tenths of a second for the California state junior college 880 title. By the big oak tree.

The program suggested that Spurrier might run the mile before the half mile. Even so, the dope sheet within the meet pamphlet forecast that Spurrier and Wilson would finish first and second in the half mile. This would mean eight points for Cal, one point for USC. I had no idea then how much beating USC meant to Spurrier. As the captain of the Bears, Spurrier led his team into the meet that Saturday afternoon with the belief that they could upset us. It was televised in Northern California on NBC. Although the weather was cool, overcast, a good-sized crowd filled the western grandstands of Edwards Stadium. The honorary referee was United States Senator Tom Kuchel. I knew that he had been a Phi Psi at USC. My fraternity was proud of having a U.S. senator from the house.

As I watched the early events, my positive mood held and I remained confident. I was there to beat Spurrier. This was real USC history. No driveway fantasy. The first running event brought the crowd to its feet as Spurrier and Len Simpson sprinted away from the Trojan entries in the mile. Score it: eight points for Cal, one for USC. Then the Bear javelin thrower, Bob Richter, let the spear fly way out there and moved ahead of Des Koch. It was the second best collegiate toss in the nation. More excitement for Cal fans. The upset was happening. Then, in the event just before the 880, a lesser-known high hurdler from Cal, Ron Dozier, beat Willard Wright of USC. Wright will place second in the NCAA final later in the season, but on that cool afternoon in Berkeley, he was only second behind Cal.

I walked across the infield and over to the starting line. It was down by the tennis courts. We would run the first 220 on the straightaway in front of the main stands. The meet officials kept us waiting. A long time. The running events are to follow a pre-set time schedule. Cal was legally resting Spurrier. He wasn't used to running both the mile and the half mile. Finally, it was time to race.

The two great Cal runners set the pace. I heard a slow time for the first lap. Really slow. A slow pace favored Spurrier. It helped him with the fatigue he still felt from having run the mile. And he had more leg speed than I did, meaning he could run faster over 440 yards. Just before we entered the backstretch that passes in front of the stands, I took over the lead. I don't do this; I wait for the kick. Mal Whitfield told me before we left Los Angeles to "jump Spurrier at the 550 mark." Was the Olympic champion behind this untested move on my part? At the 550 mark I moved up front. I think it was the slow pace that encouraged me to do so.

Two blue uniforms

I led this major 880 race down the backstretch in front of the crowd. It was a three-turn half mile. The finish was far across the field, down past the beginning of what is normally the final turn. I just kept a comfortable pace. When we came off the last turn, I began my long finishing kick toward the tape. I gradually measured it out. The fact that it was a long way down to the finish helped me. I had more strength left than Spurrier. I could see the two blue jerseys out of the corner of my eye. I didn't tighten up. It was like the state trial heat two years before when I upset Casper: I just let out more and more.

They stayed there. The two blue uniforms. All the way down that long finishing stretch. Then, with maybe thirty yards to go, I only saw one blue uniform. It was the proud captain, Spurrier. I can still see the string stretched across the finish line. I didn't know if my chest touched it first or not. It was very close. Within seconds, an official informed me that I had won. I had delivered. Cal couldn't beat USC now. Instead of eight points for a one, two finish, Cal received only four for second and third place.

In that moment I had found a place in USC track history. My Trojan immortality. Spurrier was in sad shape. There was an ambulance parked near the finish. I saw them giving him oxygen. When I was congratulated by Senator Kuchel, I slipped him the Phi Psi grip. The U. S. senator warmly completed the secret fraternity handshake.

It was April 24, 1954.

Taylor lauded

On Tuesday morning, I picked up the *Los Angeles Times* and saw my name above a feature column written by the former Stanford mentor, Dink Templeton. Its headline read, "Taylor Lauded." Dink Templeton, a legend in the sport, had coached the famous Ben Eastman and other great runners. I found it hard to believe what I read: "Of all the USC stars the one who made the greatest impression on me was Bill Taylor, not much speed and not much stride, but a guy who just refused to fold when the great Spurrier and Wilson started past him on the homestretch."

This was too good to be true. I didn't care for the "not much speed and not much stride" assessment, but I understand it now. He meant that I did not have elasticity, that I lacked the looseness of stride that produces world-class half milers. Spurrier and Wilson both were gifted with elasticity. Especially Spurrier. And I beat them in a race that really counted. Templeton went on in his column with "the Stanford runners from the 440 up would have done well to have stayed home from Oxy just to get one look at what a real exhibition of guts can do; out of 41 points in the four events and the relay, they grabbed off a grand total of 3, and just seeing that battling Taylor would have done 'em a lot more good than the 3 measly points." I see now that Templeton was using me to spank the Stanford track team for a lackluster performance. But he was impressed with my fortitude, determination, and fight in a feature race.

The *Los Angeles Examiner* write up did give me credit for ending the Bear scoring surge, but it diminished my victory for me by saying I beat a "sapped Spurrier." He looked damn sapped to me after the race.

Why does something always take your good moments away? Why does life never let you stay happy?

The USC campus became my home; it was the center of my world for two years. The practice track was only a short block from the much-photographed Tommy Trojan statue, and Coach Mortensen's office was just across that trafficless street.

I had my own FM radio sports show in the spring of 1954. The telecommunications building was diagonally across the street from the famous statue. Was my career going to limit me to sports?

A book titled, *Thirty Days to a More Powerful Vocabulary*, captured me. It challenged my one-dimensional sport life. I remember many of the words today: egregious, indefatigable, vicarious, garrulous, wanton, obsequious. I found *Martin Arrowsmith* by Sinclair Lewis tedious, but worthwhile. It was required reading in a literature course.

I declared a major in communications after the initial semester. I thought that sports announcing would offer me an exciting profession, one where I had confidence, unusual ability. Speech, linguistics, phonetics, drama, and telecommunications formed my curriculum.

For me, Jesus was a man

When I went home on weekends, I would sometimes go down to a Presbyterian church on Victory Boulevard for the Sunday morning worship service. I liked that little rustic chapel. It had wooden beams; it could have been a lodge in the Sierras. The minister was warm, almost too friendly. His enthusiasm made me uncomfortable. He became hyper when he prayed.

As is said, I felt better after attending the worship services. This led to my reading the New Testament on my own. No Bible-study class. I became familiar with the sayings of Jesus without others providing their interpretations. I did not go beyond Matthew, Mark, Luke, or John. The letters of Paul were too religious for me. For me, Jesus was a man. I did not view him as "the Lord," or "Christ." Ultimate respect, yes. Some mystery, yes. But "God"? No.

That was one wonderful, rainy night with Lasley. We went out again, but she did not respond when I told her that I was falling in love with her. I had played the part, just like the cowboys do in the movies, relying on my image, moral stature, inner confidence. Why didn't she respond? I do not think I was her type. I really did not know Lasley. She was an image. And this allowed me to continue to live with the fantasy that I would win the girl. Just like the cowboy, Lou, did.

We did not drive up to Fresno to spend Friday night in a hotel like we had in junior college. There were no girls up to our hotel room, no door torn from its hinges. USC took a morning flight and then flew back late that night. We shared the charter with Occidental, Los Angeles Athletic Club, and the UCLA teams. Mal Whitfield enjoyed the chance to tease me on the way up. He collected an audience from the seats around us, then asked me, "What time did you go to bed last night?" Whitfield suggested that I was in bed by nine. That was close.

Then he asked, rhetorically, "What time do you think I went to bed?" Whitfield stood up in the plane and, rotating his pelvis, said, "I was out getting my hips loose." Mal Whitfield was considered to have the most beautiful stride of any runner in the world. This added considerably to his sexual innuendo on the flight to Fresno.

Some thirteen thousand people were packed into the stands when I lined up to receive the baton from Mike Larrabee in the distance medley relay. J. W. Mashburn led off for Oklahoma A&M over 440 yards. Mashburn was one of the top two or three quarter milers in America. Earlier that evening I noticed a newspaper picture of Lon Spurrier tacked onto the Fresno State bulletin board outside the dressing rooms. The caption said that "Spurrier had been upset by USC's Bill Taylor" a couple of weeks before. Weeeeeeee. I was recognized in the big time track world. And, seeing it helped my confidence. I wonder if Casper noticed the caption. Dave was running for Fresno State. That was his bulletin board.

Billy Heard of Oklahoma A&M was one of the best collegiate half milers in the nation and we ran against one another on the second leg of the relay. I received the baton well back. But I passed everyone except Heard coming down the finishing stretch. A couple of former Valley College students rushed out onto the track to congratulate me. They were ecstatic. The announcer reported Heard's race time. I was clocked some three-tenths of a second faster. My clocking was later confirmed in *Track and Field News*.

Stop, hold it. Within but a few weeks I had beaten Lon Spurrier and Ed Wilson, then clocked a relay leg faster than another nationally ranked half miler. My image of becoming a nationally ranked half miler was being realized. I was confident, excited about the future and about how the 1954 season would end up.

I thought of his loose hips when the stadium announcer said, "And there he goes, Marvelous Mal Whitfield." It was the final event of the evening and Mal was running the anchor leg in the mile relay. I smiled.

USC school record

We flew up to Modesto the night after the Coliseum Relays. In the distance medley relay, I moved USC into first place on my half-mile leg, leaving Eddie Shinn of Oxy and the other 880 runners behind. Terrill of Occidental College edged Fernando Ledesma on the anchor, but our time was a new USC school record. Over the years, USC had put some tremendous milers and half milers on the track—Olympians like Roland Sink and Bob Chambers, an Indian named Jim Newcome, the immortal Louie Zamparini. Suddenly I was on the best distance medley foursome ever to run for USC. It felt natural.

Remember Barnes and McMillen from Occidental, the two Olympians who, two years before, led Oxy to the national distance medley record? Our time that night at Modesto was only three seconds over their national record.

The night was young. When Rod Wilger (who normally ran the second leg on the USC mile relay team) felt hamstring soreness while warming up, I replaced him. I wanted to win a Modesto Relays wristwatch. While I had moved USC into first place in the distance medley, we had finished second in the race. With Lea anchoring, we would have a good chance. But Whitfield would be a problem. Larrabee gave me the baton right up front. Even though I flew into the first turn, those with faster leg speed flew around me, even under or over me, it seemed. Still, I ran the fastest quarter mile of my life and kept USC in the race.

Whitfield did not steal my wristwatch. Lea nipped Mal at the tape. Our winning time would have tied us for the best collegiate mark in the country just a little over twenty-four hours before, when the Trojans ran faster in winning the Coliseum Relays. Larrabee, Taylor, Smith, and Lea ran the eighth-fastest mile relay team in USC history at Modesto. The world record for the mile relay was less than four seconds faster than our time.

That night I had again fulfilled my track dreams, and then some. But it is difficult to hold on to such joy and affirmation when you are competing every weekend. What you did last week can quickly be erased or reduced by what happens the next time out. It is week-to-week judgment.

Sport nihilism

A BAD COLD STRUCK the next week. The doctor at the USC clinic gave me a shot of penicillin the day before we flew up for the Pacific Coast Conference finals in Seattle. I was going home. I was born in Seattle in July 1933. My mother was thirty-two, my dad thirty-three. Bad cold or not, I was determined to race well in the conference final. On the way up, I made the flight special, just like I did when we flew up to Cal and I faced Spurrier and Wilson earlier in the season. I flirted with a good-looking stewardess and called her "Spalding" because I was reading *The High and the Mighty*. The paperback would become a popular movie. When we arrived at Husky Stadium, I found that in a two-page spread of the program entitled, "The Mighty Trojans," I was pictured with Ernie Shelton, Jimmy Lea, Des Koch, and Jon Arnett. I really was not one of them. Lea and Shelton would become two-time national champions in a few weeks; Koch would win the following year. And Arnett, one of the greatest halfbacks to ever play college football, placed second in the national collegiate long-jump final a few weeks later. Talk about feeling fulfilled. I felt great about the picture. It fed me confidence.

USC was seeking its fourteenth straight Pacific Coast Championship. This was incredible. The year before, I was co-captain of the state championship junior college team. It still seems like a miracle: to have come from that driveway in Burbank by Warner Brothers where we made believe that we were famous USC track athletes, and to find my picture placed in a program alongside four of the greatest heroes in Trojan history.

The program picked me to place fifth. My cold did not bother me as I warmed up, but it was in my system. Fortunately, we did not have any qualifying heats. If they had been required, I would have wasted the one final effort that I had in me for the 1954 season.

The day of the finals was overcast; gray clouds hung over the sta-

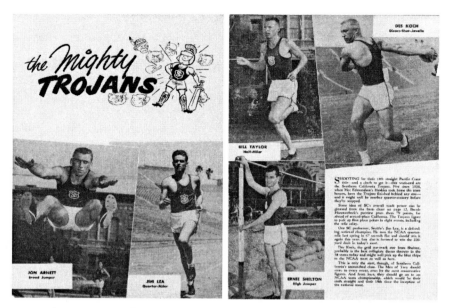

In this 1954 Pacific Coast Conference program, I am pictured with
four USC All-Americans. *Gulp.*

dium. A strong, cold wind swept off Lake Washington. The dirt track
was heavy due to rain and there was a cold drizzle during the meet.
Spurrier, foolishly, went out too fast. Shades of Casper. The wind stood
him up on the final turn and we closed in on the favorite. He did not
escape Link of Washington State or Clement of Oregon. Or Taylor of
USC. Wilson was well back. I thought that I had edged out Lonnie for
third, like at Berkeley when I won by one-tenth of a second over him.
From my view in Seattle, it was that close again. But Spurrier was given
third. I was fourth with the same time as Lonnie. Link was a Washington State half-mile veteran who had finished third the year before.
Clement of Oregon represented Canada in two Olympic Games. Spurrier will break the world 880 record the next year and place sixth in the
Olympic final a year after that. I was only six-tenths behind Link: six-
tenths of a second from winning the Pacific Coast Conference half-
mile final.

I felt crushed after the finish. And sick. One loses perspective when
one is ill. If I had been given third, I would have been one of three who

would compete in the post-season Big Ten vs. Pacific Coast Conference meet in Evanston, Illinois. This annual meet is held the week after the NCAA finals.

Coach Mortensen told me that he thought I was fourth. It was very close. Jimmy Lea won the 440, of course. But he felt sick after his race and Coach Mortensen sent word that I was needed for the mile relay. My cold had taken over and I felt terrible. I sent word back that I could not handle it.

I had to really be sick to say no to running on a USC mile relay team in the Pacific Coast Conference final. I actually cried in the locker room. A teammate came over and wanted to know what was wrong. I was sick. Did you ever see *Three Coins in a Fountain*? A lot of people seem to remember that motion picture. I do not know how it ended, but I suppose each one of the women found their guy. My kidneys began to ache so badly during the film that, midway into it, I left the Seattle theater and I went back to the hotel. I needed a massage. It took some time for Kearnie Reeb, the USC football and track trainer, to reduce the agonizing pain, but after many years a man like him was an expert. I did not realize that my season was over.

My strength was sapped

USC won its fourteenth straight Pacific Coast title in Seattle and I was a part of it. Fourth place contributed four points to our score. Thank goodness. The conference meet stays with you. If you score points, you are a part of the team victory. This becomes a part of the permanent USC record.

Next up was the Compton Invitational with its standing-room-only crowd and enormous intensity. One of the great track meets in America each season, the Compton Invitational is held in a junior college stadium with low bleachers on each side of the track. There is an intimacy between the fans and the athletes that adds an exciting dimension. The bleachers are packed and a good number of spectators are standing throughout the meet. When I was placed in the tremendous half-mile field at Compton, I had no warning that my strength was sapped, that running with a bad cold in Seattle had affected my muscles.

The thief had come

I finished next to last. Casper and that USC freshman from Canada were well ahead of me. Dave placed fourth with a national time. Cockburn broke the USC freshman school record. Good for them. My races at Fresno, Modesto, and Seattle were past history. Compton was a nightmare. The thief had come. It was not clear to me after the race that the strong, lasting ending to that wonderful 1954 season at USC would be stolen. While just the week before, I was in contact with the likes of Spurrier, Link, and Clement at the finish of the Pacific Coast Conference final, at Compton I was not able to go with the field when they accelerated. Had I been able to do so, my time would have been well below my best-ever mark.

Coach Mortensen had already entered me in the national collegiate championships that were to be held in Michigan the following week. I would be reporting to Quantico for my second Marine Corps summer camp immediately after the meet. The half-mile field offered the greatest talent of any event in the collegiate nationals, of course. Why make things easy? But Eddie Shinn made it through the trials. I had taken Eddie at Fresno and Modesto. Spurrier made the final nine, too. The two favorites in the half mile in Ann Arbor became All-Time American half milers. Tom Courtney and Arnie Sowell, along with Spurrier, would finish first, fourth, and sixth in the Olympic Games 800 meters two years later.

I will let the *Los Angeles Times* tell you how I did in my trial heat: "Trojan Bill Taylor, who has a one-way ticket from Los Angeles since he is on his way to Marine camp at Quantico, Va., was shut out in the loaded 880 field. Taylor was sixth in the second heat with only three qualifying. Also shut out in this stanza was Fresno State's Dave Casper, Taylor's old junior college rival. Casper finished fifth in the heat in 1:56.3, five seconds slower than his brilliant 1:51.3 race at Compton last week behind Mal Whitfield." Fernando Ledesma, a future USC national record holder over two miles, was the only other Trojan *not* to advance to a final. Jim Terrill of Oxy did not make the mile final. Humidity was a factor.

"Come on, Ernie"

USC won easily, scoring twice as many points as the second place team. I asked Jimmy Lea if there was anything I could do to be of help for his 440 final. The defending champion said it would be nice if I had a wet towel ready for him at the finish line. I refer to this now as my "water boy" image. The "some son-of-a-bitch stole my gal" high jumper, Ernie Shelton, just missed the world record. No one in history had cleared seven feet in the high jump. I sat with Ernie on the infield and offered encouragement in-between his jumps. After he had won the event with a tremendous clearance at 6 feet 10¼ inches, the guy who assisted me in electrocuting the movie star requested that the bar be raised to seven feet.

"Come on, Ernie." Shelton planted his take-off foot and lifted off the dirt surface with phenomenal power. He cleared it. My old Valley College teammate was over seven feet. The bar began to wiggle when he nicked it with his trail foot on the way down. As Ernie looked up from the sawdust pit below, history waited, as if it was undecided. Then the bar came down.

Where are my Marine Corps orders?

You cannot know the terror that I felt when I discovered in Washington D. C. that I had lost my Marine Corps orders. I had checked into a hotel after a midnight flight from Detroit. This was serious. I feared what would happen if I showed up without them. At a minimum, I would be singled out right from the beginning. A new drill instructor would lock in on me. Misery was ahead.

A USC teammate who had flown with me to D. C. helped me by reaching our team manager on the phone. Those going on to Evanston were just about to leave the campus. I had left my orders on the table in the room I shared with Mike Larrabee. Mike gave them to our team manager, Jack Larson, and he had already sent them by rail express to the train station at Quantico. I was to report that night. There was, therefore, some hope that they would be there at the train station. I can still picture the counter, the building by the tracks. The shelves behind it were filled with packages of various sizes. I was told that there was nothing for a William Taylor. The station clerk looked again. This time he discovered a large envelope addressed to me. It contained my order. I left the station with gratitude toward the clerk, Mike Larrabee, and Jack Larson. And with enormous relief.

Without them, I would not have felt like a Marine

I had six weeks to face at Quantico before I could enjoy the higher altitudes in Mammoth. The tragic ending for two college students who were run to death in the oppressive heat the prior summer prompted a congressional investigation. There was no Sergeant Dawley waiting for me this time. The word was firm: reduce the harassment of the officers in training. It took awhile to believe this, however. In a way, it was almost disappointing. The training lacked intensity. The smells of Quantico, the leaves dampened by the Virginia humidity in late June and July, the disinfectants in the latrines, the stench of a sick Potomac River—all seemed more pronounced during that first summer. Those memories remain in black and white. Without them, I suspect I would not have felt like I was a Marine!

By August, I was back sleeping in the bunkhouse in Mammoth. Those late afternoon runs were going to produce a wonderful surprise for me when I returned to USC a month later. You might remember that they were easy, solo efforts.

I still believed that Lasley could be won by my Western image. When I drove Bob Griffith from the Mammoth to Whittier because he was worried that stomach pains might be an appendicitis attack, I took advantage of the proximity to her home. She invited me over for dinner. Of course, I had my cowboy boots on. I enjoyed the corn on the cob anyway. Bob was okay.

As Camp High Sierra was being shut down in early September,

three of us took off on a very ambitious hike. We were going to travel eighty miles that included four passes of ten thousand to twelve thousand feet in only three days. First, there was Duk Pass. Yes, "Duk." Only 10,600 feet. Then Silver Pass at 11,000 feet. Then an even higher climb to Heart Lake and a 12,000-foot pass. Finally, Piute, only 10,000 feet. A very loud chorus of howling coyotes woke us up the second night out. My two friends were propped up on their elbows, looking out over a log to the meadow where the chorus was singing. Why is it so easy to laugh when others are scared?

I think this eighty-mile marathon with the four high passes, preceded by about a month of those high-altitude runs, had a lot to do with the astonishing improvement I discovered in my distance running when I returned to USC.

I was supposed to be back at the fraternity for rush week earlier because Jimmy Lea had appointed me chairman. When I pulled up in front of the Phi Psi house, Lea was standing on the lawn. He screamed, "Taylor, you son-of-a-bitch, where have you been?" I did not mind a two-time national collegiate champion calling me a son-of-a-bitch.

Our fraternity had talked Jimmy into being president. He was not suited for the position. Nor was I the right person to be rush chairman. And I really was late. During rush week, prospective members were invited to parties and sized up. I regret that I did not come through, but I obviously was not a fraternity type. My fraternity was the track team!

Jimmy Lea was the graduate student appointed to coach the 1954 Trojan cross-country team. Better Jimmy than Jack Davis. Our first competition was at Mt. San Antonio College. This was a big invitational with teams from the Los Angeles colleges and universities, as well as some entries from San Diego and Santa Barbara. I was running along in the middle of this large field when I experienced unusual mid-race energy. I began passing the long line of runners rather effortlessly. By the time I reached a grass field and the finishing chute, only four runners had escaped my spectacular finish. Lea came running across the field screaming, "Taylor! Taylor!" What was a half miler doing up there with the great distance runners? Altitude. Those afternoon runs at Mammoth. And the three-day hike over the high passes. I was in rare shape when I returned to USC for my final cross-country season. The use of altitude training was not in practice then; at least, I was not aware of how it could benefit long-distance runners.

We had a cherub on that 1954 Trojan cross-country team. "Little Max" Truex won the hearts of the Los Angeles track fans from the beginning. He was only 5'5", or shorter. But during his freshman cross-country season Truex set record after record, week after week, against varsity athletes (freshmen were eligible for varsity competition in cross country). We should not have been too surprised. Max had broken the national high school mile record just months before entering USC. Fernando Ledesma, who was also on our '54 team, held the national high school mile record before Max. How about that—the two most recent prep national record holders in the mile on the same college cross-country team. USC was able to land pretty much anybody that they went after.

"How does Taylor do it?" cried the soon-to-be world record holder

I was elected team captain halfway into the season. I finished second behind the cherub against Cal on the UCLA course. Then up at Stanford, when I finished fourth or fifth in a four-way meet, I had the great pleasure of hearing Lon Spurrier yell out to others, "How does Taylor do it?" It is nice to have the soon-to-be world record holder shout your name. Coming down that finishing fairway on the Stanford golf course, Fernando Ledesma, the future national collegiate two-mile record holder, worked by me. Now I was the number three man on the Trojan team. The altitude advantages were wearing down. But the next year in the Marine Corps I will run even faster times without any altitude training.

I hashed at the girls dorm, serving dinner a few nights each week to earn extra money and a good meal. In December, I noticed a brown-eyed coed in the freshman dorm. There was something special about her. She had poise and seemed more confident, genuine, than the other girls. And she had beauty.

I understood that this Betty was Jon Arnett's girl. This was confirmed when I saw her sitting with the football wives at the 1955 Rose Bowl game. USC was playing Ohio State and Jon Arnett was on his way to becoming an All-American halfback. And as mentioned, he placed second in the long jump in the nationals. So much for the new girl.

I had released Lasley to a fraternity brother. This J.B. asked me if I was still serious about her. He wanted my okay before he asked her out. His display of character impressed me. It was something I would have expected from one of my Stoic cowboy heroes. I had no right to play a fraternity brother loyalty card that might have caused him to not pursue her. And my one-sided romance with Lasley was not going anywhere.

Gary Cooper, Gregory Peck, or Glenn Ford would not have gone out of control

Stoic values were very important to me. Keeping one's word, being truthful, not bad-mouthing other people—these were my inner standards. Vulgarity bothered me, but I just rode with it. I could be at a fraternity party with heavy drinking and refrain from criticizing those who became drunk, and at times, obnoxious. At the same time, I did not partake in the booze and inwardly I did not approve of their lack of self-respect. One afternoon at the Phi Psi house my "brothers" pounded Jimmy Lea's car to death. They pushed it into the courtyard and flattened the car with iron bars. It was not worth much before the relentless attack, but they had no right to destroy it. This violent frenzy, a release of animalistic drives, seemed ugly and childish to me. I did not tell them what I thought of them. Gary Cooper, Gregory Peck, or Glenn Ford would not have gone out of control and pounded Jimmy's car into the ground. Nor would they have participated in a gang bang up at Lake Arrowhead like some of the club members did one weekend.

The way many of my fraternity brothers talked about girls bothered me, too. Women were sex objects for them. The language they used to speak about women was degrading. My direction toward a serious life was unfolding.

"Some enchanted evening, / you will see a stranger, / across a crowded room, / and somehow you will know, / you will know even then, / that someday you will see her, again and again." It was not too late for a college love story for me. The one with the poise became my USC sweetheart. Our attraction to one another was instantaneous when we returned after the winter break. When I asked Betty out, her response was an immediate "yes." Brown hair, dark brown eyes, a good figure, she was a gift of immeasurable proportions. Betty respected my serious side. And she was passionate about USC sports. Her father was the dean of Letters, Arts, and Sciences. I had landed "the dean's daughter." Our kisses, the incompleteness that we both felt when we were apart, brought forth a wonderful romance. Arnett? The All-American football player to be? Jon never became an issue. It looked like they had a very serious relationship when Betty sat with the football wives in the Rose Bowl, but there was nothing holding her back when we began dating. I never asked about Jon.

I was her Trojan

During January and early February I was carefully preparing myself for my senior track season. I began running 660-yard intervals: I ran three of them each time, walking a lap in-between each one. My times came down effortlessly; being in love reduced my weight and the legs became lighter.

My two years of active duty in the Marine Corps were only four months away. I did not even think about my future; we were completely caught up in the moment. We wanted to be together all the time. Betty had that special female quality that makes a male feel important. It was as though she was inside of me, enthusiastic about my life, hopes, dreams. My preparation for the USC track season meant a lot to Betty, too. She tried to be careful about the amount of sleep I needed, how long we stayed out at night. And she kept a scrapbook of newspaper clippings which she presented to me at the end of the season. I was her Trojan!

The Trojan 1955 publicity pamphlet presented me this way:

Bill Taylor, 880—HS: North Hollywood 1951. Bill was a mediocre prep 880 man with best time of 2:06.9. Went to Valley JC where he improved to 2:00.0. Made a big drop in his second JC season to 1:54.7. Bad cold hit him last year when he appeared primed for top effort. Finest race was upset win of Cal's Lon Spurrier at Berkeley, while fastest was 1:52.8 relay stint at Modesto. Ran best open 880 in 1:54.1 at Compton. Showed fine improvement in cross country and was elected captain.

This summed it up very well. I was glad that they noted the "bad cold." I wanted people to know why I did not place in the nationals.

There was news of the sophomore, Murray Cockburn, in the preseason pamphlet. The new frosh record holder at 1:52.7 had been lost for the season due to mononucleosis. Murray, sometimes of testy words but a damn nice guy, would not be taking over the number one half-mile position on the varsity team. But the next year he would make the Canadian Olympic Team in the 400 meters and as a member of their 1600-meter relay team.

Betty at Convict Lake over Easter break

In an early practice meet on the USC track, I out-kicked the former UCLA distance star, Larry Carter, to win the mile. Why didn't I run the mile more often at USC? In junior college, Coach Slosson ran me in the mile a number of times. I should have run it in some meets as a Trojan for distance work. And doubled back in the half mile an hour or so later. I needed the strength down the finishing stretch that this produces.

It is typical for track athletes to look back and rationalize how they could have run faster. "What ifs" seem to be part of almost everyone's baggage. My weight came down from 160 to 155 pounds. I won the pre-season half-mile time trial on a heavy track and it was two seconds faster than I had run the year before. We were still wearing heavy leather shoes with very long spikes.

I was given encouragement by teammates that I might be voted co-captain of what would become another national championship track team. I had just been elected captain of the cross-country team a few months before. But when I arrived at the pre-season track banquet, the newspapers were already taking pictures of Des Koch and Howard Bugbee. I felt very disappointed.

I took Betty with me to Frank Clark's wedding. I had not seen my old friend for some time. He told me that he was "honored" that I had come. I had become one of those USC heroes who we used to fantasize about in our youth. I admired Frank Clark. He was of character—a good person and loyal friend who once took care of my pigeons. I loved being with Betty at the wedding. She wore a suit. Her social graces were not part of my upbringing. My mother had been raised with such graces in Hong Kong, then Claremont, but they disappeared as she raised her two boys. Betty looked pretty at Frank's wedding. She did not look exactly like the girl I pictured marrying, but she had a wonderful, fun personality. She made me feel fantastic.

Greatness destroyed

WHEN WE OPENED the season at UCLA, I was assigned the familiar half-mile leg of the distance medley relay. Because UCLA was to be anchored by the phenomenal Bob Seaman, the young runner whom many felt would become America's next great miler, this relay was billed as the feature event.

The bleachers alongside the main UCLA straightaway were overflowing with spectators. Six years before, Mel Patton had run his world record 220 on this same dirt track. And there I was standing on its straightaway, waiting for the baton from Larrabee. I was a few yards behind the powder blue jersey of the Bruin half miler when Mike placed it in my hand. An outstanding quarter miler, Russ Ellis, had given UCLA the lead. The Bruin took us through a fast opening lap. I cut loose on the backstretch of the second lap and left him, opening up an enormous lead. When I passed the baton off, Jon Arnett was the first one over to me. The long-jump runway was alongside the track. He shook my hand. Betty was up in the stands. I do not know if Jon was in love with her. But if so, I was struck by his character. I wondered if I would have been such a good sport. A new USC miler, Sid Wing, ran a steady anchor leg and the great UCLA sophomore was unable to catch him. We won the relay. The next morning, the *Los Angeles Times* gave me the credit. Charles Curtis wrote: "Taylor's sparkling 880, equal to his best effort the entire 1954 season, put the Trojans far in front."

An unfolding miracle season

Out on the infield that afternoon, the 1936 and 1948 United States Olympic coach, Dean Cromwell, told me that I could "break the world record" in the 880 if I could get my hips "loose." The retired USC coach said that I ran my half mile "on power." Dean Cromwell had coached the Trojans to twelve national titles. When Lon Spurrier lowered the world record by a full second a few weeks later, it was Cromwell that the *Los Angeles Times* turned to for perspective on how much lower half-mile times could possibly fall. I think you can see why this encouragement from Cromwell meant so much to me. All of a sudden, we were not only talking about being a national runner, but perhaps even an Olympian.

My high school friend, Al Glickman, came out onto the infield and told me that he and his dad watched my relay effort. Don Hoover, my early college track friend and mentor, told me that I was "too skinny." And a USC teammate said that he had never seen me run like that before. We had new spikes. They were much lighter than the heavy leather shoes. That was quite an afternoon. It was great having old friends come out to the infield to say hello.

I ran an additional half-mile leg in another relay later in the afternoon. It felt so easy. It was as though I danced around the track. On top of the running, there was Betty's formal sorority dance that evening. Tux and all. Dance? Just hours after two intense half-mile efforts. We did not stay late. Betty tried to watch out for her celebrated Trojan.

Track Athlete of the Week with Johnson and Truex

On Tuesday morning, the *Los Angeles Times* reported that I had been nominated for Track Athlete of the Week by the Los Angeles sports writers and college coaches. Two others were nominated with me: Rafer Johnson of UCLA and little Max Truex of USC. Johnson will become an All-Time American track hero, placing second in the 1956 Olympics and winning the decathlon four years later in Rome. Max will make two Olympic teams, set American records, and finish sixth in the 10,000 meters in the games in Rome in 1960. Pretty good company! I was the hero of the USC relay team, one of the most famous coaches in American college track history had mentioned my breaking the world record, and I was nominated with two future Olympians for Track Athlete of the Week in the Los Angeles area. It wasn't just happening. It had happened.

My times on the USC practice track the next week confirmed that

I was ready for great times. I ran four seconds faster over 660 yards than I had the year before. This was accomplished without racing all out, as I was relaxed and running smoothly over the final 100 yards, somewhat like I was in my trial heats at the junior college state meets. After we walked a lap, I ran one next which was three seconds faster than what I achieved the year before. We only ran once in 1954. As we began the 1955 track season, I was clearly four or more seconds faster. Two of the Los Angeles newspaper columns included me among the Trojans who were likely to place in the collegiate nationals. This glorious, fulfilling moment would not last the week.

Coach Slosson drove down to USC from the valley every week to finish up his doctorate in geology, and to help coach the middle- and long-distance runners. On Wednesday of the Track Athlete of the Week nomination, my old junior college coach suggested that I run a full-speed quarter mile. I was not aware that Jim had mistakenly stopped his watch at the halfway mark. I finished with a fluid stride and good reserve, but I noticed some soreness in the ball of my right foot as I came around the final turn. Slosson's watch told of a very fast time for me over the first 220, as quick as I had ever run one without adding an additional 220 yards!

I began to feel sick the next day. Coach Mortensen pulled me out of a low-key meet that Friday. I checked into the campus infirmary on Sunday night with a 104 degree fever and tonsillitis. At the very peak of my running life, I found myself in a hospital bed near the Trojan track. The team flew to Arizona without me. Marshall Clark, the USC transfer from Muir Junior College (someone I liked), beat Joe Leach of Arizona (someone I did not like), in the 880 in Tucson. But Marshall did not break my meet record.

The track coverage in the *Los Angeles Times* over the next few weeks kept my name in the columns. Anybody who followed the Trojans knew that I was missing my senior season because of tonsillitis. Ironically, you receive more press when you are sick or injured. While I still felt that I would return to the track and fulfill my USC dreams, the continuous write-ups in the *Los Angeles Times* and elsewhere were my epitaph. They told of a season destroyed. The thief had come.

"Taylor's Troubles"

When I did begin training again, that sore foot became inflamed. The Oxy meet was coming up. I would have loved to race Shinn in my pre-tonsillitis form. But here is what the *Los Angeles Times* wrote about me that week: "Taylor's Troubles—Bill Taylor, the ailing 880 and 440 man, was considered to be definitely 'out' of Saturday's meet. Taylor had been ill with tonsillitis, and it was figured he wouldn't be able to run the 880 but could go in the relay. This week he has come up with a sore leg muscle and a wobbly knee so he will be up in the stands."

Wobbly knee? It had slipped out while I was stretching during practice. A reporter happened to be there at the time. One writer speculated that, without me in the race, Oxy would sweep the half mile. They finished one, two, three. Payton Jordan was still the coach. I was up in the stands with Betty. She had stayed close to me during my illness. We remained infatuated with one another. But what if her USC track hero failed? Betty had begun that scrapbook for my track articles. She drew a USC runner on the lead page. It had been a great Trojan story until the sickness.

Over the Easter break, I kept the pressure off the ball of my foot by wearing street shoes. I think the stiff, inflexible sole really helped. When back on campus, our trainer tried a combination of ice, heat, ice, heat, et cetera. It seemed to work. How long had it been since I had run? The UCLA meet was on March 5. Sometime during the week of April 4, I found that I could place some pressure on the foot. On Saturday, April 9, I would try to compete again.

But I wanted USC track immortality

A Dr. Wright had come by the USC practice track before my illness and we visited briefly. He was the pastor of a large Presbyterian church on Wilshire Boulevard. Dr. Wright was a kind man, but he made me uncomfortable with the way he talked about Jesus. I did not have a personal relationship with "the Lord." My Jesus was a Stoic man. It was his strong ethics that impressed me. And his special relationship with his Father. The magical, spooky Christianity was not for me. My Jesus was quiet. He went into a closet to pray.

On April 8, Dr. Wright wrote: "I know that you will come out well in whatever is best and finest for your ultimate character and usefulness for Christ and the kingdom." But I wanted USC track immortality. I should have just trained for awhile before racing, taking at least a couple of weeks to just gradually move back into the serious work. Dr. Wright even cautioned me not to rush back into heavy workouts and meets. Nobody else gave me any direction. I was planning on going to Denver to become a sports announcer after my two years in the Marine Corps. Why Denver? The mountains, altitude, clean air of course. Coach Slosson set me up with an interview with Robert Wood, the president of NBC. They had been fraternity brothers at USC. Mr. Wood told me that he thought they could find a spot for me in the NBC parking lot when I got out of the Marine Corps. He said I could begin spending time in the sports department when I was not parking cars. I never followed up on this opportunity.

The Cal meet that year was held in the Coliseum. No Spurrier or Wilson this time. As we approached the final turn of the second lap, I found that the pace was slow enough for me to swing out around the field and take the lead. I led past the tunnel. The long finishing straightaway was ahead. I was tired. Marshall Clark tried to come by on the inside, but I did not accommodate him. He would have to go around me if he wanted to pass me. This was the same straightaway I had fled down as a little boy, running toward my father at the end of the stadium. My little legs would not go fast enough as the monsters in the dark tunnel came after me. I won the half mile against Cal, for the second straight year. But my time was not down there where it could have been, had I not missed a month of training. Not even close. I was back in the time range of my junior season at USC.

Dean Cromwell called me over to the railing after I finished. The famous coach offered me praise, told me that I got up on the balls of my feet when I needed that something extra and that this enabled me to finish well. The early Sunday edition of the *Los Angeles Times* ran a photo of me winning the race. The caption read, "Taylor Made Surprise." And the write up told of how I was recovering from tonsillitis. Good!

The later Sunday morning edition, the paper I thought most people would read, eliminated my picture. I had been replaced by my teammate, Sid Wing. A Korean War veteran, Sid was featured on the first page of the sports section with a larger picture. He had run one of the fastest collegiate mile times in the nation.

I was disappointed. It would have meant a lot to me for my friends to see that picture. And I was jealous of Sid. He would go on to Trojan glory. And we would enjoy a lengthy friendship.

Dr. Wright wrote, "Sometimes these blows are the facts that really make us men, as we master them, and you have so much talent I think the Lord could use you greatly." I still did not like "the Lord" bit. But he was offering me meaning beyond a track at a very disappointing time in my life. And showing me that there was an important place for me in this larger world. Good timing, Dr. Wright.

I did not like it when people referred to themselves as "Christian." How did they know they were measuring up to Christian morality? They were deciding what only God could decide. I found conservative Christians presumptuous. It was not a salvation religion for me. You did something because it was right. The Stoic cowboys, or Gregory Peck in *To Kill a Mockingbird*, Cooper in *High Noon*, they exemplified this character.

Betty said "yes" when I asked her if she wanted to be pinned, serenaded by my fraternity on the steps of her sorority house. This was a college romance. I see this now. I felt awkward asking my Phi Psi "brothers" to take time to participate, in that I had not been an active member since early in my senior year. Still, the guys walked across the street and sang for the Thetas, who in return sang to us. It felt wonderful to be pinned to Betty. What was I going to do in a couple of months when I left for Quantico? She would wait for me. Is this not what they do in the Westerns? The beautiful girl waits for the handsome hero.

Dr. Wright invited me to speak at a Sunday evening service. Betty went with me. I loved seeing her out there in a pew. It bothered me that in the *Los Angeles Times* Dr. Wright titled my talk "Bill Taylor and the Christian athlete." There was that word again. I was not a Christian. I sought to fulfill Christian ethics. And there was my name, right next to the weirdo evangelists. I did appreciate this portion of what Dr. Wright wrote after my talk: "I was amazed at your facility of speech, your excellence of voice; many young men at theological seminary even in their second year could not have presented so finished and logically organized a presentation."

"What happened?"

We landed in Burbank on the return trip from Dallas that year. I was not ready for that level of competition yet. I had faded to fourth in the half mile behind a couple of University of Texas runners and Marshall Clark. Betty was right there by the gate waiting for me. The first thing she said did not feel right to me. Betty did not rush up and throw herself into my arms and say, "I love you." No, Betty wanted to know "what happened." What happened was tonsillitis. I was no longer the same runner. My moment of greatness in a USC uniform was lost. But maybe it would come back. How could I give up? Perhaps I read too much into her inquiry at the airport?

Another potential problem for the two of us emerged in a simple way. Betty's parents had me over for Sunday dinner. My fork slipped while cutting my steak and some green peas slid off my plate and rolled off the table. Then they bounced about on the white marble floor. Was I socially acceptable enough to marry the dean's daughter? While eating dinner out one night on a date, Betty taught me how to hold the fork when you cut a steak. You see, Betty did not abandon me.

The Stanford meet was in Palo Alto. I was surprised to see my picture in the *San Jose Mercury News* with a caption that mentioned my "early season sickness." I was still the "race favorite," however, according to the newspaper. I could still win meets against Cal, Stanford,

UCLA, against weak half-mile fields. But you are not remembered at USC for these two-way, dual meet victories. Nationals. The nationals. The pillars by the new track at USC celebrate the winners of the collegiate finals. (Wrong. When I was honored along with the other members of the 1955 national title team fifty years later at the USC-UCLA track meet, the announcer mentioned my having won the half mile against UCLA fifty years before. And, when he saw me earlier in the day, Sam Nicholson identified me as "the dual-meet champion" of the '55 team.)

I appreciated seeing my friend from Mammoth days, Bob Griffith, standing along the rail at the Stanford meet. Bob graduated Phi Beta Kappa from Stanford; he is a lifetime friend.

In the locker room after the meet, I noticed a USC teammate talking with a Stanford guy whom I figured was the high school friend I had heard about. If so, this fellow was Betty's old boyfriend at Dorsey, now a baseball player at Stanford. He probably was bright as hell, too. When Betty picked me up at the airport, I let myself have it by mentioning that I thought I had seen her old boyfriend in the locker room after the meet. The coloring in her face changed. Not good.

I ran a couple of good relay legs at Fresno and Modesto. In fact, my time at the latter meet equaled what I had run there as a junior. But where were my four seconds? Where was that four-second drop in my time that I was able to achieve in 1955 before the tonsillitis? A very strange thing happened in the Coliseum Relays. It was as though the gods or goddesses were teasing me. I still do not know if I ran the fastest time of my life that night. I was handed the baton fifty or more yards behind the best collegiate half milers in the country. Once again, somewhere around forty thousand fans were in the 1936 Olympic Stadium. The anchor runners went out very slowly, waiting for someone to take the lead. I kept making up the distance that separated me from this elite field, then I began to doubt whether I could hold such a pace. I was running down some of the best half milers in the country. I passed a couple of them before the finish and USC ended up in fifth place. My teammates were all over me at the finish. They were ecstatic.

I was told that Slosson clocked me in my fastest-ever half mile. When it was announced that USC finished in fifth place, there was substantial applause from the large crowd. For fifth place? No, it was for me.

When I came out of the Coliseum locker room into the tunnel, Coach Mortensen said that he clocked me three seconds higher than what Slosson had reported. I do not think he knew the time that Jim's watch had read. I turned away and said, "Shit." A week or so later, a USC freshman hurdler, Wayne Bithell, told me that my Coliseum Relays anchor leg was the greatest running he had ever witnessed. He was serious. I thought it was because he liked me. I will never know what really happened on that anchor leg. But going into the Pacific Coast Conference Championship meet in Eugene, Oregon, it brought hope. A comment by Slosson in a Los Angeles paper stated that he thought I was ready to run under the USC school record. He must have believed that he had the right clocking for my anchor leg in the Coliseum Relays.

Betty and I were still in love. I had her lips, those brown eyes. And her playfulness. She was enormous fun. I really loved her. And it looked like I was returning to form on the track. I flew up to Eugene expecting to possibly win the half-mile final. While I was warming up for my 880 trial, I noticed him. This Oregon runner was an Australian. His name was Jim Bailey. He was more mature than the rest of us. He presented a casual image as he kept tossing a rock up in the air. I did not know that he was one of the best milers in the world.

Bailey was in my trial heat. He eased away from me as we came down the finishing stretch. As the hometown Oregon fans roared their approval, my legs felt a bit heavy. I finished second, advancing easily, however. In the final the next afternoon the field got away from me over the initial lap. Then, on the backstretch of the second lap, I used up some of my kick when I moved up into a better position. But unlike in 1954 when I was only six-tenths of a second out of first place, in Eugene I was two seconds behind the winner. Of course it was Bailey.

Bailey won the national collegiate mile title three weeks later. Then in 1956, the Australian defeated his famous countryman, John Landy, in the first sub-four minute mile ever run on American soil. And I returned from Oregon without the fastest USC half-mile time for the season. Down the finishing stretch, Bailey, Clement of Oregon, and a runner I had taken the year before from the University of Washington stayed in front of me. When I tired near the finish, a USC miler, Marty Montgomery, eased by me. Finishing fifth, I was not invited to run the half mile at the Compton Invitational. I would only be running a mile relay leg. This hurt. USC had me lead off. I would have produced a better time by running second, but the coaches did not want us to fall too far behind. At best, my effort could be described as mediocre. Two years before, I had run on that great Valley Junior College mile relay team at Compton. Our time was the best in the United States for junior colleges for the year. But when I left the track at Compton that night I was aware that my place in Trojan history was not going to happen. It seemed so unfair. I cried uncontrollably in Betty's arms when we reached the car. I think I lost Betty that night, too.

The 1955 NCAA finals were held in the Coliseum. I made up my mind to do everything I could to advance from my trial heat into the final nine. If I stayed up on the pace, was in a good position coming around the final turn, I just might qualify. And placing within the top six in the final would mean achieving what was expected of a USC track scholarship athlete, i.e., a place in the collegiate nationals. Betty had a job, so she missed the trials on Friday afternoon. Had I been a likely qualifier, I believe she would have made arrangements to be there. Too harsh? Let us wait and see.

I drew what appeared to be the easiest trial heat. The defending champion, Arnie Sowell, was running in the one ahead of mine. It happened quickly. A concerned crowd seemed to plead with history. Sowell was trapped on the inside near the finish and he might not break out in time to qualify. He did not make it. The race favorite was gone. Other USC entries did not come close to advancing to the final. When it was my turn, I did stay up. The pace was tactical, so it was not terribly hard to stay close to the front. As we came around the final turn and approached the tunnel, the stadium announcer said, "Shinn and Taylor." We were in position to qualify for the final. I passed Eddie coming down the closing stretch, as I had passed Casper two years before. It seemed that I might be in the top three. But I finished fifth.

My time was the thirteenth fastest out of twenty-seven entries spread out over three heats. Casper did not advance from his trial heat, either. My time was lower. Strange, just two years before, we were the two hottest junior college half milers in the country. It was hot and muggy that June afternoon in the Coliseum. I was nauseated. I walked over by the entrance to my tunnel and sat down. It was over. My USC dream ended in failure!

The next week it was off to Quantico for two years of active duty in the United States Marine Corps. Time to say goodbye to Betty. We were in my car, parked in front of where my mother lived in Toluca Lake. When our lips touched, she did not respond. I had lost more than a place in the nationals.

I went off to Quantico without asking for, or receiving any commitment from Betty. How could such a beautiful romance end so abruptly? I would see her at Christmas time. The inevitable was too painful for me to see. It was over, but I would not give up on the relationship. It made no sense: one day in love, the next not in love. I left for the Marine Corps already wounded, in sport and in love.

A man called Peter and _the_ Wes Santee

My teammates did win the seventh straight national championship for USC. I took off my running top with the coveted SC aegis one week, placed the golden bars of a Marine second lieutenant on my shoulders the next.

This gave me, instantaneously, a new identity. The Marines were "the greatest fighting force in the world." I would take the image, but please, no combat. I was not gung-ho about the Marine Corps. The lieutenant in _South Pacific_ was more to my liking. I was touched by the tenor singing, "Younger than Springtime" to the pretty native girl. Oh, I was proud of being a Marine, but it did not please me to hear a Quantico instructor say that he was "looking forward to the next war."

Nor did I care for when a captain said, "I hate my mother because she is a civilian." While this sounds inane, even funny, I think the captain was partly serious.

Hold up on my track obituary. The Olympic year was coming up in 1956. I asked Dean Cromwell to write the commanding officer at Quantico to request that I be given a chance to train. Based on that early season effort at UCLA when I was nominated for Track Athlete of the Week with Rafer Johnson and Max Truex, I was in the company of soon-to-be Olympians.

What might happen if I had a healthy season running for the Marine Corps? Dean Cromwell did write the general more than once. He wrote personally to me as well, saying, "You are mature enough now to become a champion half miler." God, the dream was not over. Another running miracle could happen.

Betty only wrote once or twice. I ignored what was clearly a terminal sentence: "I love nature, and I love God, but otherwise we do not have much in common." I did not "love" God. That is being too familiar with God. I have told you that I was not comfortable with religious people who spoke of their personal relationship with "the Lord." I did love Betty. And, as hopeless as it must seem, I felt that when I returned at Christmas time our love could return. How could it just disappear?

Some time during that year, I saw the movie, *A Man Called Peter*. A Shakespearean actor, Richard Todd, played Peter Marshall. Richard Todd brought utter sincerity and conviction to the Presbyterian minister he portrayed. And his Scottish accent made him even more unusual. The real Peter Marshall believed that religion was not for sissies. To Peter Marshall it took character and courage to be a Christian. You did not talk about it all the time; you lived it.

I was notified that I was to report each afternoon to running workouts because Quantico was going to field a 1955 cross-country team. Until mid-afternoon, I would be in a classroom or out in the boondocks with my company of fellow officers. We had a six-month officers program to complete. I still had to attend classes, take exams, pass the scrutiny of the training officers. My company commander did not ap-

Coach Rosandich speaking to me and Wes Santee
before the Naval Academy meet.

prove of my leaving the unit each afternoon to run. A veteran of the
recent Korean War, a career officer, he gave me poor leadership chits
and had it in for me. I did feel sheepish about leaving my fellow officers
every afternoon. But, for the most part, they supported me. I even became their Olympic hope. One of them even told me once that I was
going to beat Wes Santee.

The biggest name in American track and field was waiting for me
in Quantico each afternoon. In June I was on the USC national championship track team, in September my teammate was the notorious
Wes Santee. Yes, Wes was the one in the cowboy boots at the Compton Invitational barbecue. At one point in time, Santee had run three
of the four fastest mile times in world history. Again, three out of the
four fastest mile times ever recorded were run by the long legs of the
Kansas cowboy.

I immediately became the second best runner on the Quantico
team, thus Wes and I were viewed as stable mates. And because of this
number two position I was usually mentioned along with Santee in the
heavy press coverage. I fed on this recognition. Our top six runners all
had been captains of their college teams; we came from Villanova, Ala-
bama, Notre Dame, Dartmouth, Kansas, and USC. In that we were

also Marines, the news media made a big deal out of this. But Santee was the show.

One of our early meets was at the United States Naval Academy in Annapolis, Maryland. Shortly before we started the three mile race, Wes said, "Let's go out fast over the first half mile and lose everyone." This was playtime for Wes Santee. For me it would turn into the fastest three-mile race of my life. We quickly parted from a large field of Naval Academy runners. It was fun. We flew across a portion of a golf course, then onto a dirt road. Wes bade me farewell there. I never saw him, or anyone else, over the remaining two-plus miles. The fast early pace led to that unusually quick time for me. Wes was twenty-five seconds ahead at the finish. My three-mile time was under fourteen minutes. In reality, my chances of making U.S. Olympic Team were slim. This was largely because America had the best half milers in the world. Tom Courtney, Arnie Sowell, Lon Spurrier, and the two-time Olympic champion, Mal Whitfield, were the prohibitive favorites to challenge for the three spots on the team. And if Santee doubled in the 1500 and 800, he could make the team in the latter event as well.

Maybe another event would open up for me? This was a stupid hope. I should have gone after the 800 meters from day one and took whatever resulted with pride. How long had it been since I sat down by the tunnel in the Coliseum with a sense of failure? Only three months!

When we raced in Pittsburgh, a paper told of a record crowd because the best half miler in the country, Arnie Sowell, was racing the top miler, Wes Santee. Wes brought me right into the center of this head-to-head competition when he told me to take over the lead at the two-mile mark. The overall distance was 4.3 miles. Wes said he would hold back, for Sowell would stay with him. Santee loved playing "cat and mouse" games with the fields. The strategy was that if I could get far enough ahead, build up enough separation from Sowell, maybe Arnie would not be able to catch up to me. Wes could win two races at once! At the two-mile mark, I heard the timer shout out a clocking below ten minutes. I still had 2.3 miles to go. But with the confidence of Wes Santee within me, I led the large field of runners up a mile-long hill; a television camera was mounted on a jeep immediately in front of me. The red light was on. I was running "live." My three-mile time at the summit was fast enough to win collegiate cross-country races. Before we descended a narrow path that took us through a heavily wooded area, Wes went past me. He simply encouraged me with, "Come on, Billy." Arnie did make it by me. But at the finish I was only ten seconds behind the top American half miler. Be impressed.

I was obviously getting stronger. It seemed realistic to believe that I could become the "champion half miler" that Cromwell forecast. However, I never followed his advice. He told me, in a personal letter, to run over hurdles at the end of my workouts, to work continuously on my speed. He finished the letter with, "Just keeping sprinting, champ."

No hurdles were brought out to the Quantico track; no sprinting took place. From September into December, it was all cross country.

When we ran in New York for a race against NYU, we were introduced from the audience on *The Ed Sullivan Show*. Wes was up on the stage with the popular Sunday night host. The rest of us just stood up from our seats when Ed Sullivan directed the cameras our way. My mother, brother, friends back home saw me.

Santee was news. He brought excitement to the season. Wes had to be different. While the rest of the Quantico cross-country team wore cotton/polyester warm up sweats, Santee pranced around in fluffy Orlon. He was Wes Santee! At the same time, Wes was personal with his teammates; he cared about us. And he was a special friend to me. He even did my laundry for me once. Married, living in a home in Quantico, he had a washing machine. I was living somewhat out of my car, driving in from our camp in the "boondocks" to train with the cross-country team, then back out to the camp and rack in a hut where I studied and slept.

Our coach was Tom Rosandich. A captain, Tom was one gung-ho Marine. As a promoter he was tremendous. The combination of Santee and Rosandich brought about exciting meets with maximum publicity. During the cross-country season, in addition to Annapolis and Pittsburgh, we raced in Philadelphia; Lawrence, Kansas; and South Bend, Indiana.

Richard Todd, in *A Man Called Peter*, made organized religion tolerable for me. Before his untimely death, Peter Marshall was the popular down-to-earth chaplain of the U.S. Senate. Pastor of the First Presbyterian Church of Washington, D.C., he was so popular that people would stand out in the rain, hoping to find a place in the sanctuary in order to hear him preach. I did not like the word "preach." I began to measure, very privately, whether I should be a Presbyterian minister. I weighed this very carefully over the next twelve months. I did not want people to think I was religious. Therefore I did not discuss the possibility with others. But if I could be respected like Peter Marshall, have people stand in the rain to hear me preach, tell them that they did not have to be religious, that a moral life—not conversion—defined the person, I could be a second Peter Marshall. And this would make my life significant.

The trip to South Bend was of the unusual. The cross-country race took place before the traditional football game between Navy and Notre Dame. The course was on the campus golf course. It was very cold. We even ran with some sleet. My image of running successfully against other Olympic hopefuls was not hurt by my finish that day. Here is how a newspaper accounted for my effort: "Although losing to the Irish, the Marines gained consolation in the fact that Santee finished far ahead of Bill Squires, acclaimed as an Irish All-Time great. In fact, Squires was pressed for the third position by Quantico's number two man, Bill Taylor, who ran the best three miles of his career Saturday." There I was again, up there in print with great names in the sport. A veteran runner, Bill Coleman of the Chicago Athletic Club, finished second behind Santee that morning. Coleman made the U.S. Olympic Team in the 1500 meters nine months later!

We got to watch the football game on the famous Notre Dame field; we sat right behind the Navy bench. I was taken back to those Saturday mornings in Toluca Lake when, as a kid, I would listen to

Notre Dame-Navy or Notre Dame-Army football games on the radio. Out on the field in 1955 was a soon-to-be All-American quarterback for the Irish. Paul Hornung, who became an All-Pro running back for the Green Bay Packers, led Notre Dame to victory that afternoon. Like Santee, Hornung had a bit of flair, too.

The afternoon before we were to run in Philadelphia against two international stars on the Villanova cross-country team, the wire services reported that Santee was under investigation by the American Athletic Union. The reason will sound ludicrous today because it was over a couple thousand dollars of excessive expense money, nevertheless it called for an immediate suspension of my teammate. An Associated Press photographer found us when we arrived on campus and took a picture of Santee, Rosandich, and me. It went out to newspapers across the nation. The caption told of how "the number two man on the Quantico team, Bill Taylor, would replace Wes Santee." Replace Santee?

One of those Villanova runners whom I was to face the next afternoon was Ron Delaney. Unknown at the time to the American track world, this Irish lad with the pink cheeks would go on to win the Olympic 1500 meters in Melbourne the next year. I was not able to handle the top three Villanova runners. Two of them because of their international credentials, the other probably because I did not have Santee to orient and inspire me.

I was invited to speak at the New York track writers dinner about the American track and field heroes on the West Coast. The Trojans would be going for their eighth straight national track and field title in the spring. And the writers were familiar with my name because of my running with Santee. The restaurant was packed. I spoke confidently to the journalists in a dark, smoke-filled banquet room, telling stories about Parry O'Brien, Ernie Shelton, Jimmy Lea, Mal Whitfield. They loved it. Except for Whitfield, these were names from far across the United States. I personalized the heroes. I knew the gods. They were eager to hear how Parry O'Brien worked out by himself in the Coliseum. I told them how he returned to the Phi Psi house after dark and ate a steak prepared for him by the fraternity cook. He liked honey with his steak. O'Brien won two straight Olympic gold medals in the shot put. Parry was eccentric. He would place a towel over his head during the warm up for the shot put, never looking at a competitor. Went completely into himself. They liked hearing how Ernie Shelton had placed a high jump bar up at seven feet in his bedroom when he was in high school. And now, surely, my quiet, unassuming former teammate would be the first person in history to clear that height. Not in his bedroom, of course. And the writers never got enough of Santee. He was top box office, their bad boy. The one who drew the big crowds at the indoor meets. I told them some nice things about Wes. How he took a personal interest in his teammates and was not haughty with us. He sure as hell was a good friend to me.

My talk was overwhelmingly received. The intensity in that crowded room was enormous. A New York businessman who owned a company told me that I was ready for television right that moment. The man gave me his card and said to come and see him when I got out of the Marine Corps. Captain Rosandich told me afterwards that the New York writers really loved me.

At Quantico I lived out in what was called "the boonies." This would be so until I completed the required courses for all Marine Corps officers. Some instructors informed us that their course was the most important one because it could save the lives of Marines under our command. While I was running for the Marine Corps, I was also being prepared for war. We began at 7:00 a.m. and continued right through the day. Some of the weeks had night exercises. I missed several of these evening maneuvers because of my running workouts. I felt quite uncomfortable being in my rack when my fellow officers returned late at night. Fortunately, this did not happen too often. I did not drink beer like most of the other guys, so the nights out in the boondocks were lonely. I was not interested in polishing my shoes again and again, or my boots, or my belt buckle. Some of the officers planned on making the Marine Corps a career. I wanted to talk about a serious moral life with the other officers, not about how to stay alive or kill others. And because of my base notoriety, much of the conversation was about the Olympics and my races with Santee.

Social life? I did have several dates, a couple of which were with a cute little blonde in Washington D.C. One night, Hope put it perfectly when she told me that I had "a one track mind."

Coach Rosandich entered Quantico as a team in the junior nationals in Philadelphia. The distance for the championship race was 10,000 meters. I do not believe I had ever run that distance before. Anyone who had won a major U.S. running title was excluded from the medals. Wes could not run due to the ongoing AAU investigation, plus his numerous American titles. However, a couple of national distance runners did make their way into the field.

We began the six-mile run from the Penn Boathouse. Almost immediately, the course took us up a long, gradual hill. At the summit, about three miles up the park road, we turned back. I was surprised how easy the pace felt. I had no trouble staying with the leaders. While the event was officially the AAU junior nationals, the entries were almost all from the New England and Mid-Atlantic states.

I managed to stay with each burst by the leaders as we raced down the hill. The only runner ahead of me at the finish was Fred Eckoff from Norway. I was the first American. Less than two years before, I had run against Eckoff and his Oklahoma A&M record-setting distance medley team in the Fresno Relays. The paper said that "he may run for Norway in the 1956 Olympics." Only fourteen seconds separated me from this international distance star. My time was just over thirty-two minutes. Those reading this who run road races today will recognize the time as being quite good, especially given the long climb up the hill and my being a half miler. And this was back in 1955, over fifty years ago.

My large silver medal from the official U.S. junior nationals was a real one. And Eckoff was for real. But at the same time the medal was also bogus. The field was not national by geography. I ran a very good time for a half miler. Nothing more should be made of it.

It all seemed so cruel

When I arrived at the Los Angeles airport, I went immediately to see Betty. It was early in the morning due to the all-night flight from Washington, D.C. We were still on prop planes in 1955. Betty saluted me when she met me at her front door. No embrace. No kiss. We drove a short ways from her home in the Baldwin Hills and parked. Still no embrace, no kiss, only words that I did not want to hear. I had lost the girl I really loved. I got out of the car and walked along a ridge above the city, fighting off crying. When I felt that I had control of myself, I returned to the car and drove Betty home. It all seemed so cruel.

I had the indoor track season to look forward to when I returned to Quantico. Santee had hired a lawyer and a judge reinstated him until there could be a trial. I still had a month or so of officers training left in the boondocks. I took the map-reading exam very seriously for two reasons. First, Marine infantry lieutenants are the ones who call in the jets to blast targets close to their own troops, and second, I was motivated by the word that this was the exam that could cost one their commission. You were out if you did not score a seventy or higher. Add to this that I had always found math difficult. Fortunately, I was smart enough to study for the exam with some of the guys from the Ivy League colleges.

We were given a photograph of a landscape taken from the air and completed the math work in the classroom. You placed your compass on the photo and recorded data that you would use to locate certain numbers in a forest. We were then blindfolded and driven out to the woods. The challenge was to locate the correct numbers on the trees based on your classroom work. This meant using our compasses in the jungle.

I scored over ninety on the exam. This was one of the few times that I had experienced the pleasure of academic satisfaction. It was a good feeling. On top of that, the company commander who never approved of my running was transferred and my leadership marks went up instantly.

Taylor to Santee

When you stuff one hundred or so recent college graduates into an all-day classroom for nine months, boredom and cynicism result. A John Templeton placed paperback books in a drawer and read them during the lectures. John thought his book-concealing routine very clever. He managed to escape detection for some time. With one elbow on the table, his head resting on his hand, John would look down, wanting to appear that he was thinking. He was reading his paperbacks. Then came the day when, after returning from a smoking break, John found a chit on his desk. It read, "Captain Robb is watching you." John turned slowly around, surveying the back of the room. Perhaps this was only a prank? Maybe one of us filled out the chit. But when John looked up to the projection booth, there was Captain Robb staring down at him.

The daily stack of classes included: offensive and defensive tactics, emergency medicine, military justice, firing and caring for the weapons, and map reading. We were being shaped to lead in war. I escaped by mid-afternoon in order to drive to Quantico to run, but only after being in class since 7:00 a.m. As the day heated up, the flies arrived. The odor told of a nearby dairy. It was summertime in Virginia: humid, hot, awful. One day I killed a number of deserving flies with my dungaree cover during a lecture. A dungaree cap is similar to a baseball hat. No, we didn't wear them backwards. Or sideways.

Near the close of a boring presentation, the major said, "Will Mr. Taylor come forward after the lecture." God damn it. What did I do? This particular major looked like a spider monkey. I still can see him swinging by one arm from a tree limb when we were holding a class out in the field. He hung there like a monkey. Why did he want to see me after his lecture? He put it directly: "Lieutenant Taylor, will you refrain from killing flies while I am lecturing."

Santee took me to Boston with him. I was to set the pace in the feature event, the one-mile run. The famous Boston Garden would be packed. I was excited over the opportunity to run in a major indoor meet. Wes Santee and Ron Delaney were to collide in an Olympic Games preview. The bashful, rosy-cheeked Irishman was up against the brash, outspoken cowboy from Kansas. And I was to set a fast pace for over half the race.

Wes and I flew up to Boston in a Marine Corps reconnaissance plane. Just the two of us and the pilots. I had never run on the boards before. There was no indoor track at Quantico. We had been using the basketball gym. Or trails near the Potomac River, if the weather was not too cold. Wes had been away most of the time working on his defense with a lawyer, so I did not get to benefit from training with him. Nor was I giving any attention to the speed base that I needed to be developing. None! It was too cold outside and the basketball gym did not offer the opportunity to go over hurdles in order to "loosen my hips" as Cromwell had suggested. But I did not improvise or even try to figure out ways to increase my flexibility. Wes was not in top shape. And he had a muscle strain in one calf. But he was not going to miss this chance to race in the Boston Garden for perhaps the last time. We took a taxi into Boston. When we heard the "Santee-Delaney mile" being hyped on the radio as we drove to the hotel, Wes asked the driver what he thought of Wes Santee. Wes toyed with him; I did not approve of this, but I loved the intensity and excitement of the moment.

The atmosphere was absolutely electric in Boston over the race. The AP and UP wire stories mentioned how Santee had brought "his fellow Marine Corps leatherneck" to set a fast pace. The UP mentioned that I was a "former Southern California cross-country captain." They called me "Billy Taylor." Where did the "Billy" come from? Santee called me Billy. The AP said I was "handpicked," a "1:52 half miler while at Southern California."

I was all caught up in the American sport media. I had reached the national scene—as a pace setter for a Marine Corps friend. I had no idea that "rabbits" who were not running to win the race were frowned upon by some AAU officials. Bannister had two pace setters when he ran below four minutes for the mile. I do not think that there is any question that Bannister would not have done so on that particular day without the help of his teammates.

So, I did not realize that some AAU officials would scorn my role. Not that it would have stopped me from going, had I known. I was helping a teammate. And I loved being a part of the big-time track world. We had pre-race steaks served to us in our hotel room. Everything had to be "first class" for the Kansas farm boy. Wes wore the Marine Corps dress uniform that was normally reserved for formal occasions. The one with the dark blue coat, a single red stripe down the trousers. Santee knew how to dress with flair, how to present himself. I was never a dresser.

The overflow crowd was there to see the Irishman whip Santee. We were in Boston Garden, where the Celtics played and won NBA basketball championships. And in the Garden that night there was one noisy, opinioned track and field crowd. Santee asked me to run the first half of the mile in two flat: a four-minute-mile pace. No one had come close to breaking four minutes on an indoor track yet, and Wes was certainly not in condition to do so. But Santee wanted to escape from Delaney's tremendous kick at the end. We were to run eleven laps on a track with steeply-banked turns. How would I know if I was running at a two-minute pace? I had never been on the boards before, and all of the miles I had run were over four laps. Without banks.

I nailed the half mile in two flat. Unfortunately, it did not work. Delaney hunched his shoulders, flapped his arms, and began to catch up with Santee. The overflow crowd came to its feet well before the finish as the Irishman caught and went by the Kansas "bad boy." I can still hear the pounding on the boards. Delaney made a lot of noise. This was the most exciting moment of the entire 1956 indoor track season. The AP, UP wire stories told of my fast pace. I was being swept up in the world of Wes Santee. But what about my training, my preparation for the outdoor track and field season? What seemed significant at that moment was running with Wes when he needed me. I let it absorb me. When the New York track writers gathered the following week, there was praise for my Boston effort because it helped to bring about a faster mile time. A few attacked the use of a pacer. At the time, I liked the attention.

Wes lost the court battle. There would be more appeals. But he was not allowed to run in Madison Square Garden the next weekend. I would be down on the indoor track, however, for the meet director of the Melrose Games said he wanted me in the half mile there. The two gardens were the most famous indoor arenas in the country. The meet director told me that he was impressed with my form. Tom Courtney would require more than form.

Many of my USC teammates were in the military service, too. I would run into them at some of the indoor meets and also during the outdoor season. Jimmy Lea, Des Koch, and Parry O'Brien had gone from the ROTC program into the Air Force. Jack Davis was a Navy officer. Ernie Shelton was an enlisted man in the Army. I was on a first-name basis with not only my teammates from college, but also with a lot of other American track stars who were expected to make up the 1956 U.S. Olympic Team. While acquainted with Mal Whitfield and Bob Richards before the Marines, Tom Courtney, Arnie Sowell, Dave Sime, and others began greeting me by name because of my proximity to Wes Santee. This was fun. I did not mention Spurrier. I do not think he has ever called me Bill.

I was not prepared to run a fast half mile in the famous Melrose

Games. I was not anywhere near the form I had been in the year before, when I began my senior season at USC. I finished well back.

It turned out that I was able to run with Santee a few more times indoors without losing my amateur standing. The AAU allowed this exception for military athletes. Club and college athletes did not want to take this risk. This led to my pacing Wes two more times.

I was not happy when a New York writer, Lou Miller, called me "Billy 'Cottontail' Taylor." Lou had traveled around New York with us when we were competing there during the cross-country season. Santee was the reason, of course. It was great having a kind of in-house New York writer covering your team. Lou went with us to restaurants, to the Radio City Music Hall, pointed out the Rockefeller Center as we drove by. I had no problem with being identified as Santee's teammate. But the rabbit tag bothered me. I felt that it compromised my track image.

Wes and I flew to Milwaukee and Cleveland to run before packed arenas in a kind of surrealistic final appearance for Santee. An AP wire photo went out showing Santee and I boarding the plane to Milwaukee.

I felt uncomfortable when the Reverend Bob Richards yelled across the hotel lobby, "Been reading your Bible, Billy?" But I liked an Olympic champion recognizing me. Richards was the 1952 Olympic pole vault champion. The flying pastor appeared on the back of Wheaties boxes claiming that he was "vaulting for the Lord." Bob was quite a showman. And quite an athlete. We had connected up one time in the Coliseum when he asked me to run the 1500 meters in the decathlon in order to help the pace. I did. And it was likely the fastest ever time run in an official decathlon. I did it as a workout. My time, of course, was not legal. But I guess I was a pace setter even before I met Santee.

A very special dinner took place after the Cleveland indoor meet. At the table were Santee, Richards, Otto and Kay Graham, and I. These were three of the greatest names in the history of American sports. You know about Santee and Richards. Otto Graham was considered by a lot of people to be the best quarterback to ever play pro football. And there I was having dinner with the three of them. And Kay. The three

Bill Taylor and two-time Olympic pole valult
champion, "the Reverend" Bob Richards

men spoke so quietly to one another. It was as though they were close
friends. I think it had more to do with their mutual respect for one
another, each recognizing that the others were the best in the nation in
their sport or event. They included me in the conversation as though
I was one of them.

I did get a chance to run a few more times on the boards just for myself. One race went fairly well. In the New York Athletic Club indoor
meet, I had a strong finish over one thousand yards and just missed
second place. Santee and Rosandich were watching from the stands.
Their picture went out across the country on the wires with a caption
that told of Santee not being able to run in the meet. I wore Santee's
special white USMC track uniform with red and golden trim. I felt
great in it. But there was nothing Olympian about my just missing tying for second with an only decent college runner from NYU.

Just before that meet, while walking alone in Times Square, I noticed a picture of me pacing Santee in Cleveland. It was displayed in
the show window of a Movietone News theatre. Some of you will remember those hyped news reports. I went in and watched the race,

heard my name. Any feelings of anonymity in Times Square were reduced, but was this what I wanted for my track legacy?

It was at one of the indoor meets in New York that Dan Ferris, the
head of the AAU, approached me. He wanted to tell me that the governing body of American track and field would not have banned Santee for life if he had not hired a lawyer and made it an international
story. The "Silver Fox" told me that all they would have done was "slap
Wes on the wrists." Why did he approach me and tell me this?

Before the outdoor season began, before we trained on the dark
soil of the Quantico track, one of the gods of the sport showed up at
the Quantico gym. The Reverend Bob Richards said that he stopped
by for a workout since he was preaching in the area. We did not have
a vaulting pit in our gym. So Bob asked for some wood and nails, and
built a pole vault box. Then the versatile pastor stacked gymnastic pads
on top of one another for the landing. It was not very long before he
was swinging up and over the pole vault bar at a pretty good height.
But this is not why he stopped by our gym that afternoon. After he
finished his workout, he revealed the real reason for the visit. This conversation between Santee and Richards would have led to headlines
in newspapers across the country had it been leaked. We were sitting
on benches in the loft of the gym. Just the three of us. Bob suddenly
became very serious. The "flying parson" wanted to know if Wes was
going to talk, provide names—the names of other American track
stars who had taken what was considered excessive appearance money.
Richards mentioned that such a disclosure could destroy the 1956
U.S. Olympic Team. Santee's response was right out of a Western. The
Kansas cowboy said, "I am not built that way." Gary Cooper could
not have delivered the reply any better. As Richards walked away he
turned, looked back, and said, "Remember, 'Vengeance is mine, sayeth
the Lord.'" The warning, hearing the "flying parson" twist the Bible for
his own ends—this was an incredible scene for me to witness.

I moved into the Bachelor Officer Quarters in Quantico after completing officers training. I had a small room with privacy. And I was

officially assigned to special services. This meant that for five months I was to train with the Quantico track team for the Olympic Trials. Now I was on a full "athletic scholarship" in the Marine Corps, and the monthly checks were much higher than what USC paid.

Coach Rosandich assembled considerable talent for the 1956 Quantico team. Santee would be able to run in the military competitions. Al Cantello, a little javelin thrower from LaSalle, became my good friend. Al would break the world record the next year. Josh Culbreath, a 400-meter hurdler from Morgan State, placed third in the 1956 Olympics.

I was elected co-captain. And I didn't vote for myself. Why didn't I? I wanted to be one of the captains. I had recently read *Magnificent Obsession* by Lloyd C. Douglas, and it suggested a different attitude toward self-promotion. The message was that if you do good for others without thinking of yourself, then good things will come back to you. I had missed out on being the USC track and field co-captain, so this vote by a mature, talented, post-college team made me feel confident. Those troubling negative chits about my leadership from that captain who disdained my going to run in the afternoon were cancelled out.

It was lonely in that small BOQ room. I played musicals on my little portable record player. *Brigadoon* was one of my favorite records and the music from *The King and I*. I read about the positive thinking that Norman Vincent Peale touted. And the parables, sayings of Jesus in the Bible.

Sometimes I would go over to the colonial base chapel where an extremely warm, charismatic minister, Chaplain Embry, preached. He wore a white robe and he always looked like he had been freshly scrubbed. I found him a bit unreal, like he was too perfect. Yet he was warm, handsome, personal. I did not know it at the time, but Wes had been seeing Chaplain Embry for counseling during the time he was fighting for his track life.

I wanted that "something" to feel right

I wanted that "something" to feel right in me about religion. But the church pamphlets in the little chapel did not do it. I kept turning the pages of *A Man Called Peter*, hoping to find peace, direction, that which felt right. This book on the life of Peter Marshall tells of how he was saved from death by God calling his name out. Walking through a thick mist in Scotland, Marshall was one step away from falling off a cliff when he was stopped by this voice. Peter Marshall believed that God saved him for the ministry. I did not buy into the belief that God gave special treatment to some people. Santee told me that after we left Quantico, Chaplain Embry had stepped backwards on an aircraft carrier and fallen to his death down an elevator shaft. So much for God and special favors.

Quantico remained cold throughout March. Even with all that free time to train every day, my preparation did not include speed or hurdle work. And where were the gradual 660 yard efforts that had produced great results for me the year before? In great contrast, when Josh Culbreath showed up late because of his having attended Marine Corps boot camp for enlisted men, he immediately went into twice-a-day workouts. He had a plan; he knew what had to be done.

The Quantico press thought I was great. My reputation was established during cross country as the running partner of Wes Santee. After a couple of outdoor meets, I was described as "the workhorse" of the base team. Tom Rosandich would tell me years later that I "won a lot of meets" for him. Tom would put it that way. It was fun to run against colleges like Princeton and Yale. I won the mile and half mile against those two Ivy League schools in a tri-meet at Quantico, then came back with a much-praised mile relay leg. But I was up against virtual novices.

Up in Happy Valley on the Penn State campus, I won the mile and the half mile. We ran early in the day because of a spring football scrimmage that was scheduled for their alumni in the afternoon. I was winning against well-known colleges, but how fast was I really running?

I did not always compete in the mile relay, because of a strained

After my fastest ever 800 meters, this USMC general remarked to
Wes Santee, "Tell Taylor to get a hair cut!"

hamstring. The injury took away that important speed training. But
also I had no comprehensive plan. I should have been engaged in a
speed-oriented program that included the hurdling that Cromwell
suggested at the end of the workouts and progressed toward the big
meets in June. After the Penn State meet we went for brunch at the
university faculty club. I met Lenny Moore, the former All-American
halfback at Penn State and then an All-Pro wide receiver for the Balti-
more Colts. He knew my name before we were introduced. Moore and
Santee knew one another; they were of the elite in American sports.
Wes was not able to run with us because if he did it would threaten the
amateur status of the Penn State runners.

That afternoon, I was really looking forward to seeing a special televised event held in my Los Angeles Coliseum. John Landy, the new
world record holder for the mile, was going to try and become the
first person to break four minutes on American soil. Guess who won?
Jim Bailey—the same guy who surprised me by being in the half-mile
field at the Pacific Coast Conference in Eugene the year before. Santee

watched without suggesting that he would have won. No bravado.

Even with the lack of speed training, the hamstring strain, and my disregard of the hurdle advice, I still ran my fastest ever half-mile time. The All-Marine finals were held at Quantico. Wes told me he was going to go by the initial quarter at a very fast pace. A former Ivy League middle-distance star, Walt Clarkson, would try and stay with him. Once again, Wes was thinking of his teammate. The Olympian did produce the swift pace. I came by the 400-meter mark feeling relaxed, three to four seconds behind Wes and Clarkson. On the backstretch of the second lap, it was akin to chasing after Casper again.

Around the final curve, Clarkson turned into a noodle. His legs were gone. Santee had lured him into running death. I closed the gap dramatically on Santee down the finishing stretch. He ended up only one second ahead of me. My legs felt rubbery over the last ten to fifteen yards. Within minutes I was told that I had run the fastest official time of my life. I was standing by the first turn, feeling a bit nauseated when I heard this. The sunken track at Quantico has steep grass banks at that end of the stadium. It was a vivid moment for me—despite the strained hamstring, inadequate training, not much elasticity. I should remember, however, how Wes set this up. While he was running for himself, fighting for conditioning that he would need in the All-Service final in a couple of weeks, he also was thinking of me.

Before we flew to Los Angeles for the All-Service meet, it was decided that that I would make my attempt to qualify for the Olympic Trials over 1500 meters. This was utterly stupid. True, there were no Sowell, Courtney, Whitfield, or Spurrier equivalents in the metric mile, but I had never demonstrated that I could sustain a fast pace over the longer distance. It was inane for me to flee the half mile for the 1500 meters. While my time in the All-Marine final over 800 meters was the fastest of my life, I was almost three seconds over what it would take to make the U.S. team. But, had I stuck with the half mile, I could have finished up by running my own event in the Coliseum, back where it began one night with my father.

Our flight from Quantico to the El Toro Marine base near
Camp Pendleton took over twelve hours. No problem for me. I located the bed that the pilots use right behind the cockpit. I slept virtually all of the way across the country. My brother Harold met me
at Fort MacArthur in San Pedro, where the Quantico team would be
staying.

Coach Rosandich had us entered in three meets, then, depending
on how we did, there might be the Olympic Trials. The All-Service
meet was held in the Coliseum. The 800 meters took place on Friday
night. Courtney of the Army, Spurrier of the Air Force, and Santee
of the Marine Corps, were going to fight it out. I was in the stands. It
was legal for Santee to run because this was solely a military competition. Courtney set a new American record, while Santee and Spurrier
battled around the final turn for second place. There was some bump-
ing and Santee was disqualified. How ugly. The great American miler,
while running the half mile for what turned out to be the final time,
was disqualified. Wes still had the 1500 meters on Saturday, but this
was hardly the way the great champion wanted to finish his last half
mile. A couple of years earlier, Wes had run a time in Europe that was
only a couple tenths of a second above the world 880 record.

The next afternoon, I did not run a bad race. Santee won easily. I
was jealous that he helped his former Kansas teammate, Art Dalzell,
instead of me, to an Olympic Trials qualifying spot. The first three
military runners advanced to the trials. I believe I was fifth. With
Wes ineligible for the Olympic Trials, the fourth-place finisher in the
1500 meters moved up and advanced as one of the top three. Was I
just one place away?

After the All-Service meet, Captain Rosandich was going to send
me back to Quantico. Had I left, I would have missed the Olympic Trials in the Coliseum. When Santee heard this, he took off to find Tom.
I still can see Wes racing into the barracks at Fort MacArthur to locate
our coach. I was able to stay.

A couple of weeks later at the U.S. Olympic Trials, Courtney, Sowell, and Spurrier made the Olympic Team in the 800 meters. Whitfield,
the two-time defending Olympic champion, ran fourth. In the 1500

meters, Bill Coleman, that Chicago Athletic Club veteran whom I had run against at Notre Dame, made the team. So did Jerome Walters, the Compton runner who had held the national junior college 880 record that Casper and I threatened three years before.

My old USC teammates, Jimmy Lea and Des Koch, made the U.S. Olympic Team. So did little Max Truex. And the Trojan veterans, Jack Davis and Parry O'Brien. The USC freshman 880 record holder, Murray Cockburn, who had kindly come down with mono my senior year, before my tonsillitis brought me down, made the Canadian team in both the 400 meters and the mile relay.

Someone else was supposed to be on the team. Who was missing? It was Ernie. My Valley College and USC teammate did not have quite the same lift in his leg in 1956. Nobody had cleared seven feet yet, but Ernie Shelton was not coming as close to the record height as he had in the two previous years. In utter agony, Ernie lay face down in the sawdust of the high jump pit after his final attempt. He finished fifth in the trials. No Olympics for the two-time collegiate national champion. The world leader for the two preceding years, Ernie owned that Coliseum pit. Note—for the final cruelty, a junior college jumper from Compton cleared seven feet the night of the high jump trial. The lanky, likable, shy, freckle-faced friend who joined me in shocking Rusty Tamblyn lost two lifetime goals that night.

I heard later that Bob Richards went home with Ernie after the high jump trials. The Wheaties man came through for him. You cannot always fit people into a neat little package, can you? Richards, the showman, took the time for Ernie.

We "hedge hopped" back to Quantico on military flights after the trials. In Denver we saw the movie, *The Fastest Gun Alive*. Before we took off for what turned out to be Akron, Ohio, the future world record holder in the javelin, Al Cantello, recreated a scene from the movie at the Denver airport. Al could be hilarious. In the film, Broderick Crawford tries to lure a retired gunslinger, Glenn Ford, into drawing on him. In the lobby of the terminal, the ruddy-faced, stocky Cantello approached Rosandich with a water pistol hanging out of one of his trouser pockets. As usual, Tom was in uniform, captain bars on his shoulders. This did not stop Cantello from repeating the line Broderick Crawford had addressed to Glenn Ford in the film. It was, "I hear you are fast?" Rosandich wanted no part of this scene. Irritated, impatient, Tom said, "Come on, Cantello." They stood there facing one another. In the movie, Glenn Ford responded to "I hear you are fast?" with, "What do you want to know for?" He had promised his beautiful wife that he would never draw his gun again. Cantello had his hand on the water pistol. Crawford, I mean Cantello, is ready for the great line. He steps closer to Rosandich and answers for Ford with, "What do you want to know for?" and then for Crawford with, "I gotta know." It was a quick draw. In a split-second, water was dripping down Tom's face, dampening his Marine Corps uniform. The captain bars on his shoulders were of no help.

Cantello hung on to the water pistol. Akron, Ohio had a major Air Force base and we were able to obtain private rooms in the BOQ. It was late when we arrived. I was about to go to sleep when I heard noises from the rafters. Someone began shooting water out through the vents. Cantello was up there. We were quartered with some high-ranking officers. When I heard some voices in the hall I looked out and discovered two senior officers complaining about having been targeted. You do not do things like this in the military! Al Cantello was delightful, one fun travel companion.

My orders said to report to Camp Pendleton. I left the smells of the Marine base at Quantico, the Potomac River, the heavy summer air. "California here I come, right back where I started from..." Hoot, one of my closest friends on the Quantico team, drove across the country with me. We drove in separate cars, but we stayed in view of one another. When we reached a main intersection in Colorado, Hoot turned north toward Greeley. We had only stopped for gas and quick meals before we waved goodbye. I can still picture his station wagon heading up the road toward his hometown.

Camp Pendleton is south of Los Angeles, north of San Diego, along the Pacific Ocean. I had a little time before I had to report for duty, so I drove up to see my idealized Western couple, Lou and Mary.

Thinking back, I do not remember identifying with any marriage except this one. None of the parents of my friends come to mind. Frederic March and Myrna Loy had a wonderful marriage in *The Best Years of Our Lives*, but images of sex and power dominated the male-female relationships in the movies I saw while growing up. *The Outlaw* with Jack Beutel and Jane Russell, displayed the physical conquest by the male, the female protest, then arousal and passion. Same story when Jennifer Jones broke down and gave herself to the bad guy, Gregory Peck, in *Duel in the Sun*. *The Fountainhead* with Gary Cooper and Patricia Neal found an architect forcefully taking a female in a high rise apartment instead of a barn. In *Shane*, on the other hand, Alan Ladd respected the marriage of Jean Arthur and Van Heflin. Even though Jean Arthur had clearly fallen in love with him. Shane (Ladd) could have taken advantage of her. I identified with Shane. I saw the aggressive male who forced his way on the female as crude, vulgar. But I was bothered by the disloyal female. These were strong images that I took from the movies.

Lou and Mary were operating a pack station out of Bishop (up at South Lake). How quickly things had changed for me. Just a few weeks before, I had been in Los Angeles for those track meets, watching the Olympic Trials. Now I was back in California and up in the mountains with my idealized couple.

We sat at a table in their rustic cabin for two or three nights. This was not a movie, even if the two people were film-like images for me. We talked about values. And about religion. Lou told me why he admired a Presbyterian minister in Tucson. A young clergyman had stood up against racism in the pulpit. We did not discuss the Bible, or Jesus. Unknown to them, I was being forced from within to make a decision about whether Jesus was Jesus, or just another man. This pressure had been building up in me for a year or longer.

The cabin was near a rushing stream. It was a scene right out of a Western. Once again, I came alive in the rarified air. I missed Mammoth the summer I was swatting flies in Quantico. It was very special being back in the High Sierras. Lou provided me with a good horse and took me with him over a high pass to pick up some mules from way down in the canyon below. There I was, an officer in the USMC riding a horse alongside my Western hero. It was good to be away from those track images. I was ready to distance myself from the sport. Lou and I spent the night by a stream, talking some more about a moral life. I wanted to feel like I was of some use as we drove the mules back over the pass the next morning. I did not think of the song I composed as a little boy in Newhall about a singing cowhand just a-riding all day. But it was there, a part of my identification with the cowboys and the West. On my final night at the pack station, I went out by the corral to think. A brilliant array of stars encouraged questions, as did the silence within the darkness. Lou and Mary were of the mountains, of the natural. I was torn between wanting an independent life in the mountains, and wanting to become a Peter Marshall down in the city. If Jesus was who he claimed to be, I did not have a choice. I would have to be a minister. Jesus did not equivocate. He said, "I am the truth, the way, the life." When I pondered my future that night by the corral, Christianity either had to be true or false. One way or the other.

This was a private matter, although I may have shared with Mary and Lou the question I struggled with: Was Jesus the son of God or not? If so, I had to be a minister. There was no in-between for me. I was careful, however, to not sound too religious to them. Going into the ministry was still too peculiar an image for me. It was that night by the corral that I decided to become a minister. I did not say anything to anyone for months. I just let it settle. My trip to the mountains to see Mary and Lou was wonderful. Their marriage seemed so real. When Lou did not like the way Mary cooked something and they quarreled, briefly, I did not want them to fight. But each held their ground. It was a marriage secured by the mountains. To this day, I will add. What a beautiful life they have lived—wholesome, loyal, moral, honest.

Lieutenant

I WAS A REAL LIEUTENANT now. No more officers school. No more track identity. Well, not completely. My USC image was frequently mentioned in conversations. My having known and run with Wes Santee was of unusual importance to those who followed sports with any intensity. But I was just another infantry lieutenant at the large Marine Corps base. I had the good fortune to be assigned to the third battalion of the First Marine Division which was located at Camp San Mateo. This meant that I could live off base by the sea in the resort town of San Clemente. The quiet little beach community on the Pacific was a charming place to spend a year. And San Clemente put me closer to Los Angeles sporting events and home, which meant I could save some driving time. Our USMC training schedule usually ended around 4:00 p.m. It was not very long after the training day before I would be in the Pacific Ocean. That summer was filled with fluffy white breakers, the smell of the sea, the lightness of air that made San Clemente so special. I was far away from the humid, heavy air of Virginia.

Unlike my friends, I did not drive up to the Sand Piper bar in Laguna Beach at night to pick up girls. That did not appeal to me. I wanted a relationship with someone I found attractive and I did not see myself finding her with a cocktail in her hand. Yes, I was straight, moralistic, but not "holier than thou." I sought to live my values in a Stoic way and did not try to convert others.

I liked being a real Marine Corps lieutenant. At Quantico, there was always that conflict between my basic school courses and running practice. At Camp Pendleton, first as a platoon leader, then as the company executive officer, I was given the responsibility of training Marines for possible combat. The Korean War had ended, Vietnam was still eight years away, but one never knew when the Marines might be sent to fight somewhere. I enjoyed running the infantry company.

And, literally, running them. I was quite fit, having run my fastest ever half-mile time just weeks before I reported to the base. With a .45 pistol on my hip I would race up the hills, leading my men on maneuvers. Nobody else, of course, had my speed or endurance. Now, if there had been real bullets, land mines, mortar rounds coming in, well, I do not think I would have wanted to be so visible. Running became part of the identity of Delta Company. My troops got into a fight with another company in the showers because they were being teased about this unusual amount of running. I would hear later that my men had a nickname for me. It was taken from the television physical fitness personality, Vic Tanny. My troops apparently referred to me as "Tanny Taylor." But I never heard them say it.

I discovered that a good way to handle discipline was to threaten to run my men. One afternoon on our way back to the San Mateo base, a cherry bomb was tossed out of one of the trucks. We had been on maneuvers and we were using firecrackers to simulate grenades. The cherry bombs could start a brush fire. I stopped the convoy and told the sergeant to inform the men in each truck that if the lieutenant heard any more cherry bombs going off, they would run the remaining five miles back to our base. There were no more cherry bombs! I was surprised to learn later that the gunny sergeant had been getting the men up before I arrived at the camp each morning, taking them out for exercise runs. I had no idea that I was usurping his role with the troops. If we had gone into combat, I would have been very dependent on Sergeant Skinner. I was a rookie lieutenant; he was a seasoned Marine.

Mammoth had a rival

I lived with three other bachelors in a two story beach house just a block up from a wonderful surf. The beach was of fine, white sand. The temperature of the water was perfect around 5:00 p.m. What a way to end each day. Sometimes we rode the waves on our USMC-issued air mattresses. They could produce some exciting rides. At the crest of a big breaker, you could sometimes see the sand churning up far below. Then you would be tossed around in the puffy white foam, possessed by a power that was completely beyond your ability to control.

There were times when I would stand in the surf and watch the sun set over Catalina Island. It was paradise. Mammoth had a rival. However, the beach was empty of females. Nor did I see any prospects in the pews of the local Presbyterian church. That minister was dippy. Why are so many of them so strange?

There would be lengthy breaks on the maneuvers. I read Rachel Carson's *The Sea Around Us* while resting in the midst of scented sage above the Pacific. I enjoyed the book. I found science, as she presented it, very interesting.

Frequently I was picked to lead the aggressors, the guerilla unit that would seek to ambush the friendly forces during our war games. One afternoon I directed my unit to crawl up a slope and take a look at what was on the other side of the ridge. We were surprised to find enemy tank officers and their crews outside of their vehicles immediately below us. I signaled for my men to hold up, to wait until I gave the order to begin firing. I felt tense, excited. When I gave the command to fire, our victims ran frantically toward their tanks. They would have all been killed. Every one of them. I was aware of the sadistic pleasure that I received from the war fantasy.

"The pilot is over there"

I was given command of Delta Company one afternoon. Colonel Williamson said, "Okay, Taylor. It's yours." Almost immediately, I was put on a chopper to observe the number of enemy troops who had landed on the beaches. We were conducting major war games. As my noisy helicopter returned to the area where I had left my new company, I saw a funnel of pitch-black smoke rising from the ridge. Had my men started a brush fire? As the chopper set down, I could see that my men were bivouacked on other side of the road. Then I noticed part of a jet wing. Jets had been simulating an air attack on our position. I jumped out of the helicopter and within a few steps I was looking down at two severed legs. Each one was cut off at the calf. Someone said, "The pilot is over there." My dad? I did not consciously think about what I might have seen if I had ridden my bike out to the black smoke. I walked through some thick sage to where he had been thrown. One of his legs was shooting perpendicularly from his body. I did not get close enough to see his face. As said, I was not conscious of the parallel with my father's death.

A couple of other Marines were killed, and a fellow lieutenant had his face disfigured. He had been rushed away before we landed. A sergeant had his pack ripped off his back by the tip of a wing. There was no blood, no torn flesh. Just bruises. He said that he was not especially religious, but that he had "met his maker" through this narrow escape from death. I did not buy his battlefield confession. What about the pilot? What about the Marine who had been attached to those legs? How could people believe in a God who discriminates between a sergeant and a pilot? I had my own theological views well before I enrolled at a seminary.

During my time at Pendleton, the image of a Marine lieutenant was being romanticized in a new television series called *The Lieutenant*. Gary Lockwood played the role. The young officer was presented as intelligent, vulnerable, honest, caring. This image helped me to get through some mundane days. I was the lieutenant. It felt good to not be competing for my track identity. That fall I missed my first cross-country season in five straight years.

During the winter our battalion traveled by convoy to the USMC cold weather training station in the High Sierras. The freezing deaths in Korea were a recent memory for the Marine Corps veterans. On the way up, I passed by familiar memories along Highway 395. Lone Pine was where Des Koch had rescued me from the thugs after my knee was guided back into place by a doctor. The Convict Lake turn-off brought back the morning that Betty and I walked alongside the frozen lake. Then the convoy went past the road up to Mammoth, the paradise of my college summers. On the way up we had bivouacked on an old airplane runway in Lone Pine. Twilight was rich in the smell of sage. The dark presence of the High Sierra mountains formed a silhouette against the emerging evening sky. I wished that I could have been riding a horse. Twilight is my favorite time of day. The convoy moved slowly up 395. I rode in the front seat of a jeep. I was "The Lieutenant."

The All-American from Oklahoma

I loved that week up in the snow. Running around in snowshoes was fun. True to form, I set up a company competition. Sergeant Skinner tripped and plunged head first into the soft white powder on a relay leg. Only his legs and the snowshoes were sticking out. The troops roared. The sergeant took it well. Once again I was given command of a free-roaming guerilla force. We opened fire on a column of troops in the woods, and I felt that sadistic excitement again. Seeing them become frantic and confused was hilarious. I slept by an old wooden stove in the large command tent. Placed my air mattress in a snow sled. Only my nose was exposed outside my mummy bag. I have never slept any better.

That was the week I got to know Jack Ging. A recent All-American defensive back at Oklahoma, Jack was the commander of Echo Company. He played for the famous football coach, Bud Wilkinson. Jack was the most gung-ho of the officers in our battalion. That is how he played football, too. Jack was not big, just tough. And oh how he believed in himself. We hit it off. Our sport images had everything to do with it. We both could claim having been on national champion teams in college. Jack was a lot of fun, much like Bill McCormick, my junior college teammate. Ging was married to his college sweetheart, Gretchen, a tall, warm blonde with a deep Oklahoma accent. They made a great couple. We grew to be very close friends.

When we returned from the snow to the sage of Camp Pendleton, the hills began to look alike. Week after week, the same. The image of being a lieutenant was wearing off. One day the desk sergeant called to my attention the possibility that a private by the name of Joseph Matigliano was underage. And that he had misspelled his own name. Not Matigliano. His first name. A likable chap, he had spelled Joseph, "Joesph." The sergeant had Private Matigliano report to the company headquarters and stand in front of my desk. I asked him, "How do you spell your name?" He quickly spelled Matigliano correctly. I said, "No, not Matigliano...your *first* name." He answered, "Ah, lieutenant. That's the one that always throws me." When I led Delta Company through a required physical fitness test, my time over some 330 yards was easily the fastest; I felt exceptionally strong. I ran this sprint distance in cut-off boots, Marine fatigue trousers, and a cotton white T-shirt. I did not think of track. It was rewarding to me to just feel that good physically.

One of my roommates in the beach house was that lieutenant who had been caught reading paperbacks at Quantico during the lectures. The one who hid his Bantam books in the desk drawer. John Templeton told me one morning that he and the other guys living in our beach house had almost hired a prostitute the night before and sent her up to my room. It bugged them that I did not go drinking in the bars with them and that I went to bed early.

A serious-minded lieutenant invited me to a party. Just married, Pete Nimkoff was moral, sincere, philosophical. We had some good conversations. Pete had rented a beach flat on the Pacific side of the coastal railroad tracks. Pete said something very nice to me a day or so after the party. His bride had mentioned that I was quiet. It pleased me to hear that Pete told her that I was "deep."

Jack Bylin and Darlene got married when Jack returned from the Philippines. Darlene had been the faithful girl who waited for her man. I was Jack's best man at the wedding. I felt very close to both of them and very proud. It meant something to me to have some of those high school guys who were members of that rival social club see that Jack held me in such high regard.

A rattlesnake was a couple of feet from my boot

In track and field there isn't a record for the sideways long jump, but I probably would have broken it with my reaction to the rattlesnake. I looked down and saw it a couple of feet from my right boot. I was walking through some sage in the afternoon, looking up at a hill that we were to attack during maneuvers that evening. I happened to glance down and I discovered a large snake head drifting away from me. The rattlesnake was coiled. I went up in the air, and sideways. Surely a new

Lieutenant Taylor in his Camp Pendelton coaching role

world record. An incredible rush of adrenaline took me far away from where I had placed my boot. I was limp, drained. A sergeant, hearing some primordial sound burst out of me, rushed over and asked, "What's the matter, Lieutenant?" I loved being called Lieutenant.

It was a very large rattler. Camp Pendleton should have a rattlesnake for its aegis. They are all over the base. Big thick long ones. Did I mention that I was growing tired of playing war games? The hikes, inspections, parades, were repetitious. Gung-ho Jack Ging was not around to hype the day anymore. He had finished his tour of duty and gone to Hollywood with Gretchen to become an actor. Jack was also thinking about trying out with the Los Angeles Rams.

I only had a little over three months before being discharged. A big intersection in my life was ahead. What was I going to do when the Marine Corps image was over?

I received a call at company headquarters from a person who identified himself as a senior officer. This colonel wanted to know if I would accept a position as the base track coach. I almost made a terrible mistake. A Marine Corps friend, Mike Traynor, was very playful. Out of absolute boredom, Mike could easily have been pretending to be the colonel on the phone. Some of you will remember Mike's father, the Chief Justice of the California Supreme Court at the time. It turned out to be a real colonel on the phone. I shudder when I think of what I almost said to the senior officer. I accepted the coaching position, of course.

It was March and the 1957 track season was already underway. The year before, Bob Mathias competed for the Camp Pendleton track team. I liked being appointed the head coach at a major Marine Corps base, the respect I received from others for being named to the position. Motivating athletes was a role that came to me quite naturally. And I could still live in San Clemente. But there would be less time in the surf because of the driving distance and the length of the track practices.

The announcement that I would be coaching the Marine team was run in the *Los Angeles Times*. My best times were noted. When Pete Kokon heard that I might be the coach, he wrote in the *Valley Times* that "the Marines couldn't pick a better man." I received the highest possible marks on my fitness reports as the executive officer of Delta Company. Captain Jim Landers, the commanding officer of Delta Company, not only gave me superior marks, but my relationship with him provided me with evidence that I could work well with someone else in authority. Captain Landers was a good man. His low-key Idaho maturity made for a comfortable time as his executive officer.

I loved taking command of the Camp Pendleton track team. About a hundred Marines tried out. Mostly enlisted men. This was not Quantico where the teams are largely made up of officers who had run college track. Almost all of those on my Camp Pendleton track team were enlisted men without a college degree. And black. I put Corporal Pervis Atkins in charge of barracks. The future Oakland Raiders halfback was a strong leader. He would handle the enlisted men until I returned the next morning. Three other officers, two from the 1956 Quantico team, were going to be on the team. But I was the head coach. This separation was important to me. I wanted my own command.

Forget that fast 330 time from the fitness test at Camp San Mateo. I felt lousy in our initial track meet. We had only been training a week or two. I initially thought that I would run and coach. But my time for the half mile was so bad that afternoon that I announced after the meet that I would just be coaching. When Corporal Atkins heard this, he nailed me with, "Lieutenant, if you won't get yourself back into shape, how do you expect the rest of us to get back in shape?" So I trained, coached, and competed.

During this time, I timidly began telling people that I was going into the ministry. The immediate response was usually one of respect. Again and again I was told that I had chosen to fulfill "the most important profession on earth." I felt confident about my decision. It had not been rushed. I had let it come forth from within me. Gradually. It felt right. I needed a sponsor, a home church, in order to be admitted to a Presbyterian seminary. I did not like the word "seminary." Creepy. But President Eisenhower had been a Presbyterian. And, of course, Peter Marshall. I arranged with the minister of that rustic little chapel on Victory Boulevard in North Hollywood for the church elders to nominate me.

I had a basketball player with elasticity and speed on the Camp Pendleton team. Anderson had never run track before. And I had a former California high school 440 champion from Fresno. In that I could still run a good quarter-mile relay leg, I began looking around for a fourth mile-relay runner. It could be our ticket into a big meet like the Compton Invitational. And that particular meet could provide some nice closure to my track life. I really was not training for the half mile; it was too late a start. I was enjoying the coaching.

During this time, John Templeton was yanking off calendar pages when he returned to the beach house each day. He desperately wanted out of the Marine Corps. Mike Traynor was harassing his desk sergeant about making sure his discharge papers would arrive in "good order."

Max Truex suggested that we double date after the Coliseum Relays. The little Olympian was entered in the mile against major talent. Max did not have the leg speed to run a fast mile. True, he had broken the national high school record before he came to USC. But he was so slow over 100 yards that I used to tease him about how I could beat him "running backwards." Max did not really get going until two miles and out. That night he still managed a mile in just three seconds over four minutes. I think he ran all out over the whole way. Max had a specific USC coed in mind for me. Linda Nelson was a tall blonde with brown eyes, not a typical plastic USC sorority type. I liked her. The four of us met for a snack after the meet. I was interested in seeing Linda again.

I won the SPAAU 880 at Balboa Park in San Diego. I did not beat any top U.S. runners but it was gratifying to win a regional AAU title. Just like I had at Bakersfield when I won the junior college conference 880 title, I asked the queen for a kiss on the lips on the victory stand. I had told some of my men that I would do this, but they did not believe me. She responded warmly. I was told by my troops that her boyfriend became very upset.

Our mile relay time ran fast enough that night to gain us entry into the Compton Invitational a few weeks later. I was going back to my track of pathos. Where I had cried in Betty's arms after my final USC mile relay. I felt marvelous warming up. Some ten thousand fans were crammed into the bleachers on each side of the track. That afternoon I drove up with Tom Rosandich. He was coaching the third Marine division team from the Far East. They were at Camp Pendleton for the All-Marine meet that would take place the following week. It felt great to be Tom's equal. We both were head USMC track coaches.

On our opening leg, I ran the tall black lad with the elasticity. I would go second. As Anderson came off the final turn, Camp Pendleton was in second place. The strategy had worked: we were in the race.

I took off at full speed and cut over. Only Brayton Norton of Occidental, a national decathlon star with considerable speed, was ahead of me. I flew down the backstretch with him, unaware of what was lurking behind me. How in the hell did I end up back on the track again? I had retired. Well, not for long. The USC runner on the second leg had broken the national junior college half-mile record that Casper and I had approached breaking five years before. And the Los Angeles track club named the Striders had the fastest-ever national high school half miler and former collegiate champion waiting to strike.

The crowd warned me of their approaching presence as we went into the final turn. With about 150 yards to go, Chuck Kirkby and Lang Stanley turned it on and flew past me to the joy of the spectators. The crowds love the relay races. I came in, however, with the top three teams. Tom clocked me in a time that matched my best-ever quarter mile. Our third and fourth Pendleton runners lost contact. But it was good to have been back at Compton again. Enormously more satisfying than the way my USC track life ended there two years before.

I took Tom with me to the post-meet barbecue. The two-time Olympian and All-Time USC great, Jack Davis, was there. Jack had won the high hurdles once again at Compton. Guess who was on his arm? Betty! I had heard they were engaged. I walked up over and confidently offered my congratulations. It did not hurt. I did not feel jealous. I had an exciting future ahead of me. I was going to be a Presbyterian minister.

A new image was ahead

It felt great to be the host officer for the All-Marine final at Camp Pendleton. I was in charge. The Quantico team, led by a new group of Marine Corps officers, wore our classy 1956 synthetic white warm-up uniforms. I had no trouble winning the All-Marine 800-meter final. And our mile relay team took Quantico, even with Olympian Josh Culbreath on their anchor leg. We gave Anderson a big enough lead so that Josh could not catch him. After the meet, Josh fired off a sarcastic, "Thanks, Bill." He blamed me for the order of events. The

220-hurdles final was the event before the relay. I had not set up the order of events. I was puzzled. Why would an Olympic bronze medal winner be upset over losing a somewhat inconsequential relay? Well, at least it irritated an Olympian!

I felt fulfilled as I hung up my spikes for the last time. A new image was ahead. One week I was an officer in the United States Marine Corps, the next I was a summer assistant minister at Trinity Presbyterian Church. I began my preaching in the rustic chapel near Laurel Canyon and Victory where I had occasionally gone to worship in college. I had to be there in the pulpit! I had to be a minister. I felt as if I did not have a choice. I was scheduled to be in the pulpit in August when the pastor was on vacation. I think you know by now that I did not like the word "preach." It reminded me of Bible-pounding evangelists. To me, those "Jesus saves" types were an embarrassment to Christianity. Their preaching style was abhorrent; their Jesus, too personal. How presumptuous it was to claim such closeness. The manipulative tactics of a crusade were an insult to the teachings of Jesus. I did not want to appear religious; I did not quote the Bible, nor did I carry one around with me.

That summer in the pulpit and with the young people, I emphasized living a wholesome life. I wanted Christianity to be seen as natural. I spoke of being honest, clean-cut, a person of integrity who was not presumptuous about being close to God. At the same time, when I invited my close Marine Corps buddy, Jack Ging, to speak to a packed sanctuary of young people one evening, I found his message too man-centered. Ging emphasized the power of the individual and left no role for God. At the time, Jack and Gretchen were living in Hollywood. He was taking acting classes, still thought he might try out for the Los Angeles Rams. We met a few times over at the North Hollywood Park to toss the football around. When we did some short sprints, Jack would get out slightly faster than me, but I would go by him after thirty or so yards. It had only been a couple of months since I was running for Camp Pendleton in the All-Marine final.

The two of them were stimulating to be around. I spent a lot of time at their apartment that summer. Two of their acting friends, Art and

Millie, were always warm and personal. Actors have a way of making you feel like you are the center of the world. Our conversations with their friends at the apartment usually turned out to be serious. People in Hollywood were more open to talking about religion than most other people I met. When friends of Jack and Gretchen stopped by their apartment they introduced me with, "Bill is going into the ministry." And out it would come. Each one of them had some religious baggage that they wanted my view on. I would tell them that you don't have to go to church to be a good person.

I received a lot of admiration that summer. Having run for USC provided me with a touch of Los Angeles sport immortality. And my being a Marine Corps lieutenant, just months before, fascinated people. While people kept saying that I was going into "the most special professional position on earth," I let them know that I would remain one of them. I did not see the minister as being separate. But I had to be one!

One Sunday evening, Jack brought his former teammate at Oklahoma, Clendon Thomas, to speak to the young people. Clendon was an All-American running back in college and he would go on to play pro football for the Los Angeles Rams. Thomas was tall, of a strong frame, clean-cut, humble, and comfortable in testifying that he was a "Christian." I did not like testimonials. Again, how did he know he was Christian? In my view, that was up to God to decide.

Clendon told the kids not to be afraid of carrying their Bible around campus. Jesus, I was telling them the opposite: Do not try and convert other people. Let your life speak for you. However, Thomas did not come across to me as a phony. He was a man of integrity and conscience, straight out of the Bible Belt. That summer was filled with pool parties, beach trips, park picnics, and recreational sports. I made sure that each young person felt important. I constantly worked at including every individual. The size of my youth group increased rapidly. And I was given the credit.

Less than two months after my discharge from active duty in the Marine Corps, I went up into the pulpit of the rustic little chapel to preach my first sermon. I privately asked God to speak through me. I was absolutely sincere. This freed up my delivery. There is power behind what one says when one believes they are part of something greater than themselves.

Two of my first sermon titles reveal my pre-seminary values. One was, "Judge not, that you be not judged," the other was, "Be true to yourself." I believed that I let God speak through me. Not emotionally. The sermons were simple, moralistic, and very well received by both adults and the youth. I chose hymns that made me comfortable. They were, of course, the less religious ones. "Stand up, stand up for Jesus" never had a chance. The young people told me how much they liked them and how they could finally feel enthusiastic about singing in church.

Years later I was told that my "Judge not..." sermon had deeply affected a California Highway patrolman. Stod Herbert blamed himself for the deaths of his two teenage children. He had let them drive a jeep in a campground on a family vacation. The vehicle rolled over, killing both a daughter and a son. What could be worse?

My sermon spoke of how we are not to judge others. Captain Landers, the Marine Corps skipper that I liked so much, had this American Indian saying on his desk: "Do not criticize another, until you have walked in their moccasins for awhile." This was in my sermon. What Stod heard that Sunday from me was: Do not judge yourself, either. He would say to me years later, many, many times, "Do you know the best sermon you ever preached?" And then this tough-looking motorcycle officer would repeat the title again: "Judge not, that you be not judged." How wonderful that he heard the sermon that way.

My sermon on being true to yourself allowed me to join Jesus and to condemn religious hypocrites. I felt that I had a grasp of what God wanted me to say. I told the congregation that the Pharisees were phonies, that religious fanatics were too narrow and judgmental. To illustrate how Jesus was hard on them, I told of how he whipped them in front of the temple in Jerusalem. And how he attacked their rigidity, their placing the law over compassion. Jesus said it was okay to help a donkey out of a ditch, even if it was the Sabbath.

I ran into Richie Morse, and his older brother Terry, after a Sunday service that summer. Richie and Terry told me that they had heard about the tremendous job I was doing with the young people in the community. They were full of praise. I felt fulfilled.

The future was bright. I had found my way. In September, I would begin my studies at a seminary.

Hold it. There was a snag. I was shocked when I read that my acceptance into the San Francisco Theological Seminary depended on an interview with a psychologist. The questions I had answered as part of a psychological profile had triggered a red flag. This was a blow. While everyone was telling me what a tremendous minister I was going to be, my answers to some questions were threatening my admission to the seminary. Lefty, who was just back from his two-year Mormon mission, scoffed at this required interview. He was fearful that seminary would change me. He thought I would develop a theological vocabulary and distance myself from people. Lefty respected the natural way that I presented religion.

I was interviewed by a female psychologist in downtown Los Angeles. At first I felt defensive, quite anxious. But she was friendly and I settled down. I had made the decision to become a minister and did not see how I could back away from it. My decision to be one was a private matter between God and me. The psychologist gave me some tests, asked questions. When she showed me a picture of a nude female and asked for my reaction, I replied, "Beautiful." She said, "Good."

Next up was Dr. Glen Whitlock. This Presbyterian minister and psychologist at UCLA was to interpret the test results and okay or delay my entrance into the seminary. Dr. Whitlock was more formal. He did not make me feel as comfortable as the woman did. He said that I might be repressing hostile feelings and that I should consider some counseling once at the seminary. I did not reflect on what these "hostile feelings" might be. All I wanted was to be granted admission and to become a Presbyterian minister. I was thrilled when I received the letter welcoming me as a member of the student body.

PART III: EDUCATION

A town called San Anselmo

I COULD HAVE APPLIED to Princeton, gone to that more conservative Presbyterian seminary. But I fit much better in the liberal one some twenty miles north of the Golden Gate Bridge. The photographs in the brochure made the campus and its setting look natural. Peaceful. Set on a hill above the small town of San Anselmo, the San Francisco Theological Seminary had Gothic castles rising above a forest of redwood trees. Those castles would be my classrooms for the next three years. I was going to gain the college education that I had passed up at Valley College and USC. This was exciting.

John Snider, who had been attending the church services in North Hollywood that summer, was going to be attending the Presbyterian seminary. John asked if he could ride up with me. The problem was he brought along a guy who looked like a chipmunk. The little fellow was not going to be a student; he just wanted to see the campus. It disturbed me to hear him say more than once that he was going to be a minister. Great! Exactly the image that I was afraid of finding at the seminary. On our way north, we drove well out of the way because I wanted to make contact with Mammoth before I left the normal world and began my studies with those religious types. I could smell the pine, breathe the fresh air, feel alive in Mammoth. But it didn't work this time. I parked the car in the forest near the Mammoth pack station. While John and the chipmunk went for a hike, I read small portions of *A Man Called Peter*, but only felt emptiness. Something was wrong.

I felt nothing as Marin County came into view when we crossed the San Rafael Bridge. My feelings were dead. We arrived in San Anselmo and I drove my Chevrolet up a hill to castles that had stood there since late in the nineteenth century. I pulled my golf clubs out of the trunk, a tennis racket, my leather track shoes, even a sixteen-gauge shotgun. It was not a typical array of seminary luggage. Later I heard that my entrance was observed closely by certain older students. Unknown to me, I was scrutinized. Something a fellow Marine Corps officer told me seemed to fit my early impression of the theological students that I was scrutinizing. The Quantico tennis coach said, "Some people never make the varsity." The seminary was full of them.

The little town in Marin was quaint and quiet. The woods and lakes brought my feelings back. There were carpets of soft, fertile leaf mold under the great trees that surrounded the campus. Old wooden homes with fireplaces would fill the evening air with the scent of burning wood when Christmas approached. John Snider and I were given a room in one of the castles.

"God could have made us carrots"

Many of the professors were disappointing. Out of the past. My fear of the seminary being filled with unnatural clergymen was somewhat realized. However, there were a couple of new ones who had recently obtained their doctorates from prestigious German theological seminaries and they stood out in stark contrast to the older ones. Professors Hamilton and Reist were sharp, challenging. I was ready to be educated. My zilch college education was completely my fault. But now I was studying for a profession that was without compromise. You do not cheat God.

Professors were required to pray before their lectures. Pray? In a classroom? But I heard a sense of awe and incredible respect for God from the younger professors. God was separate from man. Not your friend or buddy. My own views were confirmed.

Dr. Reist was one of the new young scholars. He taught our opening course on Reformed theology. One morning he leaned out over the rostrum and told us, "God could have made us carrots." The theology of the Reformation was in line with my perception of the Holy. I went to the seminary with the understanding that even Jesus did not mess around with God. Did he not say, "Don't call me good; only God is good"?

Richie Morse died

I received word that Richie Morse had died of stomach cancer. The best athlete in our graduating class in high school was dead before twenty-five. I wrote Mrs. Morse a letter expressing my deep sorrow and respect for her son. I did not receive a reply. It had to be a devastating death for her. I did not tell Mrs. Morse that her son was with God. It would have been dishonest for me to say something that I did not believe. I entered seminary with a view that there were no automatic entrances into heaven. That it was presumptuous for us to make such a determination for God.

The professor of systematic theology, Dr. Arnold Come, had been at the seminary for a number of years and was considered a prominent theologian. While dry and slow of speech, the depth of his thought made waiting for his words to finally arrive worthwhile. Dr. Come informed us that "God so loved the world that he did not send a special delivery letter." This, of course, would be changed to an e-mail today. I did not catch it then, but Jesus was being conceptualized into a theological event. The Incarnation. Christology. The study of Jesus as a concept was underway. Lefty had warned of this. I find it ironic now that Dr. Come, who spoke of such a personal God, was one of the least personal men I have known.

John and I moved down to a much larger room with a fireplace. It was in a two story wooden home below the Gothic castle where we had been staying. Six or seven of us lived in "the annex." One of them was Eddie Shinn. Only a little over two years before, I had heard the Coliseum announcer at the NCAA trials say, "Shinn and Taylor" as we came around that final turn together by the tunnel. I had heard when I was at USC that Eddie was a religious "mystic." A damn fast one.

Perhaps the most regular guy on campus was Bill Frederickson. Bill had just been discharged from the Air Force and he enjoyed teasing the religious types by being sacrilegious. For example, he wore an old sweatshirt to class with an Acme beer logo on the back. The president of the seminary, Dr. Jesse Baird, was about to retire. Under his piety, smoking and drinking were forbidden. A little different than the USC fraternity row or the Marine Corps. One afternoon, I thought Bill went a bit too far with his teasing. Shinn went for a walk around the campus with Hilda. I think it was a first date for both of them. When Eddie returned, Frederickson asked, "Did you get in her pants?" I found this crude. And funny.

I was not attracted to any of the women studying Christian education at the seminary. So I dated a girl whom I met at the Presbyterian church by the Cal campus. We went out several times, but I was too liberal for her. She wanted to marry a conservative minister, one who took the Bible more literally than I did. I would pick and choose what I liked in the Bible, ignore the rest.

God damn it, you see I belonged at the seminary

Don Schilling had played baseball in college and he was one of the few on campus who "made the varsity." Schilling was natural, a bit too serious, but a healthy guy. Even though I was a first-year student, this senior asked me to help him with a theological question. Some of the campus conservatives had pressed him on whether or not he was "saved." I told him that I did not buy the question—it was too self-centered. God does not have to take anybody. Don went to ask Dr. Come and when he came back he said, "Dr. Come agrees with you."

God damn it, you see, I belonged at the seminary. God had a purpose for me in the ministry. I had my theology straight from the very beginning. When an older student announced to my classmates after my first sermon in the chapel that I was going to be "the next great preacher in the Presbyterian Church," I felt even more certain that it was happening. Perhaps people would stand out in the rain to make sure that they found a seat in the pews to hear me, like they did for Peter Marshall? This was supposed to happen. I came to the seminary with this destiny.

I knew from that prior summer in the pulpit at Trinity in North Hollywood that I knew how to deliver a sermon. I resented when the Scottish preaching professor, a Dr. Esler, only gave me a B grade. When I questioned him about this, he told me in his heavy accent that "Rome was not built in a day." He added that I had not structured my sermon in the prescribed way. A sermon is not about being orderly. It was my natural, honest delivery that impacted my classmates. A three-point sermon was stuffy. Lefty was right. The seminary wanted to structure me.

I joined the Marine Corps Reserve in nearby Kentfield for extra money. It only required a commitment of one weekend each month. During the summer break, I would need to go to a two-week summer camp. The United States government paid well. I appreciated the friendships that I was able to form away from the seminary. On campus, I was the lieutenant who rushed off in his USMC fatigues. At the Marine unit, I was an infantry officer who was studying to become a Presbyterian minister. Both images made me special.

Dr. Hamilton was one of the bright new professors who had received his doctorate in West Germany. His brief prayers at the beginning of class gripped me. A sense of the Sacred was nurtured in me through his sense of awe. Dr. Hamilton asked me after his seminar one day why I did not have more confidence in my own thinking. While I felt secure with my theology, I was intimidated by the intelligence of my professors and classmates because of their high academic credentials. Would you believe I had never footnoted a paper before seminary? Believe it.

Eddie Shinn and I were contacted by the San Francisco Olympic Club and asked to run for them that spring. Lon Spurrier wore their uniform when he broke the world half-mile record in Berkeley three years before. Bud Held, while attending classes at the seminary a year or two before me, and wearing the Olympic Club aegis, set a world record in the javelin. Who broke his world record? My Marine Corps friend, Al Cantello. It appeared that we might be able to put together a fairly competitive mile relay team out of seminary students. Darrel Griffin was part of that USC mile relay foursome in 1953 at the Compton Invitational along with Lea and Sorgen. Shinn was quick. We needed one more decent quarter miler. The Air Force veteran with the Acme beer sweatshirt tried to be that runner. Bill, who at a later time would do extremely well in the masters meets for senior athletes, was not fast enough at the time to make our foursome competitive for the big relay invitational meets. When Griffin hurt his Achilles, the mile relay team folded. But it was responsible for having lured me back to the track. I had no serious intentions for the half mile.

Over the Easter break when I was in Los Angeles, I went down to USC and worked out, even ran a 330-yard sprint with a new Canadian star on the Trojan track team. When we finished in a virtual tie, and with a fast time, Coach Mortensen commented, "Bill, I don't remember you being that fast."

"Now that's prayer"

A visiting professor from Stanford taught our course on ethics at the seminary. Dr. Alexander Miller made me feel like I belonged there when he told this story in his New Zealand accent: "A farmer nurtured his crops faithfully, did everything he could to insure a good harvest, then suddenly the clouds darkened, the winds increased, and a heavy storm washed his crops away. The angry farmer raised his fist to the sky and shouted, 'Damn it God, if I were God, I wouldn't be such a goddamn fool.'" The class became very still. Such strong words to be directed at God! Miller waited. Then he said, "Now, *that's* prayer." I could live with that kind of theology.

Hope and Doris Day

Back home in Toluca Lake over the Christmas vacation I found a job with the North Hollywood post office. Like the Marine Corps Reserve, the pay was very good. And Bob Hope, Ann Blyth, William Holden, and Doris Day were on my route. When I took a parcel that needed a signature to Bob Hope's door, the sound of his voice from inside the mansion made it seem like the radio was on. When her signature was required for a package, Doris Day greeted me with a face covered with white lotion.

Biblical Greek was difficult for me. Hebrew was easier. I was not planning on graduate work, so I did not feel the pressure to do well with language courses. And I ignored the classes taught by the old timers: how to be organized as a pastor, hymnology with conservative hymns, Protestant church history in America, etc. My interest was in systematic theology and philosophy. And then, because of another new professor arriving on campus, psychoanalysis.

A classmate at the seminary told us that he had run a very fast 100-yard dash when he attended UCLA. I questioned his claim that he ran under ten seconds. Frederickson did not believe him. One afternoon on the Sir Francis Drake High School track in San Anselmo, I spotted him a two-yard advantage for our race over one hundred yards. About sixty yards down the track, I went past him. My speed had definitely increased. In fact, I was looking forward to running a quarter mile in a meet that weekend in San Jose under the aegis of the San Francisco Olympic Club. Then it hit. An extremely sharp pain shot up my left hamstring. Track athletes, coaches, fans, know that a hamstring pull stands you straight up. It did. I hopped over on one leg to the grass and sat down. I had run my final race. The journey from the driveway by Warner Brothers ended on a high school track in San Anselmo. What irony. I have been the head track coach at that high school over the past thirty years.

Jeanne

W[HEN I LOOKED] over the women on the seminary campus as possible dates, only Jeanne stood out for me. Fairly tall, full lips, green eyes, well-formed breasts, Jeanne was in seminary to become a Christian education director. I decided to ask her out. When we spoke to one another, she made me feel important. Some of the guys on campus were saying that Jeanne would make "a great minister's wife." This did not impress me as I was not church oriented. Jesus wasn't church oriented, either. On our first date we went for a walk at night above the campus and climbed part way up the mountain. Her full lips were responsive. I liked how easily we could talk with one another, her intelligence, inner beauty. Another night we drove out under a full moon through the beautiful countryside, then over to a bar/restaurant in Petaluma for dancing. Feeling her full body close to mine made me want to sleep with her. But the summer would soon separate us, as Jeanne was to assist the park ministry in Yosemite and I would return to the North Hollywood congregation.

Trinity Presbyterian had a new sanctuary and I was really looking forward to preaching from the pulpit come August. My sermons, however, would not have the same impact. No longer would I deliver a simple, moral message, perhaps even with a quote from Reader's Digest. My emerging theological sophistication would distance me from those who did not want to think in a worship service. Nonetheless, I believed it was my charge to bring the seminary to the pew and to share with the congregation the depth of theology. Once again, Lefty was right. Those fresh, moralistic messages were of the past. Those who wanted to think would thank me after the service. I am sure others wondered what I was talking about.

The youth programs were more recreational than educational. We had a great time together. This led to a clash with the pastor's wife, since I made no attempt to coordinate the youth activities with the

Christian education program. I felt like I knew what I was doing. The size of the youth group grew and I received more and more compliments from the community.

One day Gretchen Ging told me that she had always wanted to teach Sunday school. Gretchen was beautiful; that alone was enough to capture the attention of the kids. When Gretchen disregarded the Presbyterian curriculum and taught her values, this did not go over well with the pastor's wife. I saw Gretchen's warmth and vitality as more important than the study materials. And I really did not care what the pastor's wife thought. A strong wish for independence kept me from being diplomatic, sensible.

While my sermons were increasingly abstract and theological, my feeling about heavy church curriculum for young people was different. I wanted them to have a wholesome summer and to care about one another. The serious thinking could come later.

The cowboy Lou, and his wife, Mary, were spending the summer out in a canyon in the far end of the San Fernando Valley. No pack station for my favorite couple that summer. When I told Lou about Jeanne, he became excited and urged me to go after her immediately, to not let her get away. He would settle for nothing less than a marriage proposal. I suppose I made a good case for being in love with Jeanne. Those warm summer evenings with Johnny Mathis singing, "I want you with me, all the time," encouraged romantic feelings. To this day, I can feel the memory of her full lips on mine as we kissed on the side of the mountain. Jeanne was a complete woman. Her intelligence, the way she made me feel about myself, her commitment to life—all contributed to a woman worth marrying.

Lou was relentless. It was only a few days before I sent a telegram to Yosemite asking Jeanne to marry me. I found a small jewelry store in North Hollywood and bought an engagement ring. I told Jeanne that I was coming up to Yosemite after my two weeks of summer duty with the Marine Corps Reserve in Coronado. Lou was beside himself. He would call some nights as soon as he got home from work, wanting to know if I had heard anything.

Lou and Mary, my favorite couple.

Jeanne was paralyzed. I did not know that she was scared to death of trusting me because earlier that year she had been briefly engaged to another guy at the seminary. Lou and I were completely taken up by this love story. I kept playing the music from *Pal Joey* over and over on my little recorder. I could not wait to see her.

I met up with my reserve unit from Kentfield down at the naval base in Coronado, right across from San Diego. One morning, I watched the Navy Seals doing endless one arm push ups next to where we assembled. What a rough bunch. Our training exercises that summer were to include a landing on the beaches of Camp Pendleton. But first, we had to practice climbing up and down a net so that we could later handle lowering ourselves into a landing craft during choppy seas. I did not care for the bulky Mae West life preservers that everyone was supposed to wear. I felt a lot freer by not tying the straps together. This gave me a kind of casual John Wayne appearance. An open collar and white T-shirt under my green USMC fatigues made me more comfortable.

As I waited with our company to climb up the net, a colonel called to everyone's attention my casual appearance over the loudspeaker with, "Lieutenant, your tie-ties are untied." That was me. Thus I became known by my fellow officers as "Tie-tie Taylor." Not just at Coronado, but even after we returned to Kentfield. I appreciated this male companionship away from the seminary.

It was eerie being out at sea at night. The destroyers and cruisers kept silent company. I thought of the war movie *Victory at Sea*. Each time I went out to sea with the Marine Corps the evening movie was, *Mildred Pierce* with Joan Crawford and Zachary Scott. A few of you may remember it. Scott with that thin mustache, Crawford, a consummate actress, without beauty.

I was apprehensive the morning we climbed down the nets and into the landing crafts. I had seen those war movies. I knew that they would circle around and around in the swells. And that the air would be filled with exhaust fumes. Being an officer, I was free to position myself where I wanted to be in the landing craft. I found a place where I could focus on the lights along the California coast. This would help me to avoid becoming seasick. Some of the troops who had no view began to vomit. I continued to look at the shore lights. I still do when I am out to sea, even on large Greek ferries. And if I do not, seasickness begins.

I felt enormous relief when we finally began moving toward the beaches that morning. But when we reached the shore the landing ramp would not drop down. I said, "Over the...", but a safety NCO on the beach said, "No way, Lieutenant." Our landing craft was backed off the beach and moved out beyond the breakers for safety reasons. We had climbed down into it at 5:30 a.m. It was 9:00 a.m. before we were finally allowed to come onto shore and disembark. If anybody had told me I was going to be kept out at sea for three hours in that bobbing craft, I would have really worried about handling it.

My knee locked while I was crawling under live machine gun fire during our time at Camp Pendleton. Lethal rounds zipped about thirty inches over my head. I could not move. And I was next to a demolition pit where explosives were being set off with regularity.

When the NCO in charge of the training exercise eventually called for cease fire, he noticed me lying out there. I resented his saying over the public address system something like, "Get that Marine out of there." I had to be carried to the base infirmary. The doctor was quick about working my knee back in place. I always felt so grateful when it was put back. I could have sung the doxology (e.g., "Praise God from whom all blessings flow, praise Him all creatures....")

As soon as we were free to leave Coronado, I set off for Yosemite with the engagement ring. I had to pull over a few times that night because it was a long drive from San Diego and I was worried about falling asleep at the wheel. I left at about nine in the evening, arriving in Yosemite early in the morning to meet Jeanne. She approached me cautiously. I remember that she had the habit of dragging one foot behind her. Just a little. The sun had not reached the canyon floor yet. There was that wonderful smell of pine, the freshness of the mountains early in the morning. I could only stay for the day. I needed to drive back that evening. The two-week Marine summer maneuvers had broken up my work as the summer assistant at Trinity Presbyterian Church. And Jeanne had to work at the Ahwahnee Hotel that evening. She was the receptionist for the popular lodge.

Below the powerful Yosemite falls, I pulled the ring out of the glove compartment and showed it to her. Then, I put it back. She told me later that I barely let her see it. Jeanne said that she needed time. The response of her lips to mine told me that she loved me. But I drove back to the San Fernando Valley that night with the ring in the glove compartment. Jeanne did agree to visit me for a couple of days in early August.

The pool was straight ahead

I took on a few summer jobs in addition to my work at the church. I had saved up a good amount of money as a bachelor in the Marine Corps and used it to pay for my seminary tuition. No track scholarship. So I obtained extra cash from odd jobs. A couple of them involved clearing weeds from the backyards of homes. At one house, there was a lower yard below a swimming pool. I rented a large rototiller from up the street and backed the trailer with the tractor into the driveway.

The pool was straight ahead. I would need to swing the large rototiller to the right in order to avoid it. Without taking the time to locate the clutch, or the break, I started up the engine. My brother Hal had just stopped by. Hal was working in that part of the Valley for a hospital supply company. Things were going well for him.

The two of us tried to change the course of the tractor. It had bolted forward, moving directly toward the pool. I held the steering handles while Hal grabbed onto the front of the machine and attempted to pull it to the right. Everything was happening so fast. This huge tractor plunged into the swimming pool. Hal held on too long and was flipped—with slacks, wallet, and shoes—into the water. As my brother climbed out, I watched the tractor begin to slide down to the deep end of the pool. Slowly. Gas and oil rose to the surface. A long black tire mark on the floor of the pool told of its route.

How would I get the tractor out? I asked my brother to back up his car to the pool. Then I dove down and tied a garden hose to the tractor. The oil and gas in the water stung my eyes. When Hal was ready, I dove down again and took hold of the steering handles. There was a moment of hope as we approached the steps. Then, the garden hose snapped. The tractor, of course, slid back down to where it had been in the deep end of the pool.

We had to get a rope. A horse stable was up the street, so I drove up and borrowed a thick one. Then I called the home of a church family and asked that they send some of the young people to help. When the kids arrived, I went down under the water again. Did you see Dustin Hoffman at the bottom of the pool in *The Graduate* when he walked around under water with those flippers? There I was. My predicament seemed hilarious to the young people. A couple of them were assigned to hold wooden boards down on the pool steps so that the tractor could be pulled up and run over the planks. What does wood do when it is released under water? It rises quickly to the surface. One or more of their arms got whacked, but we got the machine out. How much was the soaked tractor going to cost me? I was surprised when the proprietor said, "Nothing." He believed it would "dry out." What about the family that owned the pool? I heard that there was no more swimming that summer.

Movie stars

Rusty Tamblyn gave me a call and asked if I wanted to go with him to MGM. Rusty was nominated for the Academy Award for Best Supporting Actor in the movie *Peyton Place* that year. A few years later he did the tumbling in *West Side Story*. As we approached the studio entrance, a very serious looking Keenan Wynn and his gang rode through the MGM arch on motorcycles. Moments later I was introduced to the actor, Richard Anderson, who played endless numbers of supportive roles in the movies.

Then I was introduced to James Mason. The well-known British actor of dignified roles seemed to appear from within the movie sets. Nobody else was around. Do the actors live there? Just before we entered the cafeteria, a young woman came running toward us, yelling out, "Bill, Bill!" It was Barbara Ruick, the daughter of Lorraine Tuttle. When I was twelve, our Toluca Lake gang would sneak into Lorraine Tuttle's swimming pool. I bounced off her diving board as the sirens sang out the end to World War II in Europe. I did not realize that Barbara knew me, as she was in an older class at North Hollywood High School. Some of you might remember the movie, *Carousel*, with that handsome and likable actor, Gordon McCrae. Barbara sang, "When I Marry Mr. Snow" in the musical. I liked having a Hollywood actress run toward me at MGM yelling my name.

I was counting the days until Jeanne would arrive by Greyhound bus from Yosemite. Finally the morning came. She arrived at 5:30 a.m. I watched her wait for the driver to pull out her suitcase from the compartment under the bus. She was wearing a brown cotton summer dress. Jeanne was a woman, not a college girl. This would be a relationship for life.

First, I drove to the church to show her the new sanctuary. It was still dark outside. I unlocked the church door; inside it was still and quiet. Then I showed her the new pulpit that I would be preaching from. The next morning, we drove over to Sunset Beach, near Malibu. It was there that Jeanne told me that she loved me. It came out suddenly. I was not as thrilled as I thought I would be. Maybe it was the hour of the day, or that Jeanne was wearing a bathing cap. Or was it my discomfort when direct, personal feelings are shared with me?

I did not look forward to going back to San Anselmo without the ring on Jeanne's finger. I did not want jealousy to interfere with my studies at the seminary. Other guys would be after her. While I was confident about my ability to compete with those seminary types, I was still afraid of losing her. Where would she sit in the dining room for lunch and dinner? And, if we had the same class, would we sit next to each another? Would we study together in the evenings? I wanted that ring on her finger!

I located an afternoon coaching position in Kentfield. Right next to where my Marine Corps Reserve held its meetings. The coaching proved exciting, fulfilling. We won and won. I viewed myself as a tremendous coach. When I was in high school, I had coached my brother's junior high football, basketball, and track teams. They never lost. I later realized it was not just me—my brother had gathered together outstanding athletes from his class. One person Hal brought to this team was Tommy Maudlin, who went on to become the starting quarterback for USC. I went to see him play against Stanford in Palo Alto that fall. Tommy provided the tickets. So, in a distant way, I did end up playing quarterback for USC.

Harold was a better all-around athlete than I was. He made All-League in baseball at Hollywood High School, hitting over 370 his senior year, and he was a starter and one of the leading scorers on the Sheik basketball team that made it into the Los Angeles City finals. After two years at Valley College, where he excelled in basketball and impressed anyone who saw him play golf, my little brother transferred to USC. But he did not go to USC on an athletic scholarship. Our mother, the grammar school music teacher, paid the tuition.

He could have possibly been a four-sport letterman. Four? Harold was exceptional in basketball, golf, and baseball. And when he cleared 6 feet 3 inches in the high jump at a USC track practice the first time he ever tried that event, it was clear that he might have lettered in that sport as well. But Harold would never fulfill his potential in any one of these sports. He did letter in golf at USC, playing on an outstanding team with a two or three handicap.

During the summer basketball league, he played with the top USC guys and it appeared that he would be a part of the team, but the old coach, Forrest Twogood, who was a season away from retirement, favored the athletes on scholarship and never took a look at Harold. When he came to his locker the day after the first practice, it had been cleared out. No conversation with the coach, just dropped from the team. The coach of multi-national championship baseball teams wanted Harold to play second base, but my little brother thought that the sport was boring—that you "stand around too much."

Hal was injury prone, self-destructive when success was in reach. A friend of my brother told me that Hal was seen by his fraternity brothers as "the nicest guy" they knew at USC. This was nice to hear, but I recalled what Leo Durocher, the former Dodger manager, once said: "Nice guys finish last."

I meant a lot to my younger brother. And a number of times I really came through for him when he faced some serious difficulties. He was my biggest fan when I ran in college. Mom, too, of course.

I took Jeanne's father, Stan Standring, to that football game at Stanford when Tommy Maudlin provided the tickets. Stan and I had a good time together. A self-made businessman with no college years, Stan owned a moderate-sized company in Sacramento. His work and his daughter were the ultimate meaning in his life. Driving to their Sacramento home after the game, Stan tried to caution me on going too fast with Jeanne on the wedding night. I found this a bit strange.

Jeanne was an "only" child. Her parents owned a fairly large suburban home in Sacramento. Mrs. Standring was controlling, dominant, neurotic. She used her sickness to control both her husband and her daughter. Yet Sue drove a sporty Thunderbird convertible. She and I hit it off pretty well. I did not have to suffer too many weeks after returning to the San Anselmo campus before we got the ring on her finger. We? Sue liked me. Jeanne and I were up at her parents' home in

Sacramento when, after a long talk with Jeanne, Sue came out from the back of the house and told me that Jeanne was going to marry me. It is not supposed to work this way. I had not asked why the prior engagement was broken off. Red flags were waving, but I just wanted that ring on her finger. Being married would complete something in me.

When Billy Graham was invited to speak on campus it divided the student body between those who came from very conservative church backgrounds and those of us who felt that the popular evangelist was manipulative. I saw Graham as conducting a holy circus. I liked what Karl Barth said when asked about the Graham crusade when it came to Basle, Switzerland. Barth, the most respected Reform theologian of the twentieth century, believed that Graham, by pressuring many people at once to convert with his soft, luring "come forward" at the crusades, was "placing a gun to God's head." This was consistent with the theology that I brought with me to the seminary. Again, my sense of destiny, of having made the right decision to be a minister, was supported.

The wedding was set for the beginning of the Christmas break. I would not have to face campus jealousy anymore. Jeanne was going to be my wife. We would have a home. Jeanne had secured a teaching position in Fairfax, a small town next to San Anselmo. She would support us while I prepared for the ministry.

On November 10, when I picked up Jeanne to go to the Marine Corps birthday ball, she really made over my uniform. I did not like the way an officer uniform—in this case first lieutenant bars— could excite a female. What is it that attracts women to military uniforms? How can you trust them if they are so shallow?

Jeanne looked fabulous that night. It turned out to be a great, festive ball. Everyone seemed hyped, excited. I really enjoyed being with my fellow officers that night. I was happy that I was going to be a Presbyterian minister. And that I would soon be in bed with Jeanne.

There were times when I thought I might be making a mistake. One Saturday morning I saw Jeanne walking with her seminary lady friends in downtown San Anselmo. They had been out shopping for the wedding ceremony. Seeing them together made me uncomfortable because the other women were church types. Nice classmates, but not striking in appearance. And, at that moment, Jeanne did not look like the girl I wanted to marry. The tall baseball player from Montana had said to me before Jeanne and I were engaged, "She is not the one you are looking for."

I did not sign up for the easy courses. Landing high grades was not my objective. If I was going to be the best preacher in the Presbyterian church, I knew that I needed to be well grounded in theology. I went after a solid base. I took the electives that I thought would contribute the most to my worth as a minister. Dr. Come offered a course on John Calvin's *Institutes of the Christian Religion*. How could you be a Presbyterian minister and not study Calvin? The class was in Geneva Hall, named after the Swiss city where Calvin ruled. I earned a B from this tough professor. The *Institutes* helped to build my theological base. Human behavior cannot surprise you if you know your Calvin. God alone is supreme and man is a creature unable to save himself.

My understanding of what the Reformed Church meant by grace developed in a small classroom within Geneva Hall. It was in my second year that a new professor, Dr. Edward V. Stein, introduced psychoanalysis to me. The course he taught, "Psychotherapy and Religion," sent me into orbit. Dr. Stein was a psychologist as well as a theologian. This man will figure prominently in my life. Receiving an A in the course was easy. I fell in love with the subject. The professor of philosophy, Dr. Surjit Singh, gave me a B, then an A, in the two courses I took under him. These grades were a clue to my aptitude for philosophy. But at that time I was oriented to theological metaphors. I did not yet know of Socrates, Plato, and Aristotle of ancient Greece, nor of the late-nineteenth-century philosopher, Nietzsche.

The weekend before the wedding, the plan was for me to drive up to Sacramento and stay in Jeanne's home. She had ceased to take seminary classes. When I was having my car serviced, the mechanic informed me that he had stripped the opening to the oil tank. I kept having this fear of Jeanne changing her mind, so I felt like I had to make it to Sacramento despite the condition of my car. Jeanne had been teasing me about changing her mind. I let her emasculate me to some extent. I understand now that this was a test: she needed my certainty. The mechanic shaped a wooden stick and used it to plug the oil container. It would take about ninety minutes to reach Sacramento. I made it past Vallejo, but then a stream of smoke warned that I was leaking oil. I did not stop. Just short of the Nut Tree, near an airfield, my engine exploded. Parts came up through the floorboard. This whole wedding engagement had been peculiar. I hope you are enjoying this threatened twenty-four-year-old Marine Corps officer racing to Sacramento to hold on to his reluctant bride.

My old Chevy from Quantico days was dead. Stan drove out to pick me up, and then bought us an inexpensive replacement car for $350. Because I was stealing his daughter from him, Stan told me after that Stanford-USC football game that he sometimes wanted to crack me on the jaw. Now he was helping me. There were good feelings between us.

The Reverend Bob Ferguson conducted our marriage service at Jeanne's home church in Sacramento. Bob was not a very good public speaker. And I was not pleased with the service. Good friends drove up to be in the wedding party. My brother Harold was my best man. I was uncomfortable asking a certain classmate, Ted Pickett, but I did. He looked like someone who would go to seminary, but I put friendship over my being uncomfortable with his image.

Why do women change hairstyles, especially for their wedding? I did not like her perm. And then when she changed from the wedding gown to the honeymoon departure outfit, she wore a business suit with a short skirt. Things didn't feel right to me. Sue let us take the Thunderbird. We spent our wedding night halfway to San Francisco; in the morning we drove to a charming inn in Carmel. Once in bed, Jeanne froze up. She could not let herself go in Carmel, either. It was a dismal honeymoon—for both of us. And things would only get worse.

Marriage

I LOVED THE LOCATION for our first home. Jeanne did not share my enthusiasm about the place. Located below a house where a retired couple lived, it consisted of two rooms and a bath. A corridor of heavy green trees led up the road to this quiet location near the seminary. Beautiful ferns and moss surrounded me as I walked down to the campus for my morning classes.

I loved having a gold wedding ring on my left hand. I never considered giving up on Jeanne or annulling the marriage. She asked for time. I did not feel as though I had a choice. She would pick me up at about 5:00 p.m. at the school where I was directing the athletic programs. I usually ran the two miles over to the campus in mid-afternoon. Jeanne took our car to the elementary school, used it for shopping, then picked me up.

Just after the wedding, Stan became very depressed. He had to be hospitalized in a psychiatric wing in Oakland. The doctors were afraid of suicide so they even had taken the belt to his pants away. Stan had told me before the wedding how the labor union was ruining his company. He saw himself as a generous employer and felt that his workers, by joining a union, were being disloyal.

While things were getting worse for his business, he lost his daughter to me. Stan and Jeanne had a very close relationship. I thought that they made too much of how close they were. Then there was Sue. She was in endless therapy. Sue was the authority in the family. She was a pretty good gal, too. People are not always what they want to be. Sue told me that if she could have one wish fulfilled, it would to be to know peace.

I was standing on the Kentfield football field coaching the seventh and eight graders at the middle school. A large man approached. It was Bob Ferguson, the pastor who officiated at our wedding ceremony two months before. What in the hell was he doing there? He told me that he had been at the seminary for a meeting. Then he told me that Jeanne was over in the car and that her father had killed himself.

Sue had gone to the market. When she drove the Thunderbird into the garage, she found Stan hanging over her parking space. The sick son-of-a-bitch had to be one angry husband to do such a thing. But who knows what his intent was when he wrapped his belt over the beam and put his head within the loop?

We drove up to Sacramento that weekend so that Jeanne could be with her mother and attend the funeral. She chose to sleep with her mother. While the poor woman was surely tortured by darkness, frightened to her core by the ghastly scene of her husband hanging from the rafter in the garage, I felt abandoned by my wife. This will happen two or three more times on our visits to Sue.

Jeanne, of course, withdrew even more from me physically after the suicide. Guilt finds many victims with a suicide. Did she at some level feel that I had killed her father? Or that our marriage was to blame? In a perverse way, Stan actually won his daughter back.

We enjoyed going to the movies together. One night a film triggered a deep emotional response in both of us and after the movie, Jeanne came alive in bed. In *Some Came Running*, Shirley MacLaine played the part of an innocent, trusting prostitute. The Hollywood actress was young, fresh to the screen. Everyone in the movie except Ms. MacLaine was a manipulative son-of-a-bitch. Each played an angle. But she was pure goodness. Her employment as a prostitute was a job. She was a genuine, captivating person. When she was killed by a stray bullet at the end of the movie, her death seemed so unfair. After we had gone to bed that night I started to cry when I began telling Jeanne about how I felt, how it was so unfair. My sobbing reached the out-of-control state when I asked, "Why did the only good person in the movie have to be killed?" Jeanne was responsive in bed that night. It was a start.

"Why did the little boy have to die?" Or Leonard Denti, the nicest person in our high school class? Or my father? I sought out Dr. Stein for counseling. Remember my psyche tests? After evaluating them,

Dr. Whitlock suggested that I seek out some psychotherapy. I was also motivated to approach Dr. Stein because of the free-floating anxiety that was disturbing me. Perhaps my prime motivation was my fascination with the "Psychotherapy and Religion" class?

While Dr. Stein would suggest that my running was a sublimation for my anger, we never touched the most obvious reason for my present anxiety. We both failed on that one. How could a Freudian counselor not ask about my sex life?

We also did not explore my compulsive feelings about going into the ministry. Why I did not feel like I had a choice. Things are much clearer with hindsight. Ironically, it was Dr. Stein who said to a few students on the steps up to Geneva Hall one morning, "You do not have to be a minister to be a Christian." I did not like hearing that. It confused, even haunted me.

Only 'regret' was left

I experienced a tremendous breakthrough in academic confidence during a seminar on Sigmund Freud. The other fellows in this class were straight-A types. Just four or five were taking the elective. Dr. Stein was the instructor. One afternoon we were searching for an alternative for the word "guilt." Each time someone came up with one, Dr. Stein wrote it on the blackboard. I suggested, "regret." Regret turns the focus to the victim, not the one who is feeling guilty. Guilt can be self-centered. Teenagers are given to saying, "I'm so sorry, I'm so sorry," when they do something wrong. What they are likely saying is: *Don't blame me, don't blame me*. Like, *I don't want to feel guilty*. Their focus is on themselves, not on the one who has been wronged. My classmates discussed each of the words up on the blackboard. One by one, the words were erased. Then, to my great surprise, only "regret" was left. My word won the day. I could think! I look back at this moment as the most significant day in my intellectual development.

Another elective proved of tremendous value to me. "Hebrew Words Study" was taught by a new professor, too. A very young one. Dr. David Alexander completed his doctorate in his early twenties.

Tall, lean, academic looking, he was bright without pretense. When I first came to seminary, I felt that conservatives and fundamentalists were missing the deeper meaning of biblical passages with their literal, shallow translations. The course took Old Testament interpretations to a much deeper level. Even the Ten Commandments became exciting. "Thou shalt not kill" is not limited to taking another person's life. You can murder someone by ignoring them. "Taking the Lord's name in vain" has nothing to do with swearing. It has to do with the attempt to manipulate God. U.S. presidents violate this commandment every time they suggest that "God is on our side." Same for coaches who ask for God to be with their team in football games. They claim the prayer is to prevent injuries, to have a fair game, but we know it is frequently to bring victory. To gain some more divine help. A swear word might be crude, but swearing does not violate one of the Ten Commandments. This should make a lot of U.S. Marines happy. At the time, I did not swear.

Dr. Alexander soon became the youngest person ever to be president of Pomona College, my mother's college. The Pomona campus is in the quiet town of Claremont, where my grandparents retired after returning from China.

Between my second and third seminary years, I took a position as the summer assistant at North Long Beach Community Presbyterian Church on Orange Avenue, a few miles north of downtown. I had a favorable impression of the pastor, the Reverend Richard Irving, when we met in front of the church on a June evening. He was tall, soft spoken, looked directly at you when he spoke. And he led the worship services with dignity. For me, worship was a serious confrontation with the Holy. The prayers by the new professors at the seminary addressed the Sacred. Or, better, the Sacred addressed the new professors. How could one have a cozy relationship with God? A certain terror needed to be present in worship as a part of one's encounter with God. Maybe ultimate respect is a more acceptable way to communicate this point. The Holy did not offer a buddy-to-buddy relationship with God in my theology.

Jeanne and I had college students over to our apartment on Sunday evenings. They liked Jeanne. I felt good about her being my wife. The discussions at these Sunday night seminars were serious. We applied theology to movies, books, contemporary life. Thus began my love for teaching. I found it challenging to connect the best of what I was learning at the seminary with their questions about religion and life. I did not have to force life into religion. Rather, theology spoke to life.

My brother showed up at the door of our apartment one evening with a good-looking blonde from USC. Harold would marry Lesley later that year. And I would assist with the ceremony. Because I was not ordained yet, the minister at the La Cañada Church officially led the service. Many of those seated in the pews were Hal's fraternity brothers from USC. It was clear that they really liked Hal. And they showed a very special respect for me, because of my status as a former Trojan track star about to enter the ministry. It even impressed me!

We rented the upper rooms of a wooden home on Butterfield Road when we returned for my senior year at the seminary. The rustic house rested in a grove of trees. We had a bedroom, living room, kitchen, and bathroom. And a private entrance. I set my books on the windowsill above a desk at the top of the stairs. My library was building. I would stay up late; studying for my classes felt good. I had a sense that I was preparing for an ultimate role in life. And I loved being married.

Jeanne had a miscarriage. She told me the next morning. Just like that. It was very early in the pregnancy. Did we lose a son? Or a daughter? This seems ominous as I reflect back on it now. Our marriage was deepening. Jeanne was a great companion. But she still could not let go fully in bed.

Sue came to visit us. As she was about to leave, Jeanne's mother collapsed on the couch. I guess she wanted to stay. We called a Dr. Stubblebine because he was the most respected psychoanalyst in the county. He had lectured to my class at the seminary one time. He made it clear at the beginning that he was an atheist. I remember respecting his honesty, but the concept of an atheist was foreign to me. It even seemed dangerous. Dr. Stubblebine came up our narrow staircase and looked over Sue on the couch. When she did not answer his question, I told him, "She is hard of hearing." He responded with, "She hears what she wants to hear." Hearing that made me feel secure about having chosen him.

This woman was one very damaged person. Not everyone pulls into a garage and finds their mate hanging from the rafters. She did try to maintain some distance from us, not wanting to wreck her chances of seeing her daughter by alienating me. Sue eventually left Sacramento, spent time in the psychiatric wing of a Marin County hospital, then lived in a series of apartments in nearby Kentfield for the rest of her life.

If I had entered seminary a year earlier I would not have heard this large, strange-looking man with thick glasses. His words found themselves as they stuttered out in an amazing array of clarity. He asked the seminary student body, "What is God up to with his world, and why are you here?" I was on the edge of my pew. He told us that "God has a history, and He does not start over with you." It was fantastic.

His words hesitated before they were released. When delivered, they drew you into his fascinating mind. Leaning over the pulpit that day was the new president of the seminary. Dr. Gill told us that "Presbyterian ministers are to be scholars because the Word has a history." Then he told a suspenseful story about his drive across the country with his family to San Anselmo. How, one day his mind was elsewhere and he was not concentrating on the road. They were crossing the Colorado Rockies when suddenly the car started sliding on a mountain turn, the wheels spinning on loose gravel. The Gills were precariously close to the edge. As Dr. Gill spoke, he hesitated, stammered as his words sought their place. He told of how they came out of the spin and discovered, painted in large print on a rock, "Jesus saves." Dr. Gill leaned out over the pulpit and asked us, "What does it mean to say 'Jesus saves'?"

At that moment I was not alone in my discomfort with traditional

Christianity. A theologian was up there in the pulpit saying what I went to seminary to hear. This is why I was there. The Word was not about being saved, going to heaven, the Word was about God. For it is through grace that God gives man his dignity and freedom. I went up to Dr. Gill after his address and asked, "Where have you been?"

He was marvelous. Like when he told us about how he almost missed a saint because of her cigarette smoke. They were seated across from one another in Istanbul with a view of Asia across the Bosphorus. This woman had saved thousands of Russian refugees and Dr. Gill suddenly realized that he almost missed recognizing this saint because of the thick smoke. Dr. Gill loved to dance words, to illustrate points with charming attacks on conventional Christian morality. For example, he was confident that God loved Emily Post, "but he didn't give a damn about her book."

It was not just Dr. Gill who brought forth dynamic, relevant theology. We had a guest Lutheran theologian speak in our chapel one morning. Brilliant colors decorated his academic cape and robe, evidence of advanced degrees from European soil. I thought such displays overdone, un-Stoic, even pretentious. He looked like Superman. Or Captain Marvel. He was a peculiar looking scholar, but he drew me into his mind. I was especially intrigued when he asked us, "Do you know why I am Christian?" He waited. Taunted us in silence. Then said simply, "I am a Christian because my mother was a Christian." Things were really getting exciting now. Theology was vibrating.

I would soon go forth to tell of that Word, that man made flesh, which tells and makes some sense of the complexity and terror of life. At the same time, I could not have defined existentialism when I graduated from the seminary. I was building the words, the vocabulary that would enable me to do so shortly, however. Dr. Reist led us through two volumes of *Systematic Theology* by Paul Tillich. Yes, another elective, not a required course. Tillich's metaphors of 'being' and 'non being' were the most useful ones for me. I would later discover that the ancient Greek philosophers preceded the Christian theologians by centuries. But my climb up the Acropolis at night in Athens was still eight years away.

I felt trapped

Shortly before I graduated from seminary, I received a standing ovation at the awards banquet for the middle school athletes I coached. The applause reflected their appreciation for the passion and leadership that I put into the sports program. I was touched. The kids framed a thank-you letter that is in our garage today. A particular line defines what I am still doing through my present age. It read, "You ran us in 100 degree weather, but we loved every minute of it."

As I approached graduation from the seminary, my brother wrote that he was never more proud of me. So why did I have my first attack of claustrophobia at the graduation ceremony? I felt trapped, panicked, even though we were seated outdoors. At USC, because I didn't work at the academic, I passed up the ceremony. I did not even go. But I was very proud of my academic effort at the seminary. I was not graduating with honors, but I respected myself for having taken the tough electives that provided the meaningful grades. Why these feelings of terror? The anxiety attack was awful. It was difficult to not just get up and bolt the ceremony.

The North Long Beach church sent me a telegram. They had created a new staff position so that I could be their assistant pastor. It seemed like the right place to go. I liked the senior minister and the people. I did not relate to the religious jargon about being "called" to this church. I admired the Presbyterian view that the minister assumes an office, is employed by the congregation to do a particular work. But this view was compromised by a spooky ordination ceremony. Most parishioners want their minister or priest set apart. To be that special link to God. While some want their minister to be human, most really want their clergyman separate. I wanted to be special, but I felt that my task was to challenge the communicant to remove the minister from their charm bracelet. The clergyman does not have any special powers. There was no holy blood transfusion when I was ordained. Oh yeah? Then why did they "lay their hands" on me, set me apart by ordination? Mankind is terrorized by the uncertainty of life. The minister is too often ordained to provide magical rescues.

The 1960 United States Olympic Track Team had a few practice track meets in California before they left for Rome. One of them was held in Long Beach. It was highly satisfying for me to have my youth group hear a good number of the Olympians say, "Hi Bill," when the team walked to their bus after the competition. Ron Morris, Al Cantello, Dave Sime, Max Truex—these four stand out. Ron would earn the silver in the pole vault at the Olympics. Al would lead the javelin throwers in the preliminaries, but miss placing in the final. Sime would just miss winning the 100-meter final. And Max would run a tremendous 10,000-meter race and place sixth. I did not feel track pain over not being on the U.S. team. I felt proud of greeting them as a Presbyterian minister.

Iconoclast

THE DAUGHTERS OF the Evening Star wanted to sit close to their deceased sister, so they chose the front pew of the sanctuary. With the casket open. They were not members. When they called and requested a Christian service, Pastor Irving gave them to me. They were not happy when I informed them that the casket had to be closed once we began the worship service. I was not going to feature the corpse. Not after our focus turned to God, the inexplicable, the Holy, the eternal. According to Jeanne, who was sitting in a back pew, the women sat gazing at their dead friend while I waited in the pastor's office for the time to begin the service. This was the first funeral I would conduct as a minister. It felt good to have Jeanne there for support and companionship. Before I entered the sanctuary, Jeanne told me that the women stirred with discomfort when the mortician came down and closed the lid on the casket right in front of them. But, the lid would not stay shut. It kept rising back up each time he tried to close it. Finally he banged it hard enough for it to stay down. The Daughters of the Evening Star were upset. They, of course, called the church office and complained about the service. Thus criticism began.

My charge as a pastor was to threaten people. To tell of the God who requires justice. To inform people that their wish for personal salvation is not Christian. Well, one best tread lightly with this one. People frequently seek religion for a deal. And eternal life is the big selling card. I was charged to face the questions of life, not try to escape them. To, in faith, wrestle with existence. Remember the farmer protesting to God when he lost his crops? How the Stanford professor said, "Now *that's* prayer"? Christians were to wrestle with God. Dr. Stein told of how, for many people, the church is like a big teat "where they come to suck." I had no trouble sticking my neck out. It affirmed my being in the ministry. I was not about to compromise and preach a less offensive gospel. Yet the criticism ate into me.

Jeanne thought the funeral incident funny. Her conservative faith had ended. People become resentful, even bitter, when they realize that they were duped by fundamentalism. They become uncompromising critics of religion. This change in Jeanne made her an even better companion. I had the devil's advocate in bed with me.

Richard Irving was not a revolutionary. The senior minister was fair, patient, unemotional. He had come out of the Bible Belt in West Texas. While compassionate, he hid his personal feelings. I do not think he ever shared any doubts, fear, or anger with me. I was working alongside a non-controversial minister as the sixties began. I was catapulted out of a dynamic seminary with the charge to take the Word into the marketplace. Mission accomplished! But it did not feel this way until much later in my life.

"Now you have Christmas"

The Reverend Harry Chase named us the "Young Lions." Older, very bright, Harry was the campus minister at nearby Long Beach State. He delivered many insights. Perhaps my favorite one was, "Heaven is a relation, not a location." Harry sharpened our fangs while we moaned about the religiosity in our parishes. At times, an older pastor in the area, Paul Aijian, was equally challenging and insightful. There were damn sharp people in the ministry. It was not the freak house I feared.

There were four of us Young Lions; one was Bob Peterson, a brilliant iconoclast. We were seated around a Christmas nativity display at the Emmanuel Presbyterian Church in Los Angeles one morning when the assistant minister of the host church offered some platitudes about the baby Jesus in the crib. Peterson got up, took a cross off the wall, and slammed it down on the baby with, "Now you have Christmas." Peterson fed my sense of value in being of the ministry. I loved it when he told of counting the bricks on a wall outside the window of the head pastor's office during the lengthy daily staff prayer sessions.

Jeanne and I found a home to rent over in Lakewood, to the east of Long Beach. A dairy was on the other side of the backyard fence. On my birthday, she handed me a paper sack. Inside the bag were two black and white tumblers. Pigeons! Like Tuffy, they had feathers on their legs. I cannot think of any birthday gift that has meant more to me.

Jeanne and I both enjoyed the couples who came to the adult education classes. My love for teaching took precedence over preaching. In addition to some very solid church literature prepared by the Presbyterian Church, I reached for important theological books that I wanted to read and understand. I would be a chapter or two ahead of the class. The book that had the greatest impact on me was *The Courage to Be* by Paul Tillich. I did not realize then that the philosopher/theologian was existentializing Christian metaphors. I had not met Nietzsche yet. The "God is Dead" quote on the cover of *Time* magazine does not appear until the mid-sixties. My theology advanced with the classes I was teaching. In the summer of 1961, this led to shocking sermon titles on the message board in front of the church. Anybody driving by the church on Orange Avenue could view them. Each one was a result of my having led the class on *The Courage to Be* ("God is Dead," "The Illusion of Immortality"). Each spoke to the kind of Christianity I could respect. I did not realize it, but I was thinking my way out of the ministry. Yes, the church office did receive at least one call about the sermon titles. Take your pick.

The claustrophobia went with me to Long Beach. Thick fog closed in on me late one night when Jeanne and I were driving home from a movie. I had to lean out of the window in order to see the white line that divided the two-lane road. Suddenly I was overwhelmed by claustrophobia. There had been a seductive, appealing sexual scene in the movie. I am sure that's what triggered the frightening episode of claustrophobia.

A second attack was set off by a sexual scene in the movie, *La Dolce Vita*. A sensual woman is pressured into a strip tease at a party in

Rome. While reluctant at first, she gives in and begins to remove her clothes. The party crowd cheers her on as each item is discarded. She ends this exciting sex dance under a fur coat that Marcello Mastroianni quickly places over her nude body. It was time to see a psychiatrist and the thought of seeing one terrorized me.

Shortly before seeing a psychiatrist, I had a dream where I was in jail for murder. Dr. Stein came and paid my bail. My favorite seminary professor, the one who introduced me to Sigmund Freud, paid the ransom.

My worst bout with claustrophobia hit me on a flight to San Francisco. Jeanne wanted to go up and see her mother. We were on a crowded PSA jet when I suddenly wanted out of that narrow fuselage. I had never felt such overwhelming panic. Not even at the seminary graduation, or from *La Dolce Vita*. The panic was so bad that I was not about to fly back as planned. I talked the husband of Jeanne's closest friend into driving me all the way to Long Beach from San Francisco. I had to preach on Sunday. What was going on?

I made the appointment to see a psychiatrist. No more counseling just so that I could be a better minister. I had my own terror to face. This led me to a Dr. Flint in downtown Long Beach. I paced back and forth outside his office before the first visit. It was not time for the appointment yet. My anxiety exceeded any pre-race nervousness. I wanted to flee. The psychiatrist was young, fairly tall. He had me lay on the couch while he sat in a chair behind my head, smoking a cigar. I suspected that he was playing like he was a Freudian psychiatrist. And I found the heavy smoke in his small office insensitive. But I did not tell him how I felt. Jeanne also started therapy.

Therapy did not move quickly with Dr. Flint. One day I felt he was defensive when I complained that he was late. You are supposed to say whatever you feel in therapy. Right? It took courage for me to complain. The son-of-a-bitch pulled out his records to see if I had any unpaid bills. He informed me that I was two or three payments behind. I did not tell him that I thought he was being defensive.

It was a cold, bleak day in the Coliseum. I went to see the UCLA-USC football game with my seminary friend, Bill Frederickson. A low, gray overcast sky hung like a blanket over Los Angeles as though a field of ice extended out from the Coliseum. I felt cold, encompassing fear. What in the hell was happening to me?

Bill and Sally Frederickson were our good friends. His church in Inglewood was not that far from Long Beach. One day we drove down the California coast to the San Diego Zoo together. I liked being with Jeanne. She was wearing her hair in a darling way that day and looked good.

I could not know that I was beginning what has turned out to be a lifetime of trip adventures with young people when, in the summer of 1961, I took a group from the Los Angeles Presbytery to Mammoth Lakes. A Presbytery is made up of Presbyterian churches in a geographical area. I wanted recognition beyond the North Long Beach community. I asked Bill Frederickson to go with me. And I took our dog, Moochie. I would quickly discover that Bill did not care for dogs. Jeanne and I had found this black poodle-like character at the Long Beach pound. We loved Moochie. I had not told Frederickson that I was bringing our dog to Mammoth. He screamed, "No way!" when he saw the dog climb up the steps into the bus. Moochie hiked along with us to Shadow Lake, high above the canyon that runs down from Thousand Island Lakes to Devil Post Piles. We spent a night or two up there, below Mt. Banner and Mt. Ritter, the Minarets. Bill and I got along well. And he tolerated Moochie.

One of the Young Lions was desperately trying to escape Christian fundamentalism. When I assembled the staff for another conference for the Presbytery, I asked my friend to join me. We went into the mountains east of Los Angeles for that retreat. This tortured man told me that it was a sermon that I gave at the North Long Beach Community Church that had given him his first glimpse of escaping from his religious imprisonment. Jim had come to our worship service at North Long Beach while on his vacation.

There were far too many young people at the conference. There would be a control problem. They were from churches all over the Los Angeles area. Jim was frantic when he woke me up in the middle of the night and told me, with great alarm, "They're running around outside of their cabins!" It was damn cold out there. We were up some six thousand feet in the mountains in the winter. I said to Jim, "So." In a state of panic, he warned me that "they could be having sexual intercourse!" I told him, "If they can enjoy doing it in the freezing weather outside, well..." I turned over and went back to sleep.

Jeanne and I went to see Rusty Tamblyn in the *West Side Story* at Grumman's Chinese Theatre on Hollywood Boulevard. Rusty was the leader of one of the two New York gangs in the popular musical. He did his usual tumbling routine in one of the musical numbers. Again, I liked going to movies with Jeanne. We were a couple. She was smart, easy to talk with about the intellectual issues raised by the films. We found *Dr. Strangelove* hilarious. Especially the scene in the war room at the Pentagon. In the film, World War III was about to begin with an American plane heading for Moscow to drop an atomic bomb. And there was no way to call the jet back. The Soviet Union would, of course, retaliate. The officers in the war room at the Pentagon were feeling helpless when a general, played by George C. Scott, took command of the moment. He brought his staff to attention, closed his eyes and said, "Let us pray." Marvelous.

The movies from 1960 to 1962 were unusually memorable. The Swedish film director, Ingmar Bergman, used biblical symbols and scripture to bring existential questions to the screen. *Through A Glass Darkly* and *The Virgin Spring* were filled with theological correlations which I shared with the college students. The final line in *Through a Glass Darkly* remains with me. An impersonal father finally hears his son and the son says, "My father finally spoke to me." Theology was alive on film.

Gregory Peck was of supreme moral character in *To Kill a Mockingbird*. *A Raisin in the Sun* was deeply moral in its portrayal of character and self-respect. The challenge of relating theology to the culture, through film or books, was exciting and rewarding. Religion was not about another world. It was about the moment.

The greatest worth of Christianity in my view then was that everyone matters. That human life is sacred. This opinion holds. This meant fighting for justice, having the courage to confront discrimination and the loss of life brought by military powers. Films brought ethics to the pew. My life was alive, exciting, with personal satisfaction. During this time, a church elder became upset with me because I had recommended *The Misfits* with Clark Gable and Marilyn Monroe. I had told him the movie raised human questions about relationships. I did not tell him to take his kids.

In June, 1961, near the end of our first year in Long Beach, Jeanne came back from seeing the doctor and told me that we were going to have a baby. I was going to be a father. I felt incredible fulfillment and happiness.

The great one, Wes Santee, got in touch with me when he was going to be in Los Angeles. I asked him to come on over to the church and speak to our young people. It pleased me to introduce them to this national athletic hero whom I knew personally. Wes arrived with film of some of his indoor races on Movietone News. It bothered me slightly that he was wearing his all-white Marine Corps dress uniform. Wes had been at a Marine Corps event. It was summertime. Why not wear the white uniform? Self promotion bothered me. I couldn't relate to how some people could take pride in how they dressed. Likewise, it seemed incongruous to me how, when Mary and Lou came to the North Long Beach to present their slides for a pack trip we were planning out of Mammoth, they wore matching suede jackets. In my mind, Mary and Lou were of the natural. Now they tell me that they never owned such jackets.

Most of the church members walked the short distance into the backcountry on a conference out of Mammoth that I organized and led. Lou and Mary provided the mules to bring the food and equipment to the site. I think some forty to fifty people attended this family

retreat. Jeanne did not go because she was pregnant. My favorite professor, Dr. Stein, drove over the Sierras to be our campfire speaker over
these few days. Lou and Mary had purchased the pack station at Mammoth. The cowboy and the girl who met at a square dance nearly ten
years before had returned, with their children, to live in the mountains
where they had fallen in love.

I liked being in charge at the Mammoth conference. The "assistant
minister" title bothered me, for I wished to be independent, to be seen
as an adult. I think back to what that woman said after my father was
killed, that I was now "the man of the family." At age ten?

When it was time to leave Mammoth and return to the city, it bothered me when Dr. Stein asked for a speaking fee. I thought he came to
be with us out of friendship; paying him did not feel right. And as I
returned to Long Beach I continued to ask myself why Lou Roeser got
to do what he wanted to do; why did he get to live his life up in the
High Sierras while I returned to the marketplace?

My psychiatrist pointed out one session that my mother's name was
Mary. He raised the question of whether her name (i.e., the mother
of Jesus) and her father's vocation were prime factors in my choosing
to be a minister. I thought that Dr. Flint was reaching. Dr. Charles
Hager died in 1917. I was not born until 1933. It was decades before I
learned that my grandmother's first name was Maria. When I entered
the ministry, I was not conscious of any significant influence that they
exerted on my life. But was the psychiatrist close? Was I trying, by going into the ministry, to live up to my mother's father? When I sought
understanding from this doctor about some of the criticism that had
come my way at North Long Beach, he asked me if I was aware that
football coaches were sometimes hung in effigy. I wanted support. He
hit me with realism. I felt no empathy from him. Today I see it as a
decent response. Maybe his timing was off, however.

Dr. Paul Aijian became the resource pastor for the Young Lions
when Harry Chase returned to the East Coast. Harry went to that
well-known Riverside Church in New York. That was where one of

America's most dynamic preachers, Henry Sloane Coffin, held the pulpit. Coffin would soon become a leading critic of the Vietnam War. Coffin had been a campus chaplain, too. It was told that while at Yale he greeted those who assembled in the chapel on Christmas morning with, "We are here to remember a bastard who was born on a dung heap." Bravo! I found this provocative, delightful, solid.

Dr. Aijian told us that he chose Christianity because it gave him a context to work from. That made it a relative choice in my mind. I was perplexed—Christianity was still absolute for me. But I did not forget this disclosure, for it repeated itself over the years ahead.

When I conducted a funeral for non-church members, I did not personally know the woman who had shot herself. Or the family and friends who came to the church for the service. As with the Daughters of the Evening Star, a minister had been requested to conduct the ceremony. Because it was suicide, her Catholic priest would not perform the funeral. Afterwards, I was attacked for saying that her suicide was a result of sickness. A mother in her late twenties, the woman had become more and more depressed before she took her life. I felt compassion, not condemnation, toward her final act. It was chilling to experience the way some expressed their disapproval. I saw anger, even hate in some of their eyes. Dr. Aijian told us that sometimes the apostle Paul stayed and confronted a mob, and other times he went out the back window, being lowered in a basket to the street below. Hard-hitting Christianity meant criticism. Being a minister required courage. I was not too good at going out a back window in a basket.

Jess

JESS WAS BORN at Long Beach Memorial on Atlantic Boulevard on February 16, 1962. Before I drove Jeanne and our baby home, John Glenn was in orbit and circling the earth. I had a son and I was glad it was boy. I realized this as soon as I was told. I had a son to look forward to seeing each day when I returned home from work. I loved having a family! It became clear that Jeanne was going to be a great mother. One could see this in the way she held Jess. Her self-confidence increased. At the same time, her feelings toward Sue were

Jeanne and Jess

growing more and more hostile. Jeanne was beginning to realize that she hated her mother. She ceased defending her family. This change in Jeanne brought the two of us closer together.

I invited a psychiatrist I had heard at a mental health conference to come to our church to speak. Along with my favorite theologians, Freudian psychiatrists were way up there in my pantheon. However, when this particular doctor told members of the congregation that one should strive for absolute honesty, I felt it overplayed our human capabilities. W. H. Auden wrote that "the one thing I know about man is that he lies." Very Calvinistic. And Freudian. When I wrote a thank-you note to the psychiatrist for having taken the time to come and speak to our church group, I asked him how one could be "absolutely honest" if repression was normal for all people. I felt a boost in my self-confidence when he wrote me back accepting my qualification. I felt pride in being able to converse with a psychiatrist as a fellow professional.

Bill Frederickson remembered me saying once that I had always wanted a goat. One Saturday morning, Bill called and said that he was about to buy me one, but I had to agree to keep it before he spent the money. Jeanne said no. I can still hear his laugh. Bill had gotten my goat.

Moochie had long black hair that covered his face. And bushy paws. When he moved from one place to another in the house, he left a pile of dust on our wooden floors from where he had been sitting. One night there was an outdoor party next door to our house in Lakewood. The guests became alarmed when something smashed into the wooden fence with force. Then the black paws and black hairy face of Moochie appeared through the wooden slabs at the top of the fence. I was told that there were frantic screams.

One Saturday night, we had a number of campus ministers over to our home in Lakewood for dinner. There was considerable noise, laughing—largely because of Jeanne; our new friends liked her. People felt comfortable around her. That evening, there was a serious discussion about life after death. A husband and wife from LSU who were visiting Long Beach intrigued me when they said that they did not believe in life after death. This was the first time that I began to seriously think about death being death. Tillich attacked the belief in immortality; he said it was not a Christian belief. Harry Chase had said, "Heaven is a relation, not a location." But no more time? Existence canceled? Harsh!

Jeanne was perhaps ahead of me in accepting this. She was a very intelligent person. I still laugh when I think of our quarrel in the kitchen one evening. How I baited her over something. She really got mad. Frustrated, she blurted out with, "Who in the fuck do you think you are?" My reply was fantastic: "Thou hast been with so long, and thou dost not know me?" She actually took a swing at me. I mean at my jaw. Jeanne was becoming a great wife.

Deep in the heart of Texas

A TEXAS MINISTER called me in April, 1962. He said that one of my seminary classmates had told him that I was "the hottest young preacher in the West." The man on the phone was Bill Jablonowski. He was the controversial pastor of a large congregation in Fort Worth. It was made up of business executives, professors at Texas Christian University, wealthy ranchers, lawyers, doctors, upper-class folk. I was being asked to share the pulpit with one of the top preachers in America. As an associate, not an assistant minister. The parish was building a $5 million Gothic cathedral. Their Reformed worship strongly appealed to me. The congregation worshipped God. Services were not broken up with special announcements about church picnics. Jablonowski was caustic, blunt, human. Very, very different from Richard Irving. A graduate of the University of Texas, he studied law, like John Calvin.

I did not weigh how I would react to his authoritarianism. It looked to me like I was on my way to becoming Peter Marshall. I felt somewhat like I did after I was nominated for Track Athlete of the Week in Los Angeles. It was happening. The opportunity to become a popular and respected American preacher was being offered to me.

I was not happy about flying to Texas. I had not been on a plane since that horrible attack of claustrophobia on the flight to San Francisco. I flew to the Lone Star State alone. Jeanne stayed home with Jess. It was hard for me to leave our two-month-old son. I was bothered more by a feeling of being separated from the earth on the long prop plane flight to Fort Worth/Dallas than one of being trapped.

Bill (Jab) was there waiting for me at the gate. My first impression was that he was ordinary looking. He had a crew cut. All of this changed when Jab opened his mouth. A lashing tongue was linked to a brilliant mind. In the ministry, Jab was a man among boys. Within moments of our meeting he uttered, "Shit." It was the right word.

Richard Irving never swore. Jab took me around Fort Worth, introduced me to prominent people in the city. It was an overwhelming array of professionals. Ironically, in an old cow town. These were the people who made things happen. Probably like those who waited in the rain to hear Peter Marshall in Washington, D.C. The nice, simple, blue-collar folk back at North Long Beach were no match for the ones I met on that trip to Texas. When I went into the pulpit at St. Stephen, the congregation would be made up of those who influenced life in the city.

Worship at St. Stephen was right out of John Calvin's sixteenth-century Geneva, Switzerland. I was overwhelmed by what awaited me if I took the position as their associate minister. On the Sunday morning when I attended the worship service, I witnessed silence, awe, respect, the numinous! God was God.

St. Stephen already possessed a large Gothic sanctuary. It easily took care of the flock that attended the one worship service. Jab would not divide the "body of Christ" into two services, except on Easter. The congregation came together to worship God at one service. On the cornerstone of the Gothic sanctuary was a quote from Calvin: "Everything with decency and order." Just like on St. Pierre's in Geneva.

The office for the associate minister was almost enough by itself to get me to go there. It had a large executive desk with tall bookshelves extending up to a high ceiling, and a fireplace. I thought I was in a medieval castle when I looked out of the window through its square, thick glass panels and iron bars. Jablonowski was never cheap. Everything had to be "first class." Like Wes Santee. In contrast, my narrow office at North Long Beach was a former maintenance room; at one time, it stored brooms, buckets, mops. This did not bother me; it fed into my Stoicism. But the office in Forth Worth was something else. The Texas Christian University campus was only a few blocks away. I had wanted to be a campus minister and this meant that professors and college students would be there when I preached as part of the congregation. Jablonowski was "a pro." Like any power figure who makes things happen, Jab stayed in close touch when I returned to Long Beach. He called one Sunday evening to tell me that he had witnessed two pigeons fornicating through the stained glass windows at the back of the sanctuary while he was in the pulpit that morning. Any final doubts that were holding me back were swept away by the fornicating pigeons. The man was really human!

I still had to convince Jeanne. If I accepted the position, it would mean leaving California at a time when she was still very anxious and phobic. But I had to go.

Mr. Irving looked shocked when I told him I was leaving to take a position in Texas. He was raised in West Texas and warned me about how my liberal theology might not be appreciated with the home folk.

Jab drove out to see us on his vacation, pulling up one afternoon in front of our home in a brand new powder blue Cadillac convertible. Jab traded his "Cad" in every year for a newer one. This bachelor was really something else. His driving to Long Beach on his vacation was all about Jeanne. She still had to be made comfortable about the move to Fort Worth. He took us to dinner at an expensive restaurant and immediately won her over. Within the month, Jeanne and I, along with little Jess, were on our way to Texas. I had to give up Moochie. I loved that dog. But Jeanne was not going to drive all the way to Fort Worth with him in the Rambler with the baby. My final view of Moochie was seeing him jump into the back of a van with some excited children. I had discussed the family's attitude toward acquiring Moochie with their father. He was going to a good home with his new friends.

I had wanted to see the Grand Tetons ever since I had seen the movie *Shane* in the early fifties. That spectacular backdrop of sharp mountain peaks, river, the sage, had become my image of a Western paradise. But I could not feel the magnificent setting when we arrived. Something was not right. We spent the night in the wooden cabins at the Grand Teton Lodge. For the first time in my life I came down with the shakes. I did not have the flu. It was fear.

I loved driving with Jeanne and young Jess to Texas. It was wonderful to turn around and see the little guy in his crib. Going through a town in Wyoming at night, I saw little Jess propped up on his elbows so he could check out the street lights.

After he had visited us in Long Beach, Jab came down with hepatitis in Idaho and was hospitalized there. From his bed he managed to make a local minister look like a fool. This pastor, upon returning from what he described as the "Holy Land," told of his journey in the local newspaper. Jab seized the moment from his hospital bed and wrote a scathing letter to the editor. Bill had his theology straight: God is the God of all land. There are no sacred parcels. Bigotry and hate result when special real estate is staked out by religions. However, I did not admire Jab when he bragged about attacking this lightweight minister in his hometown. As the world continues to kill over "holy" real estate, Jablonowski does not seem as vulgar. Bill was still suffering from hepatitis when he returned to St. Stephen. We were staying at the Holiday Inn until we located a home. A church elder, Winston Taylor, took us around. An "elder" is a lay church member on the highest court. Winston walked with a cane; his Texas drawl seemed gentle and kind. Watch out for "Judas."

The low real estate prices in Texas enabled us to rent a large new home with a huge yard. The size of the yard was important because I was going to send for my pigeons. A friend at the North Long Beach Church, Glenn Putnam, was taking care of them for me. Just like John Burkert had watched out for my birds when I was put in the orphanage. And how Frank Clark watched out for my birds when I was forced to remove them from the area around our apartment in Toluca Lake.

The women at St. Stephen seemed taller and very seductive. They walked with a proud strut. I broke out in a sweat at a church function one night when a very sexy one, with a heavy Texas accent, said that she would like to come and talk with me about "some counseling." Her breasts pressed against the silk of a white blouse. She wiped me out. Two of the taller young women stopped by my office one morning. They just wanted to say hello. Both carried sexual confidence.

St. Stephen was a special place. I had "made the varsity." During the initial weeks, I was introduced to the key players in the congregation. Their talent, intelligence, and commitment to the church were impressive. I was somewhat intimidated by the wealth. My clothes seemed skimpy and cheap, to me. This was a very unusual congregation. They took life, religion, and football, very seriously. It was hard to not want to be a "little Jab." He had such a command of language, was brilliant, and he carried himself with authority. I wanted his approval as I fought to maintain my own identity.

Bill did not preach from notes. He would think the sermon through during the week, then, making eye-to-eye contact with the parishioners, he would communicate the message. My delivery was going to be measured against his seasoned rhetoric. One of the conditions that had brought me to St. Stephen was the opportunity to share the preaching with Jablonowski. He lied.

Two young Presbyterian ministers in the Fort Worth area invited me to have lunch with them. I especially liked Bill Barnett. We had Chinese food that day. Why do I remember what we ate? It was because of what they told me over lunch. When I mentioned that Bill was going to share the pulpit with me every other Sunday, they gagged on their chop suey. One bluntly smashed my pulpit dream with, "Jablonowski has an orgasm when he preaches." I was stunned. Shocked. Were they jealous? Both admitted that they had wanted my position. But they would be proven right. I only had the pulpit when Jab was away. The rest of the time it belonged to him.

I did not take the time to analyze the "political" structure, the hierarchy of the church. In North Long Beach, nobody questioned me about what I wanted to do. But I was in Texas, in a church with very intelligent, capable adults. I soon unknowingly crossed two of the powerful church females with my go-it-alone attitude toward working with the young people. These two were the directors of the Christian education programs at St. Stephen and they went after me when I did not clear some new directions with them. One of them, Nancy Smith, headed the youth activities committee. Nancy was always friendly. How could she suddenly turn on me? The more lethal one turned out to be the dowager of St. Stephen, Mrs. S. Gardner Endress, head of the Christian education committee.

I was criticized not only for excluding them from my plans, but also for planning to take the young people on a short trip. We intended to write a play together and take it to other churches. We'd be away for a few days, might even miss Sunday corporate worship at St. Stephen. This was verboten.

What I did not realize for awhile was that the parishioners reflected Jablonowski. It was his pride that led to their making St. Stephen so special. Jab purchased those large, round light bulbs from Pershing Square in Los Angeles for the walkway that led up to the church office from the parking area. In the months ahead, Bill would describe me as "the best young minister of Christian education in the United States." The organist, Elza Cook, was "the best church organist in the country." John Watts, a Negro, was "the best gardener in Fort Worth." And out in the parking lot, at the end of the row of light bulbs from Pershing Square, was his new powder blue Cadillac convertible.

Jab let me dangle when the husband of the dowager, S. Gardner Endress, went after me at a session meeting one night. The St. Stephen session met in a room that could have been used in a motion picture for medieval kings and their courts. It would have seemed normal if Peter O'Toole or Richard Burton entered at any moment. Dr. Endress seemed really angry as he complained to the church governing body that "our associate minister did not find it necessary to attend the prior meeting of the church court." I was confused, unsure whether he was really upset or pretending. I had missed the earlier session meeting because I had chosen to go to a gathering of campus ministers in Denton, Texas. As I walked out to the parking lot after the scolding, I said in an offhand way to an emerging ally, "Was he really mad?" The insurance executive put it this way: "If he wasn't mad, I would hate to see him when he was." Then, before we said goodnight, he asked, "What woman did you cross?" Jab never gave me any understanding, sympathy, or direction during these attacks.

Jab was a speed reader and cardboard boxes filled with books were scattered on the floor around his office. He let you know that he devoured books. There was a bathroom with a shower between our offices. The Fort Worth Zoo was an easy run from St. Stephen. This meant I could fit a light workout into my schedule and then shower before any evening activities. There was no entrance fee to enter the zoo. I made some animal friends. Both a rhino and an owl noticed my fairly regular runs past their enclosures. The owl would look at me with its flat face upside down. When explaining these regular encounters to church friends after worship one Sunday, Bob Adcock teased me, of course, about my running fantasy. Adcock and a Bob Sweeney became important friends to me at St. Stephen.

Those early months with Jab and the congregation were dynamic as well as threatening. There was a very positive response to my insights into *The Fall* by Albert Camus, *Franny and Zoey* by J. D. Salinger, *Rabbit Run* by John Updike. I had offered an evening seminar titled, "Theology in Fiction" and there was a big turnout. That night, I made it with the St. Stephen folk. My participation in the dignity of the worship service at St. Stephen remains, to this day, a positive memory. The organist would begin with Bach or Mozart. Then I would call the congregation to worship with "Let us worship God," or "Hear oh Israel, the Lord our God is..." The numinous was there in the music, the verses; there was awe.

I was criticized by an older member of the church for wearing white socks under my robe. It was just a request to change the color. While I felt that she was being petty, that the color of my socks had nothing to do with Christianity, I cooperated. Now I see her point. I would have fared better if I had been raised an Episcopalian, gone to one of their seminaries, and been ordained a priest. St. Stephen was about status, politics, the sacraments, and money—a profile of an Episcopalian church. My clothing and lack of social graces were a handicap at St. Stephen.

I preached on a few occasions that fall. One time I had the pulpit when Bill was there. It was the only time I did not use any notes. He raced into my office afterwards, dark eyes flashing, shot out his hand, and praised my sermon delivery. I think again of Bergman, and his film, *Through a Glass Darkly*, and that line, "My father finally spoke to me."

The congregation felt my sermon that Sunday. My ministry at St. Stephen came alive. And I made sure I made it to subsequent session meetings. It might have been the next meeting of the church court when a hot young trial lawyer in Fort Worth came up to me afterwards and said, "Don't be so serious." While he meant to be helpful, his comment only made me more serious. I never saw him again. He jumped out of his office window on a Sunday morning in downtown Fort Worth precisely at 11:00 a.m.—the exact time that St. Stephen worship service began. I learned through my "Deep Throat" insurance executive friend that Jab had refused to see the lawyer when he had asked for counseling. Bill told him that his problem was with God and that he would see him in church Sunday morning. I found Jab's treatment of this man wrong, indefensible. But I kept this to myself. I did not share my thoughts and feelings about Jab with members of the congregation.

I was loyal even though I felt so cut off from him. One evening I drove over to his apartment to try and make contact in a personal way. He looked surprised, puzzled, even somewhat disturbed over my suddenly appearing at his door. I wanted understanding, approval, a human response. To hear that things were okay. He offered nothing. Basically treated me like he did the lawyer who went out the window. I drove away even more worried.

When a pronounced attack of indigestion did not go away, I went to a drugstore and picked up something for the stomach. Then a few nights later, while watching television, the most horrible fear I have ever encountered swept through me. I thought: *I could lose myself.*

I called a Fort Worth psychiatrist and the doctor told me that he was not far enough along in his own therapy to handle what he described as my "deep-seated fear." Great, now that was really encouraging—I am feeling terror and a psychiatrist says that he cannot handle my fear. He then told me that none of the psychiatrists in Fort Worth were far enough along in their own therapy and that I would need to see someone in Dallas. That was hardly any better. His tone was friendly, however, even helpful. God, all I wanted to do was go into the ministry, have people admire and respect me. Instead, I found myself in this state of panic. What was happening? Jeanne was haunted by her own fears. She literally felt like she could fall off Texas because it was so flat. We were in great shape. This was not like the Peter Marshall movie.

Questioning being in the ministry

W E WENT TO DALLAS. The psychoanalyst I saw looked like the British actor, Michael Wilding (the one who was married to Elizabeth Taylor for awhile). I found him a bit peculiar looking. He had a handkerchief tucked into a large, fancy cuff. His dress shirt had ruffles. Not very Texan! He listened for over an hour. Then, in one sentence, he gave me back my life. It was simply, "I think you are questioning being in the ministry." As I drove back toward Fort Worth with Jeanne, it felt like a piano, maybe two, had been lifted off my shoulders. Could I really do what I wanted to do with my life? For years, I had pushed aside the question, "Why does Lou get to do what he wants to do?" On a freeway between Dallas and Fort Worth, I pondered my freedom.

I was disappointed that the psychoanalyst was fully booked with patients. He referred me to a Dallas psychiatrist and suggested twice-a-week therapy. I was not in serious trouble. My life, and what I valued most, were not going to be taken away from me.

I liked the new psychiatrist. Dr. Simmons and I worked well together. We fought the Jablonowski battles from the couch in Dallas. For example, when I told him that Jab had the loyalty of certain elders in the congregation, and that my reactions to Bill might be wrong, Dr. Simmons told me that "Hitler had little Hitlers."

Once my birds arrived, I raised a flock of young pigeons. When they were six weeks old, I let them out for the first time. They timidly were exploring the roof of their loft when a fleet of Army helicopters suddenly roared right over our yard. The untrained birds scattered in all directions. I lost about half of them. It was the first time I saw any choppers coming over our home. Dr. Simmons told me that if he had raised the pigeons he would have become very angry. Oh? It sounds so obvious now.

I played golf with the St. Stephen friends I mentioned. Bob Adcock, the one who teased me about the owl and my rhino, was a very successful contractor. Sweeney was a boyish-looking church deacon and co-owner of a Fort Worth lumberyard. His college major, of course, was literature. They were my good friends. I had no idea that my time with them was going to be so short.

I loved going home to Jeanne and Jess. I would sometimes find little Jess pushing cardboard boxes over the slick wooden floor. We went to drive-in movies; one time we saw a funny John Wayne movie about Africa. I can still hear the musical score from *Hattari*. Maybe you can?

Jeanne and I took the freeway between Fort Worth and Dallas to see our psychiatrists twice a week. We would drive there on my days off. I did not feel that it was necessary to explain how I used that time. I knew that I was a responsible minister. Jeanne and I saw *Lawrence of Arabia* one afternoon after our appointments. We saw another film the night we stayed over in Dallas without little Jess. Jeanne became so anxious in the motion picture theatre that we had to leave before the movie was over.

I do not believe I ever discussed our therapy with Jablonowski. When Bill and I went over to the new Texas Christian University indoor arena to see a basketball game, I told him that I felt somewhat claustrophobic. His wonderful response was, "Anybody who feels claustrophobic in here has to be sick." What a guy.

St. Stephen had morning prayers a couple of days each week before work days began. I was given the 6:00 a.m. prayers in one of the smaller chapels. And I was surprised to find this early morning focus valuable. Those who could stay for awhile would have coffee and rolls in the church kitchen afterwards. One morning I shared a harmless religious joke with them. The older women did not laugh. I thought the joke hilarious. I told of the three wise men bringing gifts for the baby Jesus. After setting down their presents, one of them stands up and hits his head on a beam in the manger. It really hurts, so he screams, "Jesus Christ!" Mary reaches over, grabs Joseph by the arm and says, "That's a much better name than Floyd."

The USC football team was undefeated in 1962. The day after they beat Notre Dame 25 to 0 in the final game of the regular season, I hung my USC letterman's blanket from the door of my office. Between football being a religion for most Texans, and the St. Stephen claim to having the best church, ministers, organist, even groundskeeper, my display was not out of place and was accepted with a certain pride.

One afternoon I was with Jab when he made a quick stop to see a male parishioner in the hospital. He asked that I wait in the powder blue convertible. When he came back he said, "The Holy Spirit finally got to that son-of-a-bitch." I thought this both compelling and harsh. I would drop the "harsh" part today. What Jab was surely saying was that the man had caught a glimpse of his humanness. That he was not so sure of himself anymore and this gave him a deeper awareness of what matters in life. Jablonowski was the most outspoken man I have ever met. I admired his forthrightness and his down-to-earth religion. I did not admire the way he would show off. He called me into his office one day so that I could hear him speak with John Glenn on the phone. Eventually America's first astronaut was on the other end of the line. Glenn was orbiting the earth when I brought Jeanne and Jess home from the hospital. It turned out that he was not available to speak at the St. Stephen annual building fund banquet. Instead, Dr. John McCord of the Princeton Theological Seminary would have to do. I sat next to him at the head table. When I told him whom Jab had initially asked to speak, and that he was the second choice, Dr. McCord found this funny. He understood the bravado of Jablonowski. I had a nice conversation with the brilliant theologian. I felt comfortable with myself. I was beginning to realize that I was not the problem in the confrontation with Jab.

Remember the California Highway Patrolman, Stod Herbert? The father who lost two of his teenage children in the jeep accident? He gave me a large oil painting just before I left for Texas. It was of a sad, suffering Jesus. A dark Jesus with Semitic features. Stod had painted this Jesus during his intense suffering. I did not even think about how a dark Jesus would be viewed by a Texas congregation. I innocently hung it in a hall just off to one side of the entrance to the sanctuary. Just a couple of months before, James Meredith had tried to enroll at the University of Mississippi. One St. Stephen woman was so disturbed that she took to her bed for days. To Jab's credit, he gave her no sympathy. But at the same time, no blacks worshipped with us at St. Stephen. That elder who helped Jeanne and I find our house when we arrived in Fort Worth walked me over to the painting after worship one Sunday and told me it was awful. Winston said he was telling me this for my own good. Sure he was. When I did take it down, Jab said, "I wondered how long it would take you."

Bill began his sermon one Sunday with, "Good morning Adam and Eve." I felt that he was massaging their guilt. A quick whipping would make them feel better about being privileged and wealthy. I would not let them off so easily. The following Sunday I had the pulpit. A certain boldness came forth. I began to express myself existentially, using the metaphors of philosophy instead of traditional Calvinistic language. And with my Freudian bias. I was challenging the Calvinism of St. Stephen and William Jablonowski. I did not mention his "Adam and Eve" greeting from the prior Sunday, but I spoke of the sickness of man instead of guilt. I was not conscious that the congregation was aware of our rapid separation. I was definitely fighting for my identity.

When a rancher told me one morning that St. Stephen had "two Bills locking horns," I became more aware that the congregation realized that I was standing up to Jab. I felt that this was healthy. Certainly it was for me. I still did not talk about my feelings toward him with church members. Nor did I have any sense of how fatal this confrontation would be.

I received great praise for the summer adult education classes I structured. Key church members were to teach a variety of courses from the Presbyterian curriculum. And I would teach a six-week course on Paul Tillich's *The Courage to Be.* Over thirty adults ordered the book and signed up for the evening class.

Bill and I drove down together to Brownsville for a meeting of the Presbytery. I was feeling my oats; I felt far more confident around him. But shortly into the drive he expressed his disappointment in my work at St. Stephen. It went something like this: "I am sure that you are a good minister for Jesus Christ, but things are not working out." I asked for clarification. Bill told me that I did not hang around long enough in the late afternoon to see what more needed to be done for the parish. True. Nor was I encouraged to do so. And the bachelor did not have a wife and young baby waiting for him to come home.

I hung around with the younger ministers at the conference. I did not sit with Jab in the general meeting. He turned around a couple of times and gave me his big fake smile. I loved being independent. The younger ministers offered exciting ideas. Their theology challenged my thinking. I was not ashamed being a minister around such open and creative thinkers.

I did preach again without notes. One more time. Jab was not there. It was the best sermon I would ever deliver. An unusually large congregation was in attendance that Sunday morning; I do not know why. Unfortunately, because I did not use notes, I do not have a copy of the sermon. I know that I said that love has to be experienced, that God is not love for someone who has not known love. I separated myself from Calvinistic man, spoke of psychoanalytic man. And what of God? I told them that God is in every act of healing, justice, compassion. It all came together for me in one sermon. Freud, Tillich, Gill—each found their way into my words that morning. I did not quote them. I delivered this sermon in my words. I no longer was a little boy.

I could feel the intensity of the congregation. The sanctuary was alive when the service ended. When some of the college students from Texas Christian University filed out past me afterwards, they were virtually jumping up and down with appreciation and joy. I had spoken to them. I felt tremendous. Today I realize that the sermon consummated my reason for being in the ministry. When I returned to my office, I was told that the foremost religious writer in Texas had been in the congregation and that he wanted a copy of the sermon. He was looking for me. For Peter Marshall? But we did not make contact with one another.

I had not pleased everyone. The elder with the limp was waiting for me. He told me that it was "awful." I did not let the comment bother me. I felt tremendous. The *Courage to Be* class was packed. Maybe thirty-five to forty adults showed up. The praise over my educational leadership and that enormous response to my sermon had to be the reason. I went into the ministry for this to happen.

"Either Taylor or me"

Two church officers, the man with the limp and a TCU professor of literature, asked me to please stay for a moment after a Christian education committee meeting the week after the sermon. They were the appointed assassins. A third fellow made it clear before they spoke that he was not part of what they were going to say. The two elders told me that Jab had told them that it was "either Taylor or me." *Panic.*

It happened so fast. So suddenly. There was no way I could challenge Jab for the pulpit of St. Stephen. I called a respected minister in the Los Angeles Presbytery, and he told me to "come home." Dr. Simmons looked shocked. As we parted, my Dallas psychiatrist left me with, "Now you can help other ministers grow."

We drove through El Paso like Moses went out of Egypt. It felt great to be driving back to California with my wife and young Jess in the Rambler. Being a family was the most important thing in the world to me. My mother came through as usual, reserving a motel room in Toluca Lake for us, just a block or two from Bob's Big Boy and Warner Brothers. The June weather in Toluca Lake was most pleasant, temperatures softened by an ocean breeze. I was grateful to have left that sticky oven-like heat of Fort Worth. Just like that. One moment I was the associate minister in Texas, the next I was back in Toluca Lake without a church identity.

All of our friends in California, of course, wanted to know what happened. Thus began the legends of Jablonowski. He was going to take awhile to shake. The tyrant had thrown in the towel. I had been in Texas for just under a full year. People found the Jab stories provocative. I was the hero who stood up to an abrasive dictator.

We found an apartment on Magnolia Boulevard in North Hollywood. A fellow from Belgium had racing pigeons just across the street. I did not bring any of my birds from Texas. The pink apartment building with the wooden house and pigeon loft on the other side of Magnolia became my little neighborhood. In June of 1963, I did not have much perspective about how I challenged Jab and the way he was leading his congregation. It is clear today. I needed to affirm myself. If I had stayed on for awhile, it is likely that a Texas pulpit would have been located for me. Jab would have pulled that off. Better that we raced through El Paso.

I left Fort Worth with enormous anxiety because the "Taylor or me" was such a dramatic Oedipal encounter for me. I had taken on the powerful "Father." Today I see this behavior as my kind of Oedipal victory. And I believe my final sermon at Stephen was worthy of Peter Marshall.

Now what would I do? The Presbyterian process for placing ministers is slow and deliberate. Intentionally so. Calling a new pastor is a process supervised by the Presbytery. You do not even know if a nominating committee from a church looking for a pastor is out there in the congregation. If I had been an Episcopalian priest or a Methodist minister, a bishop could have appointed me to a vacant pulpit. Several pastors in the Los Angeles Presbytery did try to help me. But Richard Irving was not willing to let me preach at North Long Beach. I needed a pulpit so that I could be evaluated. I could have taken a position as an assistant minister at any time. For example, I turned down a favorable opportunity with a well-liked pastor near Santa Barbara. But I knew I had to have my own church. My friend Don Hartsock, the UCLA campus minister, was a sharp, unusual man. Don was a speaker on one of the Mammoth Lakes youth conferences that I organized. At the time I returned from Texas, Don was looking for an associate campus minister at UCLA. I became very uncomfortable when their nominating committee interviewed me. I did not have to be in a pulpit to be checked out for that position. A professor, noticing my anxiety, reassured me. He put it in an unusual way—"We are benign."

Before I learned that the UCLA committee had voted to invite me to work with Don on the Westwood campus, I decided to take a less active role with Chuck Doak at USC. This fit in with my decision to acquire a teaching credential. My former university had really come through for me by giving me credits for some of my seminary courses to fulfill educational requirements. This meant I could obtain a teaching credential much faster. My part-time job with the Presbyterian ministry on the USC campus was less than half a block from my old practice track. I did not take the associate campus minister image seriously. I tried to help Chuck, but it was my relationship with him that was valuable for me. I had no impact on students.

Substitute teaching was a quick way for me to earn some immediate cash and begin teaching in public classrooms. I was able to start right away in Glendale and Burbank, substituting in high school and junior college classes. It was not a big leap to a secular identity for me. And teaching was already in my blood. Circumstances had given me a life without a robe. And a new image. There was a new series on television about a high school teacher that Jeanne and I looked forward to watching each week. Just as *The Lieutenant* series had given importance and flair to my image as a young Marine Corps officer, so did these high school teaching episodes present a vital, moral, relevant instructor. In the mid-1950s Glenn Ford played a classroom teacher in *Blackboard Jungle*. Ford was courageous. While up against the thugs in one tough high school, he did not compromise his values.

A jolly Joe Kraft had become the pastor of the Trinity Presbyterian Church in North Hollywood. He asked me to preach for him when he was out of town. Joe, a big, heavyset man, did not take himself too seriously. So between the substitute teaching and fairly regular "substitute" preaching, I earned some money while I prepared for a teaching career.

Jeanne and I were thrilled when my former USC teammate won the 400 meters in the Olympic Trials in the Coliseum. Jeanne enjoyed sports; she was a companion in the stands. I felt pride and identification with Larrabee. More than once, I had taken the baton from him in a major relay race, like I did ten years before in Modesto on that school-record distance medley. And there had been a recent personal note. Mike came over to see the pigeons across the street from that apartment. As a kid, Larrabee raised pigeons, too. Mike was selected as a co-captain at the end of the competition that afternoon and stood with the U.S. Team at attention holding the American flag at the open end of the Los Angeles Coliseum. When pigeons were released and circling over Mike's head, I could not help but think of all the Larrabee pranks I had witnessed or heard about during my two years at USC. I just thought, "Son-of-a-bitch." Well-liked Mike was the roommate in Ann Arbor who started my Marine Corps orders on their way to Quantico after I had left them behind.

Leaving the ministry is not like just changing jobs. People continually asked me, "Why did you leave the ministry?" I told you that the "laying on of hands" set me apart, for them. People want to know why, because, to varying degrees, they believe in the spooky powers of the priest or minister. To this day I am asked that question.

A few kids cheered when Kennedy was killed. I shut that down immediately. I was out on the football field at Burbank High School with a physical education class when someone raced over from the gym and told us that President Kennedy had been shot. I, like a good part of the world, was deeply shocked. President Kennedy had captured me with his brilliant speeches, sense of humor, grace, intelligence. I wanted to be with Jeanne, watch the news with her. But I had to finish the school day. That night we felt his death together. Jesus, there were still Texas plates on our Rambler. I had left St. Stephen just five months prior to November 22, 1963. I suspected that Texans would be blamed. I read in the newspaper that one automobile in Los Angeles with Texas plates had a window smashed.

Joe Kroff happened to be out of town that weekend and I had the pulpit at my home church. The sanctuary was, of course, packed. I spoke of loss, not hope. I felt strong, capable of not rationalizing the death of this incredible leader. On that Sunday, I belonged in the pulpit. I could not know that five years later, in June of 1968, I would be speaking at the Unitarian church in Marin County about the death of his brother, Robert Kennedy.

While standing outside my old church in North Hollywood that Sunday after Jack Kennedy was assassinated, I was told that Lee Harvey Oswald had just been shot. I remained calm. I did not think the world was falling apart. My seminary preparation plus the three and-a-half years I spent in the ministry provided me with perspective. It felt good to be someone who people were depending on for strength and judgment.

Teaching and psychoanalysis

WHEN I SAW some blood in the toilet, I went to see a doctor. A hemorrhoid problem was developing. My blood pressure was way up, too. I had never experienced high blood pressure readings when I was in the Marines. I needed a psychiatrist. But this time I wanted a psychoanalyst, like the one I saw that one time in Texas. Freudian psychoanalysts were the high priests of the profession. Only they could handle my "deep-seated" feelings.

USC did come through with the teaching credential. I finished up all of the requirements in just a year. I felt badly that I was not any real help to Chuck Doak and his campus ministry work. I enjoyed him during that transition period, however. One night we went to a Stanford-USC football game in the Coliseum. It was one of those times when the Trojans won in the last few seconds with a field goal. Night games have much more intensity than day ones. Chuck pointed out how a football game was the real American worship service. He related the symbolism of the pageant to me, how the football players act out the "holy" sacrifice for the crowd. I realized that the ancient rituals with the animal having its throat cut were not dissimilar to a player scoring a touchdown. Or, in baseball, hitting a home run. In each instance, there is a kill, or score, or decisive moment, when one team wins and the other loses. Cheerleaders serve as the maidens of the sacrifice. In ancient times they were part of the sacrifice, carrying water and grain in jars to the altar. Now they have dance routines. Chuck Doak said he was an atheist. I was intrigued. While traditional religion was unacceptable to me in most respects, certain Judeo-Christian symbols still had meaning for me. I preferred them in secular language, however.

Dr. Theodore Schoenberger, a graduate of the University of Chicago, was the real thing (i.e., a Freudian psychoanalyst). The graduate program at the university was the lead school for psychoanalysis in

America. I had found my Freudian. And a new hero. Dr. Schoenberger decided to have me sit in a chair and face him, instead of lying down on the traditional couch. I was up against a pro. When I told him that Dr. Simmons bade me farewell from therapy in Texas with, "You can now help other ministers," he reacted with, "He still had the cross up his ass." I did feel that his criticism of my Dallas doctor was a bit harsh. I liked Dr. Simmons. He had helped me through some very rough times. There will be many other classic lines from Dr. Schoenberger. One of my early favorites was, "It is an insult to have certain people like you." I sure wish I had that one stored in my wallet in high school. It would have helped me to ward off wanting everybody to like me.

We began to work on my relationship with Jeanne. When I told him that she had complained about having to walk several blocks back to our car because it was up the street being worked on by a mechanic, Dr. Schoenberger asked, "Does she have legs?" Oh! Jeanne was a wonderful companion. Her psychiatrist asked that I be patient with her fear in bed. We never considered her working. It was biblical Freudianism that the mother be at home with the child.

We had moved from the apartment on Magnolia to a house right next to Stod and Bonnie Herbert. Just a couple of blocks down from the Trinity Presbyterian Church. Frequently I would see Stod ride his motorcycle up his driveway after a day's work as a CHP officer. He loved the motorcycle image. And he looked formidable when riding his powerful bike with his golden helmet and shades. Bonnie Herbert was a special human being. Almost too perfect. Not artificial. She was such a genuinely good, giving person that I wonder if Stod was ever able to get mad at her. She was a great friend to me.

Stod would invite me over at times to show me something in his studio. The painter of the black Jesus liked being dramatic, shocking. One time he pulled a photo album out of a lower drawer very carefully. On the cover, engraved in gold, was the title, "Assholes I Have Known." He then turned the pages slowly. When we came upon a photograph of a former police chief that he disliked, Stod pointed his finger at the picture and said, "This guy was a real asshole." And so it went. Page after page. Photographs of people he judged to be phonies.

Stod did not need a psychoanalyst to tell him that it was an insult to have certain people like you.

I heard the Beatles singing, "I want to hold your hand..." as I drove west to the San Diego Freeway, then past the UCLA campus and over to Westchester High School for my practice teaching. Because of my educational background and actual classroom experience, USC sent me to Westchester to be part of the first team teaching ever attempted by the Los Angeles City Schools. I found the co-teachers, the classes, and the opportunity to teach from literature stimulating. And I discovered that the novel offered me an excellent way to reflect on psychological man. The other three teachers included me as their equal. I took my turn with the lectures. They impressed me with their professional skills and dedication.

My USC track coach, Jesse Mortensen, had died. Vern Wolf was the new head coach. I appreciated how warm and friendly he was to me. Vern even let me take home a couple of the films of the old USC track meets from when I competed. As he handed me the large canisters with the reels, he reassured himself about the loan by saying, "If I can't trust you, who can I trust?" We were in the same office where Jesse Mortensen, upon hearing that I was going to be a minister, had cautioned me with, "Not much money in it, Bill."

Many of my teammates felt quite warmly toward Coach Mortensen. I was less enthusiastic about my feelings toward him. He never approached being a father figure for me. He was a fair man, but he offered nothing in the way of middle-distance coaching, nor, when sickness deprived me of my Trojan potential, was he personal or sentimental about it. From the standpoint of having a top coach training me, I should have been over in Eagle Rock with Payton Jordan. Just two years before I ran for USC, Jordan had coached those two great middle-distance runners to berths on the U.S. Olympic Team. What a difference that could have made in my times. But I never would have worn that special USC uniform. Payton has told me a couple of times that over thirty of his former runners have named their sons Payton.

He would have been very helpful if I had been hit by tonsillitis while running for him.

I was hired to begin teaching at Reseda High School, which is west of North Hollywood, out past Van Nuys. I began my teaching career in my San Fernando Valley. I never even had an interview for the position. The Westchester principal had sung my praises so well that all it took was his phone call and I was hired.

We found out that Jess was going to have a brother or sister. Jeanne was becoming a happier, more self-confident person. She took an evening class and began to paint oils in vivid, bold strokes. Jeanne was talented. There was a sharply painted branch with a blue background. Then, as my first teaching year was about to end, Jeanne painted a large canvas with slashing reds and blacks. Many reacted to the almost violent strokes on this canvas.

I really liked teaching high school, having my own classroom. And I liked being in a profession that people did not see as ultimate. I was just another public school teacher. An educator. I initially taught world history. But I was willing to take on any other course within the department curriculum. This kept things more interesting for me. My seminary education and the books I taught from as a minister had developed my capacity to reason and identify connections, but I wanted to increase my knowledge in each area.

I was familiar with several of the key existential writers, psychoanalysts, the prime theologians. But I was unfamiliar with many parts of the world and I wanted to learn more. Except for the two world wars, my grasp of French, German, and Russian history was nil. And ancient Greek, too. I had a lot of catching up to do. I loved it. I loved this chance to teach five days each week. Communicating with people fulfills me.

I was required to take twelve units of graduate work in my teaching field of history and I received an A in each course. These marks really contributed to my confidence, and to my sense of being in the right occupation, counteracting my fears that people would judge me to be fickle because of my career change.

I did not have any trouble with student discipline at Reseda. Remember, I had been a Marine Corps infantry officer. The classes were large, with sometimes over forty in a course. But I loved them. Any size would do. I wanted to teach, to be alive through sharing knowledge.

One of my favorite teaching stories involves two girls who had no academic confidence. I told their class that they could either see the motion picture, *The Spy Who Came In From The Cold*, or read the book. They were then to write a paper on what it meant to them. The girls naturally chose the movie. But, as the essay paper deadline approached they kept coming up to my desk, asking for specific direction on what to write about. Both were used to sliding by class after class through high school. The novel/movie was a complicated spy story with double U.S. and Soviet agents during the Cold War entering or exiting through Checkpoint Charlie. The Berlin Wall offered strong images of danger, mystery, and suspense. At the end of the film, a young woman is killed as she attempts to climb over a wall. It was an eerie, complicated, very well acted motion picture. The girls begged me for help. I said no. I held my ground. Of course they both wrote exceptional papers. Two of the best out of the entire class. I gave them something very special. They could think for themselves. I was a teacher! Teaching gave me these wonderful rewards. I felt fulfilled, happy.

Jeanne was a good mother. This meant everything to me. It felt good to be with her. There was something special about Jeanne, so much talent, depth, personality. We went to movies, read books, spent time with friends. People liked being with her.

A student from St. Stephen flew out to spend a week with us. Kay repeated what I think I had already heard via a phone call, that Jab had really caught hell from the congregation after I left. The church session made sure that the next minister would carry the title of assistant, not associate minister. This gave me some satisfaction. I did not try to stay in contact with the communicants at St. Stephen. This was largely because I respected Presbyterian polity that when ministers leave a parish they should, except with the closest of friends, make it a clean break so as not to interfere with the life of the parish. And I am sure that my

angry feelings toward Jablonowski had something to do with my keeping St. Stephen at a distance.

There were some sharp teachers on the faculty at Reseda. I made
some good friends. We ate our sack lunches together. Just the guys.
One was Sol, a towering figure with a brilliant mind. He would leave
Reseda shortly to teach economics at the community college level. A
non-practicing Jew, Sol was very curious about my background. He always had questions. About theology, Christian ethics, politics, sports,
or a drama production. We became lifetime friends.

We addressed a variety of topics at the lunch table. The teachers I
ate with were not lightweights; each of them had fifteen or more years
in the classroom. All were older than me, but I was able to fit right in
with them. The noontime jokes were supreme. Especially those told
by Milt. Sol put the finishing touches on this one just before we went
from the hall into our respective classrooms after lunch: "A gorilla grabs
this hunter from behind and is about to squeeze him to death. The
hunter, who is on an African safari, reaches down and yanks the penis
of the gorilla again and again. The ape suddenly releases the hunter,
and falls backwards. The hunter, not noticing that the ape has ceased
chasing him, frantically swims across a river. Exhausted, he looks back.
Where was the gorilla? It had not moved. It remained back where it
had clutched the hunter, waving for him to return." When I went to
close the door of my classroom after lunch I saw Sol down the hall
waving for me to come back. Having these kinds of people to relate to
five days a week, and the fulfillment of teaching young people to think,
made for one of the most rewarding times in my life.

My own personal thinking moved back and forth between religious
symbols and secular metaphors. Sol would say over the years that I
never gave up the Absolute. Dr. Schoenberger didn't think I ever believed in religion in the first place.

When an English teacher at Reseda described himself as a nihilist,
I mentioned this to Dr. Schoenberger. My psychoanalyst asked, "Does
he value books?" I knew this teacher to be passionate about literature.

When I related this to Dr. Schoenberger, he simply said, "Then he is not a nihilist." Psychoanalysts are archaeologists of language. My therapist was not a philosopher or theologian. He was more of a philologist. A psychoanalyst hears and plays with words. Their insights into what is hidden within the human vocabulary can be incredible.

Cory

I WAS AT RESEDA High School when Bonnie Herbert called and left the message that Jeanne had begun labor. She was going to drive Jeanne over to the Van Nuys hospital that very moment. Cory entered the world on March 5, 1965. Jeanne looked absolutely beautiful when I saw her sleeping after delivery. She was sedated. I can still picture her. Cory looked exactly like his older brother did when I first saw him. I was thrilled to have a second son. We did not know the sex before the birth. It was an incredibly satisfying feeling for me. As with Jess, we had not decided on a name prior to delivery. But we took the baby home as Cory.

I was taking a shower when I began to cry uncontrollably. What triggered it was the thought: *What if Jeanne and I have to separate?* What if our marriage problem led to divorce? It would mean being separated from Jess and Cory and that was the worst possible thing I could imagine happening to me.

Ironically, this horrible thought came at a time when Jeanne seemed to be finding herself. She was becoming more self-assertive. For example, she decided to go down to the Burbank studio and stand in line to get herself picked to be on *Let's Make A Deal*. My inhibited wife had informed me that she felt confident that she would make it onto the television show. I went with her. She was chosen. After Jeanne answered a couple of questions correctly, she looked up to me in the audience wanting to know if she should go on. I signaled *stop*. The refrigerator she won lasted into the present century. Some of those tall, poised women from St. Stephen saw Jeanne on the show. One called to tell Jeanne how beautiful she looked on television.

The clinging mother, Sue, had lost her grip on my wife. Jeanne was changing. I really loved her. There were still no big breakthroughs for us between the sheets, but there was some progress. Remember Jeanne's painting class? She told me that when her art teacher leaned close to her one night, she felt excitement. My reaction was: *Why is she telling me this?* I think now that it was because she felt secure with me. It was not a tease or threat, but a sign of sexual life. Jeanne's paintings were striking. Those powerful, blazing strokes represented strong, bold feelings. She would take her oils to Mammoth that summer.

Mammoth had to figure somehow into our summer vacation plans. I recruited my Long Beach friend, Glenn Putnam, and my former USC teammate, Ron Morris, to form an educational youth camp with me. My old neighbor, Stanley Klein, had become a lawyer and he wrote the legal contract for us. We would have the use of a lodge in Mammoth for the summer without fee at the same place where I held the Presbyterian youth conferences. Lou and Mary Roeser had put me in touch with the owners of the lodge originally, explaining that Don and Barbara Humphreys wanted to do something for young people. The lodge was available because Don and Barbara wanted to spend the summer months down at Huntington Beach.

We had a full summer to spend in my High Sierra paradise, two sons to share it with. Jess, who turned three in February, would be able to hike with me. The air was precious; the pine scented woods provided a natural perfume. I had a family and a profession that was of value; my world was wonderful. We had put a down payment on a property off Topanga Canyon Boulevard, farther out in the San Fernando Valley, so we had our own home to return to in September.

Glenn and Mary Lou Putnam shared the lodge with us that summer. I loved the large front room with the big fireplace. You could see the Mammoth ridge through the big windows. The five lakes—Mary, George, Horseshoe, Twin Lakes, and Mamie—were just several miles up the road. Mary and Lou Roeser were up there. My Western love story was fulfilled. The fantasy was reality. Thus I entered this summer feeling complete.

We did not market the youth camps well. We only had enough young people to form two sessions. Pete Kokon of the *Valley Times* gave us a plug in his column. And we ran an advertisement in the newspaper. But it was going to be a skimpy beginning. This did not really matter. Spending a summer with free time at Mammoth would be one tremendous vacation break.

Pete Carroll was being sent by his parents from Kentfield, all the way over in Marin County, to attend the second youth camp. I had coached his older brother, Jim, on those victorious middle school teams when I was in seminary. The parents wanted their youngest son, Pete, to be inspired and to learn from me. I was to meet the future USC head football coach at the Casa Diablo bus stop, down where 395 passes the Mammoth Lakes turnoff.

A motion picture set was put up to the south of the Laurel Lodge and Jeanne began painting this Western town from the porch of the lodge. Behind the stores, saloon, and livery stable were the peaks that I had seen on my training runs eleven years before. I surely passed the lodge on my way back to the jeep trail. Steve McQueen was in Mammoth to make what turned out to be one crummy movie, *Nevada Smith*. When he began racing his motorcycle on the trails of the national forest, the local people became very upset. Many of us will remember his motorcycle exploits in *The Great Escape*. The initial Mammoth student group saw Steve McQueen when I was parking the Rambler above the popular hot springs in Owens Valley. As he approached, they began screaming, "Steve! Steve! Steve!" McQueen was wearing chaps and spurs, and carrying two six-guns. I was amused when he did a quick little dance step for the girls as he passed by the car. It was followed with his cute little mischievous smile.

The young people who attended that first summer session were not impressive. They should have been screened. They offered little in maturity or personality, and they seemingly lacked any intellectual interest. It was a weak beginning. What did begin to work, however, were the adult activities. I had mailed out a few flyers and a former Marine Corps reserve friend, Ed Wachsman, drove over from Marin County. Ed was married to an attractive blonde from Sweden. I sent them up to the Roeser pack station to ride horses around the lakes.

Later I enjoyed showing them some of the enormous craters to the north of Mammoth, just off Highway 395 on the road toward Reno. A couple of books on the area gave me enough information to be somewhat informative. I discovered that sharing a little geology and locating Indian arrowheads could satisfy my teaching need. No theology. No morality. Just craters and rocks and arrowheads.

We had plenty of new rooms available in the lower lodge. Ron Morris's parents came up. They bought Ron's brother, Steve, with them. This was fun.

Jeanne and Mary Lou began cooking dinner for guests who responded to the sign we had placed out by the road going up to the lakes. It advertised "home-cooked meals." A few vacationers decided to stay at Laurel Lodge. I was able to give them fishing direction, like which canyons offered what kind of hikes, lakes, trout.

Lou and Mary suggested that Jeanne and I drive down to Bishop with them for the rodeo one Saturday night. Before we left the Mammoth area, Lou pulled off to the side of the road so that we could watch the light from the setting sun spread out over the Owens Valley. Jeanne and I expressed our love for one another with a complete kiss. Her lips met mine, the same full lips that I had first touched that night on our hike up above the seminary, seven years before. Lou and Mary, my idealized couple, were in the front seat. The wonderful moment closed the day as the valley floor darkened.

She looked pale

Jeanne looked a bit pale when we went to bed on Sunday evening. She told me that she felt unusually tired. Jeanne was reading the third or fourth book of the *Alexandria Quartet* series by Lawrence Durrell. I can still picture her in bed that night in Mammoth. I know that we shared affectionate words before we said goodnight. The early morning light began to bring me into the next day. Suddenly, at about 7:00 a.m., Jeanne let out a terrible groan and sat straight up in bed. It was a primeval sound. As though she was fighting off a demon. Like a raging protest. I watched her die.

Foam from the mouth, the telling twisted hand, then her glassy, fixed green eyes. She died next to me in bed within seconds. I closed her eyes and went to call the medics. I also yelled out to Glenn and Mary Lou that something was wrong with Jeanne.

I was not thinking about death. I was too bewildered, stunned. The medic arrived quickly from the ski clinic just up the road to Mammoth Mountain. He put a breathing device on her, worked at restoring life. Then he shook his head. She was gone. The realization came slowly to me. For, Jeanne, it had ended quickly with that raging scream. She was my companion for six years of marriage, the mother of our two sons. Suddenly she was no more. My life could never be the same.

Cory was five months old. Asleep in the next room. Jess was three and a-half years old. He remembers the morning when death took his mother. I was left with inexplicable questions. Jeanne had her life stolen from her. And I was alive to know this. With terrible irony, this happened at a time when Jeanne was feeling increasingly confident that she was going to be able to live a full life. She literally said this to me within a day or so of her death.

What killed her? There had been no warning, no medical history to explain the convulsion, the seizure. A day or so later, the sheriff reassured me that even though our bedroom was sealed off with those wide yellow police ribbons, that "there was no criminal investigation." Huh?

The autopsy in Bishop did not produce a cause of death. There was the water (edema) on the brain. This gave evidence of the convulsion. But what triggered it? Guilt arrives with death. Remember, there were signals that I might want out of the marriage. I had to handle these feelings along with the sudden death of my wife. Jeanne was a wonderful person. From that morning forward to this very hour I measure the world by her death.

Glenn suggested we drive down to Mammoth Creek to visit with a psychologist who was vacationing in the mountains. The doctor graciously made time for me. I asked him if I should be taking anything. I meant a tranquilizer. I really felt strange. The doctor wisely advised, "I believe people should feel their emotions at a time like this." That felt right. I coveted the authentic. Something very real had happened.

There were no thoughts that Jeanne was somewhere else—with God, or at peace. They took the body. Drove away with the one I had slept with for over six years. And then they cut into it down in Bishop. Her body was personal to me. I was asked for permission to send the brain to the University of California, Berkeley, to test for poisons. I, of course, gave approval. Ironically, Jeanne was a graduate of UC Berkeley. I had the two boys. Jeanne lost everything. I do not know if our marriage would have lasted. I will never know. Dr. Schoenberger told me years later that he did not think so. However, when Jeanne's psychoanalyst called me at Mammoth after hearing of her death, Dr. Lerner told me that "Jeanne was prepared to live a full life."

Never again would I be able to accept that there is a personal caretaker of life. Jeanne was a mother who would never see her children again. I held an uncompromising grudge, initially against God, then against an empty universe. Her loss of life will always remain vicious, violent, and ruthless for me.

Sue asked for the burial location to be in San Rafael, said that she would pay the cost of transporting the body across the mountains. Sue helped me out a lot. We both grew from the tragic death of her daughter. I let her have the memorial ceremony.

I wanted the casket in the ground when we arrived at the cemetery. It was horrifying to think of Jeanne's body lying in a casket. Dr. Stein was out of town, so I asked Dr. Come to conduct the service. I told the theologian that I would appreciate as little religion as possible. He said that he understood.

I held Jess's hand as we walked up to the folding chairs by the grave. Cory was back at Sue's apartment in Kentfield. Dr. Come read from the Psalms. I just wanted it to be over. Then I saw Stanley Klein standing by a tree behind me. The lawyer who had helped us initially with structuring the youth summer camp had flown up from Los Angeles. Ron and Paula Morris were there, too. Dr. Stubblebine—the doctor who had said, "She hears what she wants to hear"—came with Sue. He was by her side. Dr. Gill arrived just after the service was over. But the one who formed those marvelous stories with engaging metaphors, the one who made theology so vital just before my graduation, did show up. When I offered some metaphysical framework for the death, he brushed it aside and said, "This is not the time for cerebral reflections." I was trying to let him know that I was okay. I think he missed the point. I never found Dr. Gill personal.

Several years later, Dr. Come told me that Dr. Stubblebine had written to him after the funeral, criticizing him for not talking about Jeanne's life in a personal way. The psychoanalyst wrote, "You would have thought you were burying God." I thought that was harsh. I didn't need any more of the personal at the grave. The burial was terrifying to me.

I stayed up at Laurel Lodge for the rest of August. I called off the second youth week, phoned Pete Carroll's parents and told them not to send their son on the bus. So I never got to know the future USC coach. I listened continuously to records in the big living room at the lodge, to music that reminded me of Jeanne. I could smell her physical presence in one of her summer dresses for weeks. It was so sad. I was so sorry for her. I placed Cory's crib alongside of the bed right below where I slept. I had moved into the main bedroom where the Putnams had been sleeping. They had returned to Long Beach. The bedroom where Jeanne died was still sealed off, making her death even more ominous.

My mother came up and was a great help, as was Lesley, my brother's wife. They sorted out Jeanne's clothing and jewelry, and took what they wanted. I did not pay attention. Where did the paintings go? I know that Harold and Leslie ended up with the one with the tree branch against a pale blue background. And, I think, the flaming red one.

It was very strange to return to San Fernando Valley without Jeanne. I continued to feel depressed; the sadness weighed heavily on me. Especially when I was alone. Or even when I was with other people. Sol had me out one Sunday afternoon and although I was with good friends, I could not escape that feeling of emptiness. I put Jeanne's photographs up on a board in a little duplex I had located in Van Nuys. I needed to back out of buying the home. A real estate woman watched out for me.

It was a time of grief.

At the same time, strangely, everything was new. When I saw Dr. Schoenberger for the first time since Jeanne died, I looked carefully around his office. I was not afraid to examine what was on his desk, the paintings on the wall. I asked, "What's different?" He said, "You are." Then, "You have grown up." It was true.

My old junior college coach, Jim Slosson, asked if I needed any money. I did and I borrowed $2500. Jim helped a lot of his former runners out. The wife of my friend, Jim Keefer, helped me place an advertisement in the newspaper for a daytime babysitter. Jim was one of those Young Lions in Long Beach. I wanted the best mother replacement I could find. When I interviewed an academic-looking Madeleine, she asked if she could bring her young son with her. My initial reaction was negative because I wanted Cory to receive all of her attention. I asked her why she wanted to bring him. Her answer revealed that she was the right one. Madeline said directly, "Because he is my son."

Jess was at pre-school during my teaching hours. Madeleine would send him off and greet him when he returned home. The world began falling into place. How ironic. I felt that weight, that heavy sadness of Jeanne's death, yet my mind was never clearer, my thoughts sharper. And my sense of humor, too.

I was feeling.

My world had changed. Jeanne's death gave me a lasting grasp of time. I began to realize that life was going to go on without her. It goes on without all of us. However, I felt disappointed, even irritated, when people did not continue to mourn Jeanne, share with me feelings about her death. The report on the brain indicated there were no toxic substances. Dr. Schoenberger asked to see the autopsy report. He shared his personal reaction to the empty death. There would be no known cause. Just like that, Jeanne disappears.

Trisha

I NOTICED TWO new female teachers at Reseda at the first faculty meeting. We were in the library. It felt good to be back. Of course, the death of my wife over the summer was the prime faculty news. It had been just over a month since Jeanne's death. Jesus, this seems so strange, but I actually thought about asking one of them out. When I brought this up to Dr. Schoenberger, asking when could I begin dating, he said, "Who makes the rules?"

My life in the little duplex in Van Nuys, along with the heavy feelings of sadness, had a special meaning for me. I liked being both mother and father to Jess and Cory. I needed them and they sure as hell needed me. I went shopping, cooked, changed diapers, spent my evenings with a three-year-old boy and a six-month-old baby. Madeleine would arrive with her Mark just before it was time for me to head off to Reseda High School in the morning. I felt comfortable leaving Cory with her. I had picked the right one.

One of those two new teachers at Reseda was right across the hall from my classroom. Not too many days after the semester began, I walked over and introduced myself. Patricia Allen was sitting at her desk. She knew who I was, even mentioned that she knew that I had been a Presbyterian minister. She had a good figure. She was pretty. She looked a bit British. Her poise and confidence made a strong impression on me.

Patricia made it clear that she did not want to be called "Pat." I was told that, immediately after she received her general secondary in education from UCLA (which was only three months before I met her), she flew to Europe with a girl friend. Later I learned that when her companion was afraid to go into East Berlin, Trisha drove through Checkpoint Charlie alone. A precise use of language and boldness in travel define Patricia to this day.

She was an active member of the conservative Hollywood Presbyterian Church, and yet she wanted life now. I doubt that she would wait for God. Her loyalty to this conservative Christian church seemed incongruous with her flair for life. While the well-known church on Gower Street in Hollywood emphasized eternal life, Patricia received more immediate help. Unable to count on her family for support, she had to work while attending UCLA. The congregation and an insightful minister had provided her with dependable support and friendship during her college years.

We fell in love quickly. On the first date, we had dinner at an outdoor restaurant in the hills over Burbank. Patricia wore a black dress. The more we talked, the more beautiful I found her. We saw the world very much the same way, both politically and by personal values. Later in the evening, I held her close when we danced at the Coconut Grove.

I could not wait for Patricia to meet my boys. I was so proud of them. Cory was one cute, happy, blond baby. Jess was warm, friendly, quiet, intelligent, and with sandy brown hair—Jeanne's color. The first time Trisha saw Cory, he was on the floorboard of the Rambler. I had driven over to her apartment in Culver City. The little blond cherub was strapped into his plastic port-a-chair. He was exceptionally cute. I did not weigh the fear and confusion that would hit Patricia when a widower presented his two small boys. Why would a twenty-four-year-old woman who has just begun her professional career want to even get close to such a situation?

When I suggested that the two of us might go away for a weekend, Trisha said, "When?" To this day she says, "When?" if I mention a possible trip. Thank goodness for my mother during this courting time. She took care of Jess and Cory frequently. Unlike Jeanne, Patricia had warm feelings toward her mother. Florence was simple, uneducated, a very sweet person. She worked at the large department store at Hollywood and Vine. Patricia had zero respect for her father. Roland had been a private detective, then a used car salesman. He never held a job for very long and did not provide financial security for his wife or daughter. I found Roland nice, a warm, genuine guy. Patricia was their only child.

The church at Gower meant a great deal to Patricia. She sang in the church choir and was part of an active young-adult group. The Reverend Richard Langford, an assistant minister at the church, was a psychologist. He had an unusual influence on the college-age females that he counseled, helping them psychologically. It surprised me that a conservative congregation would have such a liberal-thinking minister on their staff.

Patricia and I went to La Jolla for the weekend. It was not long before Dr. Schoenberger asked me if I was "trying to set a record." Great.

Trisha never liked that the little duplex. I loved it. She did not move in immediately. There were some tense, testing moments ahead, even panic attacks. Patricia was faced with the decision of marrying a thirty-two-year-old man with two young children before she turned twenty-four. I had a lot of confidence in myself. My therapy sessions with Dr. Schoenberger were moving. Things were different! I continued seeing him twice a week. This helped me to avoid making mistakes with Patricia. She was young, intelligent, beautiful, and emotional.

Trisha expected me to go to church with her on Sunday mornings. I had not disclosed my emerging atheism. I did notice during the prayers that her psychologist, Dr. Langford, did not lower his head. I remained non-committal about God and religious faith. My goal was to marry Patricia. She did not press for my position on religious questions. The Hollywood church had been an extremely positive community of faith for her. She naturally wanted to share it with me. I did not have a Father in heaven to pray to anymore. He was gone. And any God would have to answer to Jeanne's death. I went along with her wish to go to church on Sunday mornings.

We wanted to be together all the time. During the lunch break at Reseda High School, we would drive over and look at Persian cats in a pet store, and drink thick milkshakes. Patricia added malt. You lose weight when you are in love, so the thicker the shake the better. Our wedding was set for December 18 at Hollywood Presbyterian. Langford was to conduct the ceremony. This would be 138 days after Jeanne died.

Dr. Schoenberger felt that it was best that he not attend the wed-

Patricia and William

ding. He said that he did not want to "upstage" the bride or make her uncomfortable. He did know virtually everything about our relationship. It was a good idea. The boys stayed at home with my mother in a newly-rented house in Encino. This proved to be disappointing to friends from the Long Beach congregation who were invited, and certain relatives. They, of course, cared about how Jess and Cory were doing.

Hal, Mom, and me,
at my wedding to Trisha

Trisha was the goddess who lifted me out of my remorse. I was not through the emotional journey from death. But life pressed to go on. I could not change the fact that Jeanne's life was over. I was free to marry Patricia. But this was not so for the bride. Jeanne began to haunt her. The ghost came into our Reseda home after the wedding and honeymoon. Dr. Schoenberger related Patricia's fear to the movie, *Rebecca*. I had grown up through Jeanne's death. While it was brave of Patricia to enter East Berlin alone a few months before becoming an instant mother of a young boy and a baby, it obviously was far more ominous for her to suddenly become a wife and a mother.

Trisha did not have the power of death working for her. In certain ways, it was just the opposite, for Trisha would be measured by Jeanne.

My knees felt weak just before I walked out into the sanctuary for the wedding service. My brother, Harold, was my best man for a second time. I just wanted to get through the service, to take this beautiful woman and be off on a honeymoon. Jeanne had not looked "right" to me at our wedding; Trisha did. We drove up to San Francisco along the gray winter coast. It was a real, fulfilled honeymoon. However, I did miss the boys, felt the pain of separation.

We drove over to Marin County after staying at the expensive Fairmont Hotel in San Francisco. Ed Wachsman, the Marine Corps

Reserve officer who came over to Mammoth with his Swedish wife, talked me into visiting his insurance company offices in San Rafael. Ed was dead-set on recruiting me out of teaching for his firm. The Wachsman Building was evidence of his emerging empire. But I loved teaching. And, I did not want my image to be one of someone who jumps around from career to career. I had only recently left the ministry to become a teacher.

Patricia became extremely jealous of Jeanne when we returned from the honeymoon. Her emotional outbursts produced some threatening behavior. I found her actions selfish, even cruel. Nonetheless, I directed the marriage. The weekly sessions with Dr. Schoenberger were vital. Trisha continued to teach at Reseda that spring. She did not really care for the high school classroom. Madeleine was still spending the days with Cory. This gave Patricia time to adjust to being a wife and a mother.

Ed Wachsman was persistent. At some level he needed me. Not just in his business. Psychologically. Ed argued that the walls of a high school classroom would eventually close in on me, and that with financial independence I would be able to still teach when I wanted to teach. Time has proven that Ed Wachsman was correct.

I did not accept Ed's offer right away. Patricia wanted time alone with me, the chance to be a bride. I always found it painful to leave the boys on those weekends. Trish and I went up to Arrowhead, Big Bear, down to La Jolla again, to various other locations in the Southern California area.

Wachsman did not give up. One night he woke me up with a call around 11:00 p.m. and before I hung up I had agreed to join his company. It felt right to build a new life with Patricia and the boys away from the San Fernando Valley. Why not leave the horrible smog, the crowded freeways, and live in quiet San Anselmo? The forests and lakes were nearby, the quaintness of the town just below the old castles a delightful memory. I could become the financial counselor for my former professors. This image appealed to me. It felt like a more adult world.

When I told Dr. Schoenberger that I was going to leave teaching and move to San Anselmo, I asked him if I was dodging anything. He said, "No, you are what we work for." And that I was "flying out of the nest with wings." Bravo! Great. I even asked if I should consider another therapist and he told me, "Just seek out authentic people."

Beginning

IN JUNE OF 1966, we loaded our two cars and drove north. I felt enormous happiness in our new home in San Anselmo with my family. We rented a narrow redwood house with a small backyard on a quiet back street. Just around the corner was 160 Butterfield where I had lived with Jeanne. But that was over, gone, no more. Patricia and I were in love.

The gold wedding rings we found at Farmers Market in Los Angeles were unusual. Thick, branch-like strands connected irregular spaces within a wide golden ring. I always valued beauty. And Trisha was beautiful.

My bride of just a little over six months shared my view that the mother should stay home with her young children. Cory was only fifteen months old when we arrived in San Anselmo. Only twelve months before, Patricia had driven through Checkpoint Charlie. I offered no apologies. Jess and Cory were exceptional children. I believed that being a mother was a natural, fulfilling time for a woman. I was confident that I could make Patricia happy. Romance was alive in our marriage, but there would be threatening moments in the immediate years ahead. I coveted our home life. Patricia wanted the two of us to break away on weekends as much as possible. Separating the family was painful for me, but I needed to come through for her, for us, and we did spend quite a number of weekends away. Sometimes we went into San Francisco and stayed at a motel overnight, or across the San Rafael Bridge to the Claremont Hotel. Our favorite destination was Carmel. Before every Christmas, we went there for a long weekend, staying in one of the charming inns. The air would be crisp, the stores decorated for the holidays. Carmel became a marriage tradition. I did my best to watch the pro football playoff games, but this was not easy.

Baby ducks and bantam chickens soon joined us under our bedroom window. The rooster did not last very long. The ducks were fun

Jess and Cory

pets. We eventually took them to Golden Gate Park in San Francisco, letting them swim away in one of the ponds. I thought of Huey, Dewey, and Louie, my Toluca Lake ducks.

Patricia would bring Jess and Cory over to a quiet little park on Mission Avenue in San Rafael at lunch time. She enjoyed swinging higher and higher with Jess. That's Patricia—no boundaries. I loved seeing them having fun together. We drove out through towering redwoods, over to the beaches at Stinson and Bolinas. On one weekend, we rented a room at a motel that was right on the beach. This family time was precious for me.

The Presbyterian worship service did not work for me anymore. I did not feel guilty for being alive. But this is what greeted one in the liturgy. Patricia remained a Christian for awhile; I went to church once or twice with her. I nixed Sunday school for the boys and this hurt Patricia. Jess wonders today whether it might have been valuable to have experienced some religious orientation, but this does not haunt him.

We were told that Jess, then Cory, tested gifted. They were bright, but I was suspicious of the promotional interests of preschool entrepreneurs. It was Trisha who made sure that Jess, then Cory, received this private instruction before they began their public school years. But I wanted the boys to experience a more diverse group of students when they reached the ages for public education. And, this avoided the high tuition of a private school.

The Wachsman firm claimed expertise in estate planning, but their objective was to sell life insurance. This was not going to hold me for very long. I needed a larger world and more excitement than I could find by selling death protection and being seen as just another salesman.

I needed to locate clients, build a business base. I figured out how to identify bridges to prospective clients, to utilize my images to gain their interest and confidence. I had intriguing images: a former half miler on USC national championship teams, an ex-Marine Corps officer, and a graduate of the Presbyterian seminary. This led to appointments with track coaches, theologians, ministers, etc. I discovered that many in the Bay Area had respect, admiration, for the USC sport teams. Yes, Cal and Stanford folk hated them, too. My images provided me with that something different. I was not just another insurance salesman.

Theological professors and clergymen were scattered all over the Bay Area. I figured out how to guarantee appointments when I called them. I identified myself as a graduate of the San Francisco Theological Seminary, then used an almost magical word by saying that I would "demythologize" their life insurance. It almost always landed me the appointment.

I separated from Ed Wachsman after only six months. My style was not compatible with the national life insurance company Ed represented, and I wanted to be independent. I did not see myself as being more moral than the traditional life agent. But many clients praised my anti-industry image. I had found the right sizzle. It was only a matter of months before I realized that a license to place investments would be useful as well. And a hell of a lot more exciting.

Seeing Patricia dancing with other men made me extremely jealous. On three occasions I saw to it that we left a party early because this threatened me. We did not know the people at the party well. When it became obvious that my bride was going to be a very popular dance partner for other men, I had us leave. Patricia did not appreciate my jealousy to put it mildly. Her dark brown eyes fired disapproval, resentment for wrecking an evening of fun. Trisha never hesitated in letting me know how I made her feel. She could be a wildcat. And I let her know about what made me comfortable. I was her husband. Fortunately this meant a great deal to her. Our religious backgrounds were actually working for us. We both viewed marriage as a covenant. I wonder, without this commitment to marriage, if we would have made it through those early years.

My mother would fly up for Christmas. Trisha's folks were living way up in Crescent City, a town in the northwest corner of California. They would drive down for the holidays, too. Sue would send over expensive gifts for the boys. Trish was still too threatened by Jeanne's ghost to have her over. And Sue was afraid of losing out altogether if she completely alienated Patricia.

Trish could only take so much of my mother. Me, too. Mary Elizabeth could be abrasive. She heard everything, but that does not mean she listened. Trisha did work at being warm and considerate to her. The daughter of missionaries actually liked her nickname, B-doll. It was taken from a character in the movie, *Baby Doll*. Our boys called her "B-doll" and "Grandma." If I called her "Grandma" she would say, "I am your mother." A real character!

Trisha did not forgive her father for not helping with the wedding expenses. She made it through six years of college without any financial help. Moreover, she disapproved of the way her father treated her mother. Nevertheless, Trisha's parents were genuinely happy to see their grandchildren every time they visited. They were careful not to intrude, always showed up with a sack full of groceries. Jess and Cory enjoyed their visits.

I became known as a sharp, liberal, investment counselor. By August of 1967, I had that securities license and was placing mutual fund business. I appreciated the intellectual relationship with the professors, be they at the San Francisco Theological Seminary or across the bay at the Pacific School of Religion. A fair number of theologians became clients. Dr. Stein told me that the Holy Spirit was in the insurance files before I ever came into the business. My former professors became clients. This allowed for my seminary education to continue through a portion of the time set aside for the business appointment. When you have a background, quick snapshots can update you on what is hot, moving in the theological world.

My marketplace was the Bay Area. I would even drive over fifty miles to San Jose (at least a one-hundred-mile round trip), to see a new prospect. At the same time, I became involved in community activities in Marin in order to come into contact with more people. My family came first, however. It was the center of my world. Fortunately, a good number of my clients were the kind of people Patricia and I wanted to have as friends. A Unitarian minister and his wife invited us to dinner; that evening, I met two women in his church, Phyllis and Ann, and each became a client and good friend. A Bob became a client and referred me to others for business. One was a Cal professor. I had lunch with Bill Sharman, former USC All-American and the coach of the San Francisco Warriors. Funny, I used to imitate him in my backyard on Toluca Lake Avenue. A Warrior player bought some term insurance through me. Both Cal track and field coaches became clients. And several of my friends: Bill Frederickson, Don Schilling, John Snider, and others from USC track and seminary days. Even the psychologist who interpreted my psychological test before I was given clearance to enter the seminary invested a significant amount of money.

I could not ask for referrals. That routine never felt right to me. It seemed to me to be presumptuous to pressure people. I was placing my mutual fund business through a hot Denver firm. A couple of their recommended "go go" funds made over one hundred percent in 1968, then again the next year as well. I lacked the investment wisdom to know that we were very likely near the peak of a major market rise, because I had no experience with investment risks. The up-and-coming market correction that would continue for some five years would soon test my capacity to take on guilt.

I felt a part of history

I BECAME WELL KNOWN in the county because I anticipated that
the country would seek to resurrect the dead president with his
brother. I formed "Citizens for Kennedy" with a lawyer from Palo Alto
and a businesswoman in Sacramento because I knew that Bobby Kennedy would be forced to run for president, whether he thought it was
wise, or not. Bobby's harsh, unscrupulous image was changing. The
wounded brother matured through death. Bobby had Kennedy charisma; he exuded pathos and moral resolve. His greatest appeal was to
moderate liberals, blacks, and Mexican Americans. Although Senator
Eugene McCarthy was the legitimate Pied Piper seeking to lead America out of a Vietnam, I knew that only Bobby Kennedy could successfully challenge a sitting war president, Lyndon Johnson, and win the
nomination.

We held a Citizens for Kennedy press conference and it aired on
Bay Area television. There was newspaper coverage, too. The tragic
history of the Kennedy family was always news. Two brothers, Joe and
Jack, each killed. The horror and fascination of seeing Jack Kennedy's
head being shattered in Dallas in 1963 with the beautiful queen of the
nation by his side was too painful, too nihilistic to just be left behind in
the pages of history. There had to be another Kennedy. President Johnson had expanded the war, and was in serious trouble with the country.
I did not have an opinion on whether he would resign or not, but I felt
strongly that the emotional identification with Bobby Kennedy would
force him into the race. Was I a liberal? On human rights, yes. Actually,
I was more of an iconoclast riding history with a sense of the moral!

Each night on television, the nation watched American servicemen being killed and wounded by an unseen enemy. There were vivid,
horrifying pictures of napalmed Vietnamese people: the old men,
the mothers, and their children. Our nation was in serious trouble.
I believed that only Bobby Kennedy, emerging from the blood of his

brother, could heal our divided country. Theology served me well. I was right. Right about where history was going. And so I became a grassroots leader for the unconvinced, unannounced heir to the presidency.

I felt sadness and pain when I came home from work one afternoon and heard on television that Martin Luther King had been killed. President Kennedy and Martin Luther King were the two moral leaders in the sixties that I most respected. Both murdered.

It did not take too long before the San Francisco Theological Seminary bells rang out over San Anselmo, celebrating the announcement that Lyndon Johnson was not going to run for a second term. With confidence, I watched on television the unfolding drama that Saturday morning when Bobby Kennedy announced that he would be a candidate for president of the United States. Lightning struck. People wanted in on Citizens for Kennedy. Thirty or more strangers gathered in my office the next morning so that they could become part of the exciting Kennedy myth.

I was not a passive young man in 1968. Dr. Schoenberger once told me that my anxiety stemmed from not being aggressive.

Jess Unruh, not Bill Taylor, was named to head the Kennedy campaign in California. He was the most powerful Democrat in the state. Unruh was credited with saying, "Money is the mother's milk of politics." This hit me personally when Congressman Phil Burton's office called to inform me that I was "under consideration" for the Kennedy delegation. Consideration? What the hell was going on? I was a co-leader of Citizens for Kennedy. What was happening was that, for the four delegate seats in my voting district, I was up against Burton; Libby Gatov, the former Treasurer of the United States under President Kennedy; George Moscone, the future mayor of San Francisco; and a political upstart by the name of Willie Brown. I was angry. I had been the early prophet. Bobby Kennedy belonged to me. I let it be known that I was not happy and the *Marin Independent Journal* reported my displeasure.

Two liberal professors at the seminary, Ben Reist and Robert Lee, felt I had made a political mistake. Wrong. I called attention to myself.

I was aggressive. While Burton, Gatov, Moscone, and Brown had to be given the delegate seats for political reasons, they named me co-chairman of the Kennedy campaign in Marin County and included me as part of the delegation as an alternate. This pacified me. I had changed a lot since Jeanne's death in 1965. It knocked the passivity out of me. I was truly riding history. Ted Sorenson, who wrote the speeches for President Kennedy, came to Marin to help the campaign. I was given the role of introducing this brilliant lawyer at a fundraiser. I was seated next to him as we drove over to San Rafael for the event. This was fun. I asked him questions, like, "Is Senator Kennedy prepared to be president?" Ted Sorenson told me that Bobby was more prepared than Jack was when he took office, especially from the moral standpoint.

Riding with Theodore Sorensen gave me a sense of touching history, of being a tiny part of it. Who knew where it might lead, if Bobby Kennedy became the president of the United States? Members of the delegation for Northern California were to meet Robert Kennedy after he spoke at the University of San Francisco one Sunday afternoon. I was going to shake the hand of the brother who walked with Jackie to the Arlington cemetery, looked into those gray blue eyes that told of that tragic moment in American history. Now there was hope again; I was excited. There were some nasty peace radicals in the packed USF auditorium, and Kennedy began his talk with, "That was nice; someone just spat on me." The secret service hustled him away as soon as he finished his speech and I never shook his hand. Nor would I ever look into those gray Kennedy eyes. I would have met him in Chicago for sure, but he was not going to make it there.

Just before the California primary, I took the boys over to the Civic Auditorium in San Francisco to see him. The Northern California delegation was told to be there again. I held little Cory on my shoulders so that he could get a glimpse of his father's hero. Jess was six, Cory three. Cory remembers seeing Bobby Kennedy. Kennedy, along with several others like Martin Luther King and Ghandi, would become a part of a moral pantheon for our Cory. We got up fairly close to Bobby after his brief campaign speech that night. I noticed his shining brown hair. Even Ethel looked stunning that evening.

I had to settle for a limp handshake from Ted Kennedy at a cocktail party for my only direct contact with a live Kennedy. I had received another one of those delegation "be there" calls. The youngest brother carried the family name, but I was not impressed with him. He lacked the personal, did not attempt to meet your eyes. He was not Jack or Bobby. I had no trouble washing my hands after touching him. I respect Ted Kennedy as a man and as a politician today. He has grown into a strong moral voice as a United States senator.

Trish was a political science major at UCLA. She was not into Kennedy-ism. Being practical, she probably voted for Bobby. But the intellectual Senator Eugene McCarthy was more to her liking. A poet and former university professor, McCarthy was the eloquent presidential candidate who was early in seeking to lead America out of the Vietnam War. I knew that McCarthy could not win in Chicago, that he did not have enough of the mainstream Democrats behind him. Bobby Kennedy was the one who could win the nomination, heal the nation, deliver us from Vietnam.

We waited at our headquarters in San Rafael for the final results of the California primary. McCarthy might still win the state. A loss in California would make it difficult for Bobby to win the Democratic nomination in Chicago. And I would not be going there as a member of his California delegation if he lost the state. My moment in time would be lost.

On June 2, 1968, around 10:00 p.m. we learned that Bobby had barely edged out the poet. I watched Bobby raise two fingers in the victory sign on television and then say, "On to Chicago." I learned as a kid the fight song for the University of Chicago: "On Chicago, on Chicago, plunge right through that line, take the ball..." His ending at the Ambassador Hotel that night had this familiarity.

I went out to our Rambler with my sense of destiny. I had called it right. I was going to Chicago! And my candidate was going to be the next president of the United States. I lit up a cigar and turned on the radio, but as I drove away I heard the *pop pop,* then the sound of panic, chaos. *Senator Kennedy has been shot.* The next twenty-four hours I felt the chill of death while we waited for him to die. Marin was wrapped in an early summer fog. My bones ached. Death returned. History was stolen.

Do you remember how we waited for that final, fatal announcement from Dallas in 1963? Bobby lasted longer. But he died, too. Bobby Kennedy would have defeated Richard Nixon. There would not have been an Operation Linebacker; our bombs would not have still been falling on children in Hanoi and Haiphong at Christmas time, for we would have been out of Vietnam much sooner. There would have been no Watergate, for Nixon would never have been the president. Karl Botterman, the pastor of the local Unitarian church, asked me to speak at the Sunday service as a tribute to the dead senator. I stayed up until around 2:00 a.m. on two successive nights, writing out what I could say, to them and to myself, about history being ripped away.

Maybe there were some present that morning who appreciated my realism, but I think most of those who were at the service wanted to hear something more positive, perhaps something about hope and finding some meaning through his death. I saw Bobby Kennedy as irreplaceable. An insignificant man had changed the world with a senseless shot. I felt it a matter of authenticity that we face his senseless death with courage and integrity. Our character depended on it.

As I walked around the Rambler upon reaching the carport of our home, I noticed the Kennedy bumper strip below. I reached down, tore it off, and dropped it in a trashcan. I had dealt with death.

Bobby had won the California primary so the Kennedy delegation still went to Chicago. I went expecting to support the poet, Eugene McCarthy. He had barely lost to Bobby in my state; their goals were compatible. Just after we took off on the flight from the San Francisco airport, Jesse Unruh conducted a poll to find out how many of us wanted to place the name of Senator Ted Kennedy in nomination. Huh? I was the only one who voted no. Were these people crazy? Maybe two hundred people voted. Not only was the kid brother too inexperienced to be the president, he was emotionally distraught due to the death of a third brother. I felt that the California delegation voted as they did because they were unwilling to accept Bobby's death, to take on its nihilism. And, McCarthy was still the enemy for many of them. It bothered me that they could not tear off their Kennedy bumper strips from their cars and go forward.

I had a chance in Chicago to tell Shirley MacLaine just how much I liked her in the film, *Some Came Running*. When I saw the actress at the cocktail party in Chicago I went up to her and introduced myself. She looked beautiful. And I personally received the Shirley MacLaine smile. For a few moments, it was just the two of us. She told me that it was her favorite role. There were a couple of times when I was able to visit with her on the floor of the convention, too. Being aware of her interest in India and mysticism, I let her know I had been a Presbyterian minister. She told me that we would have to talk some time.

When our California delegation heard last-minute campaign speeches off the convention floor by Hubert Humphrey and Eugene McCarthy, I noticed a young man seated next to Shirley. It was her younger brother, Warren Beatty. How could one know that he would, in future years, see himself as a presidential candidate, and be a leader in film and political life?

Humphrey's eyes searched the California delegates for some contact, a sign that he could bridge the gap between the mourning Kennedy delegation and Lyndon Johnson. The Democratic nomination of Hubert Humphrey for president was decided the moment Bobby Kennedy was killed. The convention show was posturing. There were floor fights with Mayor Daley of Chicago screaming at a liberal speaker, Unruh rushing his California delegation abruptly off the floor in a sophomoric protest, etc., and all the while the Texas White House (i.e., Lyndon Johnson) was in control of the nomination. There was no way the philosopher-king, Eugene McCarthy, was going to be the Democratic candidate for president. A delegate from New Jersey told me that they "could not sell McCarthy" in his state. I was educated in Chicago in realpolitik to question the "democratic" process itself.

When the chaplain of presidents, the Reverend Billy Graham, began the invocation at the opening session, I noticed a tall, curly haired

Shirley MacLaine, (*left*); Rafer Johnson *(center, back)*;
and Bill Taylor *(right, front)* at the 1968 Chicago Convention.

fellow who looked up at the evangelist and muttered, "Oh shit." I went over and congratulated him on his theological taste.

I did not become involved in the protests outside the convention hall, where police clubs came down on the heads of McCarthy teenagers.

The morning we checked out of the Hotel LaSalle, I stood for a long period of time next to George Moscone. The California senator would become the mayor of San Francisco; he too would be assassinated.

I sat next to a black newspaper publisher from Oakland on the flight back to San Francisco and he deepened my political education. Do you know how they got out the black vote in Oakland? On flatbed trucks. The publisher described how they would drive up and down the streets, piling black voters onto the trucks, and delivering them to the polls. I viewed this as manipulative, even un-democratic. Today I see it as reality.

Shortly thereafter, I learned that in the birthplace of "democracy," the citizens of ancient Athens were fined if they did not attend the meetings of the assembly and exercise their votes. A rope soaked in red dye was dragged through the marketplace, staining the garments of any truant citizen. No flatbed trucks in Athens in the fifth century B.C., and no pure democracy, either. Shirley MacLaine, being a woman, would not have been able to attend their assembly, let alone vote.

Before I left for Chicago some politically active Marin Democrats were vehement about my not letting Humphrey be nominated. They hated him. When I returned from Chicago, one of these Humphrey-haters called and wanted me to hate Nixon. Tricky Dick was now their anti-Christ, and Hubert was the good guy. I said, "No, thanks."

I spent considerable time writing in my weekly newspaper column about Bobby Kennedy and my experiences in Chicago. In my columns, I questioned direct democracy, qualifying our "democratic" method of government.

My firm, William Taylor & Associates, became better known in the county. And my production with the brokerage firm earned Trish and I a trip to Europe in June of 1969. A good amount of this income was a result of my joining the local Rotary club. My association with business and professional leaders in San Anselmo led to more clients.

Why Rotary? I saw the club rituals as "Mickey Mouse." However, the San Anselmo club offered me the opportunity to meet a variety of interesting people. There were three medical doctors, a lawyer, a couple of seminary professors, a newspaper publisher, a furniture store owner, two dentists, an eye doctor, an architect, the owner of the largest department store in town, a CPA, veterinarian, minister, etc.

It was a men's club then. No women. The humor was rewarding. Phony comments were slaughtered on the spot as one was quickly brought down to earth. This was good for me. The weekly pot shots helped me to see myself as "just another guy."

On one of my business visits to the seminary, Professor Neil Hamilton pulled me into his little office in order to "update" me on theology. Hamilton was one of those bright, young professors, the one who questioned me once about my not having confidence in my own thinking. Once we were in his small office in "the castle," Dr. Hamilton went right to it—"It doesn't matter whether you say, 'yes, God,' or 'no, God;'

what matters is whether you stand with Jesus and cry over Vietnam." I held onto that one.

The newspaper publisher in Rotary, Peter Edwards, was responsible for my weekly column. Edwards was blunt, sharp of the tongue, from a working class family in Wales. While it was only a throwaway paper, over the next thirty-plus years I frequently heard from people that they read it on a regular basis. Peter titled it, "Theology and Politics," and that was the way it was for awhile.

I became far more interested in thinking and writing about politics than in participating in them. Just as I had done in the pulpits in Long Beach and in Texas, I used the column to think out loud. My column was a voice in the marketplace. It seemed that I could not meet a new person without them asking if I was *the* William Taylor who wrote for the paper.

From time to time, I would read in the letters to the editor how I had irritated someone. I never answered these attacks. In March, 1971, Ms. Barbara Boxer attacked me in a letter to the editor of a local newspaper. Accusing me of "preachy prose," she chastised me for my "putting down all those who have firm convictions on any important issue." In some ways, guilty as charged. But I saw Barbara as a demagogue. Her certainty and lack of self-doubt disturbed me.

A seminary professor chastised me when I wrote that a particular self-righteous liberal was not all that different than the right winger he was up against for election. They both claimed a certain ideological purity from opposite ends. I loved having the chance to share my thoughts on a weekly basis. And I enjoyed the attention, even being at the center of controversy. One week I took on *Jonathan Livingston Seagull*. I saw this lofty flight of a bird as separating us from the earth and its harsh realities; it was Gnostic, a fantasy.

I found myself still thinking about Lou, the packer, and Mary, up there in the mountains; they were living where they wanted to live. I was down in the marketplace. And it felt right. I went to Chicago, met Shirley MacLaine, wrote newspaper columns, visited with theologians, and was making enough money to do what I wanted to do.

Travel : The Gift of Patricia

B EFORE THE SIXTIES closed, there was another monumental event. In June of 1969, Trish and I flew to London for a four-day business conference. This came at the time when the public passion for buying stocks was beginning to falter and the markets began a serious decline. The financial sessions in London had intensity for me. Several of the speakers who addressed us were mutual fund managers. It felt great to be part of an earthy profession. These were professional men with intelligence. I found them blunt, honest, mature. I liked being seated in the midst of some of the leading producers in the industry. I did, however, think that it was ostentatious when one of the owners of a new mutual fund company arrived in a limousine. I liked him, however. He said he knew the stock market was "near its bottom" because of the level of sickness he was feeling. Unfortunately, we were years away from the end of the down market.

We had ten days before the charter would return. Trisha had been in Europe five years before so I let her choose where we would spend those ten days. Thanks to Zeus, Apollo, and Athena, she chose Greece. I had quoted Plato in a paper in seminary, but I really knew nothing about him, or Greece. Some of you surely saw the movie, *Never On Sunday*. The motion picture was about a prostitute who sought to humanize a Western tourist. Wally Cox played the American "Boy Scout" type who wanted to intellectualize with the prostitute, Melina Mercouri, about ancient Greece. While he wanted to think Greece, she wanted him to feel Greece.

Trisha felt Greece. She had seen *Zorba the Greek* a number of times, and read the book by Nikos Kazantzakis. Zorba was passionate, spontaneous, natural. In the movie, Alan Bates played a writer who lived in his head, careful to not expose his emotions. Anthony Quinn not only played Zorba, he became Zorba. Some will remember when Zorba said to the writer, "Come on boss, dance." Zorba felt Greece.

Trisha's passion for Greece was of music, the sun, blue skies, the sea, dancing, the food, retsina, archaeology. While I reflected on Greece with a book, Patricia dove into the blue Aegean.

We took the bus into Athens from the airport. I was intimidated. A seemingly harmless older man picked up our bags when we got off in Syntagma Square and walked us over to the Pan Hotel. Not the expensive King George or Grande Bretagne on the other side of the square. Many a spy story placed the characters in their bars. We were given a room near the top of a very narrow building. I was edgy. The height bothered me. Down in the streets of the city, I was xenophobic. The military junta was in power in 1969 and the dramatic, intense, revolutionary music of Nikos Theodorakis was stirring audiences in the Western world. Theodorakis composed the score for the movie, Z, while he was in exile in Paris. The world knows him best for his masterpiece, *Zorba*.

I felt inspired when I climbed up the slick marble to the Parthenon one night. I knew that Socrates, Plato, and Aristotle had touched the same surface over twenty-three hundred years before me. Athens became the center of my world that night, a new philosophical home. Socrates was the prime figure for me. Plato and Aristotle were only names then. Like Jesus, Socrates never wrote down his thoughts. Plato, his student, recorded in writing the probing questions that Socrates asked in the marketplace immediately below the Acropolis.

I found Greece sensual, too. The warmth of the faithful summer sun, the emotional music, a light blue sky over the crystal clear water every single day. But it was the staggering intellectual contributions of Greece that claimed me. Their fifth and fourth century B.C. philosophers and writers of tragedy (e.g., Aeschylus, Sophocles, Euripides) are unique. How could one not be swept up by the Greek architecture and sculpture? Unlike Jerusalem, Athens became man-centered. Sex was not dirty; the human body was admired. Greece was the antithesis to Christianity in this way.

In 1969, when there was a full moon, you could climb up onto the great rock in the evening. The famous temple was not roped off like it is today. We were able to lie down on our backs within the Temple of

Athena and look up through the roofless sanctuary at a glittering array of stars with nobody else around. This view was unique, glorious, forever.

I was ready for the symbolic power of Greece because Christianity and "Jerusalem" had betrayed me. Greece was delightfully pagan, ornery, and playful. Even the gods had fun. Christianity doesn't laugh. There was no place for Jeanne's death in Christianity. Belief in an afterlife would deny it and be cruel. My source of power came through the senselessness of her sudden loss of life. It was definitely time for Athens and the base, corrupt, dishonest, deep-thinking Greeks.

My athletic dreams had been somewhat mystical. I wonder if an athlete can have it otherwise. My early visions of the ministry were supported by my compulsive belief that I had to be a minister. While I told people that one can be human and religious at the same time, I was still personally relying on fate. The morals of the stoic Jesus still carried some weight with me when I went to Greece with Patricia, but a personal universe where God cares for each individual ended with the death scream in Mammoth.

We left Jess and Cory with friends when we flew to London and this was very painful for me. On the airplane flight over the Atlantic, I felt waves of angst, sweaty palms, separation from the earth. But this was the price of foreign travel for me at that time.

I returned to San Anselmo from London and Greece with an international image. Very few people in Marin had traveled to Greece and some felt that it took courage to go there. The business conference in London enhanced my investment image. At the same time I was viewed as being independent, not the usual salesman. The fact that I was part of the notorious Chicago convention still has an impact on people. So my need to gain attention, and clients, was well fed as we entered the 1970s.

My successful transition from the ministry to the marketplace drew clergymen to my firm. First as clients, then as business associates. Six of them came to work with me. When one of the co-owners of our national firm met them at the initial William Taylor & Associates conference at Lake Tahoe, he told me afterwards that he had never seen a more impressive group of young men.

Often when I met someone new, I'd hear, "Do you know who...?" Yes, I knew. While I may have given up on Moses, my appearance suggested that I looked like him. Or better, like the actor who played Moses. Charleton Heston was not known as an arch-conservative at the time, so this comparison did not make me uncomfortable.

Over time these comparisons became infrequent. But one day I was eating lunch in a Chinese restaurant near our offices in San Anselmo. "Ben, Ben Hur!" I heard a woman say. She was seated behind me, up against a wall. I knew of this woman, of her unmeasured behavior, even psychotic condition. She kept the town on edge. I ignored her calls. But when I heard, "Where's your chariot?" I turned around and smiled. Fortunately she left things at that.

William Taylor & Associates had a second business conference and this time we gathered up the coast at the Heritage House in Mendocino. The lodge overlooks an active sea where waves crash and spray dances off the rocks below. The conference, however, was spoiled by guilt. There was such anxiety over market losses that all but one of my associates would leave the business shortly. The guilt load was just too heavy. I had to "leave the dead to bury the dead" in order to survive that monumental decline in stock prices. Once people lose money, you lose their trust. Your business relationship is usually over. I had to possess the strength to take on the guilt, and move on. What were financial losses compared to Jeanne's loss of life? Unfortunately, my ministers carried too much guilt. Only one of them stayed in the business. Bob lived in Colorado and he joined another firm for logistical reasons.

I became used to hearing at sales conferences: "How do you get away with it?" They meant my beard, and sometimes my not wearing a tie. Trish was behind the beard. It was okay to have one in Marin. An iconoclastic business image in the San Francisco area could help a practice.

"The" Dr. Schoenberger called and wanted to know if I had a "good investment" that would also reduce his taxes. He made it clear that he would never hold me responsible for an investment. He would not keep his word.

Freudian psychoanalysts do not form friendships or business relationships with former patients. Ted told me that I was his "only exception." Why did this orthodox Freudian choose me? I was flattered, thrilled, still in awe of my psychoanalyst when this post-therapy relationship began. When Trish and I were going to visit Los Angeles, he invited us to his home for dinner. It turned out to be a wonderful evening. Ted, his wife Elsebeth, their sons, Steve and Tommy, and an older daughter, Karen, were all there. I was very impressed with how they listened to the words that they spoke to one another at the dinner table. In the words was the person.

Ted was funny. The one who listened to me from 1963 to 1966 was suddenly an entertaining, delightful friend. Both he and Elsebeth said several times that they found me "so human." My liberal views appealed to them. Thus began a deep and lengthy friendship.

Trish and I took the two boys with us to Lake Tahoe and Mammoth during the summer. I continued to love being together with my family. Late one afternoon, shortly after swimming, Trisha noticed that her wedding ring had slipped off her finger. The one from Farmers Market. The search had to be postponed until the next morning due to darkness. With little hope, we began traversing back and forth in the beautiful clear blue water. One could see the bottom clearly, even in five feet of water. But all I saw was sand. Recovering the gold ring with the unusual crossing patterns we had chosen together was extremely unlikely. Losing it felt like a threat to our relationship. The disappearance came at a time when Trish and I were still fighting for our marriage.

Hold it. I touched something with my toe. I dove down and clutched an object under the sand. It was the ring.

We drove south from Tahoe to Mammoth. I did not say anything when we passed the lodge where Jeanne died. This was my first trip back. Patricia and I rode a couple of horses up toward the Rim where we could look out over the lakes. Leslie, one of the Roeser daughters, took care of Jess and Cory back at the pack station. When we were well up into the forest I suggested to Trish that we make love. Nice memory!

Family Trips

MY POLITICAL EDUCATION continued when the people who ran the Democratic political campaigns in my county asked me to be co-chairman for two U.S. Senate races. John Tunney, the first candidate I backed, did not show up to speak to a packed auditorium of supporters. I was told that his meetings in the City with major financial supporters usurped his Marin County appearance. Congressman George Brown, the other candidate I was endorsing, seemed more like a teddy bear than a Washington politician. Respected for his conscience, Brown did not make political deals. Therefore, he was not a part of any significant legislation.

My connections with the Democratic Party ended when I backed a former sea captain for a non-partisan state office, unaware of how much liberals hated him. My good friend Gene Burris recruited me to help this Kett. Gene stood fully behind his character, so I lent him my name. In politics, every move has to be calculated, measured for its political impact. Power brokers play chess with people. You cannot afford to cross certain people because you might need their support at a later date. I was not playing the game.

In 1970, Patricia found us a home in the hills of Sleepy Hollow. We paid $41,000 for a three-bedroom house overlooking a quiet residential community. The hill behind our house has since been declared open space, a protected area for wildlife and for recreational use.

When my firm presented new products to its national sales force, I paid special attention to the quality of the people who would be running the investment. I believed I was able to read people well and to identify those of high ethical principles and intelligence. Back then, I tended to respect anyone from Harvard or Stanford, and I did not allow for the possibility that even academic professors could be bought. Not to imply that they were immoral—they just wanted to make some big money and see their ideas work in the marketplace. This meant they turned to firms like my broker dealer for funding. With the stock markets being victimized by successive years of losses, people were receptive to buying alternative products.

My mutual fund broker had been sold to some wealthy, bright entrepreneurs from the Harvard and Yale law schools who provided products that increased my income considerably. These innovative investment vehicles were guinea pigs. They were not shams; there was no fraud. But "guinea pigs" carry a higher risk than conventional products.

Part of my financial success was related to the business instincts of a new friend, Jerry Ledzinski. Jerry, a graduate of West Point, was decorated for courage in Vietnam. He was building up a lush practice in Carmel and it was his image of integrity and his marketing skills that enabled me to create the income that provided my family with the funds to travel.

We went to Europe as a family in 1972. Cory's soft little hand tightly held mine as we walked through the Tuilleries in Paris. Later in the morning, feeling the weight of jet lag for the first time in his brief life, the cute little blond fell asleep on a bench in the Impressionist museum. The baby was now seven.

In Germany, we picked up a new 250C Mercedes, drove it over the Alps, through Italy and down the Yugoslavian coast to Greece. Thanks to Patricia, I had discovered this model at a showroom in San Rafael. I loved its body style.

Off the Yugoslavian coast, I watched Trish playing with Jess and Cory in the beautifully colored Adriatic Sea. This, of course, was of monumental satisfaction for me. It felt like home when we entered Greece. It was not too long before we came upon the archaeological ruins where Alexander the Great grew up. As we drove slowly past the site I thought of how the young Alexander could not have been any prouder of a new chariot than I was of my Byzantine gold Mercedes.

When we arrived on the island of Corfu, the new Mercedes made an immediate impression. Shortly after arriving and checking into a hotel, I received a phone call from Helen, the mother of Spiro (a Greek friend whom I had met in the insurance business). She told us that she was coming right over to the hotel to take us to their villa to stay. We would be their guests for over a week. Trish and I were given a warmly decorated guest bedroom. The maids cleaned each day, leaving the scent of garlic behind. We drove to three wonderful, different beaches while on Corfu that week, but we did not discover much in the way of archaeology.

My being a member of the Kennedy delegation in Chicago was not lost on our host family, or their friends. Jack and Jackie Kennedy were seen as royalty in Greece. Bobby's death completed the Greek tragedy. We left Corfu excited about being invited to return to the island the next summer. They told us they would host a Kennedy party so their friends could meet this delegate from the Chicago convention.

In the remote mountain village called Kosovo, I noticed Jess and Cory watching television with some Greek children. The set was mounted on a pole in the small town square. Older men with shepherd crooks were sitting at their nightly "reserved" locations along a wall. The Greek children, along with Jess and Cory, were watching *I Dream of Jeannie*. I thought of Jeanne and what she was missing.

People remained curious about why I left the ministry. Behind this frequently asked question was the big one, "Do you believe in God?" The Presbytery in Texas wrote and wanted to know whether I planned to retain my ordination. I did not appreciate the formal request to either affirm or reject my church office. I told them to drop me. Then they wanted to register me with a congregation. I was not even given the option of limbo or hell. I reluctantly said to release me to the Presbyterian church in San Anselmo. I wasn't worried about where I stood with God.

Jesus was still somewhat special for me. His parables and sayings retained some power. Jesus said, "Where can the son of man place his head?" Is this not a question that any person who seeks an authentic life must ask themselves at times? As a young man, I had cathected on

Jesus. You do not unglue such a placement casually. Does that mean that I was still a Christian? You could say that I remained one because I still held some Christian values. But I was not a believer in a personal God who intervened in history. And I did not believe I needed Jesus to save me from my sins.

I was at a cocktail party in Scottsdale, Arizona, when my insurance wholesaler surprised me with his joke about Jesus. I thought such humor was reserved for theologians: those who understood that God had a sense of humor. On the floor of this mundane insurance convention, my wholesaler and friend told me this hilarious joke: "Jesus is standing at a table, his disciples seated around it. He breaks off pieces of bread and tells them, 'This is my body, broken for you; eat this and you become me.' Then he lifts up the cup of red wine, and says, 'This is my blood, the new covenant; drink this and you become me.' Peter is embarrassed. He reaches up and tugs Jesus' sleeve, saying, 'Sit down Jesus, you're shitfaced again.'"

This does not mean that I did not feel guilt

A friend and client asked me what I attributed my success to, in that my career began with considerable investment trauma. There was a lengthy and agonizing down market in stocks between 1969 and 1974, then consequences for some of those alternative-type positions either formed or blessed by my New York firm. I gave the question some thought and then answered that it was because I was able to let go of many clients, move on to new people. I stayed with anyone who showed me a measure of trust. But I concluded that there were others who could not move forward with me. This does not mean that I did not feel guilt. Guilt remained, but I was able to act in my interests nonetheless.

We returned to the villa on Corfu the next summer. At the Kennedy party, I was the living relic from the Chicago convention. There was a new wrinkle in the sheets, however: Jacqueline Kennedy had married Aristotle Onassis. I had a hard time placing them in bed together. But what did I know about power and wealth? How does a woman follow up being married to Jack Kennedy?

While driving across northern Greece, we spent a night in Thessaloniki. In the morning, I went out into the busy streets of the large city and began asking for a bookstore. We had decided to go to Istanbul and I needed historical information. In English. I had come a long way since those first couple of trips when I felt vertigo if I was separated from Patricia. I asked Greeks along the street, "poo-EE-nay vib-LEE-o?" *Where is book?* I take great liberties with foreign languages. After a couple of requests, I was directed to a store with books. In it I found a copy of *The Fall of Constantinople* in English. Now we could go to Istanbul. Our family trips always found us with books. Trisha made sure that the boys were well supplied too. Jess read an enormous number of pages.

The Greeks still proudly refer to Istanbul as "Constantinople," even though they lost the city, five hundred years before, to the Turks. Istanbul carried a foreboding image for me: Moslems cutting off the heads of their enemies, displaying them from the entrances to their cities; harem girls obeying the sexual whims of the Sultan. The id was not held in check.

My knowledge of the Ottoman Empire was close to zero. I did not know that some of the sultans could be tolerant after a conquest, not require people of other religions to convert to Islam. Nor did I know about the Islamic Golden Age of poetry and science that came forth before the West experienced the Renaissance. I carried the same fear and prejudices toward Moslems that most people in the Western world continue to this day.

We stopped in several towns before we reached the Turkish border. Our best type of day in Greece would include a visit to an archaeological site in the morning, lunch at a beach taverna, followed by swimming in the blue sea. Trish would swim with the boys, snorkel, explore the underwater world made so vivid by the marvelously clear water. I would enter from time to time, float, then go back to a book or my portable typewriter. I felt refreshed, even baptized by what was be-

On the morning of my fortieth birthday, I felt anger in Istanbul; in the evening, I felt love for Patricia.

coming an annual ritual.

At the border, we were told that Greek insurance for the rental car did not cover us in Turkey, but that we could buy coverage in a town some 100 kilometers up the road. Decision time. Should we forget Istanbul? Not our travel style. In the town that was supposed to provide us with insurance, I was ignored when I asked for help. No one would even speak to me. It was on to Istanbul without coverage. Do you know what the traffic is like in Istanbul? It approaches Naples in its chaos. We were greeted with dented '42 Chryslers and other discarded American models from the 1940s. Traffic lanes did not exist. I felt elated when we finally pulled up in front of the Hilton. All I wanted was insurance. The Blue Mosque, sultan's palace, a view of the Bosphorus, could wait.

The Hilton had an insurance desk. The insurance would cost about $500 because you could only buy coverage for a year. Our budget could not handle the extra expense. I left the car in the parking lot over the next couple of days while we walked around Istanbul. Then I would face the perilous drive to the Greek border.

I woke up on my fortieth birthday very angry. It hit me that I was halfway through life. I did not think about my birthday in this way before I awakened that morning. I just woke up with the realization that I was really mortal. And this meant that I would some day cease to exist. I was very angry for a time that day. Patricia took me to a very nice birthday dinner in the main Hilton dining room. I had made the transition. Fifty, sixty, seventy would be easy compared to forty. Existence had dealt with me!

The most precious moment of our family life on the Greek beaches came a year or two later on Crete. We were out on the eastern tip of the large island when I saw Cory running toward Patricia. I was seated at an outdoor table of a taverna, shaded by palm trees. The thin, long trunks told of the continent of Africa immediately to the south of the large island. As little Cory ran toward Patricia, I could hear him calling, "*Mee-TER-ah moo, mee-TER-ah moo.*" In Greek, this means "my mother." Tears filled my eyes. Little Cory had a mother.

The national conferences held by my investment firm continued to

Cory yelled out, "my mother" in Greek on a Greek beach.

give me a sense of stature. I mingled with the best in the business. Then, upon returning home from New York, Florida, Colorado, Arizona, or Hawaii, I would inform my clients about the professional talent that was assembled. My favorite and biggest investment weapon was the Vietnam Special Forces officer from West Point, the one who was developing his own practice in plush Carmel. We first came in contact when my firm asked me to call this Jerry Ledzinski to recruit him for our company. I was flattered that New York had chosen me for this task. Loaded with charisma, this son of a West Virginia coal miner was surprisingly comfortable with wealth. Jerry was genuine and down to earth. He became the star producer for the company. Everyone wanted to sit next to him at the conferences; perhaps his sales ability would rub off on them?

Jerry sat by me. He felt comfortable with me because I was not in awe of him. I teased Jerry, called him "the god." He was of enormous help to me with business perspective and the passion to place certain products. I sold off his enthusiasm and charisma.

Jerry Ledzinski and I agreed that the selling world lacked integrity. While my marketplace guru was a believing Catholic, we could still talk frankly about "God, or no God." Fluid conversations between us resulted. Jerry was the number one celebrity of our brokerage firm due to his sales and war record. I was their national sports star who had helped build the company through my early production.

My interest in locating exactly where monumental thinkers—those who greatly influenced history—slept, walked, died; was not confined solely to Greece. Switzerland is usually seen as the place to observe magnificent Alpine peaks, hike, eat cheese, and yodel. True. But for me, tiny Switzerland also burst forth with Nietzsche, Wagner, Einstein, Lenin, Calvin, and Jung.

Nietzsche was up there in the Alps. The ascetic prophet of the late nineteenth century lived in a small boarding house in the village of Sils Maria, just down the road from St. Moritz. Today, St. Moritz is a playground for the very rich, receiving jets with royalty aboard, but only a short distance away is a village that receives holy pilgrimages to an iconoclast of staggering controversy.

Friedrich Nietzsche lived in a small room at the top of the stairway in that boarding house. The village was his Alpine home every spring and summer in the 1880s. Then the snow and ice would chase him down to Turin, Nice, or Genoa. Tortured by ill health, Nietzsche pondered the questions of existence as he hiked in the forests and along the lakeshores that were at his doorstep. The "retired" professor of philology and philosophy from the University of Basel thought out his terrifying responses to Plato, Socrates, Christianity, German-ism, and Wagner-ism in one of the most beautiful locations on earth. He told of a certain respect for Buddhism and the Old Testament, but he slaughtered Plato and his Socrates. Christianity was a sick, destructive, dishonest, anti-life religion for Nietzsche. He did not just ridicule the faith of countless millions, he annihilated it. He warned of the militant Germans as they marched to the increasingly war-oriented pomp of his former father figure, Richard Wagner. It was Nietzsche who condemned anti-Semitism.

Nietzsche screeched like an eagle out over Europe with, "Now it is time to love the earth." Nietzsche informed me that my health, success, and freedom were due to my overthrowing the Christianity in me. What Schoenberger began, Nietzsche finished. (Nietzsche is most famous for warning Europe about the "death of God." Few understand what he meant by this. He saw the foundation of Western values collapsing and the resulting vulnerability of weak humans who could be recruited and rounded up for destructive ideologies.)

I ran alone one afternoon above Sils Maria. The day was idyllic. The trees in the forests and around the lakes are the highest in Europe. It is thought that Sils Maria is the perfect location because it is forested but also high in elevation. As I returned to the village along a narrow path next to a swift-flowing stream, I suddenly felt that Nietzsche's Zarathustra was standing in the shadows behind me. Before I turned, the image of him wearing a tall hat with a wide brim pulled down over a portion of his face flashed before me. A cape fell off one shoulder. When I did look, my fantasy was not there. I continued down the narrow trail but Zarathustra was not through with me. As I crossed the meadow filled with flowers, before reaching a paved street, he challenged me to go more deeply into myself, to personally take on existence. This was not an academic exercise. I was being given the chilling challenge to leap into the abyss. Sigmund Freud once said that no one has ever gone more deeply into their psyche than Nietzsche. Quite an endorsement!

It was not easy finding the address in the charming Swiss city of Berne where Albert Einstein recorded his theory of relativity. My prime motivation in searching for the apartment of the most popular scientist of the twentieth century wasn't only related to physics. It had even more to do with the word "relativity," and its place in philosophy, existentialism. I felt that people too easily avoided a struggle with the responsibility of making moral judgments, hiding behind the conclusion that all things are relative. Words like "justice" and "truth" raise absolute questions for me. I didn't appreciate Einstein's conclusion that "God didn't throw dice" in constructing the universe. What of Auschwitz? The problem here for me was not Einstein's certainty related to physics, but that he inferred the existence of a personal God. For if there is an active God who sometimes rescues some, and other times disregards others, then this God has to answer for Auschwitz.

Tourist groups gather 200 meters up the street from Einstein's apartment in Berne in order to watch in wonder as a mechanical bear and other figurines come out and make appearances on the face of the large town clock each hour. On my numerous visits to Berne, I never saw any group of people gathered in front of Einstein's apartment. This bothered me. Were tourists unaware that Einstein's apartment is just down the street? When I traveled, I sought to enhance my own awareness of history and time by visiting engaging locations. In future trips with youth, I wanted to share my knowledge of these locations with others—just as, in the ministry, I sought to bring the seminary to the pew.

Our base hotel in the old town of Zurich was a regular summer home for our family. Just up one of the narrow passageways from the hotel was the apartment where Lenin stayed before he raced back to Russia to lead the revolution in 1917. History rushed by while tourists shopped.

I had a feast in tiny Switzerland with these historical giants. As I walked around old Zurich, Lenin or Einstein could appear (the physicist left Berne to teach at the University of Zurich). Carl Jung lived in an expensive home along the northern shore of Lake Zurich. Freud came to see him before they went to war with one another and they rode by carriage along the quay just in front of the hotel where we stayed seventy years later.

The *San Francisco Chronicle* announced a lecture at Cal, Berkeley about a Greek archaeological site. Trish and I decided to go. The archaeologist who gave the lecture was Dr. Stephen Miller. The summer after Trish and I heard the lecture, we went to visit Steve at Nemea. Nemea is close to the classical sites of Mycenae, Argos, and Corinth. The ancient track was still buried when Trish and our boys walked on top of it in 1974. The entrance tunnel was filled with centuries of dirt. Several years later, when Dr. Miller reached the ancient starting grooves where athletes placed their bare feet 2300 years before, he told me that I was the first person he thought of. This was a rather nice sport link up for me.

Dr. Miller was in favor of my writing a guidebook on ancient Athens for the same reason I felt that I should write one—there weren't any that put the traveler in touch with the vital locations in that city. I did not care how many columns supported the roof of the Parthenon. I wanted to know what the symbols on the goddess Athena inside the temple represented. What did the Greeks of the fifth century B.C. really believe about Zeus, Apollo, Athena, Pan? I wanted to locate where Socrates taught Plato, go to the cemetery where Pericles delivered his famous funeral speech. Steve told me that I would have to write the travel book because university professors were required to publish academic texts only. It would be up to me to connect the scholarship with the historical sites in Greece.

Jess and Cory did not spend their summers watching endless cartoons on television. They did not run off every day to play with their friends. Instead, they traveled with us overseas and we were together as a family—at meals, archaeological sites, and in the Aegean Sea.

One time, in the village of Zermatt, Switzerland, the four of us took a somewhat risky hike up to the Matterhorn hutte at 10,600 feet. The winter snow had left considerable ice on the trail. At one stage, we worked our way carefully along a very thin path with a pale blue ice-covered lake some 500 feet straight down. The edge was only two feet from where we placed our boots at times. I held onto Cory's hand and was careful with my trick knee. These were lasting family moments.

I whacked little Cory across the head when he lost interest in hearing me read a portion of the Pericles funeral speech on a hot afternoon in the ancient cemetery in Athens. Cory was nine, maybe ten. According to Dr. Miller, we were likely standing within 200 meters of where the famous Athenian orator delivered what has been proclaimed the greatest speech in history. The guide books did not contain this kind of information. I wanted to be close to where history took place, to visualize what happened at a specific location. One needed an informed archaeologist for this kind of information. I had one.

I wrote a good part of the book, *Athenian Odyssey*, on the 1976 family trip. Trisha was not too happy about spending thirteen straight days and nights on the island of Santorini, but I cannot think of a more dramatic or inspiring setting for writing a book on ancient Greece. White and blue homes rest precariously on the slope that descends from the village of Thera to the deep blue water of the caldera. When I asked the hotel manager how he lives with the threat of another eruption from the volcano that peeks up from under the vast sea, he responded with, "One day at a time." The last eruption was in 1926. Our room at the Atlantis Hotel had a small balcony that enabled me to look out over the enormous body of water as I wrote. The fresh morning air was even Alpine. It was there that I assembled my guide to the glittering Golden Age of ancient Athens for travelers.

Late one summer afternoon in Athens, I suggested that Jess and I run a mile together around the track of the 1896 Olympic Games. Not a race, just an afternoon run in a very special stadium. Jess was a year from beginning high school. I was forty-three. This was the stadium that the Olympic Games returned to in 1896. A Roman emperor had closed them down in the name of Christianity sixteen hundred years before. The running surface in 1976 was made of gray cinders, just like my practice track at USC. Two ancient herms stood on the turn at the closed end of the stadium near a tunnel from which the athletes and officials entered.

Jess and I ran easily together for three laps, then on the backstretch of the final one, the young deer took off. As we approached the final turn, I realized that I was not going to catch him. You can see the Acropolis as you go around that tight curve. As Jess sprinted away, I thought of the son surpassing the father. Then it hit me: the Theater of Dionysus is at the foot of the south wall of the Acropolis less than a mile away from where we were running. There, the play *Oedipus Rex* by Sophocles was presented for the first time! This was twenty-four hundred years before Jess surpassed his father. I smiled as I trailed my

Jess surpasses his father on the Olympic track in Athens

son to the finish. Jess was willing to take his dad, and I had a son who could run!

The boys played well together on those wonderful summer trips. At times, Trish and I would have dinner alone during our travels. We saved money that way, for Jess and Cory were happy to stay in their hotel room, eat breakfast cereals, and play with their toy Greek soldiers. During the day, besides swimming with their mother, they engaged in endless soccer, sometimes with Greek boys. That was special for them and for us. It was gratifying to watch them making friends.

Cory could be innovative and funny. In Wengen, Switzerland, he dressed himself up in a makeshift costume and suddenly appeared in a quiet, rather stuffy hotel lobby, looking like a Martian. Our son just popped out of the elevator with a flimsy antenna wire circling over his head. Cory could really tease his older brother. One morning I heard them playing soldiers outside a bedroom window and Jess, as the senior army officer, was inspecting Cory, who was standing at attention. Upon receiving his orders, he saluted Jess and said, "Okay, five star nothing."

These family moments during those summers throughout the 1970s were wonderful. There were the many hikes in the Alps when we carried lunches of nuts, bananas, delicious strawberry yogurt, peanut butter and jelly or salami sandwiches. All four of us enjoyed the *pa-go-TOE* (ice cream) in Greece.

I felt enormous fulfillment when Steve Miller gave me permission to use the following endorsement on the back cover of my book:

"All too few leave Greece with the feeling that there is little significance to be derived from the old marble. Such disappointment is due partly to the fact that very few Americans have a significant background in the history and literature of ancient Greece which has been common since the Renaissance. *Athenian Odyssey* cannot fully solve these two problems, but it can help to correct them. It provides a background that is necessarily incomplete, but which helps to breathe life into those old stones. It also provides a balanced picture of the vices as well as the virtues of fifth century Athens. *Athenian Odyssey* will be stimulating and challenging to the thoughtful reader."

Gulp. My book can help to correct the lack of appreciation and understanding of the significance of ancient Greece? Can "breathe life into those old stones"?

Dr. Stephen Miller was one of America's leading Greek archaeologists. His praise made me feel that I was a part of the academic world, as a writer of Greek history. This was incredible. Life was good.

With the publication of *Athenian Odyssey*, and the favorable reaction I received from travelers, I felt that I was on my way to becoming a respected travel writer. *Athenian Odyssey* sold out immediately at the Cal bookstore. My publisher/editor wrote to the highly respected Artemis Press in Zurich, Switzerland, to explore with them whether they would publish *Athenian Odyssey* in foreign languages. When we returned to Zurich after our annual summer joy in Greece, there was a phone message for me at the hotel. I was told by a woman representing Artemis that the answer was yes. They did decide to publish my book in European languages. In addition to this fantastic development, a distributor in Greece ordered five hundred copies. One of their accounts was the Hilton in Athens. My publisher told me that I had "many books" in me. I thought I was on my way. Just like at UCLA that fantastic day when I blew the relay race wide open, or right after my final sermon at St. Stephen when so many people were excited.

Each time I arrive at one of those significant moments in life, it is taken away. Just as travelers to Greece were reporting back to me how much they appreciated and admired my book, my American publisher declared bankruptcy! The royalties would never be paid. A second major disappointment arrived by mail. Artemis Press informed me that my book was a victim of budget cuts. Another important image was stolen from me.

Part IV: Gift of a Lifetime

An unfinished track life

A MARIN LAWYER told the local high school track coach that I should be recruited to coach. Warren Perry, having attended Occidental College, and Cal Berkeley in the 1950s, was aware of the USC track image during the Golden Years of the sport. This coaching opportunity came at the time when Jess was entering high school. My "young deer" from the track of the 1896 Olympics became one of my runners. I did not realize it at the beginning, but I was returning to my unfinished track life. While I still received recognition for having run for USC, my unresolved "what if" syndrome was toxic. People wanted to know if I had run in the Olympics, or set a world record. Thus the search for my track worth was thrust upon me. It had been largely dormant for over twenty years.

In addition to the track questions, people continued to ask me about leaving the ministry, religion, God. I adjusted the Christian metaphors to secular concepts and words. Is Luther's experience of grace different from what is experienced for others in psychoanalysis? Luther accepted God's acceptance; the psychoanalytic patient accepts themself. This power of being does not discriminate against the religious or non-religious. I could not believe in a God who plays around with nature, or football games. I did not see how Rotarians can thank God in prayer at their luncheons for a beautiful day, and neglect holding God responsible for natural disasters. Life after death? Jeanne was dead. There is no other acceptable conclusion. I would fail her if I rationalized her early death.

A Canadian company was willing to take over the distributions of *Athenian Odyssey* and royalties began to arrive. Not much money, but evidence that my book was in circulation, alive in the marketplace. I obtained an agent, Linda Allen. She went after contracts for a travel series. Rome, Vienna, Berlin, and Zurich were potential locations to write about. At that time, Jacqueline Kennedy was an editor for Doubleday; she wrote to Linda that I had "pertinent credentials" and "a fascinating background." But their "budget" prevented them from investing in a series at the time.

The investment business was not enough for me

Track workouts split my business days. I begin work early in the morning, and closed the office down at noon. Track was a diversion, a chance to balance my day. The investment business was not enough for me.

Twenty-six years after I won my first individual conference championship in Bakersfield, I returned with a high school girls' mile relay team for the California state finals. This track meet is almost always the most competitive one for prep athletes in America. Two of my girls had never run high school track before the 1978 season. A third liked softball as well as or better than track. Only the tall, lanky senior had impressive credentials. We trained for months with the goal of making it to the state finals. I ran the workouts with them. At age forty-four, I could even pull them along.

I was not intimidated by this high level of competition. I drew on my experience at two state meets to help the girls. Eight other teams were in the mile relay final. As race time approached, my tension increased so much that I could not stay seated and kept moving around. Over ten thousand fans awaited the exciting relay races that would end the championship meet. Who would have thought that my skinny, frightened freshman girl would be the one to thrill the crowd the most on that warm evening in Bakersfield? She moved us all the way up into third place as she roared past all but two teams on the backstretch of the second lap. The next two girls held this position and my team placed third in the California state final. Not a bad coaching beginning!

We jogged around the track under the sprinklers after the crowd had left the stadium. The five of us had accomplished something very unique. At the track banquet a few nights later, I told Jenny and Jenny, Lisa, and Lori that I would take them with me to Europe the next summer.

On one of our last family trips together in the seventies, Patricia wanted a week alone in Paris. This would split us up. How would I handle separation anxiety? What if she met other men? Trisha taught me to trust. What else could I do? I concluded that I could torture myself or I could trust her. Over the years I have chosen to trust her.

While Trisha went off to Paris, the boys and I headed for West Berlin. We made a brief stop in Nuremberg in order to locate the parade ground where those huge Nazi banners were once displayed by powerful searchlights. He was there—the monster of the twentieth century, Adolph Hitler. Next we stopped in the peaceful community of Bayreuth; the opera house there still annually receives pilgrims from all over the world devoted to Richard Wagner. Later we visited West and East Berlin and viewed the mound over Hitler's bunker between the walls. I impressed on Jess and Cory the evil of the man who was responsible for the death of millions of people.

Berlin was a divided city in 1978. The western wall displayed fresh death wreaths that identified where people had been killed trying to escape. One afternoon in West Berlin, Jess and I took off on a run through the Tiergarten, running down the wide, smooth paths toward the ominous wall. The final moments of World War II in Europe had been fought where we were running. When we reached the wall, Jess and I swung to the right at the Brandenburg Gate toward Checkpoint Charlie. We continued on the thin path, gliding along with unusual energy. On the other side of the western wall was "no man's land." And under a mound, the covered headquarters of Adolph Hitler, the place where he shot himself. For me, on that run, Evil was on the other side of the wall.

Jess had recently set the school freshman/sophomore mile record and I had spent a season training with those swift girls. We passed a bombed out building just off the path; over the wall I could see the upper portions of the drab apartment buildings I remembered from *The Spy Who Came in from the Cold*. In the movie she does not make it. Richard Burton could only watch her die helplessly.

As Jess and I approached Checkpoint Charlie, we noticed an East German guard tower. The soldiers wore those distinctive helmets that extend down over the ears. Jess told me that one of the guards in the tower kept his machine gun trained on us as we ran below. Suddenly the thin path delivered us right in-between Checkpoint Charlie and the East German customs shack. U.S. soldiers were to our right, East German border guards to our left. We were in-between the barriers in "no man's land."

We kept running. Jess said that the East German soldier in the tower continued to follow us with his machine gun until we were through the passageway. I could almost feel the bullets ripping into my back at any second. As it turned out, we were no big deal.

Gift of a lifetime begins

In the summer of 1979, I took the four girls of the mile relay team, plus six other members of the Drake track team to Europe. I called this adventure Arête West. On this first trip, we hiked in the Alps in Switzerland and we ran in eight track meets.

Since that initial trip, I have taught and led Arête West trips every other year to this day. Rather early on, I began to emphasize not just running, but also thinking. The students are required to attend seminars every other week for nine months prior to lift off. Then we spend about five weeks exploring five to seven countries per trip. Whether or not we race in meets, we always find special locations to run, including the ancient tracks at Olympia, Delphi, Nemea; through the park in Athens to the 1896 Olympic Stadium, even through Swiss Alpine forests where Nietzsche walked.

I had dreamed of running for the U.S. on the summer tours in Europe. Small clusters of outstanding American athletes were chosen to travel from city to city in Europe and compete. Ernie Shelton was selected. So were Jimmy Lea and Ron Morris. I never made it into one of those summer tours. So it was a thrill to see Jess, in 1979, win a competition over 800 meters in Basel. There was my son, along the Rhine, outrunning entries from Switzerland, Germany, and France.

He started blowing kisses

On the 1979 trip we abruptly decided to leave Switzerland and take the night train to Paris. As soon as we reached the hotel I told them, "I will meet you downstairs in your running gear in fifteen minutes." They complained, but they knew that I meant it. It had been raining so the air was fresh. As we began our run we could see patches of blue sky beginning to appear through puffy white clouds. Invigorated by the weather and the atmosphere of Paris, we raced through the Tuileries toward the Arc de Triumph. I was very excited, fulfilled, running with my track family in Paris. We jogged in place at the Place de la Concorde because six or so lanes of commute traffic would suddenly be upon us if we tried to cross the large traffic circle at the wrong time. When there was a break in the flow of cars we made a run for it, but the mass of automobiles appeared again, coming right at us. The drivers slowed as youthful goddesses sprinted past them. Then a Frenchman stood up in his small convertible and started blowing kisses to the girls, charmed by this display of nymphs running through his city.

Vienna was the "Mecca" of my psyche. To some extent, Sigmund Freud had replaced Jesus for me. I felt that psychoanalysis had saved me from that horrible panic attack in Texas. Trish had taken "her week" away from us before we met up in Vienna. She was somewhat late; I was a little worried. I asked Jess if he wanted to go for a run around the Ring with me. He passed. The Ring is the wide boulevard that circles the center of the old city. There was a light drizzle as I ran past the Gestapo headquarters. Adolph Eichmann had been in Vienna in 1944 arranging for Jews to be shipped in great number like cattle to Auschwitz. Some of the wealthier Jews were provided a way to escape this fate. I left the Ring and ran a couple of blocks to 19 Berggasse, where Freud lived and practiced psychoanalysis for forty years. His monumental insights greatly influenced a century of human thought. As I jogged in place in front of the entrance, I pictured Freud walking into the doorway at which I stood. Karl Jung also had passed through this entrance when he visited Freud early in the twentieth century.

Back on the Ring, I went by the university, the musical theatre, the place of city government and the parliament; each displayed a different form of architecture, e.g., Renaissance, Baroque, Gothic, Classical. Then I chose to jog below the balcony where, in 1938, Adolph Hitler had received the adoration of some eighty thousand Austrians upon returning to the city triumphantly. The rejected art student owned the city that had rejected him.

Only a furlong or so down the Ring from the balcony is the Gothic opera house where Hitler would wait for a "standing room only" ticket to a Richard Wagner concert. Freud must have passed by Adolph Hitler on his nightly walks around the Ring. One of them penetrated the Unconscious and increased the world's understanding of itself; the other unleashed his Unconscious on millions of people and murdered them.

The soft rain continued. I was still full of run when I raced through a medieval arch to our hotel within the walled city. It had been thirty-one minutes since I had started out around the Ring. I thought to myself that no one else on Earth had ever experienced a more rewarding thirty-one minutes!

Trisha arrived within the hour. It was exciting to see her. Almost like having an affair. When we went for a walk, we stopped and kissed continually. It was raining off and on. During one lengthy kiss, a driver began honking his horn. I believe he was expressing approval.

A different world

In 1981 on the second Arête West trip we found ourselves alone in East Berlin on a cool overcast morning. It was a Saturday and no one was out. Checkpoint Charlie produced some concern because one of the Arête lads had German relatives and East German customs officers kept us for awhile in the border shack. Finally they let us through and we walked into East Berlin. The grit alongside the empty streets could have been there since the end of World War II. We passed by a high wall with a mural displaying workers from various occupations marching for Socialist ideals. It offered a colorful display of a different world. We sat down on a bench with the bunker just over a partition. I began to talk about the monster of history who took his life in 1945 not far from where we were seated. Suddenly, an older woman screamed in German. Rick, who held us up at customs not many minutes before, translated her words with some excitement—"He will be shot." One of my students was trying to look through a gap in the barrier. The woman stood at her apartment, well situated to be an authority on the dangers in crossing through "no man's land." The student, Mike Fulton, came quickly over to where we were seated. It was an eerie classroom.

We took a streetcar to the 1936 Olympic Stadium and the track of Jesse Owens and Archie Williams. Williams was my friend and their teacher at the high school where I coach. Archie won the 400 meters in the 1936 Olympics. When I met Archie a number of years before, I told him that he had a famous track name. We had gone out to play a round of golf together. His response was, "I am Archie Williams." Archie was one tremendous guy. When he out-drove me by a considerable distance on the golf course that day, he offered this explanation: "Black power."

I had the students run a number of fast 220-yard strides that morning in the 1936 Olympic stadium. It was thrilling for me to see them running on the track where Owens had blown Hitler's dream of showing the world that the Germans were the superior race. I share my feelings with the young people about excessive nationalism. I have a strong dislike for unexamined tribalism.

Cory was too wrapped up with Hitler (more so than the other young people). He enjoyed being provocative, shocking, dark humored. So we were treated to some impersonations of Hitler—right from the box where Hitler had watched the Olympics in 1936. As we were finishing the workout, a guard started screaming at us over the stadium public address system. He was becoming hysterical about our running on the track. The German language can sound so harsh.

We walked over by the caldron that once held the sacred Olympic flame and looked up on the wall that named the winning athletes from the 1936 Olympic Games. Yes, there was Archie Williams from the U.S.A.!

I did not realize it until it was too late, but when our train cars were disconnected en route to Vienna from East Berlin, I lost half of the young people. This happened at about 9:00 a.m. when the train stopped in Salzburg. My car left the station and went directly east toward Vienna. The rest of the kids and my friend, Dr. Robert Griffith, went elsewhere. I was prepared to spend a night in Europe without knowing where half of my students were located. It was time to eat, with or without them. As we left the youth hostel for a nearby restaurant, around the corner came the missing half of our group, with Dr. Griffith. I was so glad to see them. They told me that upon arriving at the Vienna station they heard over the loudspeaker, "Vil der Villiam Taylor party report to der station master." About seven hours before, I had told the station master, who did not speak English, about the missing students. Where had they gone? Bob was delighted to tell me that they experienced a beautiful ride through the Alps and entered Vienna from the south. That was a wonderful evening meal together.

The next morning we climbed up the stairs at 19 Berggasse to the Freud flat and museum. This began the first of my many pilgrimages there with young people. This first time, however, was the supreme one for me. I spontaneously led them into the library of the archaeologist of the mind and told them to sit down on the well-polished wooden floor and to close the door. I did not ask if this was okay with the museum staff. There were no tables or chairs, just a smooth waxed wooden floor and some cabinets with books. A large window was open.

I wanted to share with them how valuable psychoanalysis had been for me, but I did this without letting them know that I had been in therapy. When I was growing up, it was generally believed that if you saw a psychiatrist there was something wrong with you; you would be stigmatized. These days, I speak freely with the young about my analysis.

That morning in the library I informed them that I would impersonate Sigmund Freud and try and answer their questions. Some of my own personal experiences in therapy were within my answers, but they did not know this. We had the privacy of the library for maybe twenty to thirty minutes. I shared what I had learned about Freud, like his having said, "I am not a Freudian." Of course I mentioned that "sometimes a cigar is a cigar." And the time when Freud "accidentally" smashed a gift placed on his desk. Upon reflection, Freud recognized that he was holding back strong, angry feelings toward the person who had given him the present. The damage to the gift was no accident.

When Dr. Griffith told me as we approached the Ring that my talk was "inspired," I felt an incredible sense of worth. I had given what might seem to you like a religious testimony. For me it was down to earth, real, honest.

Suddenly he was not in his room anymore. I felt a certain loneliness when Jess went away to college. While the Berkeley campus is just across the bay, it could have been the East Coast because Jess did not come home very often. But because our family years had been so fulfilling, I could let go of my son. My sons had given me the chance to provide them with a father. My life was full and I felt proud, satisfied about the way we had raised Jess.

It did seem at times like we didn't matter as much to him as he did to us. I realize now that this independence was a compliment to the way we raised him. After a threatening academic freshman year at Cal, Jess chose geophysics for his major. I was extremely proud of his ability to handle advanced math. Even calculus. The collegiate running dream did not work out for him, however. After he hurt his knee over the Christmas break his freshman year in a pickup soccer game, the "young deer" was not able to race competitively in track again. Instead, he surpassed his father with an A in calculus at Cal Berkeley. Jess was very popular with his college friends, and had a couple of serious romances. Cory is three years younger than Jess, so he did not leave home until 1984.

The Sea Cloud

Patricia told me she had always wanted to sail on a tall ship. She loves the sea. When Steve Miller suggested that we book passage with a Stanford alumni group that would sail to Greek islands on the Sea Cloud we decided to go. Dr. Miller would be the resource professor for the journey. The fact that he taught across the bay at Cal was forgiven. I expected to be included to some extent in the seminars in that Steve had enthusiastically recommended my book. Did he not write that my book would be "stimulating and challenging to the thoughtful reader"? Stanford graduates would certainly be "thoughtful readers." He never mentioned my book.

Trisha never wants to wait until tomorrow. Her life is today. She is largely responsible for our traveling overseas together over thirty times! I was not aware before the trip that I would lose Patricia to the group. It is her nature to be a faithful, supportive team member. This has deprived me of her company on trips when I would have preferred our being alone together. We are both strong individuals. We each hold our ground. The young people, incidentally, admire this. They see strength in our relationship, for we can remain close yet maintain separate identities.

Before we boarded the Sea Cloud there was a rendezvous in Rome. We had a couple of days in the city before the tall ship sailed.

I began my run in the afternoon along the Tiber on a very hot day. I stayed in the shade of the trees along the river, not thinking about the fumes from the commute traffic. Or about how much water I had in my system. Runners then were not as conscious of maintaining liquids then as they are today. When I left the Tiber, I was looking forward to visualizing Roman history as I ran past the ancient forum. But I had to leave the shade of the trees to do so.

Contact with the earth grounds history for me. And time itself. We are of the earth, as Nietzsche reminded us. For this reason, I have trouble accepting synthetic tracks. Synthetic tracks produce faster times, but they remove us from the earth.

The ancient forum came to life when I looked over to where Caesar's body had been cremated. The officers of victorious legions passed right by this exact location as they moved along the Sacred Way toward the Temple of Jupiter on the Capitoline Hill. After dumping some cherished prisoners down a hole to slowly die in the pit below, they made sacrifices in thanksgiving for their victory.

I heard no music from *Gladiator* as I approached the Coliseum. The film came out about twenty years later. I was only forty-nine, able to run easily through the busy city. I took a right at the Coliseum and passed by the Arch of Constantine. Rome watched to see which direction Constantine would take when he returned to the city from the East. Would he turn left, go through the forum and up to the pagan Temple of Jupiter, or would he make his way across the Tiber to give thanks at the altar of St. Peter?

History kept me company as I ran up the Circus Maximus. The

chariot race in the movie, *Ben Hur,* will forever belong to Charl-
ton Heston. Although I felt hot, I gave no thought to the direct sun
as I ran straight up the center of the vast track where Rome held those
spectacular chariot races as the Caesars looked down from the Pala-
tine Hill.

I should have gone up the Tiber and right back to the hotel. But
when I saw a ramp going up to the Capitoline Hill from the other side
of the forum I decided to take one last look over the ancient ruins. I
was a little over halfway up the ramp when I felt a pain shoot from the
back of the right side of my head. A second pain shot back from the
front left and I recall falling backwards. When I became conscious I
brought my hand up to my forehead and realized that my glasses were
missing. There was blood on an elbow. I was filthy and I found myself
sitting down on the base of an Egyptian obelisk. There was a hotel
entrance about thirty yards away. I went in and asked the man at the
desk if he would please tell me what city I was in. He said, "Rome." I
then asked for a list of hotels so that I could call Trisha. Fortunately we
were staying at the Rafael Hotel. San Rafael is the town to the east of
San Anselmo, so the name was easier to locate. Trisha rushed over by
cab, then back at our hotel she put me in a bathtub with a lot of ice.

I was about a half a mile from the Capitoline Hill when I regained
consciousness. I had walked, stumbled, or jogged right through the
evening commute traffic. I have no memory of how I made it to that
obelisk. None. What in the hell had happened? Back in Marin, my
doctor guessed it was dehydration. It has never happened again.

When I walked out on the deck of the Sea Cloud, I found the water
glittering under the light morning sun. We had arrived in darkness. I
had no idea that I had slept some 100 yards from the holy island of
Delos.

Dr. Miller used his Greek archaeological credentials to arrange for
our early morning entrance. I left him lecturing in the midst of some
scattered marble just inside the entrance as I took off on a run. Soon
I encountered those much-photographed lions by a small pond. I became intoxicated with this private moment with ancient Greece.

A large green lizard was on the back of one of the marble lions. The lizard looked up as if to ask, "What are you doing here?" I easily negotiated a narrow trail up to the highest point on the island. My legs were light, full of life. A soft morning breeze had come with the freshness of the hour. Above was the pale blue sky, below me, the scattered blocks of white marble that tell of classical Greece. All of this belonged to me on a private morning run.

The Stanford public relations representative on the Sea Cloud noticed that Dr. Miller had not mentioned my book and ordered copies of *Athenian Odyssey* for everyone after the trip. When we docked in Athens at the end of voyage, Steve came up to Patricia and me and apologized for not being more personal on the trip. The Cal archaeologist seems to always be experiencing some crisis. But what a talent, what a friend.

All alone for a run on Delos

He kept them in the train compartment all night

I was not paid for my column in the weekly paper. This did not bother me. Socrates never charged for teaching. The coaching positions for track and cross country each pay a couple thousand dollars a year. There is something right about doing something you love without pay. I pay my own way on the Arête trips. I do not want them thinking of me as their hired tour guide. We all benefit from the economy of scale. A van split eight or nine ways is considerably cheaper than what a family must pay for the rental.

On the third overseas youth trip, in 1983, the train did not leave Rome until after midnight. When we finally climbed up into our car the aisle was so stuffed with young people one could barely move. We found an Italian family (or families), in our reserved compartment. They refused to open the sliding doors. There was no conductor in sight. It was like being in a cattle car. And hot.

I gave up on getting the Italians out of our reserved compartment, dragged my bags to where the train cars connected, and settled down to sleep for a few hours. My longtime friend from those High Sierra days, Bob Griffith, sought revenge. A pediatrician, and Stanford Phi Beta Kappa graduate, Bob parked himself on one of those tiny pull-down aisle seats outside "our" compartment. Then, according to the students, he began staring at the hijackers in our reserved cabin. One of the boys suggested that "the Doc" take off his belt and run it through the handles of the sliding door. The Italians became his prisoners. Whenever one would plead to be let out so that they could go to the bathroom, Bob would just shake his head from side to side and mutter, "No no no." He kept them in the compartment all night.

Bob is an extremely kind, thoughtful person. He went with Arête as a friend on the first trip, then joined the next three for portions of the adventures.

Age fifty just drifted away

We walked down the road from the Delphi village to the temple of Athena in darkness. The entrance to the beautiful circular home of the Goddess was roped off. I took a chance. It would be one ugly scene if the Greek village police discovered us within the archaeological grounds. Nonetheless, we slid down a steep bank with as little noise as possible. It was pitch black. I held onto the shoulder of a young friend in order to protect that "football" knee.

I commanded absolute silence. A sense of the sacred was the reward. There remained the fear that our voices could carry back to the police

Patricia on Mykonos

in the village. I had the youth lay on their backs within the temple as I faced turning fifty the next day. It had been ten years since those angry feelings in Istanbul when I woke up with the thought that my life was probably halfway over. In silence we witnessed flashes of lightning from a thunderstorm beyond the crags that provide Delphi with the appearance of a cathedral. Pan dances in the meadows up there, in the Parnassian range. We had stolen a moment in time. I let age fifty just drift away as the lightning bolts of Zeus provided the fireworks.

Trisha met me on the island of Mykanos after the 1983 Arête trip. I felt love and excitement when I saw her walking toward me across the simple landing strip. She was wearing a colorful summer dress. It was Vienna all over for us. Only nobody honked this time.

The Olympics on my home track

Not everyone has the Olympics held on their own home track. Trish and I had been in Europe before we attended a business conference at the lush Greenbrier in West Virginia. Yes, Jerry and I sat together. Trisha flew back to Europe afterwards and I faced a flight from Washington, D.C. to San Francisco alone in the plane. A movie was playing about an ape being used for experiments. When the ape escaped from the laboratory it let out a victory cry. A few moments later, I ended up entertaining the packed DC-10 compartment when I kneeled on my seat, raised my arms and began pounding my chest. I did not realize how the gorilla sound would carry when I let out a subdued roar. The entire cabin seemed to enjoy the impersonation.

Two of my female high school runners met me at the San Francisco airport with the Mercedes. We headed immediately toward Los Angeles and the 1984 Olympic Games. I tried to catch a little sleep around 5:00 a.m. in the Hollywood Bowl parking lot, but a security guard discovered us and we were politely asked to leave. There was supposed to be enormous freeway traffic because of the Olympics. Not so. We drove down a virtually empty freeway each morning and parked close to the Coliseum.

We stayed nine nights during the Olympics in the Schoenberger home; halfway through, the initial two girls left and two other runners came to visit. I received the Freudian couch in Ted's office for my bed. Ted and Elsebeth were wonderful. I took each of them on different days with me to the Olympic track events. Ted got to see the world record holder, Edwin Moses, race past him on his way to victory in the 400 meter hurdles. Dr. Schoenberger was not a sport fan, yet he marveled at the speed and grace of this Moses. When I took Elsebeth, she was thrilled to see the flag of her native Denmark flying over the stadium.

On the opening day of the Olympics, the flame from Olympia was carried up to the caldron by Rafer Johnson, the All-Time UCLA hero. I had been nominated with Rafer Johnson for Track Athlete of the Week by the Los Angeles sport writers and coaches. Thus began nine days of many connections to my track life.

It pleased me to take my junior college coach, Jim Slosson, to the 800-meter final. Jim was the coach most responsible for my becoming a collegiate half miler. I took my brother, Hal, too. I was surprised to see him there another day with his lady friend, Margie. Harold was having financial trouble and I knew that tickets were expensive.

The U.S. Olympic committee did not provide a free pass for Ron Morris on the day of the pole vault final, so I took my good USC friend. Ron won a silver medal in the 1960 Olympics in Rome. How could he be overlooked? This was his home stadium.

How did I get all of these tickets? When the press started hyping potential terrorist attacks, Bob Griffith sold me all of his tickets. We had both applied through the Olympic ticket auction for a couple of seats each day and almost all of our requests were honored. I had four tickets for virtually every day.

On the final night of track competition, the track events in the Coliseum brought me a sense of wholeness. My great little high school miler, Katy Dykstra, was with me. She was running for the University of Arizona at the time. Jess and Cory were there, too. As the four us stood under the flaming Olympic torch after a gold medal was awarded to the 1500-meter winner, I felt that my track life had come together. The sun had just dropped below the rim of the stadium, leaving pink and red memories over the Los Angeles sky. I thought that the track below us was my track, too. It belonged to me as much, or more so, than it did to the Olympians who had just run on it. My unbelievable thrills were still down there on it. As well as a major disappointment. That night my track memories were complete, fulfilled, at peace. But not for long, for I was still coaching. As a coach, if you are emotionally involved with your athletes, you will feel their results. Hopefully, with greater wisdom. That night in 1984, new stadiums and expectations awaited me, and I had a ways to go with "wisdom."

Just before the Olympics, while Patricia and I were still in Europe, there was a car accident and my star male athlete received serious head injuries. When someone alerted me to this by phone at the Schoen-bergers, I was told that he would be hospitalized for some time. I planned to see him, of course, upon returning home.

Jerry Zieff was regarded as the athletic "stud" of the county. He carried grace: Jerry was simple, tall, fast, talented, and extremely well liked. Some sport writers and coaches told me that they thought he was "one of the three best pro football prospects" to ever come out of Marin County. Mike Holmgren, of pro football coaching fame in Green Bay and Seattle, spent an evening visiting with Mrs. Zieff, Jerry, and me in their San Anselmo home shortly before Jerry graduated. Holmgren was recruiting for BYU. In track, Jerry was the county

The great Zieff and his coach

champion in both sprints and the long jump. In addition, he set the school record over 400 meters as a junior.

I still had to face Jerry when I returned home from the Olympics. One of my high school girls went with me. I was so glad that she was in the elevator with me as we approached the hospital floor where they had this great athlete. I was fearful, apprehensive, anxious. An orderly wheeled him out. His head was shaven for they had cut into his brain; he tilted off to one side with his head hanging down. Again, I was so glad that I had company. This first visit terrified me. I returned a number of times. The visits became easier. He got better. But he would never be the same. No college football. No pro contract. Competitive sports were over.

Jerry has ended up a kind, sensitive person. The "stud" of the county, the one other athletes measured themselves by in 1984, is a proud, reflective, middle-aged man today. He works with his mother in a family business. Jerry loves to fish. I do not hear any bitterness. He still loves hearing about "the great Zieff."

My mother said, "Good."

Leslie never calls me. Why was her voice on my business phone? The former wife of my little brother informed me that Harold had tried to kill himself. He was in a hospital with a destroyed esophagus.

Remember that woman, Margie, I saw Harold with at the Olympics? She called Harold and told him that their relationship was over. My brother was a family man. First he lost Leslie, now another female was abandoning him. Leslie not only wanted me to know, she wanted me to tell my mother.

I accepted this responsibility, of course, but I decided to postpone telling her until I flew down that weekend. This became extremely difficult because Mom was a wise, alert woman in her mid-eighties. She began calling me and asking, "Where's Harold?" I told her several times that Harold was on a trip and that I would see her on Friday.

Mom was not surprised when I told her about the suicide attempt. In fact, she told me that she "figured as much." One cool cat! We had gone to dinner at a restaurant near her apartment in Toluca Lake. That frank, intimate conversation over dinner was the most direct and personal talk we ever experienced.

The plan was for me to pick Mom up the next morning; we would drive to the hospital in Glendale together. I was staying with Ted and Elsebeth. It helped enormously to be staying with my former psychoanalyst.

Before I picked my mother up, I had a call from Leslie. Harold had pulled his support wires out and was racing death. When we walked into the waiting room at the hospital, I heard *beep beep beep beep* coming from the operating room. The swinging doors were closed. It was just like a medical show on television.

Leslie, and their two daughters, Julie and Alison, were there. Every now and then, a nurse would run in and out through the swinging doors. Hal was on the other side of the wall from where we were seated. I wondered what he looked like in there. Suddenly things became frantic. Nurses began moving rapidly through the swinging doors. My little brother was obviously in real trouble. My mother said that she hoped he would not make it. She was a Hager. Matter of fact. A realist under fire. Then the *beep beep beep beep beep* changed into *beeeeeeeeeeeeeeeeeeeeeee.* It was over. My younger brother was dead.

My mother said, "Good." A frank, to the point, "Good." Mom did not cease being Harold's mother; she was being realistic about his chances to find happiness with a destroyed throat. Our candid communication continued at breakfast the morning of the service. The funeral was held at the church where I had assisted in the wedding for Harold and Leslie twenty-five years before.

My mother's trait of putting down our friends was activated even before we entered the chapel. She attacked this one man purely out of meanness. She had others to degrade. My brother Harold had just murdered himself and here she was, knocking those who came to remember him. This was a regrettable side of my mother.

My legs ached as I took the flight back to Marin. There was a coaches meeting that very night. Why weren't they more personal? But did they even know that my brother had just killed himself? Grief wants understanding, acknowledgement.

At the same time I felt harshly toward my younger brother because of what he had done to his two daughters, to Margie, and to his mother. Any warm or understanding feelings toward Harold were years away!

Jess graduates in geophysics

Patricia and I sat with the other parents and friends in a small shaded quad next to his science building on the Cal campus. Jess had successfully handled a challenging academic curriculum at Cal Berkeley and was to graduate that afternoon. He had impressed his dad with his capabilities in math and the sciences. I was extremely proud of him.

The Drake track athletes picked up on my enthusiasm over Jess graduating from Cal when I arrived in Santa Rosa later that afternoon. I was dressed differently from my normal coaching attire: slacks, a sport coat hanging off one shoulder, and a gold, red, and black striped tie loosened around the neck. The Redwood Empire championship was being held in the same stadium where I had placed second in the state junior college half-mile final at age eighteen. My elation over Jess's graduation from Cal was contagious. Again and again our athletes responded to my joy with their best marks. In the final event, our boys completed a deeply satisfying day by winning the mile relay.

Our Polish visas would cease to be valid at midnight

I stood some twenty to thirty yards from the twisted rubble of gas chambers at Auschwitz. Moments before, we walked down from the platform where Jews once were sent to the right or left upon disembarking from train cars, some to work, most to die. The inscription at the end of the rail tracks said "four million" Jews were gassed by the Nazis in the gas chambers immediately in front of where I was standing. I kept a distance from the broken chambers of death. If one listened, one could still hear their screams. My head was light, my lips silent. What could one say?

This was the fourth youth adventure and the most suspenseful one. The drama actually began before Auschwitz. We left Prague that morning at 5:30 a.m. and stopped in an industrial town in eastern Czechoslovakia in order to exchange currency at a bank. Bob Griffith and I stood in line for perhaps thirty minutes and, after moving twenty-six inches, decided to risk making it to the Polish border on our current gas levels.

The first crisis occurred when Bob and I lost sight of one another, since all of the passports were with me in my van. We were in Czechoslovakia in 1985, behind the "Iron Curtain." Veteran travelers to this day are shocked when they hear that we were able to move about freely through the communist countries at that time. I think our scheduled track competition in Prague gave me some sense of security. As I drove eastward, I was not even sure if I was on the correct route to the border. An hour later, we came upon the van Bob was driving parked along a country road. Wow. That was close one.

Maybe I shouldn't have driven through a public park in a communist police state that evening? We had been driving around this vast compound for some time, unable to find an entrance that would lead us to the youth hostel. I was surprised to see Bob following me on this wide concrete path within the trees of this Cracow park, in that he was unwilling to go with me earlier when I roared up a closed freeway in Czechoslovakia. The Polish people were out for their evening stroll when we appeared on their walkway. Yes, they looked disturbed, upset with us.

After registering at the worst youth hostel I have ever experienced, we walked over to a restaurant for a late dinner. Seated alone in the ballroom, with red drapes hanging from a high ceiling, we waited and waited for our food. When the main serving finally arrived, Bob threatened to hit little Katy with his baked potato because she asked if he was going to eat it. Bob stormed out of the ballroom. Our day had started in Prague at 5:30 a.m. It was almost 10:00 p.m. When I returned to the youth hostel, I found a note saying that Bob would be sleeping elsewhere. Had I lost the driver of our second van in communist Poland?

The next morning I discovered a note on my van and it said to call Bob at the Holiday Inn. The son-of-a-bitch had skipped the lousy youth hostel for a real hotel bed. What was a Holiday Inn doing behind the Iron Curtain?

The drive toward Budapest on a Polish road was a happy one. The sun was out; ducks were swimming in the little ponds next to farmhouses along the way. We were turned away at the border because our travel professional had not arranged for a second visa in order for us to pass through Czechoslovakia. The guards were very nice, but we were not going to Budapest on that road. They informed us that the closest consulate was in a city near where we had entered Poland the day before.

Our Polish visas would cease to be valid at midnight, so we drove aggressively across southern Poland. It was taking much longer than the map seemed to suggest. By mid-afternoon we were facing real trouble. Once in the city of Katowice, Bob relayed a message from a student in his van that we should hire a cab to lead us to the consulate. Brilliant!

I began pushing buttons on a panel in an empty lobby. Remember, it was Friday afternoon. *Please, please let someone be here.* A wooden shutter slowly came up. An old woman without any human warmth communicated to me that we would only be able to obtain transit visas to Austria. So there would be no Budapest!

We needed western currency and photographs in order to obtain the transit visas. We tore off the photographs from our visas for Hungary, then emptied suitcases, backpacks, and sleeping bags on the front lawn of the consulate, searching for all of our western currency. The frantic search was successful. We got our transit visas.

It was about 1:00 a.m. when I told Bob to wait alongside the dark Czech highway because I had to go back to a hotel restaurant to hopefully locate a backpack and passport that our future Harvard lad left behind. I was prepared to give him my American Express card and leave him in Czechoslovakia if we did not find it. Our transit visas were good for only one night.

A detour blocked our passage going back and I could not continue on the same route. Within minutes, we were lost in darkness along a country road. We came upon a man on a bike who helped us. Together we studied a map lit by the van headlights. Before long, we were on our way and we obtained the backpack with the passport.

The Czech border guards were far from friendly as we approached Austria at about 3:30 a.m. Before reaching customs, we passed soldiers stationed at checkpoints with sub-machine guns. At that hour in the morning, an officer made us take out some of our luggage from the vans for inspection.

Once in Austria my objective became to catch a little sleep. I didn't realize I had parked next to a cemetery until I woke up the next morning. Some of the Arête kids were cheerfully walking through the graves.

I had slept gratefully for a few hours under the steering wheel of my van.

We needed bathrooms, food, money, so we pulled into the Vienna airport and located a currency exchange, and a grocery store with milk, bananas, yogurt, cereal, and, of course, those clean Austrian restrooms. I was surprised to discover a youth hotel near the Ring with private rooms and showers for a moderate price. After the long awaited shower and a short nap, we walked over to the Ring. An exhibit of most of the famous Klimt paintings had just opened. Before the trip, the students had observed copies of *The Kiss*, *Judith*, *Danae*, and *Hygeia* in my office where we held our pre-trip seminars. And now the originals were suddenly before us. It was an incredible experience. The *Beethoven Frieze* had been moved from its normal home and was with us, too. Along with the music of Beethoven's Ninth Symphony.

Incredible series of monumental historical encounters in less than thirty hours

Was the '85 youth trip worth it? Yes, yes, yes! I still marvel at the historical encounters that we accumulated before those threatening travel experiences after leaving Prague. In Nuremberg, we located the parade ground of the Nazi searchlights where Hitler had screamed out his hatred of Jews. Later the same morning in Bayreuth, we were above the grave of Richard Wagner, where Hitler had once stood in reverence. That afternoon in the St. Thomas Church in Leipzig, we looked down at the grave of Bach.

Western religious materials were not allowed in East Germany. I was not orienting this Arête group to Christianity in a religious way, but we did hide some information on Martin Luther from the stern border guards. They offered no hint of our being welcomed in their country. The next morning in Wittenberg, it was the grave of Martin Luther; later that afternoon we reflected on Adolph Hitler and the bunker that was just on the other side of the barrier in East Berlin.

Before our fateful swing into Czechoslovakia and Poland, then Vienna, we fortunately met Caroline, a lovely university art student who became our guide in East Berlin. Groups were not allowed in East Germany without supervision. By the Brandenburg Gate, our pretty and articulate communist guide delivered a challenging view of Socialism. In answer to the student questions she told us why she respected her country: free education, free health care for everyone, care for the elderly. These Socialist values had consequences; it would be a long time before Caroline could own a car. Or travel freely.

I could sense as we approached Checkpoint Charlie that Caroline didn't want to say goodbye. She, of course, could not go with us in 1985. The wall would remain up for another four years. We asked if we could send her anything. She requested a poster of James Dean.

You taught me to like myself

Does a son ever escape his guilty feelings toward his mother? Mary Elizabeth Hager Taylor advanced into her later years with surprising independence and flair. She finally quit feeling sorry for herself and started doing just what she wanted to do. I asked her what had brought about this enormous change from the moaning, complaining person to the popular, well-liked figure in Toluca Lake. One year the town made her the honorary mayor. She even was able to see her name up on the Dodger scoreboard for one of her birthdays.

When I asked my mother what brought about this change in her, she said to me, "You taught me to like myself." Jesus, what a gift. All of my guilt over not doing enough for my mother and I end up with this beautiful ending. How did I teach her to like herself? I would not buy into her self-pity, would not let her lead me into feeling guilty. This worked.

Before her hospitalization for a stroke, she was living in an apartment in Toluca Lake. Close to Bob's and the Lakeside Pharmacy. The retired music teacher never asked for money. My mother always took care of her own expenses. She was a Hager—independent, proud, judgmental. When I was down in Los Angeles with my track teams she would always ask the girls, "Did you win?" At times, we would find her sitting at a restaurant bar visiting with her friends. The girls were extremely warm and loving toward my mother when I introduced them to her. This pleased me. Mom made a point of telling me that she was only having "one vodka." My mother died with dignity and self-respect. This is the way I prefer to remember her.

I returned from the incredible '85 youth adventure to maidens who would grace the county for the next four years. After winning the Redwood Empire cross-country final as freshmen, they went four straight years without losing a league track meet. And they were beautiful. One Bay Area paper began paralleling their undefeated record with the great USC streak during the Golden Years of the sport. That was a reach, but I loved it. It was both fun and rewarding to coach the black robed goddesses. The maidens wore black tops and shorts with a lightning bolt slashed across a white "D" on the front of the uniforms. Hello, Zeus.

My identity became attached to this lengthy victory streak and I found myself once again depending on athletic results to measure my self worth. At the same time, while I coveted the athletic respect, I became increasingly aware of the value of the teaching relationship. The existential moments in sport were giving each young person a confrontation with victory or defeat. As a coach, I was assigned the task of helping them to be fair with themselves, to gain perspective on the taunting "what ifs" of athletics before they left my fold. This provided me with a trip back to my emotions about my running days, the severe disappointment I experienced because of the tonsillitis. The pain was still there. But a dialogue within myself was underway through my coaching.

Islam

My trips to Spain and Portugal with Patricia in the mid-1980s provided a variety of experiences. Foremost they impacted my understanding of Islam. Moorish architecture informed me that Allah cannot be squeezed into human form because He stands far beyond mankind. The geometric patterns on the porches, shutters, and arches of the Alhambra tell of a God who cannot be compromised or manipulated. The abstract representations told of the Holy in a far deeper way for me than the cluttered ornaments in the Christian cathedrals. It was not surprising to find beautiful gardens in Granada, Spain; for the Moors had come from the deserts of North Africa and their vision of paradise naturally included an alternative landscape. Patricia and I experienced an amazing morning walk within the Alhambra among its fountains and deep red roses. Spain is existential by landscape. For me it cannot be compared to anywhere else in the world. I noticed the rich colors before the jet even touched down on our approach to Madrid. Spain is color! Its passionate blood has soaked the soil.

"This is our mass"

Salamanca suddenly arises from the highway. A river separates the city from the rest of the world. Salamanca does not have a university; Salamanca is a university. Its character and profile is that of the academic. A favorite run in Salamanca took me past where Columbus had pleaded for financial support for some kind of adventure, and I ran past where the scholar, Unamuno, had stood up to fascism. He, like Socrates, Hus, and Bruno, was a man willing to risk death and not forfeit integrity. I was surprised to learn that Unamuno was a Catholic existentialist. I did not know that they existed.

We were told in Madrid that we would see the best flamenco in the world at a particular nightclub. I was struck by the existential finality of the dance, the decisive heels that confront death and deliver life. The lead female, in a beautiful white flowing robe, performed the most graceful dance movements I have ever witnessed. It was well after midnight when the Spaniard seated next to Patricia and I gave the dance its powerful clarity with, "This is our mass."

Eleven days in Egypt

Suddenly Patricia wanted to jump onto this T.W.A. "Getaway" trip to Egypt over the Christmas holidays. I protested that we would only be gone for eleven days and it would be a waste of money. The fear of terrorism by travelers was at its height. We heard that out of twenty-three scheduled T.W.A. Getaway tours for the winter of 1986 in Egypt, twenty had been cancelled. Two airports, Vienna and Rome, were hit just hours before our departure from San Francisco. Television stations were showing pictures of the dead bodies by check-in counters as I crossed the Golden Gate Bridge on our way to the San Francisco airport. The *International Herald Tribune* carried a picture of empty high heel shoes alongside some Christmas packages. I did not want to go.

Thus began our winter trips. Every other summer I traveled with Arête, then Trish and I took our personal summer trips in the off years. To this we added another trip in December every year. Yes, two overseas excursions every twelve months. Largely because of Trisha, I have now traveled overseas over fifty-five times. She is indeed a wonderful travel goddess for me. Patricia has an insatiable need to experience new places; she is of continuous curiosity. We must go now, while we can enjoy it—that is her motivation and philosophy.

It turned out to be a perfect time to visit Egypt.

We arrived at the airport in Rome the morning after the terrorist attack. Inside the airport, I saw an Italian guard with a sub-machine gun strutting around like he was Mussolini. The jaw was thrust forward, the beret tilted to one side. We saw him just a few meters from where we checked in for our connection to Cairo.

The cancelled tours not only meant fewer lines, less people, but they gave our being in Egypt a special character. Great! I wanted our trips to require courage. I wanted to have people see that Trisha and I were traveling to unusual places.

When the jet banked over the Nile it was one penetrating sight. The river was down there; the Nile was actually below us. Upon landing, we were led across a dirt surface surrounded by airport shops. A big hulk of a man in a robe had a dwarf carry his heavy trunk. The little fellow was excited, happy about being with his master. I was in a different world.

As we drove from the airport toward Cairo, soldiers dressed in black uniforms were spaced alongside the road for miles. Perhaps this was just for show, but they were armed and the threat of terrorist attacks was quite real. We passed an enormous cemetery where thousands live in the old tombs. Camels, buffalo, animals pulling carts, old cars, and trucks were packed in the city streets. The damp air seemed to choke on itself. This dramatic drive ended with the shuttle van delivering us to a hotel immediately next to the Great Pyramid of Giza. Thanks, Patricia.

I went for my first run in Egypt that night around the massive tomb that was built forty-six centuries before. Numerous armed soldiers in black jumpsuits were just outside the hotel entrance gate. The message to me was that I needed protection. Nonetheless, I left the safety of the hotel grounds and went out into the night. As I set out running around the massive pyramid, a tall Egyptian lad began running alongside of me. He wore slacks and street shoes. I was uncomfortable with his presence until his big smile and genuine demeanor relaxed me. I still wanted to lose him so I could be alone with history and time. Via sign language, I could tell that he wanted to know where I came from. Did I want to advertise that I was an American? I told him, "California." He lit up even more and began to shout enthusiastically, "Michael Jackson, Michael Jackson, Michael Jackson!"

New Year's Eve turned out far better than I had thought it would. I have mentioned I do not like group tours. A party with a tour group was not my idea of good way to spend New Year's Eve. Patricia loves parties. She was upbeat as we were driven across Cairo to a large ship on the Nile. The people seated across from us at the dinner table were without intellectual curiosity. Things picked up, however, when the music started and the wine was poured. Trish and I enjoyed the small dance floor a couple of times. Then, back at the dinner table, a very fat Egyptian fellow came over and wanted me to dance with him. *What?*

You have to be kidding. Trish insisted that I do so. So there I was, on New Year's Eve, dancing with an overweight chap who could have been a lineman for the Chicago Bears. Ripples of fat bounced up and down under his loose shirt as we danced to the rock music. He was friendly, pleasant, and huge. I do not do things like this!

When Patricia and I went up to explore the upper deck of the ship and to escape the noise and cigarette smoke, the captain noticed us by the rail and asked Patricia if she wanted to steer the big boat. She actually turned the large cruise vessel around on the Nile on New Year's Eve. It was as though we were above time as we looked out over Cairo from the Nile from the very high deck on the cruise ship.

Back at the tables, I asked if anyone had thought about, or pictured, the baby Moses floating on the Nile in a reed basket. I did not know if they were listening. However, I gained their attention when I asked, "Have you heard of the first Jewish discotech?" I personally answered my rhetorical question with, "Let my people go-go." Not bad.

The Nile was a long way from Toluca Lake and Sinatra on his kayak

Train stations are eerie places in poor countries. We waited under a damp, moist carpet of fog for the train to take us by night to famous Luxor. While sailing on the Nile a day or so later, I heard the most consistent voice of the twentieth century singing over the ship speaker, "I'll do it my way..." As women in brilliant colors walked down to the river to fill their jars as they have done for the past five thousand years, Frank Sinatra was singing his signature song. The Nile was a long ways from Toluca Lake and Sinatra on his kayak.

The eleven-day trip was amazing. One day we were way back in time on the Nile, the next one we were in San Anselmo. Our visit to Egypt was actually enhanced by its limited duration.

The military police were standing by our broken window in Communist Prague

Bob was suffering from jet lag when he slammed his van door in Prague, shattering the window on the driver's side. He had just met up with us the day before, in Vienna. When the students walked off and left him to lock up alone, he exploded. I was waiting across the street with two Czech coaches. We observed the tantrum and began to walk slowly toward the restaurant in silence. After a few moments, one of the coaches, Vanda, offered, "A very strong man." This was especially charming because Vanda did not speak English.

We all had a great time at the outdoor restaurant with live music and a festive atmosphere. Bob forgot about his outburst. After saying goodnight to Vanda and Kathryn at the metro, we returned to the vans. The military police were standing by the broken window. Prague was still a police state in 1987. One of the young officers had his notepad out and we were about to be written up behind the Iron Curtain. They, of course, asked to see our passports. Neither one spoke any English. As I was attempting to show them how the window was broken by slamming the door, one of our more confident girls broke the tension by lifting the hat off one of the officers and playfully putting it on her head. Alyssa teased the seriousness away. The notebook was put aside and the incident was not reported.

Our next destination was Belgrade, Yugoslavia. The coaches met us at the station and took us to their sport club for lunch. They had been cut off from the Western world for almost fifty years. This clearly was a big occasion for them. A track meet was held in a large, empty stadium that afternoon. It seemed unreal or surrealistic, our being together without a common language and about to compete against one another in sport. I jogged around the track before the racing began and a professor at the university joined me in slacks and street shoes. Death was not many years away for these Serbs. Bombs were coming to Belgrade. The Arête youth wonder today if any of the young athletes they competed against were killed by American bombs.

The coaches treated us to a great meal and party in an outdoor res-

Arete '87 at the Acropolis, Athens

taurant after the track meet. They would not let us pay for anything. As we left Belgrade for Greece on the train, it was after midnight. The Yugoslavian team and their coaches were at the station waving good-bye to us.

After Cal Berkeley, Jess went on to graduate school at the University of California, Santa Barbara. Shortly before he received his master's degree, Trish and I went to hear him speak at a geological conference in San Francisco. We were struck by his poise, clarity, calm demeanor. Afterwards I asked his lead professor if our enthusiasm was bias. Were we just proud parents? The professor fired back, "Jess is very marketable."

Unlike Jess, who took to math and science, Cory was of the theatre and liberal arts. Our youngest son transferred to UCLA after two years at UC Santa Cruz. The UCLA drama department carried the image of being one of the best in the nation at the time. It was during some of his classes at UCLA that Cory became interested in social revolutions and moral integrity. College wasn't all theatre for him.

How about running around ancient Jerusalem and Troy?

I vividly remember the coastline that appeared shortly before we landed in Israel. I could see the land of the Bible. The Israeli government was firmly in control in 1988, yet we still found suspense and danger in Jerusalem. On our first night, a waitress told us to move quickly away from our table because a bomb might be in a bag near us. You chill to the bone upon hearing that an explosion might happen close to you at any second. I had never felt that kind of fear before.

Trisha suggested that we leave the Hyatt and move to the American Colony Hotel in East Jerusalem. Before we left, I had an early morning chance to run up a hill that began just outside the hotel entrance, go past the university, and look down upon the places of the Bible. I was racing the morning sun. Any later and the heat would be too strong. I looked down at the Garden of Gethsemane as I approached the Mt. of Olives. Jesus Christ! I found that there was still some life in the verses and parables for me. "Don't call me good; only God is good." That says it for me. Too bad most Christians do not make this distinction between Jesus and God. "May this cup pass from me..." Jesus struggled with his destiny right below the ridge where I was running. He was still in Jerusalem for me in 1988. Not in a mystical way. He wasn't a tour guide floating around the biblical sites. But sayings like those two I just mentioned still carried some emotional power within me.

The golden Dome of the Rock, one of the holiest sites for Islam, was in view. The sun had not appeared on the horizon yet. It would arrive over Jericho. Jericho? This was a fantastic run. I asked myself on my way back down the hill, "Why do they keep on killing one another?" I had my answer before I reached the Hyatt, and it has not changed. The Jews and Arabs kill one another because of their religious beliefs. Schoenberger was correct; religion teaches hate. Religion is behind the "eye for an eye" revenge killings. The blood of martyrs flows as freely as it did from animals in ancient times at the altar on the Temple Mount. Today they kill over sacred real estate. Religions issue holy property deeds. The bond between people and soil is permanent. Jerusalem needs UN troops. All faiths need to be protected. There cannot be peace without a complete compromise and control over the respective "holy" places. By the time I returned to the Hyatt, I knew that there would not be peace.

Early one morning after we moved to the American Colony Hotel, I decided to run around the ancient walls of Jerusalem. I began on a quiet street, running toward the Damascus Gate in my track shorts. While alongside the eastern wall, I looked up to the St. Stephen Gate, or, Lion's Gate, as it is known. I thought about my time in Fort Worth when I was a Presbyterian minister at St. Stephen, battling Jablonowski for my selfhood. The fact that Stephen was stoned to death at this gate was not lost on me. I had just passed the Garden of Gethsemane to my left. Was it there that Jesus said, "Where can the son of man place his head?" I do not feel separated from that question. It has existential meaning for me today. Nietzsche said that in the final analysis one must live life alone.

I continued up a gradual grade below the staggering beauty of this golden dome of Islam. I could only see the very top rising just above the ancient wall. Moslems believe that Mohammed rode his horse to paradise from there. On the other side of the rock-platform, and below, is the Wailing Wall of the Jews. Below the King David Hotel I passed by the Jaffa Gate where bus passengers and pedestrians had been blown apart or shot by snipers. I felt some concern at the Damascus Gate when an older Arab glared at me. His eyes told of serious hate. My bare legs did violate Moslem religious values. Dr. Gill told us that he was sure that "God loved Emily Post, but he did not give a damn about her book." I do not think this casual attitude toward manners was appropriate at the Damascus Gate that morning.

I came upon three or four Israeli soldiers in a jeep parked in the street. As I jogged past, I looked down at the driver, a good looking young kid with a sub-machine gun on his lap. He was, perhaps, eighteen? His facial expression suggested a certain amusement, like, *What in the hell are you doing running through East Jerusalem in your shorts?*

As we lifted off from Israel for Istanbul the flight was greeted with the news that an American naval ship had mistakenly shot down an Iranian airplane with over a hundred people on board. It felt very strange to be up in the air above the Mediterranean knowing that over in the air space above the Persian Gulf a jet had just been blown out of the sky.

We reached Troy on my birthday. As in Jerusalem, I ran around the walls of an ancient city. It was a short run because Troy is surprisingly small. I was well aware that across the Hellespont were the deadly beaches of Gallipoli. Thousands and thousands of soldiers were sliced in two by machine gun fire or blown apart by artillery there, right across from where, three thousand years before, the Greeks attacked Troy and bled and died on the battlefield.

After my birthday run, I placed two pages from the 1954 Pacific Coast Conference track and field program on the longest and most-preserved section of the ancient wall. Under a banner headline in the program that read, "The Mighty Trojans," were pictures of Jimmy Lea, Ernie Shelton, Jon Arnett, Des Koch, and Bill Taylor. We thus joined Hector, Odysseus, Aeneas, and Achilles as heroes at Troy. Yes, I felt silly, self-conscious about this posting. Trisha headed immediately for the parking area. I lingered for awhile, enjoyed seeing a group of tourists looking curiously at the pictures.

Who wants to be kidnapped in Morocco?

When I read that a curious Christian tourist who tried to look within a mosque in Morocco had his head slashed off by a Moslem fanatic, I was apprehensive about our flying there. It did help to know that this particular beheading took place over fifty years before I stood by the entrance to the mosque.

I felt suspense as we drove from the airport to Casablanca. Everything was in black and white—just like the movie! I noticed a man walking off to the side of the road in a jallabiya. The ground fog added a certain mystery to the scene. What was I doing there?

The French had occupied Morocco and did terrible things to the

Enjoying an annual baptism in the Aegean Sea
(Note the hat on the rock)

Moslems not that many years before. Did the Moslems remember them? Did they still hate the French for how they were exploited? And, therefore, would I be meeting people who hated Westerners?

The medieval city of Fez contains narrow, endless passageways enclosed within thick walls. I knew that, earlier in the twentieth century, severed heads had been displayed from an entrance only a hundred meters from our hotel parking area. Even with my experiences in Egypt, Israel, and Turkey behind me, I was edgy about being in Morocco. Why should I risk my life, or the possibility of being kidnapped, to see another Moslem country? And Morocco was known for endless harassments by marketplace hustlers.

Trisha saw to it that we had a room with a balcony that looked out over the thousand-year-old medina. We were situated within the walls at the well-known Palais Jamai Hotel. Not long after we arrived, sounds from the medina told of the evening call to prayer. A gradual chorus of primeval screams came from different locations within the medieval city. Hearing them was worth the entire trip. I was being treated to a symphony of raw Islamic theology. The prayers competed with one another in praise of Allah from the mosques above the narrow passageways.

Moslems throw themselves down on their prayer rugs because they know that they are no more than a grain of sand on the Sahara. A religious service is not a fashion display. Clothing is incidental. The One God is the entire focus. Nietzsche said that we are no better than worms. Dr. Reist told my seminary class that "God could have made us carrots." I sensed something in those prayers in Fez that is missing in the West.

But there has not been peace

I ran out the gate that had once been decorated with skulls. It was not completely dark yet, so I went up alongside a narrow road on a hill above the medina that meandered through scattered graves. As I neared the summit, I noticed that the sky was beginning to greet its evening stars. I came upon a shepherd with hood and crook, and his sheep. To the east was Jerusalem. It was Christmas Eve. I ran back through the gate of the skulls feeling enormous satisfaction in being able to experience Christmas Eve this way. I remembered that, as a young boy, at a few of the Hager Christmas Eve gatherings I was asked to sing a Christmas hymn. One time I sang "It Came Upon the Midnight Clear" (e.g., "It came upon the midnight clear, / That glorious song of old, / From angels bending near the earth, to touch their harps of gold; / 'Peace on the earth...'"). Bethlehem was over there, directly to the east. But there has not been peace.

We spent a very cold night in a French fort on the edge of the Sahara on this Morocco trip. A college professor had recommended it; he said that he "could not imagine a more fascinating place" to experience New Year's Eve. The setting reminded me of Palm Springs, without the golf courses. Large, dramatic, pink-tinted boulders rose off the desert floor and wealthy homes were scattered beneath their rounded domes. Paul Bowles wrote that Tafraoute "is like the badlands of South Dakota" written on a grand scale.

I went for my run in the late afternoon and came upon a narrow trail heading out into a canyon. I was alone, embraced by stillness. It was marvelous being out there at the edge of the Sahara on New Year's Eve. The weather was idyllic, softly warm and gentle. It was not long before I noticed two large black tents ahead. I had come upon desert people, the nomads. I became concerned when I noticed their dogs and turned back toward the village. I returned in time to hear the call to prayer from a lonely minaret. It closed out my run. I was thrilled with where Trish had taken me.

She and I had a pre-dinner cocktail there in a very cold bar. There was no evidence that we would have any heat in the dining room for dinner, either. Or in our room. I thought of those who had come off the Sahara to this French fort earlier in the century, with slaves, wild animals, gold.

In the dining room we were treated to unusual New Year's Eve entertainment when some old Berbers came marching through, banging spoons and metal objects against one another. Their white robes looked like bed sheets. They came around the tables twice. That was it.

I found one bite of meat hanging from the bone that I was served on that special evening. I was counting on the crème carmel for dessert, but a German group finished it off. I could already taste it.

Trish and I still faced a night without any heat in our room. It was going to be damn cold. The year closed with the sound of jackals playing outside of our freezing room. I wouldn't trade it.

Some of our winter trips ended before New Year's Eve; on those years we would celebrate with the Steins and Schoenbergers. This led to my seeing my first therapist, Ted Stein, and my former psychoanalyst, Ted Schoenberger, in conversation. One year, a French woman at the dinner table was gaining their attention because the more she spoke, the more attractive she became. When she sensed it was time to tell them of a recent dream, this engaging younger female presented the two therapists with this account: A man is standing at a railing in a loft above Claudia's bed in her home; suddenly this man falls over the barrier and lands on her; there is blood everywhere.

No one spoke at the table as we waited for Jung or Freud to interpret the dream. Ted Stein, in his familiar, thoughtful, "Jungian" tone, suggested that the man might represent her "animus," the "male side" in a female personality. Okay. A safe, predictable explanation.

We turned to the Freudian analyst. We had to wait for Dr. Schoenberger to share his view. Finally he turned to Claudia and said, "I think you needed a tampon." We laughed and we laughed into the night. I initially even slid off my chair. The conversation raced us right through midnight. We missed the beginning of a new year. A couple of hours later someone mentioned that it was past 2:00 a.m. I do not remember ever having so much fun at a party. It was fulfilling to have my two prime father figures together. I had enormous respect for each of them. I was no longer their student or patient; I was their friend.

Left to right: Ted Stein, Ted Schoenberger, and
Bill Taylor celebrating New Year's Eve together.

Trisha working her way across North Africa

When the pilot announced that the descent into Tunis had be-gun, I once again felt the suspense and awe of suddenly being trans-ported by jets to an unusual place in the world. We were returning to North Africa, for Trish wanted to see each of the countries on the Mediterranean.

We know a great deal about ancient Carthage. The Phoenicians landed in what is now Tunisia about three thousand years ago. With Algeria on one side, and Libya immediately to the east, Tunisia was a kind of "safe haven" squeezed in-between two anti-American coun-tries.

Christmas night was memorable on a dance floor at the edge of the Sahara. The dining room was crowded, but when the band started playing, nobody dared to begin the dancing. So Trish and I led off. Italians, French, an international crowd joined us. It was fun being a bit bold, helping the evening to come alive for ourselves and others.

On New Year's Eve, looking out over a dark, angry Mediterranean Sea a few miles west of Carthage, it struck me that only six months before, in the summer of 1989, I had been with the young people in Istanbul, Athens, and Rome. Virgil tells us by poetry that Dido, first queen of Carthage, leaped into a funeral pyre when her lover, the Trojan hero Aeneas, left Carthage to found Rome. Now I was standing on the North African coast near ancient Carthage with memories of having looked toward Rome from an opening in Agios Sophia in Istanbul.

Aeneas came to Carthage from Troy. Arête '89 had visited Troy, on their way to Rome. There was a soft drizzle falling as I remembered the students and our recent journey. As I looked out over that angry sea, a Moslem prayer sung tenderly over the village. Terrorized Westerners have no idea how sensitive and loving the singing of the Koran can sound. The verses took me back to Istanbul six months before, when on the final night of Ramadan I awakened to the most beautiful prayer I have ever heard. This pastoral, peaceful masterpiece hovered over the wooden homes in the oldest section of Istanbul. Now, by the sea and ancient Carthage, I was hearing another tranquil prayer.

The next morning I watched a live mass on television from St. Peter's in Rome. Trish and I were waiting for the cab to take us to the airport. When I turned on the television set, Patricia bolted out of the room and went down to the lobby to read. As I watched the Pope performing the mass, it struck me that, in many ways, a sacrifice that two of the girls on Arête '89 had witnessed in Istanbul was being acted out in St. Peter's. Alyssa and Marina watched a sheep being killed for the Ramadan meal. They were astonished to observe the ancient ritual we had studied about before the trip being acted out in exact detail. Three thousand years before, similar procedures were followed by the ancient Greeks and others in the Mediterranean world. What I saw in my room was the Pope offering not an animal, but a man for the communal meal. The rituals appeared essentially the same to me.

Sports is the prime American ritual. The supreme sacrifice around the globe is not mass, but World Cup soccer! Every four years, the summer Olympics begin with the fire being brought to a caldron by a runner before the games can begin. The gods require their sacrifice. Today we have a Dionysian twist for American collegiate basketball with "March Madness." The purpose behind these sacrifices is to experience continuation, to advance beyond "sudden death." This is why one feels let down when their favorite athlete, or team, loses. We continue the sacrificial ritual in order to ward off the fear of death and momentarily escape endless guilt. I was fascinated to watch this portrayed by the Holy Father in St. Peter's on New Year's day from North Africa.

Jess located an engineering position in Italy and one of the projects that his company spent time on was a bid to build a bridge over the Strait of Messina. The waters off Messina in northern Sicily carry powerful stories. Odysseus lost sailors to those hungry monsters on the cliffs above. Too bad about the eventual bridge. But Jess is not guilty. After four years in Bergamo, Italy, he returned to California and pursued another graduate degree, this time at USC.

Those maidens who went undefeated in the county for four straight track seasons were off to college. How could I replace them?

I did not pay any attention to him initially. It was two years before his unusual ability burst forth on the track. Even when he broke Jess's school mile record after a compromised sophomore year due to an injury, I did not recognize his national potential.

Then it happened. We were across the bay and Richie Boulet was up against one of the best high school milers in the country. With 300 meters to go in the race, Richie abruptly turned on his jet engines and flew away from the favorite and the rest of the field. No one came close to catching him. East Bay coaches immediately wanted to know, "Who is your unknown runner?" Both Richie and I realized the significance of the fast time and the margin of victory over this champion distance runner.

I was shocked when I learned at a conference in Dallas that my investment firm in New York was fighting for survival. Trish and I had flown to Texas for the annual company convention. I became highly suspicious of what the company president was feeding us. What it boiled down to was that our sales force was being sold. The parent company was collapsing due to a national banking crisis and a major change in the tax law. My New York firm was dependent on investments with massive tax benefits and when Congress changed the tax law, retroactively, those talented New York lawyers who had structured our firm were going to be forced out of business. It was Jablonowski who said, "Man does not live by bread alone, but bread helps." God damn it. After the loss of clients due to the stock market collapse of 1969-74, then the oil and gas crisis of the early eighties, how could I handle a third loss of investor trust?

My income from coaching brought in three to four percent of our annual income. Our travel and our life in Marin depended on my investment business. I, fortunately, did not have my clients buy the stock of my broker. But they would still hear the word "bankruptcy." The regulators required that it be disclosed. The real crisis for me was credibility. I had championed the New York professionals for almost two decades. Their intelligence and innovative talent had provided me with that something extra, that sizzle that every salesman knows is what moves product. And now this image was collapsing.

I had to come up with a new image, a new Gospel. And fast. I needed respect; my clients needed security. I had been recommending an investment management firm with strong international connections for two decades as part of their holdings. I even visited their offices in Geneva on a family trip in the mid-seventies. This experienced, tested firm had not yet become the centerpiece for my investors, but they knew of my respect for it. I turned to this established stock and bond management company because of its record and stature. I did not need the "sizzle" anymore. I had the clients. I needed performance with stability. This would prove to be my investment salvation. And that of my clients.

The slashing of throats in Algeria

You do not just go to Algeria. One might even give special attention to getting their personal affairs in order before going. The former French colony lives with death. Before landing in Algiers on a December night in 1990, I had read *A Savage War of Peace,* written by Alistair Horne. This brilliant author provided me with a gruesome view of the colonial war of independence fought with France in the mid-twentieth century. Trish and I arrived thirty years later with Algeria on the brink of becoming an Islamic state. The civil war and the throat slitting were only weeks away. In addition to reading Alistair Horne, I watched *The Battle of Algiers*, considered one of the greatest documentaries ever filmed.

Trish and I would be driving on a mountain road where, in the Algerian War of Independence in the late 1950s and early 1960s, a bus was pulled over, passengers ordered out, and, as is done with sheep or goats or camels, all of their throats were slashed. While abhorrent and terrifying, is a cluster bomb any better? The "terrorists" were Algerians who were demanding their own land and their own religion. The French had other plans for this country. Along with the vast reserves of gas, there was French pride at stake during the war with Algeria. The capitulation by many French citizens with the Nazis in World War II, along with the loss of Indochina in 1954, made another disaster unacceptable to a nation with a proud military tradition. Especially a defeat to inept, ignorant, colonized Moslems of North Africa. So the French fought dirty. Both sides did. If you can find a copy, read *The Centurions* by Jean Larteguy. A classic, it tells of the French in Indochina, then Algeria. Jerry read it at West Point, before he faced his "Algeria" in Vietnam.

So why did we go? Algeria was a forbidden destination of unusual beauty. And Trisha was set on visiting all of the North African countries. Only Algeria and Libya remained.

We were way down on the Sahara when I left Trish freezing in an ordinary cabin-like room and headed for the bar. I wanted a beer before dinner. The village of Timimoun is southwest of Algiers, in the fifth-largest nation in the world. From our room, we could see an absolutely smooth carpet of desert sand extended toward the mountains that separated Timimoun from the Mediterranean Sea. Immediately below the room was a lush green garden of palm trees sweetened by dates; petite little canals sent water silently flowing through this oasis.

There were a couple of journalists from Algiers talking about a vote when I sat down at the bar. They told me the Islamic party won more seats than was expected and the Algerian government was therefore canceling the election. French influence, secular power, upper class Algerians who wanted dresses from Paris and suits from Italy, tossed the ballots out and the U.S. said nothing. A decade of slashed throats was about to begin by civil war, only this time they would belong solely to Algerians.

Western newspapers stopped counting when 100,000 Algerians had been killed. The world looked elsewhere for bloody news. Many of the deaths came directly by a knife in a frenzied ritual common to the tradition of sacrificing animals. Babies, mothers, fathers, grandparents—all victims because an election result was denied.

I ran off the hill of our frontier hotel, past the oasis of cool running streams, into the magnificently smooth desert. A road parted this spectacular sea of sand. I was not full of stride, nor fatigued. This nibble of exercise did not matter, because for a moment I was separated from civilization, alone in the crisp early evening air. An incredible orange-red sun was about to drop below the horizon, in beauty more powerful and deep in colors than any human artist can create.

Upon returning to the village I ran up a gradual hill. Darkness had begun to sweep across the desert. Three tall black African women, carrying large baskets of green produce on their heads, came up from the oasis. They took bold strides as they rotated their hips with confidence. One saw me, turned, and with flashing white teeth made some remark to the others. All three turned together and laughed at me. I was not insulted. By age, beard, and running shorts I was surely an incongruity for this Saharan village.

El Oued can reach temperatures of 140 degrees Fahrenheit in the summer. That gave it an ominous image, even though it was winter when Trisha and I drove into this desert city surrounded by the endless sand of the Sahara. By the time I went on my run, it was already dark. I wanted to find a softer surface than the pavement near the hotel, so I made my way toward the southern edge of the town. It was then that I noticed some bright lights and activity up ahead. I jogged up to where a number of men were moving boxes and crates. A man in slacks, shirt collar open, approached me with a sub-machine gun dangling from one of his hands. He was pleasant, yet he turned me around and sent me back to the hotel. I did not argue with him.

I started doing some fairly fast strides on a strip of dirt in front of our hotel. Moslem women, robed, faces covered, would appear out of darkness on the road next to the path. Animals came by me, pulling carts. I felt good, fast. Running at nighttime can do this for you, make you feel faster. A young boy, perhaps thirteen or fourteen, decided to join me. I would jog back to a particular telephone pole each time after I sprinted about seventy yards. Then I would do another one. After three or four sprints, the boy made it clear by sign language that he wanted to know how many more I was going to do. I had completed six of ten so I held up four fingers. It helps to set goals for conditioning, even when you are no longer a competitive runner. The boy stopped after one more and went over and sat on the steps of the hotel. As said, I felt a lot of speed that night. This surprised me. I was fifty-seven. Was I motivated by the lad running with me, or the machine gun? When I went into the hotel lobby, I passed the night manager, pointed back to the boy sitting on the front step and said, "Your next Morceli." Noureddine Morceli had broken the world mile record recently and in Algeria he naturally was a national hero. However, the night manager corrected me. He said, "No. *You* are the champion."

The mighty legions of Rome, after their victories, were told to stay, to not return home. Caesars built them cities in North Africa so that the army would not be a threat in Rome. It was at Timgad, on the road from El Oued to Constantine, where Trish and I walked alone through the cream-colored garrison town that contained a library, theater, law court, amphitheater, rows and rows of barracks. The snow-covered Atlas Mountains rose behind this magnificent site. After we drove a few miles down the highway, I asked the driver to stop and let me out. I wanted to run back toward Timgad and absorb that spectacular setting. Except for a shepherd boy who was moving his sheep on the ridge to my left, I was alone. I was doing what I wanted to be doing at twilight on New Year's Eve.

The Algerian airport terminal was small, but orderly. Not anything like the chaotic Bombay one I would see a few years later. We escaped from Algiers just in time. Three weeks after we left that little airport in Algiers, human flesh and body parts hung from the ceiling of the terminal. Twenty-four people were blown apart. The Algerian civil war had begun.

Both Sweden and the Black Sea

During the nine-month preparation period for the 1991 youth trip, I was coaching that lad with such great potential. Richie put on a blazing kick a touch too soon in the state cross-country finals, barely losing the 5000-meter final. The Stanford and Olympic coach, Brooks Johnson, gave it positive perspective when he told me shortly after the finish, "You can always smooth out the timing of the kick."

Half of the youth wanted us to include Sweden on the 1991 trip, the other half voted for the Black Sea. We went to both. A drive to the lake country in northwest Sweden was overwhelmingly beautiful, enhanced by the musical score from the movie, *Dances with Wolves* on the tape deck. Boulet set a youth meet record in a Copenhagen 1500-meter race and the news was reported in the *Marin Independent Journal*. While what was happening on the trip exceeded the importance of a track victory, Richie was exciting and the young people admired his inner fortitude and character. So did I. But I was also riding his track image, still carrying some of my unfulfilled "national" dreams.

We held funeral games one morning before the farmers came to their fields at Troy. They were in honor of my former USC teammate, Max Truex, who had fought so courageously to prevent Parkinson's

In front of ancient walls at Troy, we built a funeral
mound for my USC teammate, Max Truex.

disease from taking his life. The students, with Homer in one hand,
and a rock from the ancient battlefield for the mound in the other,
thought dearly of the little 5'5" cherub who battled through many
races before losing life at age fifty-five.

I was captain of the 1954 USC cross-country team when "little
Max" first charmed the running fans. He was the one who fixed me up

with Linda when I was at Camp Pendleton. The two-time Olympian and American record holder came by to visit me in San Anselmo during his illness. His face looked puffy, but I did not realize that he was fighting for his life. After building the funeral mound, the youth ran for Max before the ancient walls of Troy. I sent pictures of these funeral games to his wife, Kay and she shared them with their children.

The hills of Austria may be alive with the sound of music, but a concentration camp along the Danube below the mountains tore into the hearts of the young on that '91 journey. At Auschwitz you see the broken walls and foundations of the gas chambers, at Mauthausen you stand under an actual gas vent. While I continue to include the Jewish death camps on the youth trips as evidence of how despicable and cruel humans can be to one another, I see nihilism beyond the Jews. Jeanne's death scream was my Auschwitz. The endless cries of the Palestinians hold Israel accountable. The volume of violent deaths carried out on this planet by countries and tribes is so horribly consistent that the students need to be brought before a wall of emptiness in order to know their world.

Our boys were with women; life had moved on. Jess, in addition to his masters in geophysics, obtained an MBA from USC. Cory graduated from UCLA in theatre arts in an enthusiastic ceremony that Patricia and I both enjoyed. He worked for a literary agency for a brief time, then landed a position with National Geographic. Cory married a UCLA coed who played the lead in the university production of *Romeo and Juliet*. Julie has proven to be a marvelous choice.

Our sons were well out of the nest, experiencing new friends, relationships, even values. While I was the liberal patriarchal father, their time in the wilderness belonged to them. I felt the distance, waited for time to bring them closer.

The National Geographic television offices were in North Hollywood, just down the street from where Bob Hope lived. And, therefore, close to my former pigeon loft which was a block up the street from Hope. When I visited Cory and Julie at their duplex in North Hollywood, I was able to walk less than a block and be in the park where we had played Saturday morning tackle football games. This led to some nostalgic runs under familiar sycamore trees.

When Jess wasn't working in Italy, he held positions in the Bay Area. For awhile in seismology, but today as a consultant for Fortune 500 companies. Cory, through endless hours at night on his own time learning how to use the sophisticated equipment, worked his way up at National Geographic.

The miler was over at Cal Berkeley. Richie was elected captain of the track team, won the Pacific Coast Conference 1500 meters twice, and it appeared that, as a pro, he was headed for the 2000 U.S. Olympic Team. In a newspaper article about Boulet, it was mentioned that I was "a former half miler on two USC national championship track teams." There I was back again, eulogized by sport mythology.

The Cal distance coach told one of my adult track friends that he had "never received a runner from high school as well prepared as Boulet." It is true that I did not race him to death, run his legs out of future life with excessive mileage. But there was also a little criticism that I did not work him hard enough. This does not bother me for two reasons. I did save his legs for big time efforts in college and as a pro. And

Julie and Cory

I do not think that high school running should be over-emphasized. Do you know how much time is eaten up by running ninety miles a week? Or even sixty?

During the 1990s there were several times that I needed to reinforce the confidence of my investors. My own emotional strength was a big part of the success that resulted for the clients. My effort reminded me of what it took to stay with the field on the backstretch of the final lap of the half mile, when you want to back off, or quit, due to less and less oxygen and increasing pain.

Huge round craters told of the B-52s that had preceded us in Vietnam

Patricia gave me the choice, as long as our next winter trip would be in Southeast Asia. It did not take me very long to say, "Vietnam." She would have preferred Indonesia, Bali, Thailand, or Burma. But I wanted to see those rice paddies, and the people that I watched on television night after night during the Vietnam War. I took Jerry Ledzinski with me. Or, more accurately, I took a marked map showing where my investment friend had fought in the rice paddies and a copy of the letter from a senior officer that led to his being awarded a silver star for bravery. The war not only took life from fifty-five thousand Americans, and a million or more Vietnamese, but there were thousands of Americans who could not survive it psychologically. Such a high dose of meaninglessness crippled them emotionally for life.

Vietnam was just opening up to American travelers when we flew into the Hanoi airport. The U.S. government had not officially recognized Vietnam yet. Clients and friends were very curious about what we would experience. I was still writing my newspaper column, so I brought the community in on the journey.

We came down through the broken clouds on our flight to Hanoi from Bangkok. Just a few minutes before, I had looked down at the wide, muddy Mekong River. As our jet approached the runway, familiar green rice paddies appeared, and there were huge round craters filled with water that told of the B-52s that had preceded us. When we touched down, I saw only two aircraft near a small terminal. One was a Thai jet, the other, a very large, mysterious one painted pitch black. I noticed little boxes on display, covered with American flags, as we taxied past the big jet. It struck me that body parts were in the boxes and the U.S. government was sending them home. The ominous black aircraft had a tiny label just below the cockpit that identified it as belonging to the United States.

I thought we weren't supposed to be there.

A narrow road, crowded with bikes and occasionally joined by a water buffalo, led us toward the heavily bombed city. Jane Fonda and the Hanoi Hilton were ahead. I was well prepared for this trip because of the excellent array of books that were available on the Vietnam War. I am not talking about the heavily biased, hate-America publications. Serious scholars document the catastrophe. While we bombed children at Christmas time in Hanoi, a deeply disturbed president was heard to say that the communists would advance as far as Texas and rape his daughter if we didn't stop them.

Once in Vietnam it hit me: I had been a Marine. My discharge as an infantry officer is dated July, 1960. I was in the Marine Corps just a few years before America began sending its troops to Vietnam. The horror of napalm and Agent Orange would scar our character for decades. It was during the height of the war that Professor Hamilton had said to me, "It doesn't matter whether you say 'yes God,' or 'no God;' what matters is whether you stand and cry with Jesus over Vietnam." His theological framework does not work as fully for me anymore. I would put it differently: all we can do is stare into nihilism. In that cold instance of death, there is no meaning. We are not even comforted by the warmth of caring tears.

The capacity of the American people to accept thousand upon thousands of civilian deaths staggered me. How can they enthusiastically applaud a president at dinners or speaking engagements who has killed to such proportions?

While we were waiting to take a ferry north of Haiphong, I noticed a pretty, young Vietnamese woman with large baskets of greens precariously balanced on an overloaded bicycle. I also noticed a red communist star on the cabin of the ferry above where she was standing. My attempts to make contact with this shy, young woman were ignored. I seemed to be making her nervous. One of our guides, a young man called Chin, bridged this gap and asked her a few questions for me.

President Nixon called the bombing around Hanoi and Haiphong, "Operation Linebacker." Was it just a football game for him? I thought that surely some of the young woman's relatives, if not close family, were killed or injured by the American pounding of the villages in the Haiphong area. As we were leaving the ferry, I went over and helped her balance the bike that was loaded with produce as she headed down the ramp. It looked like it was going to tilt over. I was very pleased to see in a photograph later that the girl had a big smile on her face as I helped her off.

We had arrived early to Vietnam, before the world discovered that one could travel around it safely. It angered me when I discovered that our small tour group was not interested in the war. Nobody wanted to

Helping a Vietnamese woman carry produce off a ferry ramp
(Note the smile of this previously shy woman)

go on pilgrimages with Jerry and me. They preferred arts and crafts, or going to a Buddhist temple, to locating where monks and nuns chose to protest the American bombings by self-immolation.

In Hue, I actually jumped out of the van by the Perfume River and the gates to the old city and took a cyclo to a pagoda where a nun had committed suicide. It was in a part of Hue that was unfamiliar with American tourists. To the children along the road, I was a peculiar westerner with "round eyes," cut-off pants, a beard, and a tennis hat.

Stanley Karnow, a Pulitzer Prize-winning journalist who is praised for his balanced account of the Vietnam War, wrote about my nun as follows—

"I witnessed the first in this series of self-immolations on the morning of May 29, 1966, at the Dieude temple in Hue. A Buddhist nun in her mid-fifties, Thanh Quang, had entered the temple compound at dawn. She assumed the lotus position as one of her friends doused her with gasoline. Then she lighted a match, immediately exploding into flame as another friend fed peppermint oil to the fire to suppress the stench of scorched flesh. By the time I arrived, her burning body was still erect, the hands clasped in prayer."

I entered the sparse temple grounds alone. I wanted to locate the exact spot where she had given her life to stop the bombing. I could not find anyone who spoke English. An attendant led me into the fairly small temple, but that did not offer any closure. I left, feeling the emptiness of the war.

I felt full of stride as I ran down the streets in Saigon with the morning bike traffic. Those on the scooters and cyclos did not bother me. I ran for a good number of blocks before I reached the much-filmed U.S. Embassy. The huge compound was locked up. I pictured scenes that I remembered from television as I jogged outside of its familiar gate and walls. Up on the roof was the platform where the helicopters at the end of the war had swept up the last of the Americans and taken them to the waiting ships. It was as though my reading was for them. For Vietnam. For Jerry.

At the Saigon airport, I looked out at the camouflaged military hangers that were used during the Vietnam War. It had been an incredible trip for me. Even with the group. Above a check-in counter at the terminal, I noticed an ominous destination—Phenom Penn. The Killing Fields were just a short flight away. I immediately thought of the powerful motion picture, the unbelievable brutality of Khmer Rouge. I could not see myself ever going there. Before the century was over, Trish and I flew into Phenom Penn.

Dehydrated, no water, no change for a phone call, the kids down at the dock, a triumph

One moment we had a refreshing breeze out at sea, then suddenly the suffocating heat of North Africa hit us. We had traveled by ship across the Mediterranean from Sicily to Tunisia. This was on the next youth adventure in 1993 and I was very worried that the car company in Tunis would not hold our van because we were going to arrive late.

It was near dark when we docked at the port. I took a cab by myself into downtown and left the young people at a gate by a parking area. They had never been in an Islamic country before and here they were, abandoned by the docks of a North African seaport.

I didn't ask the cab to wait which was stupid. The goddamn Hertz office was closed. A few hours before, the temperature had reached 106 degrees; I was dehydrated, I didn't have any water, it was getting dark, and I did not speak Arabic or French.

How could I call the Hilton about our reservations without money or the ability to communicate? The owner of a bar/restaurant next to the Hertz office came through for me. He gave me bottled water, changed some money for me, and called the Hilton to arrange for them to send down their shuttle bus to pick us up. The Hilton had held our rooms, but there was a problem. There was no electricity in Tunis because of the excessive heat. The Hilton gave us sandwiches and we ate in the lobby by candlelight. And flashlight.

On top of this, the Hilton manager promised to call the car company in the morning to see about having a van delivered for me. We had lucked out once again on an Arête West adventure.

The next morning, after we drove to Kairouan (the holiest city in Tunisia), the girls joined me for a run outside of the ancient walls. In their shorts. As we ran back toward the hotel, a couple of truck drivers blasted their air horns in appreciation. Given the reputation for fundamentalism in Kairouan, this salute was an incongruity.

The Tunisian van we rented took diesel; the one we stored in the port city of Trapani for our return required leadless gas. After sailing back to Sicily, it was not too long before I pulled the van up to a diesel pump in Palermo. A man filled our tank with the wrong fuel, of course. He did not notice the error until removing the nozzle from the gas tank.

Panic. We had to catch the ferry to Greece the next day. And not from Palermo. Our ferry would sail from the port of Brindisi on the northern side of Italy. Where would I go to rent another van on a Sunday morning? Would one even be available in Palermo?

It is hard to believe what happened next. The station owner began to suck (by tube) the gas out of the tank. I watched him spit several mouthfuls out. The entire process took well over an hour. But by noon we had the right tank of fuel and were ready for the drive toward Brindisi. I took out a considerable amount of lira and handed it to the man. He refused it. Told me it was his fault. Is this your image of Palermo?

I did not want to conduct the wedding ceremony for Jess and his bride, Shawn. I still carried some unexamined feelings leftover from my separation from the ministry over thirty years before. Leading the wedding ritual turned out to be good for me because I was able to go back and feel how I felt as a minister.

The wedding was held in a dense redwood grove on the way to the Point Reyes National Seashore in Marin County. I stood with Jess and Cory in front of family and friends as we waited for the late bride to appear. Once ready, I said quietly to Jess, "You son-of-a-bitch, you dumped this whole thing on me." I was struck that day with how many young men attended the wedding. They flew in from Southern California, the East Coast, even Europe. His popularity with his male friends made me feel proud and happy for my son.

You know that Trish and I raised Jess and Cory without religion. While Jess did not find it necessary to have one, Cory became deeply involved in an international Buddhist movement. His devotion to the Japanese leader bothered me because I felt it was unquestioning. It bothered Patricia as well. However, through chanting, a moral commitment, and leadership, Cory grew in stature. In regard to his devotion to the leader, I had my heroes. I quoted Dr. Stein, Dr. Gill, and Dr. Schoenberger endlessly. Cory is a sensitive, loving son. The Buddhist organization has enhanced his character. As Nietzsche said, Buddhism is one of the better choices if you are going to have a religion.

India

Going to India by tour seemed sensible. I had heard terrible stories about travelers becoming seriously ill there. Trish had wanted to go to India when she was in college, so she was thrilled about our destination. I went with little enthusiasm.

India turned out to be provocative, colorful, different, different, different. This was most apparent when we drove by bus into the most unusual city in the world one night. Benares (Varanasi) dazzled me as we passed endless shack-like shops on both sides of the muddy road leading into the city. Energized Indians in colorful saris moved about under bright, ornamental lights while music from tape decks screamed out into the night. Thousands upon thousands of people were alive to the blast of pulsating sounds.

The next morning I almost stepped on him as I got off the tour bus in the dark. A young boy was out in the streets before 6:00 a.m. on a round skateboard—or, more accurately, a piece of scrap wood with roller wheels. The boy did not have any legs. Just arms to propel him through the dung of the sacred cows. His face told of those hustling lads of cities of poverty all over the world. The young businessman was up early practicing his trade.

We found Indian men sitting around fires just before we reached the "mother" river of India, the Ganges. The current of the sacred river

moved slowly below us as we waited to step into a boat that would take
us to the cremation fires. We were on the southwestern side with the
temples and shrines. Across the river there are no structures, just flat
land. Within minutes, the sun rose brilliantly across the water.

I felt both excitement and apprehension when we approached the
place where families were burning the bodies of their loved ones. Some
were still piling wood on pyres. Soon the corpses would be given to
the flames. The guide said that, out of respect, we would stay out in
the river, not go too close. But you want to go closer, you want to see
more.

I watched pilgrims splashing and submerging themselves playfully
in the river. Undisturbed by this joyful frolicking in the holy water,
one fellow in a yellow garment, legs folded, sat and stared directly at
the sun. He sat there, motionless, in a trance. I believe he stayed in that
position the entire day.

On the way back from the river, I tightened up when I saw that
I would have to pass beggars. Below me, as I made my way up a narrow walkway toward the bus, I looked down at a woman with gauze
wrapped over her biblical disease. I was looking down on my first leper.
I kept walking. I was no Saint Francis, the little monk whom the Greek
writer, Nikos Kazantzakis, in *St. Francis*, had embrace and kiss a leper
on the lips. No, I fled with the Cox and Kings tour company.

I do not have a love affair with India. But Trisha gave me some unforgettable memories by taking me there. One came very early in the
morning in Nepal. In darkness our bus raced up to a higher location
before we saw the enormous orange sun rise over Mt. Everest and other
Himalayan peaks. China, Japan, Burma, Vietnam, Pakistan, Afghanistan all seemed to be in proximity as snow-capped mountains stretched
for hundreds of miles, both east and west. Absolute lasting beauty!

While I was running some fast strides on grass alongside a canal in
front of our hotel in Cochin, India, I thought about the white church
across the waterway where the funeral services for Vasco de Gama
were held before the great explorer was returned to Portugal. On an
earlier run in Lisbon on one of our two Spain/Portugal trips, I went
into a monastery along the river Tagus and saw the sarcophagus of the

national hero who sailed around Africa and into the Indian Ocean in 1497. Later on that run in Lisbon, I jogged by the entrance to a small dock and memorial structure on the Tagus from where Vasco de Gama sailed. What is travel without linking up time and places?

The drive at night to the airport in Bombay displayed endless bodies stretched out on the sidewalks and alongside the road. Cardboard, scraps, and newspapers were used for roofs and walls in thousands of makeshift huts.

Leaving India is separating from suffering and filth, overpopulation and disease. India is unlike anywhere else on this planet. The mix of colors confronts the suffering, the religion reeks of superstition and inner peace. Life is both inconsequential, and sacred.

Separated, without passports

It was raining fairly hard. I tried to avoid the collision. We were nearing Auschwitz. The approaching car glanced off the side of our van and pulled over to the side of the road. I wanted to drive away. But people came out of a roadside inn and I had no choice but to wait for the police.

One of my travel fears had just been realized—an accident on an Arête trip. I told the students to keep this to themselves, to not tell their parents or friends, to not compromise future trips. One of the boys said, "It wasn't your fault." I wondered. The other boy felt the same way. Still I wondered. The side of the van had a huge gash; it was not just a scrape. It appeared as though we had been in an awful accident. The police officer told me to follow him in the van. Remember, it was raining. The afternoon was in black and white.

It took awhile to reach the station. The building, undecorated in impersonal gray cement looked like it was straight out of a spy film set in Eastern Europe. I was taken up to the second floor and into a large room with scattered desks. A couple of detectives were seated at two of them. I brought Jen with me; she spoke a little German. And I wanted company. Was this really happening?

It appeared that the police officer was scolding me for driving recklessly. While it was likely an acting routine, in Polish it was intimidating. My mind raced back and forth from the dreary police station to my bewilderment that this was even taking place. We were near Auschwitz.

It was not until I indicated that I would sign the traffic ticket and accept responsibility for the accident that the young officer dropped the acting. He was a young, nice-looking man. He actually walked Jen and me down to the van where the rest of the group was curiously waiting. The officer and I shook hands. Then he wished us well. I wonder: What would have happened, had I not been with Jen Ponig and the other young people?

I waited until we were in Vienna before I asked the youth for their reflections on Auschwitz. The day of the accident and death camp ended with a multi-course dinner in Cracow with traditional Polish food. The kids needed to let go, have fun, and they raced playfully out into the enormous square after a wonderful meal. So I waited until Vienna. We had actually gone within the rubble of the gas chamber at Auschwitz. This time vertigo did not keep me a safe distance away.

We began our reflections with a view of the balcony where Hitler stood when he returned as a hero to some 80,000 cheering Austrians. I played his favorite opera, *Lohengrin*, on our portable cassette through two small speakers. The music was beautifully eerie. The poetic, poignant, honest reflections by the students were of courage and wisdom. The evening sky with a light blue tint closed out the day.

Our group became separated again, this time in Turkey. The car company had not delivered the scheduled van and we had to take two cars. Fortunately one of the girls, Amy Glenn, was old enough to take the wheel of a second vehicle. After an hour of frantic driving back and forth on the highway looking, I found them sitting on a curb at the intersection where the separation occurred. This episode threw our schedule off and we ended up arriving on the Greek island of Rhodes a day ahead of our itinerary. The assistant hotel manager, after telling us that we would need to stay elsewhere for a night due to the hotel being fully booked, took a personal risk by letting us wash up and shower in the service quarters; then he gave us a place to sleep between the kitchen and the hotel walls. The cement surface was most welcomed as the police would not be waking us up in the middle of the night and telling us to move on. I was exceedingly happy as I watched the kids spreading out in their bags for a night's sleep. Being very tired, I slept quite well. It is one of my favorite hotel rooms of any overseas adventure. And it was my sixty-second birthday.

In Prague, we could not afford the entrance fee to hear a Mozart concert in the Bethlehem Chapel. This was extremely disappointing because Jan Hus, one of the great martyrs of intellect and conscience, had preached inside. Some of the kids were especially looking forward to Mozart. Hus meant something personal to me, too, because I had been a minister. Luther had said, "We are all Hussians." Denied passage into the chapel, we stood outside in a drizzle. I began telling my students about how some twenty of Hus's students were murdered where we were standing for affirming their independence and values. Then the young usher who told us of the highly priced tickets motioned for us to follow him into the chapel. Quietly. Seated in the back pew, I looked up at the pulpit. I felt my life linked to it. It reminded me of the rustic pulpit in the chapel in North Hollywood where I preached my first sermon. I saw tears on the cheeks of some of the Arête youth as we listened to the absolute beauty and purity from the violins. We had not been asked to pay admission. A rare, special moment had been given to us, without charge.

In 1993, twenty years after Steve Miller told me I was the first person he thought of when he located the ancient starting grooves at Nemea, the two of us along with people from the village and Arête West staged the first track meet in twenty-three hundred years at the site. I jumped at the chance to put my athletes on the ancient track in an actual competition. While there were only a few races, Steve staged them as if they were the authentic Pan-Hellenic Games at Nemea. The meet officials from the village dressed in ancient robes, the winners were crowned with celery wreaths. Olympia claimed the olive leaves; Nemea had the celery. A crew from the University of California, Berkeley filmed the races of what Miller called the New Nemean Games. The film was shown on the Cal campus that fall when Steve gave his annual report to the university and friends of Nemea. Several of the Arête runners were asked to stand and were introduced. This competition was both real, and of fantasy. I think back to those "games" that Harold and I conducted by Warner Brothers when we were growing up in Toluca Lake, the hurdles we made out of bamboo poles and cardboard boxes.

Two years later, on the youth trip in 1995, we were back with Steve trying out a new event for what would become in 1996 the worldwide New Nemean Games. A five-mile uphill effort to the stadium began in a farmer's field by an ancient altar dedicated to Heracles. The crops and dust breathed history into their lungs. Village people stood alongside the road and offered them water as they climbed up the hill toward the excavated stadium.

The next year the world came to Nemea. Thousands of people from various countries ran barefoot while NBC and other media outlets filmed the event. Steve even arranged for the flame that was on its way to Atlanta, Georgia, for the 1996 Olympic Games, to stop and light up the caldron at our track.

Steve told me he seriously considered running naked!

Arête lass winning the first race in 2300 years on the ancient track
at Nemea

My friend, Payton Jordan, joined the organizing committee for the worldwide summer games at Nemea and even agreed to run in the competition. Twenty years before, I had introduced the famous coach to the archaeologist. Miller recently told me that he will forever be grateful that I introduced him to this golden god of track and field. Steve said that Payton's charisma lifted up the entire event.

Seven months before the Olympics in Atlanta, I asked the head U.S. Olympic track coach, Erv Hunt, what he was going to do with Carl Lewis. We were standing on the infield of the Cal stadium when I inquired about the prima donna of the sport. I could see it coming: Carl Lewis, the most publicized track and field athlete in the world, would demand special privileges in the '96 Olympics in Atlanta. I was sure that he would make trouble for Hunt. Erv told me that he had thought the matter through and he felt prepared for Lewis. We will see!

A few days before the Olympic track events began, I met my USC teammate, Sid Wing, at the national airport in Washington, D.C. We drove down to Oxford, Georgia, together. Sid had lived in Atlanta with his aunt when he was growing up. Not that many months before the Olympics, she had died and her home in Oxford remained vacant. Before I met up with Sid, I spent a couple of days in Washington D.C.; on one of those days, I drove down to Quantico and walked on the old track surface where I had run my fastest 800 meters. The smells of the old base greeted my senses. How many years had it been since I had been there? Forty!

The Olympics take past track and field athletes back into themselves—those who heavily identified with the sport, anyway. The Olympics can represent the finality of sport existence for their heroic dreams. And once every four years, the dream returns. Especially if the Olympics are on home soil. Sid and I were there together because our lives carried this essence of the track and field athlete. Carl Lewis had not qualified for a spot on the sprint relay team in the U.S. Olympic Trials, but he made it known that he wanted to anchor the American team. The pressure began to build for Erv Hunt to comply. The other

American and world track "superstar," Michael Johnson, endorsed this change. Both presidential campaigns lobbied for the track brat. Hillary Clinton called for her husband. Father Bush let it be known that Lewis had the Republicans behind him. Nationalism was going to take away the relay position that had been earned by another athlete.

Jesse Owens or Bob Mathias would not have done this. It was the ploy of Lewis, the leader of the media types. I was surprised to learn that the U.S. Olympic track sponsor, Nike, told Hunt that it was up to him. On the night of the 400-meter relay final, Sid and I waited in suspense, seated right above where the athletes would come into the stadium. The majority of the people in the stands around us clearly wanted Lewis to run. Would Lewis come out, or would the sprinter who legitimately qualified for the relay team appear? The tall, quiet coach from a large family in Fresno, Erv Hunt, stuck by his decision. Carl Lewis did not come out. The U.S. relay team ran second to a great Canadian foursome in the final. With honor, as far as Sid and I were concerned. Same for Payton Jordan. He told me this in a letter after the Olympics.

Months later, I received a thank-you phone call for a letter I had written in support of Hunt to the chancellor of the University of California. Because of the public reaction over Lewis not replacing the lesser-known relay sprinter, Hunt's job as head coach at Cal was threatened. Some felt that he had betrayed his country. I was told that my letter to the chancellor helped Hunt keep his job. It felt good to have been a part of this and to see ethics win out over greed.

Patricia

Trisha travels because it makes her extremely happy. She returns home exhilarated from a sailing trip on the Aegean Sea, or a trip to Mexico, Polynesia, even Burma; those are places that I choose not to go. For years I gave her a very tough time when she announced that she was going on another trip. Of course she said that I could come with her. Usually, track or cross country prevented me from considering the trip, plus they were not places that excited me.

My Greek shepherd staff and USC identity—appropriately
displayed on the high school track where I coach

Our marriage remains personal, with intellectual stimulation, physical attraction, and commitment. Trisha is very supportive of the academic side of my work with young people, in sport and in the overseas youth adventures. At the same time, she does not see any importance to a sub-four minute mile. When I was leaving one morning to go and see if my former high school star, Richie Boulet, could run under four minutes for his first time, Trish remarked, "Hasn't someone already done this?" I actually appreciate her lack of interest in sports. Our dinner table company is the BBC news, not the entries for the next track meet or the up-and-coming USC game.

Who decides "good" and "evil"?

We began in Israel, then flew to Egypt and Greece, by ship we went to Italy, by van to the Swiss Alps, Verdun, and Paris. It was thrilling to teach from this itinerary. Wow! On the final night, we celebrated along the Seine in Paris. After a picnic meal of baguettes and cheese, the young reflected on the personal meaning of the journey for them. Spontaneous dancing along the river closed our encounter with time.

Early on in this trip, we visited Megiddo, in Israel. I remember it with a certain fascination. From the ancient ruins, we could view Armageddon stretched out before us. Is life worthwhile without the moral struggle? Who decides "good" and "evil"? Megiddo was desolate, alone back in time. But not the questions.

In Jerusalem for the second time, I realized that for me, Jesus was not there. Nine years earlier, I was fascinated with the biblical locations where Jesus reportedly uttered the words that formed many of my values. But not this time. The psychic energy that attached me to him in any mysterious or religious way had disappeared.

Several weeks after we left Jerusalem, a bomb went off in a restaurant where we had stood one evening, killing over twenty students. We missed death in Cairo, too. Just a couple of weeks after we visited the Egyptian Museum, a tour bus parked in front of it exploded. Eight Germans were killed. Up the Nile, in ancient Thebes, some forty tourists were shot in a mass killing. The odds of being in the wrong place at the wrong time were virtually nil but the tension produced by television images of victims of bombings would frighten some of the parents when I organized future Arête trips. It took considerable trust by the parents to release their sons and daughters for five weeks to travel with me to the Middle East and North Africa. But to dodge and miss Israel and Egypt would have deprived the young people of an enormous encounter with past and current history.

Jerusalem was on edge, tense; Cairo was full of friendly greetings. One of the places we wanted to see in Cairo was the old colonial hotel in *The English Patient*. Before the trip the students saw the Academy Award winning film and were familiar with the Shepherd Hotel. All we found was the vacant lot where the hotel once stood, but we did not need the actual structure to appreciate the location. The magnificent hotel would have been nice to see, but in certain ways, the experience was better without it.

When we approached the earliest of Egyptian pyramids south of Cairo, I asked the driver to stop so I could place a motion picture musical score in the van tape deck. It was from the movie, *Apollo 13*. Then I asked that he drive very slowly up the slight grade that hid the pyramid. As it rose up before us from the Libyan Desert, time itself emerged. The architect of the first pyramid was joined by engineers who had sent three men around the moon.

It was never my intention to offer my blood as a sacrifice at Nemea. Several days after we left Egypt, a particular morning was heavy with heat as Dr. Miller gave the 1997 Arête students the opportunity to clear soil that covered a track even older than the already unearthed fourth century B.C. one. Their trowels inched carefully over the seventh century, B.C. clay-like surface. When our "resident" archaeologist was ready to take them to the excavated track a short distance away for his lecture, I hit my forehead on the sharp edge of a low ceiling while rushing down a flight of stairs to a bathroom. Blame it on those short Greeks. Or my bifocals. I was surprised at the amount of blood. Steve had me lay down at the entrance to the stadium while he took the students through the ancient tunnel and out onto the track. I feared what Steve was going to say when he returned. Like, "You will need some stitches."

Steve drove me over to a doctor's office in the new village of Nemea. The physician examined me and said I needed to go to Argos for the stitching. Ancient Argos? That major city-state of ancient Greece? The kids looked very concerned, as the trip could not continue without me.

Steve put me in a cab, while our oldest girl, Amy, drove the van. Dr. Miller called ahead so that the medical staff at Argos would be ready for me. Steve is well known throughout the region and the doctors were expecting me. At the hospital, I was immediately stretched out on an operating table with a couple of physicians in green medical uniforms leaning over me. I believe I told them I had been a Marine. They froze the portion of my scalp and stitched my forehead. I barely felt the needle. I was told to come back in the morning to have some of the stitches removed. The other ones would need to stay in place for five or six days.

We slept the night of my bloody sacrifice at Nemea on a roof over a restaurant in ancient Mycenae. Argos, Mycenae, Ithaca—I hope these names are dancing classical history before you. While I was still somewhat stunned by the afternoon drama, the students pulled mattresses off bunkbeds in the stuffy youth hostel rooms and slept under a vast, glittering field of bright stars. The smells of the Greek countryside overwhelmed our senses. Just a half mile up the road, the royal blood of Agamemnon had flowed upon his return from Troy. Just before dawn, a wonderful chorus of birds began to sing the sun into labor. Far off toward to the southwest, the fortress of ancient Argos was in view. I would not trade sleeping on that roof for any expensive beds in luxury hotels (at least for one special night).

When I walked out of the hospital the next morning with some of my stitches removed, I looked up at the acropolis of the ancient fortress of Argos. The sun was pressing its warmth against its golden walls. Like the heroes of old, I had been wounded nearby. The gods surely knew of my wound.

She scared the hell out of me as she approached the van. An old woman with a floppy hat, torn dress, and heavy boots was herding her goats through a village above Sparta. We were on our way to visit King Nestor at Pylos, where Odysseus' son Telemachus had traveled in search of news of his father. The woman wanted her picture taken. Fortified by the young, I complied and had her write down her name and address on a piece of paper. She was near the window, breathing into our air. The goat lady left us with a scribbled Greek name and apparently her city. There was no street address.

After returning home, I taped the handwritten name and city onto an envelope, and I placed a fantastic picture of our "goat lady" within it. I had no confidence that the letter would be delivered.

A few months later, a package arrived from somewhere in Greece. I opened it and found a heartfelt note from her. She sent each of the young people hand-embroidered golden table banners, and her love. Jesus!

Upon our arrival at the south end of the thin Greek island of Ithaca, I hired two cabs to drive us to a cove below the village of Stavros. I thought we might sleep on the beach where the goddess Athena had assisted Telemachus in beginning his search for his father. The cabs drove us down a steep road to the small harbor and dumped us out with our luggage. There was time for a refreshing swim in the calm, peaceful water before dinner. It was there that we read a few passages from the *Odyssey* under an evening-tinted blue sky.

Later, returning from dinner in the town above the cove, we needed flashlights as we walked back down the steep road. I purposely fell behind the youth and took the evening for myself. The sky was brilliant with glittering diamonds. I was being careful with each step because it was so dark. Then I heard the bells. The goats were singing to us as they moved about the hillside, with a chorus of wonderful jingles. At that moment, I was completely fulfilled.

The cab driver, Johnny, had told me that he knew a doctor who would be able to take my stitches out. I did not want to wait until Rome. I had heard frightening stories about their hospitals. He delivered me to a shack in the village above the cove. I sat down on a bench in a bare room. The doctor was an intern on assignment for the summer. She was tall, dark, and striking, resembling the Greek actress, Irene Papas, only younger. She did not speak English so the cab driver translated our words. I looked up into the face of the goddess Athena while she removed my stitches. Were we directly above the ancient palace of Odysseus?

In 1997, Nietzsche waited for us in his Alpine forest, as he did on several of the youth trips. Zarathustra appears from the shadows, speaks to the teenagers before they become adult-ized. Thomas Jefferson did not write, "All men are not equal, nor shall they become equal." Nietzsche did! Teenagers find truth in his sarcastic insights. Clever insights abound. For example: "Association with other people corrupts one's character—especially if one has none." I remember in high school how I wanted everyone to like me. I could have especially used this verse from Nietzsche then.

Almost always, during our early morning hikes above his old boarding house in Sils Maria the weather is absolutely beautiful. The hikes take us into the woods where Nietzsche thought the ideas that shook Europe (and still terrify many Christians). The night before we enter the forest, I give each of the students a verse from Nietzsche. Existential thought does not come easily to the guilt-reward oriented morality of Western youth. Inspired by the Alpine peaks that surround them, the students are asked by Nietzsche to reach higher and higher. Or dive lower and lower into themselves. Zarathustra tugs, pulls, will not compromise. Nietzsche saw that Christianity rewarded weakness. *Arête* for Nietzsche is the courage to exist.

John Lennon came along on Arête 1997 from Jerusalem to Paris by a recording. The verses in a later song turned his earlier "Imagine all the People" upside down. Shortly before being murdered, John Lennon sang, "The dream is over / what can I say? /...I don't believe in the Bible /...I don't believe in Jesus /...I don't believe in Kennedy /...Elvis /...Zimmerman /...the Beatles /...I just believe in me." God, I loved those lyrics. Nietzsche would have enjoyed them, too.

Lennon had previously joined Arête groups by tape through a medley provided by Cory. Our son included Wagner, Beethoven, the Beatles, even the USC marching band. The youth were partial to "Imagine all the People," but immediately following the concluding verse—"and the world will be one"—Cory placed a recording of Hitler screaming at a Nazi rally. A romantic view of the future was squashed on the tape deck of our van.

When we camped alongside a river between Verdun and Paris, we did not know that Boulet was racing in Belgium that very night. Richie's time that evening over 1500 meters was fast enough to qualify him for the World Championships in Athens the next month. My former high school star was realizing the dream of every serious runner: world status! My running life was still unresolved; my track identity was still intermingled with this young man. Richie became a hero for my student athletes because of my intense feelings about his greatness and his lower and lower times on the track; the young identified with him.

Jess had to separate in marriage. Blame the "minister." While he shared close friendships with others, some lonely, painful years were ahead for our oldest son. During this time his interests broadened; archaeology, philosophy, and history provided the two of us a lot to converse about. Jess is very good at fixing things, just like his mother, and like my dad, too. When he hired a construction worker to improve his San Francisco home, he handled part of the renovation himself. In this way he clearly surpasses his father.

Kirsten was tall, blonde, and trim, a black-robed goddess when competing in the girls track uniform. National magazines wanted her body when she was only thirteen and a high school freshman. Would she stay with us? Would she have the time for sports with girls of her own age? The model chose the hurdles, the high jump, and friends over early money and magazine fame. She was one of the leaders during those four years that the Drake girls track team went undefeated.

I was deeply touched, and remain so to this day, with a letter I received from this goddess in 1997. I poured myself into coaching and her reflections on what I contributed to her life are wonderful to read. Eight years after graduating from Drake, Kirsten sent me this letter:

> Last week, the Wednesday before Thanksgiving, I was substitute teaching for the French teacher at Santa Cruz High School. Ten minutes before the bell rang, I asked the students to think about the people and circumstances in their lives that they are thankful for. I reminded them that, besides eating turkey and mashed potatoes, Thanksgiving is the day to acknowledge and appreciate those who give our lives meaning. You have been, and will always be at the top of my list. Even after nine years! I thought to myself, 'What do I have to thank Mr. Taylor for?' He made me run like a dog. Sweat, cramp, cry, wheeze. Pushed us harder than I've ever been pushed. But he believed in me. He tried to separate me from my best friend—the nerve! And we are still living together after all of these years. But he recognized a neediness, an insecurity, and wanted me to find my own stability, strength, and identity. He tortured my brain with philosophical puzzles and left me speechless with probing questions. 'What's going on in there? I know something is going on in there?' Probably more than he wanted to know. Definitely more than I wanted to deal with. But he challenged me to stare down whatever evil or fear stood in my way, especially if it shortened my stride.
>
> For four precious years, you were my mentor and coach. What I aspire to be now. I honestly can't imagine what my life would be like now without your lasting influence.

The Killing Fields

She wanted to go back to Southeast Asia again. My response was, "Okay, as long as we include Cambodia." I felt I was ready for the Killing Fields. Trish and I landed on an empty tarmac in Phnom Penh over the 1998-99 Christmas holiday. There was not another jet aircraft in view.

As we drove by cab through the city I asked myself: *Why aren't the main dirt streets of the city paved or leveled?* Wasn't it the civil war two decades before? We checked into a hotel along the great Mekong River. It felt unreal being in Phnom Penh. This particular hotel had been used for the wounded and dying during the slaughter. I could see the wide river from our room. We were in a city where evil had triumphed.

I asked that the cab driver take us to see the former school that had been used for interrogations, incarceration, and torture of those suspected of Western idolatry. If you wore glasses or read books, you were a suspect.

At the school, Trish and I found hundreds of student pictures displayed, taken before they were marched some nine miles out of town to their death. At Drake High School, I regularly post track and travel photographs. In Phnom Penh, they displayed photographs of students who were sentenced to be killed.

That same afternoon we drove nine miles out of Phnom Penh to a vacant lot. I had pictured arriving at a glass partition or some other barrier separating tourists from the pit of bones and skulls that were displayed in a 1984 movie about the Khmer Rouge regime. Instead, the cab pulled up and stopped in front of a skimpy wire fence. Could this be the Killing Fields? Two boys in street clothes were seated by what might be called an entrance. There was no ticket booth. One of them, acting like a guide, immediately walked us toward a glass pagoda. It contained rows upon rows of human skulls. A sign said there were eight thousand of them. Where were the pits of the Killing Fields? I walked apprehensively ahead, becoming lightheaded. This was just too damn casual. Auschwitz retains the broken concrete of the gas chambers. The Killing Fields turned out to be like a hole in a vacant lot in your neighborhood at home. Not fifty yards from the glass pagoda, I came upon small potholes. The skulls had been unearthed from these casual pits. For a moment, I was alone with the memory, standing in the Killing Fields.

Our trip to Cambodia turned out to be one of the most memorable ones of my travel life. The wide, muddy Mekong flows quietly by the French architecture and wide streets of Phnom Penh. When I was jogging by the Mekong within the hotel grounds that first or second night, I thought of Jerry Ledzinski, my business guru. Jerry had fought (and almost died) not all that far from the shore on the other side of the river. There, during the Vietnam War, American bombs killed farmers in their fields, and families in the villages. In Cambodia! Kissinger said we were not in Cambodia. Do you want to believe Henry, or Jerry? Can brutality from the air be weighed as being any different than death by weapons on the ground? Is not the bomb an extension of the pilot who releases it? Or the general who ordered the attack? Or the president who ordered the general? These deaths should weigh on the conscience of all who manufactured and delivered the explosives, too. These are the questions that came to me as I ran along the muddy Mekong in Phnom Penh, formerly known as the "pearl of southeast Asia."

I took the death of a dear friend with me to Cambodia. The ambulance went by me when I was picking up the mail at the post office in San Anselmo, just before we were about to leave the country. It was screaming, scolding the heavy traffic that blocked its way. I had no idea that my fun friend from seminary was in that ambulance. The vehicle's frantic speed was in vain. Bill Frederickson died of a heart attack before he reached the hospital.

Was my good friend already dead when he went by me? Or, did it come seconds, a minute, later? This death really hurt. Bill had been my most consistent friend over forty years. Before we left for Cambodia, I went out and saw his wife, Sally, and their two daughters, Nikki and Toni. It was terribly sad. Bill had not reached seventy. The daughters, both former track runners at the high school, were devastated. They were very close to their father; Bill was their friend. I wish he had not pounded me on my shoulder when UCLA scored a touchdown on USC in the Coliseum back in the early sixties. We should never have sat together for a Bruin-Trojan game.

It was never a question of my not going to Cambodia because of his death. But I felt torn leaving before the memorial service. Another lifetime friend, Gene Burris, would be there to lead the worship. I gave Sally and the two daughters a poem. It closed with, "Goodnight, dear friend." Did I write that?

The Christmas music in the plush hotel in Angkor Wat was incongruous for me because Bill would be missing his final years, when wisdom celebrates the life journey. The late sixties and early seventies in age are the time when you come to see yourself with the greatest perspective. I do not know about the late seventies, or early eighties, but I suspect with decent health they can they can bring the greatest wisdom of all.

My Mother's City: Hong Kong

My mother was waiting for me in Hong Kong. And my grandfather. Mary Elizabeth Hager was born in the city in 1901; she did not leave China until she was ten. When I flew into the city it was my grandfather's famous baptism of Sun Yat-sen that defined him for me. In a biography on the founder of modern China, Marie-Claire Bergere wrote: "Sun Yat-sen was baptized by an American Congregationalist, Dr. Charles Hager, a recent arrival in Hong Kong. A real friendship seems to have linked the young minister to his convert Sun, whose religious zeal he praised and who was soon accompanying him on his mission tours."

In 1885-1886, over a decade before the emperor was overthrown, Sun Yat-sen lived for two years in the Congregational Church boarding house with my grandparents. The 1997 and 2005 Arête groups stayed in the same hotel where Freud lived when he was studying hysteria in 1885-1886 in Paris. For me, the grandfather in Hong Kong and the psychoanalyst in Paris both belong to my pantheon of father figures. I love connecting these separate locations by time, the personal with the historical.

Hong Kong's tall skyscrapers were decorated with Christmas lights. We had flown in from Thailand in business class with corporate executives returning from a day of appointments in Bangkok. The wine was exceptionally good; the attention by the female flight attendants, special. It was when I saw the lights of Hong Kong below that it really hit me that I was about to land in my mother's city. We landed on a new tarmac, away from the congestion of downtown buildings that used to threaten the approach to the old airport. Then we took a new Mercedes cab on the expressway that runs under the harbor through a tunnel and onto the island. It was a different kind of ride. Not like the one we had taken just a few days before, trying to avoid deep potholes in the road upon arrival in Phnom Penh.

Trish had us booked at the new Hyatt. Even with her travel agent discount, it still cost plenty. It was worth it. Our room provided us a sense of being extended out over the harbor, suspended above the docks and water traffic below. Off to the left as we looked down upon the massive port was the pier where my grandparents docked. I felt a closeness to their lives that I had not experienced before. The glittering city became personal. Hong Kong was striking, beautiful, spectacular at Christmas time.

Where was their mission home? Where did my mother grow up? I had some photographs with me provided by my cousin Bobby. He had been in Hong Kong several years before with the same pictures, but he could not find the Mission House.

The concierge at the Hyatt in Hong Kong tried to help me locate a congregational church so that I could begin my search for the grandparents. He was sophisticated, a hotel professional. Upon hearing the name Sun Yat-sen, he characterized him as "the revolutionary."

No luck. No listing for a congregational church in Hong Kong. I took the photographs to a bookstore, thinking that I might find pictures in a guidebook of the neighborhood that might trigger an identification. Trish joined me; together we negotiated crowded downtown streets. I appreciated her company, her sense of direction. We found the bookstore that the hotel had recommended, but on the door we also found, "Closed for the holidays." The next day would be New Year's Eve. The following morning we would fly from Hong Kong to San Francisco.

That afternoon I showed two photographs (one of Sun Yat-sen, and one of the Hagers) to a woman selling garments from a stall in a narrow backstreet. She immediately became hyper when she saw the photo of Sun Yat-sen and wanted her friends in the other stalls to see it. A man suggested that the buildings in my photographs were "higher up" on the hill. He said he recognized the neighborhood and suggested that we go to another bookstore. So I dragged Trisha around the corner to that address, but that store was closed, too.

Would there be time to find the neighborhood where my mother grew up? Trish was willing to go back to the bookstore the next day with me. The deal was that she would get to go shopping after the search. When we returned to the bookstore that the street market vendor had suggested it was not yet open, so we waited some thirty minutes. Once inside, we found two men at the counter. I had with me a photograph taken by my mother's brother, Robert, when he visited Hong Kong in the 1920s. They showed us on a map where they thought a school in the photograph still stood. Most of the older structures had been torn down. But these two men felt that a school was "up on Crane Road."

I was pumped. There is an outdoor escalator that takes you up the steep hill rising above the Hong Kong harbor. You do have to get off and walk at some of the cross streets, but it would be a harsh climb without the escalator. Trish and I had been up there the day before, wondering if we were in the neighborhood of the Mission House. Without knowing it, we ate lunch just down the street from where my mother had lived.

The photographs worked. Trish identified a balcony in the picture on Crane Road. I became very excited when we rushed across the street to a big red church with the familiar balcony. The entrance gate was locked, so I pressed a buzzer and we waited. Eventually a young woman appeared and led us into a large, multi-purpose room that I suppose had once been a sanctuary. She asked us to wait while she took our photographs to an administrator. As we sat on a bench, young Chinese children, perhaps of kindergarten age, were led past us. I thought of my grandmother. Did she start the first kindergarten in China near where we were seated?

It was some time before the young woman came back. She looked pleased, pointed to steps outside the door and on the other side of the patio, and suggested they were the ones in the photograph. But the congregational had moved to a new location. She provided us with an address and phone number for this church. It was over toward Kowloon and would require our taking a cab.

Our flight would leave the next morning; time was running out. I left Patricia in the midst of those skyscrapers to shop at expensive stores and found myself a cab. When I mentioned Sun Yat-sen to the cab driver, he called him "the father." Note that the well groomed Hyatt hotel concierge referred to Sun Yat-sen as "the revolutionary."

I was really excited when the driver let me out just past the entrance to 119 Leighton Road. At the side entrance to the church, a directory read: "Chinese Congregational..." Bingo! I had it.

The reason that the concierge at the Hyatt did not come up with the right address was because I had asked for the "Congregational Church," not the "Chinese Congregational Church." I walked up to the corner to view the church from its front and to see if a door into the sanctuary was open. A long red and gold banner was hanging down the face of the front of the church. It read, "From 1883 to 1998." I had found my grandfather.

I spoke through a voice box to a woman who informed me that the pastor, Mr. Kim, was at a meeting and would not return until late in the afternoon. By cab, I returned to the Hyatt, still wanting the location of the Mission House. Trish arrived a short time later with a couple of shopping bags from those expensive stores. What a great life. Those large hotel windows gave us a full view of the Hong Kong harbor as brightly colored packages adorned our bed.

I had left my hotel room number with the church receptionist. While I was out running, Pastor Kim called back. I enjoyed those short runs in Hong Kong. I would go down to a ferry building, by a new convention center, then back along the harbor with a view of the cluster of tall, modern buildings. Hong Kong is a stunning city. There was a pretty little park with a garden in front of the Hyatt where I finished off my run. Was my mother raised somewhere up on that hill above?

Back at our room, I immediately returned the call to Pastor Kim. He told me that they had just celebrated the founding of the church and that my grandfather was remembered with great respect and gratitude. I have a tea set of silver on the mantle above the fireplace in our home that was given to "Dr. and Mrs. C. H. Hager in 1904 by the Chinese Congregational Christians."

Mr. Kim was thrilled that I was in Hong Kong and he wanted us to meet. Unfortunately, it was the last evening on the trip and Patricia and I were going out to dinner. There wasn't a good time to see Mr. Kim. I did obtain information on the location of the original Mission Preaching House. Mr. Kim told me that the building had been torn down, but a memorial sign on the new building tells of Sun Yat-sen living there. That was enough for me. Off we went to find a Bridges Street before dinner. The traffic into central Hong Kong was very heavy. It took some time to make it into the heart of the city. Then the cab driver let us out well below Bridges Street. The escalator was some distance away. Trish, in a tight, very sexy skirt, held my arm as we climbed up steep steps. It was dark out when we reached Bridges Street; the last of the street merchants were leaving. Pastor Kim had told me that the sign was in a market. We walked past a poultry building where a man was hosing down the cement floor inside. I went looked in and saw empty crates that had contained chickens and ducks. I was careful not to slip on the wet cement. We walked a short ways down Bridges, then turned back. Where was the sign?

As we were passing the poultry building on our way back to the steps, I noticed what might be a sign above some parked motorbikes. It was oblong, unlike the others on the street. I could barely read what was on it—"On this site originally stood the three-story premises of the Congregational Mission Preaching House. Sun Yat-sen lived on the second floor of the house while he studied at the Central School

Grandfather Hager reading the pulse of a patient

during 1884 to 1886. He was also baptized in the church in 1883. He was given the baptismal name 'Rixin' from which the name Yat-sen was later adopted."

I felt congruity. Congruity with my grandfather. There was surely something of him in me. Education and the search for values drove both of us throughout our adult lives. Perhaps the greatest trait we have in common is tireless enthusiasm?

One of his friends from Oberlin College remembered Charles Hager as "athletic of body, vigorous of mind, conscientious of soul, indomitable in spirit, who showed a faithfulness in everything he undertook—in work or in play, on a baseball field or in a classroom. I never knew him to fluke, or give an excuse. "

Part V: Fullness of Being

Past comes alive

B OULET RAN HIS fastest mile in Eugene, Oregon. In the race were two of the best Kenyan runners, along with all of the top Americans. The two Africans set out to run the fastest time ever recorded on American soil. Or rather, on a synthetic track. The Kenyans went out too fast and the swift pace set Boulet up for his best-ever mile time. He was well back until late in the race, but as they tired he gained momentum and worked his way past the U.S. runners. Richie took all of the top Americans and was over six seconds under a four minute mile with a 3:53.23 clocking.

The U.S. track world was in search of another Wes Santee or Jim Ryan. Magazines began to feature Boulet as possibly the one who could restore American dignity in the event. This taunted my memory of myself. After graduating from Drake, Richie ran for the Cal Berkeley team, and after that, for New Balance, as a professional. While he was far removed from me by coaching at this stage in his development, the cathected energy that I had invested in him almost a decade before was still emotionally alive in my psyche. I could think of having a former runner in the 2000 Olympic Games. Would he remember me when interviewed on television?

Could Richie be another Wes Santee? Was he capable of being that great? My former Marine Corps teammate at one time ran three of the four fastest mile times in the history of the sport. I trained Richie over four years, I ran with Wes for almost a full year. From a physical standpoint, there is little to compare between the two. Santee was vastly superior. From a mental standpoint, they were comparable.

Among the papers that I received after my mother's death there was a letter that told of my father's death. For some reason, I put it away for many years and did not read it carefully. It was from James R. Salisbury, the cadet who had crawled away from the fatal plane crash that killed my father. Here is what the man wrote to my mother—"I have been in the Army for six months, and he is the only man I have met who gave me any encouragement and comfort when I needed it most. I was on my way out, almost defeated. He gave me many hours of his personal time and expert advice and I have not known an un-enjoyable moment with him." And then, "It was for me that he made that final plunge."

I felt his letter deeply. It brought my father to me and again told of what I had lost.

It pleased me to hear from my great half miler, Lori Saia, that "Lon Spurrier cannot shake having lost to you." The nightmare for the future world record holder in the 880 occurred in 1954 when I upset him in the Cal-USC dual meet. Four decades later, Lori wrote a letter to me. It told of how the man seated next to her at a Cal track meet suddenly announced to those close to him, "There's Lon Spurrier." Lonnie is a Cal icon. Lori then reported that this man said, "Spurrier has never gotten over losing to USC." Go on, Lori, tell us more. Lori has never been shy; she enjoyed her response. I can see her gray eyes sparkle as she told the gentleman, "It was my high school track coach who beat Spurrier that day."

I began to worry that Lonnie would not show up as the Cal crowd gathered for a luncheon in Berkeley. What was I doing at a Cal luncheon? The father of one of my former county half-mile champions kept running into Spurrier at university events and my name kept coming up. So Spurrier finally said to the dad, "Get Taylor over here." It turned out to be a good thing that he was not there earlier. As Steve introduced me around to Cal alumni, one, then another, said, "Oh, *you* are the legend." How flattering. It was getting interesting. When Lonnie did arrive, he damn near ignored me. I suggested that we sit together. He said something like, "Why not? I don't have any other plans." On our way to the lunch tables, Lon saw Ed Wilson at the bar. Ed had finished third in the race when I nipped Spurrier. They had been favored to take first and second; through April of 1954 they were ranked by time as number two and number five in the country. I was number seventeen. I remembered Wilson as a nice guy. He was the half miler who beat me by two-tenths of a second in the junior college state finals when I was a freshman. Wilson's first comment was, "I thought you were taller." Then, quickly, "I beat you in the state meet." I had two wounded Bears on my hands. This was really fun.

I had to leave the luncheon early to meet a couple of my girls for a cross-country meet. My track past danced before me as I walked across the Berkeley parking lot toward the car. I was amused. This was all silly, my being "the legend." But fun, fun, fun.

Precarious edges

Arête '99 had a tremendous itinerary; we began in Jordan, then travelled to Syria, Istanbul and Troy, Greece, Italy, the Alps in Switzerland, the Dolomites in Austria, Munich.

On the first morning in Amman, Jordan, I had the girls do hill sprints up a residential street. The girls wore shorts. It was early in the day and I kept an eye out for any trouble.

Moses may have come through southern Jordan on his way from Egypt to the "promised land." From high up in the rocks above Petra, with precarious edges only feet away, the rugged, barren landscape of biblical times extended northward for us toward the Dead Sea. The Old Testament says that God told the Jews that a certain real estate up ahead from where we stood belonged to them and they were to kill the men, women, and children and take it.

The view, however, was spectacular. One can possess time itself as the mind passes over the centuries when armies, traders, and refugees came through the gorges and canyons of this magnificent setting.

A few days later in eastern Syria, I watched the students playfully run up a steep road to the top of a mound above the Greek and Roman ruins at Palmyra. They would be chasing darkness on the way back to the hotel. I had returned to the small frontier village a bit earlier and was waiting for them. As darkness approached, I began to worry. Some of the girls were in their running shorts! As the sun fell off the earth in the west, I felt alone. We had seen road signs coming into Palmyra indicating that Baghdad was the next destination. I went out of the hotel and stood by shops in the village just in case there was any trouble over the lightly clad maidens. The proprietors did not appear interested in my presence, but they became very aware of the lasses when they came running down the middle of the street. They were full of stride and energy. The Moslem shopkeepers reacted with smiles, not condemnation. These are the precious moments for me.

On a Sunday morning in Florence, I started up the van and drove down a long driveway toward the gate. We were to arrive in the Swiss Alps before the sun went down. Before I was out of the youth hostel grounds, however, the van lost power. We were not going anywhere. I ran back up the road to the villa and faced a fairly long line of young people waiting to check out. Fortunately, I gained the attention of a woman behind the counter and told her about the lifeless van. She tried to reach road service for us, but no one was answering the phone (it was, after all, a weekend). We only had one night scheduled in the Alps. What about our Nietzsche walk the following morning? And the workout on the petite track in St. Moritz? I felt desperate. The woman asked if the van had a security system. I knew immediately that had to be it. The keychain had an unfamiliar object hanging from it, resembling a cigarette lighter. I kissed her on the cheek and raced joyfully toward the van.

That evening, we did run on our petite track under Alpine peaks. And Zarathustra was waiting for us alongside the trail the next morning.

Thirty-three years after Jeanne died, the phone rang and Cory was calling from Los Angeles to tell us that he had just won an Emmy. I thought of his origins, of Jeanne. Trisha raised Cory. Jeanne was his mother for five months; Trish is his lifetime mother. Jess was hit differently than Cory by her death, as he was three years older than his brother. Jess knew that his mother died that morning in Mammoth.

He remembers it very clearly. Cory has no such memory.

The Emmy was for sound editing a National Geographic special titled, "Avalanche." What a thrill for all of us. Cory turned down National Geographic when they moved the television offices back to where the magazine is published, in Washington, D.C. He and Julie stayed in the duplex by North Hollywood Park for awhile longer, then bought a home in Burbank. When I am down in Los Angeles for track meets, I take the team to see Cory and Julie before we head back to Marin. Cory usually gives a short talk on some film project he is working on. He captures their interest with his vitality, clarity, and excitement.

One Sunday morning we went with Cory and Julie to the Santa Monica Pier before heading up the Pacific Coast Highway to San Anselmo. It was a beautiful morning, and I had a grandson to play with on the beach of my high school memories. Liam had joined the family. As my runners enjoyed the warmth of the pleasant Los Angeles beach on one side of the Santa Monica Pier, I walked up the shore on the other side, right by where we played football in high school. Liam squealed as he tempted the familiar waves "down at the beach at Santa Monica." By chance we ran into a young man on the pier who knew Cory through the Buddhist organization. I was told that thousands of young adults look to Cory for inspiration and direction. I observed Cory's confident demeanor—relaxed, soft spoken, in charge. It was a good morning.

The terrible price of Being

I LEARNED THAT Peter Edwards was dying. Quick of mind, opinionated, sarcastic, Peter was the publisher of the local newspaper. He was the one who asked me to write those controversial columns. After he sold the paper, we were still in touch weekly through Rotary, but when he dropped out of the club we lost contact with one another.

Bill Frederickson died of a heart attack just after running; Edwards lost his life to pancreatic cancer. When I finally drove out to Lucas Valley to see him, Peter's greeting was a blunt and typical "What took you so long?" Peter and Susan had just purchased an expensive home. He had made a lot of money in real estate, and some enemies. Peter never hesitated to let someone know if he did not like them. And he especially had it in for phonies. Fortunately, he liked me. We visited for awhile the day I went out to see my friend dying. Peter would drift off from time to time because of the morphine. When it was time to go, he reached up to hug me, to say goodbye. I leaned down and embraced my outspoken friend for the last time. Peter died the next week.

I was asked by Susan and the two sons to lead the memorial service. The boys had gone to the high school where I coach. I made it clear that I could not lead a religious service. They informed me they did not want one. I was proud to remember a friend within a community of friends. Peter's death, like Bill Frederickson's, came too early for he was only in his mid-sixties. Yet it seemed natural to me. Harsh, too soon, but of life.

All of a sudden a number of my close friends were dying. And virtually all of them in their mid- to late sixties. Jerry Belanger hugged me goodbye, too. He was a special guy. Fun, loyal, a good friend and client. Because Jerry was so weak, his wife, Charneth, walked me across the house to the door. We left Jerry sitting on the couch with a blanket over him. His long battle with leukemia was about over. As I was halfway up their driveway I looked back. Jerry had made it across his home for one final glimpse of a friend. I drove down their twisting road high above Mill Valley, shaken by how casually we had said goodbye to life. Just like that.

I learned that Lefty Tamblyn had died because someone sent me a North Hollywood High School alumni newsletter. I knew that my track and Mammoth Lakes companion had lost a leg due to diabetes. It was Lefty who secured that wonderful job for me over the summer of '52, where we sang songs from the Hollywood musicals as we tossed plastic dishes about on the porch outside the camp dining room. Lefty had always taken a special interest in me. But he was not around to be hugged. The news came through an impersonal listing of the dead in an alumni newsletter. How can a close friend just be gone?

It was a heart attack that ended Jack Bylin's life in his mid-sixties. In my old town of Newhall. I had been the best man at Jack and Darlene's wedding. Darlene was the ninth-grade girlfriend. My girlfriend. But Jack became her hero in high school; he was a kind of hero for me, too. A close friend, Jack maintained a certain charisma throughout his life. She has remarried. I wrote poetry to Darlene when Jack died. It came forth by song. She wrote back, thanking me for what I captured by verse. It sang without effort. My lamentation to a friend. They will always be Jack and Darlene, to me!

Bert Convy was both my friend and nemesis. Like Lefty, his death came before age sixty. At the time of Bert's death, he was a very popular game show host and nightclub performer. The last time I saw him was on the USC campus in 1954. He had just performed with his trio for the student body in Bovard Auditorium. Bert did not seem taller than me that day. It was my campus. I had fulfilled those high school yearbook predictions about running for USC. Bert had actually written that he looked forward to seeing me running for USC and in the Olympics. While I felt that we had always been competitive with one another, our contact that day ended for me in a fulfilling way.

Both Jack and Bert, like me, were born in July of 1933. They were friendships that measured time for me.

I did not sense her potential in her at first. Morgan was so small that I affectionately named her "the Elf." However, I discovered during her initial season that she had tremendous balance, poise, and speed. And she was the premier ballerina in the county.

Morgan was a darling little girl. Just moments before the county final over 400 meters she announced in an absolutely charming way, "I think I am going to win it." This was not bravado. It was just Morgan! Morgan did "win it."

I moved "the Elf" up to 800 meters. When we reached the Redwood Empire championship meet near the end of her sophomore season, I told her to go out quickly over the first lap, and then pick up the pace as she entered the turn. On the backstretch she was to rest up a bit before letting out her finishing kick.

I was not prepared for the time this strategy produced, however. My little Elf listened to me. She risked a fast pace with a full lap to go. And she did pick it up on the first turn of the second lap. The result was a stunning new Redwood Empire meet record. An experienced official at the finish line was shocked when he looked at his watch. Clark Palmer knew the significance of the time. Others were excited, asked questions, wanted to know, "Who is she?" It was a rare moment. A new running goddess, a petite one, had stolen the headlines. And far more than I realized was happening in my psyche, for she had come to heal my track wounds.

Morgan ran away from the field the following week in the Meet of Champions. This qualified her for the prestigious California state finals. One of my closest track coaching friends, Mark Simi, came over to sit with me near the finish at the Cal stadium. So did Richie Boulet, who would be seeking an Olympic Team berth in just a couple of months at the U.S. Trials. When Morgan came down the finishing stretch with a huge lead, the announcer, my friend Keith Conning, blurted out with, "Banks is coached by Bill Taylor, former USC 880 great." A cluster of Drake parents looked up to where the three of us were located and enthusiastically applauded me. All of this in the stadium where I had taken Spurrier and Wilson.

How was my little sophomore handling this sudden fame? It was uncanny to witness her poise. I told a newspaper reporter, "She is not one of us." I asked her once if she liked being herself, and she paused, then said in all seriousness, "I like being Morgan." In some ways, Morgan was more mature than others of her age, and yet she was refreshingly younger in other ways. Morgan was a precious, innocent, charming, compassionate, funny little girl.

Three of the top ten in the nation would be in her races at the state. They were two to three seconds faster than she was, going into the competition. Morgan had already lowered her best time by four seconds over the preceding two weeks. The week after the Meet of Champions, the California website for high school track ran a photo of Morgan and me, referring to me as her mentor. Mentor? That was the right word. I was not just her track coach. We talked quietly about the early death of her father after a track practice a few weeks before, played Yahtzee on the flight down to Los Angeles for the state finals, and then at the motel we began discussing the possible Arête route for the following summer overseas. I drew a map on a piece of paper and framed some of the prime historical events and correlations.

We were staying in a motel near my old high school in North Hollywood, close to where Cory, Julie, and Liam were living. We went out to dinner the night before at a place in Studio City. It turned out that the festive restaurant was only fifty or so yards from where I used to catch the streetcar to go down to the Los Angeles Coliseum to watch Mel Patton race for USC. And less than one hundred yards from where I showed up after running away from the orphanage. My personal history was closing in on me. Delightfully so. The next morning I drove over to my old high school and ran around the familiar track. Fifty years later, I found the same grass, dirt, bleachers. The high jump pit was in a different place. Everything else looked the same.

The 800-meter trial that night was not until 7:00 p.m. We waited out part of the day at the motel, then made the long drive across Los Angeles and down to Cerritos College where the meet was held. Morgan looked good in her trial on Friday night in Los Angeles. While qualifying for the final, she did not use herself up, again revealing uncanny wisdom for her age.

The wait at the hotel before the final the next day became tense. Morgan was intimidated by the seniors she saw running in the other heats, and for the first time as her coach I was up against self-doubt. She said that she wished she could just watch those great half milers in the race. I told Morgan, "Do not be surprised if they come back to you down the finishing stretch." I remembered my state final half mile in 1952 in Santa Rosa when Casper and the rest of the field came back to me.

Morgan was used to leading her 800-meter races, but I felt it was better, due to the pressure she was feeling, to have her ride the pace, stay out of trouble and then wait for them to come back to her.

Everything seemed right to me when we arrived at the Cerritos Stadium. The weather was warm, but not excessively hot. There was a light breeze. Ironically, we ran into my old half-mile rival, Dave Casper, just as we were entering the athletic compound. A small grass area is the only place available for the best runners in the state to warm up before they go out to the track. I watched Marian Jones doing her pre-race drills there ten years before.

Casper surprised me with his personal warmth. He was not his usual cocky self. He told Morgan that he could not share any pre-race strategy with her because one of his old runners was the coach of the race favorite, an attractive blonde with tremendous speed from Newport Beach. I did not mind it when Dave said to Morgan, "Just hang on, stay relaxed." Then, "You will drop your time and be right up there at the finish." Thanks, Dave.

This moment brought the past and the present together. Morgan and I sat on the grass in the compound, nervously waiting for the final call to report for the 800 meters. I could identify the other half milers as they warmed up by their rhythm, the way they jogged. Half milers have a loose gait. Just before I left Morgan and went to the stands, she told me that she really felt scared. I told her that this would be her last race of the season and that she was "going out to pasture after this one." I walked over with her to the check-in tent, gave her a hug, then left the Elf to race against the strongest half-mile field in the nation.

I wanted to be alone up in the stands. When the 800 field came off the first turn, Morgan was running slightly behind the favorites. But as they approached the end of the first lap she seemed to have faced some traffic problems and fallen back a bit. You do not want to have to slow up, use up your kick with bursts of speed to get around other runners. And you do not want to get bumped, be thrown off stride. Or even go down. It happens. Especially in the half mile.

Down the backstretch of the final lap, Morgan eased her way up to contact with the favorites, those great ones she had told me she felt she could not beat. I discovered myself literally running along the elevated railing around the track as Morgan raced past me. When they came off the final turn, she moved into fourth place. The three favorites were ahead of her. Would they "come back"? I was ready to settle for fourth place; that would be a medal, a place in the state finals for my sophomore. With fifty meters to go, I saw a familiar black jersey with the large white "D" go around one of the favorites. A sudden burst of energy set off a finishing sprint that took her by the former state champion and into second place. The Elf won the silver medal, finishing second in the California final.

Morgan Banks and her mentor

When I looked down at my watch, I had my second great surprise. Morgan had dropped her time another two seconds. I learned almost immediately that this time moved her up to number two in the nation. Suddenly I had another national runner and she was only a sophomore. This meant that she would likely be the state meet favorite the next year. Those other three top girls were seniors.

This all happened in Los Angeles, not all that far from the Coliseum, on a track near to where most of my track memories are stored. Almost immediately after Morgan finished, Casper yelled down to me from the stands. He was excited because the Newport Beach girl had won the race. But he was also happy for me. I went up and we shared our joy. Forty-seven years before, the USC head coach had written to me: "We are looking forward to your becoming a national champion..." Was Morgan going fulfill this for me in 2001?

Lebanon

Only days after the state finals, Patricia and I were in Lebanon. I did not think that this small, thin country which stretches down the coast below Syria to the northern border of Israel could rival Morocco, Tunisia, or Algeria. Lebanon offered its own suspense and continuous coastal beauty. We flew from Cypress to Beirut with the new Middle East Airlines. I was not comfortable trying an Arab airline, or landing in Beirut. I remembered the television coverage of a T.W.A. jet being blown up on that runway, and, of course, over two hundred U.S. Marines being killed by a suicide bomber at the barracks immediately south of the airport. And for me, the most haunting memory of all was of the kidnappings of Americans in the 1980s.

Shortly before we landed, Trish became irritated because a man lit up a cigarette in our non-smoking compartment. I told her to leave him alone, for we would be landing in only a few minutes. He had thick black hair, and a dark complexion. I reasoned that he could be a hostile Muslim who would not appreciate a Western female tourist telling him to put out his cigarette.

Trisha would not leave it alone. She pressed the button that brought a flight attendant back to our seats. God damn it, Trisha. My "terrorist" was told to put out his cigarette. He did so willingly.

We dropped directly down over where the Marines had been killed. Once off the jet, a cold, impersonal passport officer (who looked to me like a Hezbollah commando) failed to welcome us to Lebanon. Dressed in camouflaged military fatigues, he damn near scared me right back to the plane. I had been processed through passport control in Cairo, Algiers, Amman, Casablanca, Istanbul, and Tunis, but I never thought that I saw hate in the eyes of those customs officers.

This fear shortly proved inappropriate. I had experienced a Western projection of terrorism—even with my travel experience. That very evening Patricia and I walked through the downtown streets of Beirut without a guide. We enjoyed dinner and music in a crowded outdoor restaurant in the rebuilt portion of the city. Not many blocks away, a series of bombed out buildings began to unfold, telling of the horrible civil war that ended in 1990. These broken multi-storied structures displayed holes from machine gun fire and walls blown apart by rockets. The people of Lebanon killed one another for fifteen years. Israel killed in Beirut during this time, too. They will forever be known for the massacre of families in a southern neighborhood of the city.

Once known as the "Paris of the Middle East," Beirut was decorated with gutted office buildings and apartments when Trisha and I drove through the downtown streets the next morning on our way to the archaeological museum.

A very different view awaited us up the coast at ancient Byblos. We stayed in a small hotel right next to a petite harbor that once floated cedars to Egypt in return for papyrus. There is evidence that these logs made their way to Jerusalem, as well, and might have been used to construct the second Temple of Solomon. Suddenly Patricia and I were three thousand years back in time with the Phoenicians, those daring explorers of the sea. Letters of the Western alphabet were carried by ship from the little harbor to Greece. Even to this printed page.

When we drove south to the ancient coastal cities of Sidon and Tyre, I was aware that Israeli jets might attack with bombs at any moment. Hezbollah resistance fighters would be their target, but Patricia and I could be "in the wrong place at the wrong time." I thought back to my visits to ancient Carthage far across the Mediterranean Sea, that petite port on the North African coast that once received the ships from Sidon and Tyre. The combination of this significant ancient history, the sounds of the relatively small Moslem cities, and the beautiful coastline turned Lebanon into a vacation feast.

Before we drove out to the incredible Roman site of Baalbek near the Syrian border, I asked a young proprietor of a well-to-do shop in Byblos if I should be concerned that Baalbek is the Hezbollah headquarters. Like, what if our tour van broke down? He told me, "Hezbollah would help you." My conversation with this young Moslem man changed my stereotype of "terrorists." When our Secretary of State, Madeleine Albright, visited his shop, she asked him if he wanted to visit the United States. He told her that he was unable to get a visa. When Ms. Albright inquired why, he replied, "Because I am a terrorist." The U.S. Secretary of State, with those hawk-hooded eyes, looked him over suspiciously. Then she said that she did not believe him. His response to her was, "Are not all Moslems terrorists?"

Before she left Beirut, Ms. Albright arranged with the American consulate for the young man to be given a visa if he ever decides to visit America.

This was quite a summer. Shortly after we returned from Lebanon, I attended the U.S. Olympic Trials in Sacramento. My former miler, Richie Boulet, had a chance of making the American team. Unfortunately, he was not at his best due to injuries that interrupted his Olympic year preparation. Nonetheless, people in Marin County were deeply interested in having a local athlete who had a chance to run in the Olympics.

I was received in Sacramento as the successful coach of the prep sensation, Morgan Banks, and the high school mentor of a genuine Olympic possibility, Richie Boulet. It was rare for Marin County to have two national runners, let alone two in the same year. It was a fun climbing up into the stands to locate my seat in the packed stadium and having people I knew from as far back as my USC days, shouting "Good luck, Bill!"

I mentioned earlier that you could not compare Boulet to Wes Santee physically. Wes was one of the greatest milers to ever live. But because of my familiarity with both of them, I knew that a comparison of their minds was appropriate. Richie could put so much into a race that he would literally collapse after finishing. When this happened, it was evidence that he had exerted one hundred percent. It happened after both of his state cross-country meet finishes, and twice on the track after his state meet races.

I went to see the movie, *Gladiator*, the afternoon after Richie failed to make the U.S. Olympic Team. He was exhausted, went down on hands and knees just a few meters past the finish line. He reached down with everything he had to give. In the film, the moral hero, unable to defend himself, was stabbed by a vengeful, unscrupulous emperor. After killing this horrid man, the hero (i.e., the gladiator) collapsed in death on the floor of the Coliseum. Alone in the theatre, I identified Boulet with the gladiator. In the movie, a Roman statesman addresses fellow Roman leaders and asks, "Who will help me carry him?" I choked up. Boulet had done everything he could to make that Olympic Team. It was simply the wrong year for him. If the trials had been a couple of years before, around the time he ran that sensational sub-four minute mile with the Kenyans, he would have been on the U.S. Team. My own personal track memories were not that far away. Were my tears in the theatre for both of us? I had tried so hard to place in the national collegiate final my senior year at USC, to fulfill my athletic dream. I did not collapse like Boulet just past the finish line

Boulet down after his 1500 m. race
at the 2000 U.S. Olympic Trials.

when I missed advancing to the collegiate final in the Coliseum. But a few moments later I did sit down, nauseated, fatigued, at the entrance to that tunnel of my track life.

Back to Bill

DID I HAVE THE FASTEST half miler in the United States to coach in the coming year? Did she realize this? *Track and Field News* listed my Morgan as one of the three best in the country, speculating that she might end up as number one.

But Morgan had not trained during the summer. She went to France, then to the state of Washington with her family, ignoring the schedule of light runs that I had given her. It is typical for most high school students to stop training during their vacation months, but the great ones have a sense of what it will take to realize greatness. Boulet would have trained.

I was really disappointed. A red warning flag was waving. A national dream was dependent on her preparation. Yes, *my* national dream. You might think that it was a matter of fear for Morgan? Or that things were moving at too fast a pace for this young girl? Morgan had other things in her life. She was the lead ballerina in the county, and valued the respect she received from this role. And Morgan simply enjoyed spending time with her friends. She was not a track fanatic. The 2000 cross-country season was ahead of us when she returned to high school and I looked forward to building up her half-mile strength through training and racing over longer distances.

Investors were deeply frightened during this period of time because of a severe and lengthy decline in stock prices. I once again faced the possibility of losing clients. I was proud of what I had done for them throughout the prior decade, but most people need your confidence and support when, once again, headlines are making it hard for them to stick with their portfolios. During these threatening couple of years, a major national investment magazine came out with a rating system that placed my international management firm at the top. That did not hurt the need for confidence. Still, it was an agonizing wait. In a way, my courage to reach down on the backstretch of the half mile race was asked for again. I did not know when the markets would recover. Nobody did.

Morgan did win the league cross-country title, but it took considerable pride on her part to do so. Longer distances can be cruel to a half miler. I was one of the exceptions. But I would have traded some of my long distance ability for greater leg speed.

Morgan opened up her junior track season with a time that was ten seconds over her state 800-meter clocking. I found it hard to hide my disappointment when I called in the *Marin Independent Journal* with the meet highlights. The sports writer caught the moment, asking, "Isn't she supposed to do better?" Three or four seconds over her best time would have been a normal place to begin the next season. But not ten seconds. Something was wrong.

Ballet legs? Had she danced her track legs away? I did not want to hear what Morgan told me before practice one day, that she "did not have the same legs." This meant that as she ran the half mile the lightness was not there anymore. I respected her frankness, but I wanted my national star back.

At a big invitational in Los Angeles the USC middle-distance coach watched Morgan race. As did my former Trojan teammate, Sid Wing. The consensus was to keep the hope alive. Maybe if she reduced her ballet practices? But that was Morgan's territory. I did not feel right about suggesting that she drop out of ballet.

To her great credit, Morgan made it into the state final six weeks later. The legs were not the same, but she made it happen. She even dared to lead the trial after the field bunched up at the 200-meter mark. This brought the stadium announcer alive. The track world worships heroes. The large stadium crowd heard over the public address system, "Morgan Banks of Sir Francis Drake," "Morgan Banks," finally, "Banks, Banks, Banks!" She led over the final 600 meters and knocked out one of the race favorites (in fact, the one who would win the event the next year). The Elf had pulled it off and track people were thrilled. They wanted Morgan back.

She was fortunate to have gained a sixth place medal in the final on Saturday night in Sacramento. The Friday night trial had taken everything she had to give. I suggested as we drove from Sacramento to Marin after the final the following evening that she consider not attending ballet classes during the 2002 track season. It was a beautiful thing to see Morgan leading a state field in the trial; it provided one last glimpse of her unusual half-mile talent.

Body change can impact the running future for female athletes. What was possible one year is many times not there the next. Helping runners, coaches, and parents to realize that this is normal for certain females is a real challenge. The desperate wish for athletic success too often postpones facing the truth. The poor athlete is left with that familiar dream where one seeks to escape from some danger and their legs will not go faster.

Morgan agreed to reduce her number of dance practices before her senior track season, then to drop ballet when the races actually started. Would this adjustment return Morgan to national form?

Lenin and "the red Christ"

I was anxious to see the eerie remains of a life that changed a good part of the world. My Arête youth had seen a huge statue of Lenin in Budapest in 1987. In 1989, the next Arête travel team saw the statue covered up, boxed in a wooden frame. The 1991 group only saw the platform where the statue had originally been standing. When we are in Zurich, I take the teenagers up a narrow passageway to the door that Lenin came flying out of in 1917 to lead the Russian Revolution.

At first I did not understand why Nikos Kazantzakis called Lenin "the red Christ." But when I stood over him below the Kremlin in Moscow, with those colorful Russian orthodox churches on each end of Red Square, it magnified my understanding of Lenin's importance to world history. Only a few were allowed to enter the black marble tomb at one time. Young soldiers stood reverently at attention near the body of the most famous Russian since Peter the Great. Patricia and I had seen Ho Chi Minh in Hanoi. I thought he looked too puffy.

Bloated. I found Lenin well preserved.

We had gone to Russia in 2001 because a former student from the 1983 youth trip had invited us. After college, Paul Wilkinson developed a very successful company in the former Soviet Union. My former cross-country runner had control of certain ground services, including escorting the VIPs for all U.S. jets arriving in Russia. When I asked Paul to take us to where Lenin had addressed the crowd in St. Petersburg upon returning to his homeland for the revolution, his wife, Angelica, told us how she and her classmates used to wear red scarves around their necks to display how they belonged to Lenin. Paul had met her in southeast Russia. She did not refer to him as the "red Christ," but her story supports the Kazantzakis image.

One of the lads wanted us to climb up on Mt. Olympus in Greece after we left Russia. I had saved a pamphlet from an earlier time that told of a youth hostel up near the home of the gods. We drove to a village below the crags of Zeus and spent the night there. The next morning, we began a very difficult climb to the youth hostel. Not dangerous, just straight up. When I came upon the young people waiting for me to catch up, the lad whose idea it had been to climb Mt. Olympus greeted me with, "You have my respect, Mr. Taylor." I responded, without expression or emotion, "Fuck you, Rory." This pleased him.

I am glad they had their time up in the mists of Greek mythology. We were wrapped in the clouds of the gods. Only at brief moments did the jagged peaks of Zeus and Hera appear. Three of the boys got up at 5:00 a.m. to explore higher up before we headed down. They ventured only as far as was safe. You needed equipment to climb to the highest peaks. How wonderful to have these young men get up so early to greet the god, Helios, as he was bringing the sun up behind his chariot.

The gods can be very playful

I headed down the mountain before the rest of them for obvious reasons. With my knees, I would need to be careful. When my blue mummy bag slipped out of my poorly arranged straps, it began bouncing down the side of Mt. Olympus. I stood still and watched it pick up speed as it raced across switchbacks. I needed the sleeping bag for camping out later in the trip.

A man and woman hiking down offered to help me look for the bag. We searched for awhile before the man located it resting on the limb of a bushy tree. He was a doctor who taught at Cal State, Northridge, and also the medical trainer for the track team. We hiked along together for a while and I was surprised to learn that his closest friend was one of the runners who had passed me in the junior college cross-country final, the time I quit.

It was not until I returned home and checked some result pamphlets that I discovered that this chap, Holland, whose buddy I met, had placed third in the California state high school mile final just six months before he passed me in the conference cross-country final. I also learned by this review that Holland was the same runner I defeated by such a wide margin on that relay leg against UCLA, the race that led to my being nominated as Track Athlete of the Week in Los Angeles at the beginning of my senior track season at USC. What a strange coincidence: hiking down Mt. Olympus led to my discovering that one of my worst running experiences, and perhaps my best, were linked. The gods of Olympus can be oh so playful.

Camel safari

Patricia for years had wanted to attend a well-known Indian camel faire on the sub-continent. When she made a special request to do so on her sixtieth birthday, I felt I should go with her even though it meant missing the state cross-country final as a head coach. In twenty-five years, I had never missed a practice, let alone a meet. And this was the state final! My time in India with Patricia was the right choice for me and for our marriage, even if I do not care to ride a camel ever again. I actually became motion sick after four hours on the beast. I chose, instead, to get off and bump along, sitting in a cart being pulled by a camel under a hot sun. So much for the exotic camel safari.

I love traveling with Patricia. This is another way of saying that I love Patricia. She is not as wild about my company on our adventures, however. Patricia likes to keep going, seeing, doing. I prefer to see, then to relax, reflect, and read. But traveling gives us a huge block of time together, away from the routine at home where our varied activities separate us. The excitement of traveling to monumental places enhances our marriage. Our visits to Egypt, Algeria, Vietnam, Cambodia, let alone Greece, bring excitement and importance to our lives.

Of all the places we visited on the second India trip, I most vividly remember Jaisalmer. It appears to be suspended in space as you look toward it from a distance. The U.S. was carpet bombing Afghanistan at the time I was within the walled city. Pakistan was immediately to the west, perhaps just ten miles. The ancient caravans turned north at Jaisalmer on their way to Kabul. An Indian newspaper reported that "an estimated 8000 courageous Muslims" had gone to Afghanistan from Pakistan and "been killed" by American bombs. The article said they went out of "a sense of religious duty." I thought of the families who would never see a father, a husband, or a son again. I drew in the soft morning air as I looked out toward where Alexander the Great had, in the fourth century, B.C., ended the eastward expansion of his empire and returned westward; then I looked north to Afghanistan and the bombs. The sky was pale blue, and clear. I belonged there with Patricia.

The terrible price of Being

John, a major client who became a close friend, died. A few days before his death, he called me one morning and asked me to take care of his wife, Bobbie. John thanked me for my friendship, then said, "Goodbye." This was it. He would not call again. This is one tough world. And it has courageous people in it.

My Marine Corps buddy, Hoot, died. I had not seen him since we were discharged from the Marine Corps. About fifty years later, Hoot wrote me a letter asking for my phone number. Instead of calling, I replied by letter, as I typically did. Hoot died before he had a chance to call me. Does the fact that we had been out of touch for some fifty years make our friendship any less real? I don't think so. Trish and I disagree on this. Hoot was as real to me as someone I know today.

Sol towered over life. An intellectual giant, my friend and fellow teacher at Reseda High School was physically tall as well. He and I enjoyed a sport connection because he had played basketball in Madison Square Garden when he attended Brooklyn College. Sol was my favorite correspondent over the years. We stayed in touch with one another from 1966 until an e-mail told me that he was dead. Ironically, the accident that killed him happened when he was shooting baskets with his grandson in the driveway of his new home. Sol hit his head; after weeks of struggle to save this rare life, he died.

Sol was on top of every moment. He saw a much larger landscape of life than many of my friends do. I was flattered that he chased our friendship. He would let me know his displeasure if I did not call him when I was in Los Angeles. While flattered, I also found this presumptuous. Before his unexpected death, Sol and I met for dinner a couple of times at a restaurant in my old neighborhood by Warner Brothers. Our years of knowing one another allowed for a richness in conversation as we reflected on our respective lives. At Sol's suggestion, on one of these evenings we walked up a few blocks after dinner to my old apartment on Toluca Lake Avenue. I showed him where my old basketball backboard had stood between the two driveways, pointed out back to where I had kept the pigeons, chickens, ducks. Sol was interested in all of the details. Another friend is absent from this world.

I was able to be of some help to his wife, Sheila. I appreciated the chance to remember this exceptional man and friend over the course of months after his death. Sol cast a long shadow.

For those of you who are my age, or older, you are likely all too familiar with this stream of deaths already. There is a heavy price to pay for existence. It can be so cruel, gruesome, horrible. But for me, an honest person faces up to the facts and does not rationalize life. It is authenticity that I treasure.

I think the greatest gift we can give a friend is to be real. A man who has observed my teaching and coaching over the past twenty-five years told me recently that the "greatest gift" I give to the young people is that I am always myself. I told him, "They bring this out in me."

Morgan was featured in the program at the Oakland Invitational mid-way through her final high school track season. The race was to be run on the track where she had won the Meet of Champions two years before. When the leaders distanced themselves on the backstretch of the second lap, she did not even go after the talented field. It was time to talk with Morgan.

I asked her if she would drive back to San Anselmo with me. We were crossing the San Rafael Bridge when I suggested that we consider moving her down in distance, lowering two laps to one lap. This would provide less time for her to think during a race, less time to experience the frustration of not being the same half miler. I have found that reducing the thinking time sometimes allows an athlete who cannot live up to past marks a chance to race better. While Morgan made it clear she wanted to qualify for her third straight state meet, she also expressed great relief over reducing the race distance.

After the county finals, Morgan dropped out of the 800 meters. People were bewildered when they heard this. She had just won the league half-mile final by a considerable distance, owned two state medals in the event, yet suddenly a future appearance in the event was cancelled. Just like that.

Gaining myself

MORGAN FELT SOME GUILT—or failure—about dropping the 800 meters. I shared this weight with her. We talked frankly about what she was feeling. The *Marin Independent Journal* wrote a feature on her the week before the state trials in Berkeley. In it she explained why she was not running as fast as a senior. To the credit of the writer, Morgan received respect. Not only for the outstanding times she achieved as a sophomore and junior, but for how she was facing the changes in her running life. This is what Morgan said about me:

> "He is my mentor, my teacher, my coach, my father figure. My father died when I was six and a-half and he stepped in for me. He will be part of me forever. I have never been so inspired by one person in my entire life. He has taught me so much about life, sport, history, and travel. Our relationship is so unique that I am thankful every day that I met him. Half the reason that I enjoy track is because of him, and I don't know what it would be like without him. I don't know where I would be without him."

The headline above the article read, "Banks Hoping to Finish Career at State Meet." People told me that they cried when they read her story. Coaches told me that it was the kind of article "that you retire on." How would the story end? Could it be a good one if she failed?

Four would advance to the state finals at the Meet of Champions. More than four of the girls competing for these coveted spots in the 400 meters had more speed than Morgan. She would need to make up for this with strength and mental toughness.

In the race to qualify for the state meet, the winner was well out in front when the field came off the last turn. Three other girls were fighting with Morgan for the remaining places. With thirty meters to go, Morgan and the three other girls were inseparable. I had positioned myself high up in the stands where I would have a good view of the finish. I thought Morgan placed second, at the worst, third. The results were held up while meet officials studied the photographs. Morgan was awarded third place, thus fulfilling her dream of three straight state meets.

Her bold athletic finish allowed me to reassess my own track history. My running life went with her around the track where I took Spurrier and Wilson forty-nine years before. Through a young goddess, I traveled back to my track image and discovered that my final collegiate race when I did not fulfill my USC dream was not my epitaph. I had so many thrills through the sport. The pain of what was lost with tonsillitis is one segment of my deeply satisfying track career. I cannot change my history. I was hit with sickness at the peak of my running life—but that did not need to dominate my memories.

There was no chance of Morgan making it through the 400-meter heats in Los Angeles and earning a lane in the final. Track is very predictable compared to team sports. Morgan arrived with the nineteenth best time out of twenty-seven runners. You do not make up that kind of difference in a speed event. I found it ironic that the finish line was the same one she had crossed when she placed second in the 800-meter final two years before. This time she was last.

The next day we drove across Los Angeles to the stadium to see the state finals. As we walked across the parking lot toward the entrance gates, I said to Morgan, "This way this year." Two years before, we walked down to a gate where the competing athletes enter. This time we went over to the other side of the stadium to watch the races as spectators. Morgan was leaving high school with a balanced track image. No endless "what ifs" were on her doorstep. She can enjoy knowing for the rest of her life what it felt like to be number two in the nation, and she can respect the way she handled disappointment. A young girl met adversity with courage. It was past time for me to do the same.

I was surprised that I felt a sense of loss when one of the track lads asked me how I felt about my leaving the ministry. We were driving back from Los Angeles after that wonderful morning with my grandson, Liam, on the beach at Santa Monica. I did not realize how much being a Presbyterian minister had meant to me. I told Rory, the very one who congratulated me on my hiking courage on Mt. Olympus, that I deeply valued the opportunity to share with people what I believed. I was somewhat surprised to feel some sadness that the ministry had not worked out. Being a Presbyterian minister had been a very positive image for me as a young man. Rory said, "Isn't that what you do now?" And, "Does anyone do it any better?"

Richie Boulet asked me to conduct his wedding service in the redwoods above the Cal campus. I was very flattered, but still cautious about accepting a priestly role. But this was Boulet. I soared back into my track past through him, went down with him on all fours at Sacramento as his Olympic dream failed. How would I handle the wedding ceremony? They did not want a traditional one, so the three of us went to work on the ceremony together.

Boulet is a genuine person. And everybody who met his bride-to-be, Magdalena, was struck by her warmth, beauty, sincerity. A Polish track star who ran for Cal Berkeley, Magdalena had just become an American citizen.

The wedding was to take place in late August, 2002. This was less than three months after Morgan finished her track life.

Richie chose a petite Greek theatre in those redwoods above the Cal campus as the site of the ceremony. A few days before the wedding, I asked Richie and Magda, separately, to write down what they loved about one another. Each one was extremely curious about what the other person had written. That was cute. Their personal respect and fascination with one another came across strongly when they stood in front of their family and friends in the tiny theatre. However, it was their sense of humor that made the wedding so personal and special. When I read their vows out loud, one by one, they would repeat them.

Here are Richie's:

> *I promise to love you,*
> *cherish you,*
> *respect you,*
> *and honor you.*
> *I promise to encourage you,*
> *and inspire you,*
> *to share my hopes and dreams with you,*
> *and do all I can to make them reality.*
> *I promise to hold you when you sleep,*
> *and give you your space when you get too hot.*
> *I will carry you on my shoulders in victory,*
> *and comfort you in defeat.*
> *Your joy will be my joy,*
> *your sorrow my sorrow.*
> *I will climb mountains with you,*
> *run ungodly distances with you,*
> *and follow you to the ends of the earth.*

They repeated the vows in Polish for Magdalena's family. I did not risk attempting any Polish, but Richie read his in Magda's native language. The Stoic miler who prided himself on saying "there is no pain" while racing, choked up and cried.

The wedding was joyful. People told me that they were deeply appreciative of the way I led the service. I felt a great sense of completion that afternoon. As with Morgan, life had moved on!

Fullness of Being

MARSHALL CLARK DIED while jogging with his girls cross-country team. My USC half mile teammate and good friend fell dead from a heart attack. Throughout the years, Marshall would call to congratulate me on one of my athletes, to run a training question by me, or sometimes to ask philosophical or religious questions. Marshall valued my theological background. Tall, lanky, a most pleasant person, he was very well liked by both adults and students. He coached at Stanford as an assistant to Payton Jordan before becoming a long time high school coach at Saratoga in the San Jose area.

Shortly before his death, Marshall took the time to congratulate Morgan on her running years and to offer some perspective, as we were walking out of the stadium after the last state meet. Over the years, it was Marshall who would call me with excitement about Boulet or Morgan, showing interest in my athletes, even though he was coaching his own successful ones.

Earlier, when we would meet at Bay Area cross-country or track meets, Marshall would tell my runners that they had "a dirty coach." We got a lot of mileage out of this complaint. Marshall had tried to squeeze by me on the inside against Cal in 1955, and I did not move over and let him pass. I had no obligation to do so. I really got him back one morning when he introduced me to some of his girls at the track meet in Los Gatos. Confident that they knew about how much he loved USC, I asked if they were aware that O.J. Simpson ran track for the Trojans. The name O.J. perked up their interest. They said that they did. Then, with a serious tone, I asked, "Do you know that your coach still thinks that O.J. is innocent?" They cracked up. Marshall looked very embarrassed.

Now Marshall was dead. The list of friends dying continued, yet this one was different. I think my identification with him as one of my half mile training partners had something to do with this. And, per-

My USC and coaching friend, Marshall

haps, because it came while running? Marshall's sudden death made me aware that my life could end in seconds. I was not more fearful, just cognizant of my mortality. It had been some thirty-two years since that birthday in Istanbul when I woke up angry about being halfway through life. Marshall's death communicated to me that it could happen on any day.

My entrance into the Hall of Fame for Marin County high school athletics was unique because I used my time at the rostrum to introduce to the audience many of the top athletes I coached over twenty-six years. This meant that I spoke longer than most, but it was worth any criticism. Only a few of the great ones from Drake will ever be selected for this honor because the Athletic Foundation picks from all of the sports. Each year up to ten athletes and coaches are picked from football, basketball, baseball, track and field, swimming, etc.

At the induction ceremony on November 14, 2003, I concluded my acceptance speech with, "My coaching life is complete, but it is not over." The next morning my new little ninth grade "goddess," Katelyn Calvelli, won the league cross-country title.

It was a wonderful night for me. Long time friends Jim Smith, Herb West, Bob Griffith, Keith Conning, and Sid Wing were there with me. Jim flew all the way across the country from North Carolina to check out his old high school buddy.

The master of ceremonies did some research on me. And he had fun telling the audience stories, like my driving the tractor into the swimming pool. He even called Wes Santee. Wes told him of how, after the two of us received our awards for going one, two in the All-Marine 880 final at Quantico, General Pollock said to him, "Tell Taylor to get a hair cut."

A very tender moment came when I introduced Jerry Zieff. His disability is still obvious. As the lanky athlete of the past stood in humility, tears filled the eyes of those who knew him. Bob Griffith and Cory told me that his presence at the banquet was the highlight of the evening for them.

I spoke of how Sid Wing called me when he turned sixty-five and reported proudly that he had just run 400 meters in a time under his age. Like, sixty-four seconds! I told the audience how I responded with, "Never call me again," and hung up. This drew a great laugh.

After introducing Jess and Cory I remarked, "Jess got the running genes and Cory, the Emmy." You could hear people at the many tables reacting to the Emmy disclosure. But it was the excitement that the two of them generated when they arrived before the ceremony that leaves the most lasting impression on me. Their confidence, dress, and pride ignited my assembly of friends and supporters.

It was a lifetime evening with my track athletes!

As though they were beamed down from Mt. Olympus

When the USC national championship track teams reached their fiftieth anniversaries in 2004 and 2005, I was invited down to Los Angeles to be recognized as a member of those teams. The ceremonies were held during USC home track meets. The first time, the excitement grew for me when I arrived at the old practice track, which is today a small track stadium named for Dean Cromwell. The immortals emerged at the entrance gate. My hero on the '54 team, Jimmy Lea, was checking in at the reception table when I arrived. Two of my closest track friends, Ernie Shelton and Fernando Ledesma, showed up moments later. The mythological figures kept coming as though they were being beamed down from Mt. Olympus. And I was one of them!

When the announcer introduced the 1954 team, he told the crowd how I had beaten the "world class" Lon Spurrier and that I had been the cross-country captain. When he gave me credit for placing "third" in the Pacific Coast Conference 880 final, I told the current USC head coach, Ron Allice, who was greeting us at the bottom of the ramp, that I was actually fourth. Ron offered, "You just moved up a place."

Both years were joyful occasions for me. The 2005 gathering had a somewhat different cast of characters; Sid Wing, Ron Morris, and other track friends showed up. Some of our teammates were dead: Max Truex, Des Koch, Mike Larrabee, and Marshall Clark.

Cory suggested that we drive the short distance over to the Coliseum after the 2004 reception. I walked over to a familiar wire fence and looked across the stadium to the womb of my track existence, the tunnel. I remember standing outside that fence when I was twelve or so, unable to gain entrance to the USC vs. Notre Dame football game.

I noticed that Cory was filming me at that moment, some thirty yards from the caldron that holds the Olympic flame. I had just been introduced as a part of a USC national title team. And in view, by imagination, was the frightened little boy as he ran toward his father. An enormous flood of emotions packed into those few seconds. I was proud of what I had done with my dreams.

Iran

People were concerned about our going to Iran. And in Iran we were asked, "Aren't you afraid?" Some of them thought we were taking a big risk. But going through customs turned out to be casual.

The traffic in Teheran was horrible; the lengthy journey through the country, spectacular. Iran offered incredible colors by desert and mountains, and by those absolutely beautiful mosaics. I had never been overwhelmed by the beauty of mosaics before, but I had never been to Esfahan. On our 38th wedding anniversary, Trish and I rode in a carriage around fountains surrounded by this Persian splendor.

I asked that the set itinerary be changed by the Iranian travel company so that we could see ancient Susa near the Iraq border. Xerxes left Susa to attack Greece in 480 B.C. Aeschylus placed his play, *The Persians*, in Susa, even though he fought the Persians in view of Athens.

How close was Baghdad? Just several clouds to the west. Actually, about 200 miles. But the border with Iraq was only twenty or so miles away. That is all I needed to visualize the American war by my proximity to it.

In a village extending back to 300 A.D., I witnessed tumbling pigeons doing flips against a pure blue sky. We were on the high desert in central Iran, Afghanistan to the east, Pakistan just south. Bin Laden was over there.

I discovered by chance on television a Moslem woman receiving the Nobel Peace Prize when we arrived back in Teheran. The award presentation was broadcast live from Oslo, Norway. In her acceptance speech this Iranian woman, Shirin Ebadi, challenged the rigid and vindictive religious clerics on human rights. And she was extremely critical of the American invasion of Iraq. While praising Cyrus the Great for his religious tolerance during his empire, Ms. Ebadi, a lawyer, told the Nobel gathering that America was violating international law in Iraq.

We had seen the sixth century B.C. tomb of Cyrus on the barren landscape of central Iran only a few days before. It rests by itself on a desert plain. Due to it being winter, there were snow covered mountains surrounding the site. The air was crisp, the sky blue. There was no fence around the tomb. Nothing close by. It is just out there!

Greece and family

BEFORE THE 2004 Olympics in Greece we came together once again as a family, for the first time in a quarter of a century. Trish, Jess, Cory, Julie, Liam, and I spent three gratifying weeks on the island of Odysseus. Jess, Cory, and I stayed over in Greece for ten more days after we left Ithaca for the Olympic track and field events in Athens.

I was asked to cover the Olympics for the *Marin Independent Journal*. The editor stressed that I make my articles personal. He wanted me to tell the readers about my many trips to Greece with my family and with my Arête students. The paper ran two lengthy articles with photographs. One picture shows Jess, Cory, and I displaying our sacramental flea market meal of *souvlaki*, the type of tasty Greek sandwich that we ate at the same location thirty years before.

Telemachus went in search of his father, Odysseus, when he came of age. Perhaps he embarked from the very cove where I suddenly thought of my father. I was floating in that precious water below the village of Stavros on Ithaca when I remembered that my dad was considered a very strong swimmer. When I changed to the breaststroke, I thought of his strength as I was looking up the steep hill adorned with cypress climbing toward the village where "Athena" had removed my stitches seven years earlier.

Cory was seven when we first took him with us to Greece. Now he was back with his son. Liam was delightful. While at a taverna table by the harbor on the other side of the island, I had occasion to remember a Ray Bradbury story. Liam had asked me for something. I handed it to him with, "Here you are, you little shit." Bradbury had admired W. C. Fields when he was a boy. One time when he asked the sarcastic comedian for his autograph, W. C. Fields scribbled it on a piece of paper with, "Here you are, you little shit." Liam, all of four, announced to anyone within hearing range of the taverna, "Grandpa called me a little shit." The next morning while he was holding my hand as we

Bill, Jess, and Cory

walked along the harbor at the cove, Liam asked, "Grandpa, will you call me a little shit again?"

After that wonderful time on the Greek island, I still had the 2004 Olympics to look forward to with Jess and Cory. For nine nights, we shared a room out at Marathon Beach. One afternoon, before the evening Olympic track events began, we took the metro into Athens. Suddenly Jess announced, "We are going through the agora." I looked out a car window and as we raced by the stoa of the chief archon, I saw the oath stone where Socrates likely stood when he was charged with corrupting the youth of the city. How wonderful to know Greek geography so well.

There was a soft summer breeze that afternoon in Athens. Green leaves below the temple of the smith god, Hephaestus, casually fluttered and shaded our outdoor table as we had a drink, ate dinner. Under our table was the ancient way to the Acropolis, unknown to the thousands of people who walk over it today. In ancient times, runners would light a torch from the altar of knowledge at Plato's Academy, then run about 800 meters to the agora, the same distance I covered when I raced. To win the competition, the runners had to keep the flame of knowledge burning.

While the Olympic track events were exciting—especially because they were held in Athens—it was my time with Jess and Cory that was the most rewarding. It was as though we were back in our home when they were young, the two brothers both playful and serious with one another. On the final night of the track and field competition, I stood with my sons and looked into the Olympic flame. The fire was captivating, deep in color. No conclusion. No ending. Just the brilliant moment of existence—complete, incomplete, engaging, separate, powerful. The flame held my stare.

APPENDIX

Running with History

(1) A machine gun was pointed at us as I ran stride for stride with my son Jess alongside the Berlin Wall. Bouquets decorated printed epitaphs of death that marked where East Germans had died trying to reach the West. As we approached the passageway between East and West Berlin at Checkpoint Charlie, our pace was free and quick, stimulated by the excitement of our location. Jess had become a fast high school miler. Suddenly we found ourselves right in-between the East German customs shack and the much photographed Checkpoint Charlie hut of the West. I could almost feel the machine gun bullets tearing into my back at any second. Jess told me later that one guard in a tower kept a machine gun trained on us the whole way. If you ever saw, or read, *The Spy Who Came In From The Cold* you will have a good idea of the kind of intensity I was feeling as I wondered if rounds from the East German gun would rip open my flesh. We exited Checkpoint Charlie without incident.

(2) Suddenly I felt the presence of Zarathustra. It was a soft, tranquil afternoon in beautiful Sils Maria. I was running alone alongside a fresh flowing stream in the Alpine forest above Nietzsche's boarding house. As I looked over my shoulder it seemed that he was in the shadows of the pine trees. A tall hat was pulled down over a portion of his face; a cape was hanging off one shoulder. As I escaped down the trail into a colorful meadow of wildflowers, I received a piercing commandment from the Alpine warrior—"Go even deeper into yourself; go all the way." It was a chilling, personal message. I was mindful that

Freud once said that nobody had gone more deeply into themselves than Nietzsche.

(3) I looked over to where the Gestapo headquarters had stood as I began my run around the Ring of Vienna in a light drizzle. It told of Eichmann and his administrative offices in the city, the carefully arranged transportation system utilizing train tracks to Auschwitz. My next confrontation with history required that I take a slight detour to 19 Berggasse where Freud practiced psychoanalysis for over forty years. I jogged in front of the two story flat, grateful for what the man had given to me through his endless probing of the human mind. Back on the Ring I went past the great University of Vienna, and the Berg Theatre where the busts of a couple of hometown musicians, Mozart and Beethoven, were displayed on a frieze high up on the cream colored building. Then came the Rathhaus, a sturdy Gothic structure of city government. Another brief detour, only one short block, took me to the door of the place where Freud initially practiced psychiatry on the road to psychoanalysis. Back on the Ring, Athena looked out of place in a gaudy way, standing over smaller statues of philosophers lining the drive to the entrance of the Parliament. I then crossed the Ring and ran under the ominous balcony where Hitler stood in 1938 when he returned in glory to the city that had rejected him. Some 200 meters further along the Ring is the opera house where the Führer waited for standing room tickets in order to see and hear his beloved Wagnerian operas. When I returned to the hotel through an old entrance to the city, I checked my watch. My run had taken thirty-one minutes. I doubted that anyone on Earth had spent a more interesting half-an-hour.

(4) On a hot afternoon in Rome, my run took me down the Tiber under the shade of heavily foliaged trees. Away from the river, I looked up to a balcony in the Piazza Venezia from where Mussolini had excited the mobs. And Michelangelo died only fifty or so meters below that balcony in his studio. To my right stood the ancient Forum, where Julius Caesar's body was burned after he was stabbed up the river in

the Theatre of Pompeii. Slowing my pace, I visualized the triumphant march of the generals on the Sacred Way as they approached their climb up to the Temple of Jupiter in order to sacrifice to the god for their successful campaigns. At the Coliseum I swung right, past the Arch of Constantine. Then it was another right and a run up the lengthy Circus Maximus under a penetrating sun. No chariot for me. Water? I never thought of my need for water; I was soaking up history. Then, instead of going back up the river to our hotel, I went up the ramp on the hill that allows one to look out over the Forum. I never made it to the top. A sharp pain hit from the back of my head, and then a second from the front left. I blacked out. When I regained consciousness I was seated beneath an Egyptian column in a city unfamiliar to me. I was dirty. Some blood was on my elbow and my prescription glasses were absent. I went into a hotel and asked, "Where am I in Europe?" Oh, Rome! I asked for a hotel list. Fortunately, Trisha and I were staying at the San Rafael, which is also the name of the town in my county. This helped my fuzzy memory. Trisha picked me up in a cab a short time later; back in our hotel room, she dumped me into a tub with ice. I had traveled about half a mile through the late afternoon commute traffic in Rome without being conscious. My doctor guessed that it was the lack of liquids in my system. I will never know the route I walked or jogged from the hill of Jupiter to the Egyptian column just 100 yards or so from the Piazza Colonna.

(5) We were jogging along on the final lap of a casual mile run when, suddenly, my 14-year-old son took off and I realized that I wasn't going to be able to catch him. We were in Athens in the 1896 Olympic Stadium. I was thrilled—my son was going to be a runner. He would compete in my old sport. As I rounded the final turn at the open end of the stadium, I looked over to the Acropolis, toward the Theatre of Dionysus below the Parthenon—the place *Oedipus Rex* had been performed for the first time in history. Smiling over the son surpassing the father, I followed Jess to the finish.

(6) I was not conscious that it was Christmas Eve when I ran out

through the gate of the medieval city of Fez, Morocco. A narrow path took me up through a Moslem cemetery to a ridge that overlooked the eerie medina. Passing through the undecorated graves, I came upon a shepherd with his crook and sheep and noticed a lone star to the east. It hit me—it was Christmas Eve and Bethlehem was over there under that star! Years before, when I was a boy, the Hager side of my family would gather on Christmas Eve, and sometimes have me sing. Above the medina in Fez I remembered singing, "It came upon a midnight clear, that wondrous song of old..." A few minutes later, I flew down the trail and through that medieval gate to the Palais Jamai hotel with a very energetic stride.

(7) Egyptian soldiers in black jumpsuits were all over the tourist site with their machine guns. Nobody seemed concerned, however, when I began my run around the Great Pyramid. It was nighttime. A tall lad with a big smile joined me, running alongside in his slacks and street shoes. When he indicated he wanted to know where I was from, I had no desire to say, "The United States." Terrorists had attacked two European airports just one week before Trish and I flew to Egypt. The young man persisted in signaling that he wanted to know where I was from. When I finally told him, "California," he immediately began shouting, "Michael Jackson! Michael Jackson!" as we ran together below a pyramid that was constructed almost five thousand years before. Oh well!

(8) I began my run around the walls of Jerusalem before six in the morning. I wanted to circle the ancient city before I would call attention to myself. I passed the Garden of Gethsemane, filled with the words of Jesus. "Where can the son of man place his head?" That is one strong existential question! As I passed by the Lion's Gate, where a Stephen was stoned to death, I thought back to when I was driven out of the ministry from St. Stephen in Fort Worth. As I ran up a slight grade I could see the morning sun touching a portion of the golden Dome of the Rock with unusual splendor. I pictured what was across and below the notorious platform: the wall of tears where Jews cry over the loss

of their temple.

After the road took me past the City of David, I reached the busy street below the King David Hotel. Next up was the Jaffa Gate, where I had read that Jews were blown up at the nearby bus stop, or picked off by sniper bullets during the endless battle for Jerusalem. By the time I had circled the entire city of ancient Jerusalem, the traffic was well into the day. At the Damascus Gate an older Moslem man stared at me with what I felt was hate. I was running in my shorts in their city. At the intersection in front of the Damascus Gate, a jeep was parked; inside it were young Israeli soldiers resting their weapons on their laps. As I ran past them I looked down into the brown eyes of a handsome young chap. His face told of a certain amazement, or amusement, like, "What in the hell are you doing, old man? Why are you running through East Jerusalem in your shorts?"

(9) When I approached some bright lights and saw workers moving crates outside of a warehouse, a man in civilian clothes came toward me dangling a light machine gun. Patricia and I were in El Oued, Algeria, where temperatures can reach 140 degrees in the summer. It was the winter of 1990 and I was running at night. I showed the man my hotel key and tried to tell him that I was headed out to locate a desert road in order to find some dirt to run on. It was immediately clear that I was to turn around and head back to the hotel. Algeria was only a few weeks from its horrible, lengthy, civil war. I found a strip of dirt in front of the hotel that allowed for some fast strides. Animals pulled carts past me as I ran, women walked by with their faces covered. A young boy joined me. After a few quick strides, he asked me by finger language, *How many more*? When I held up four fingers he quit and sat down on the hotel steps to watch me. I finished my four feeling rather fast that night. Stimulated, of course, by where I was and what had happened shortly before. When I went through the lobby I told the young night manager at the desk that the lad sitting on the steps was going to be the next Noureddine Morceli. At that time, Morceli, an Algerian, held the world record for the mile and was a national hero. The hotel night manager said, "No. *You* are the champion."

(10) I walked out of our cabin door and onto the wooden deck of the Sea Cloud and found us anchored only one hundred yards away from the holy Greek island of Delos. The sea was glittering under the early morning sun. No tourists had arrived from Mykonos yet. My friend Dr. Miller, an archaeologist, was able to arrange for us to enter before the summer crowd arrived by sea. And so we had the island of Apollo and Artemis to ourselves. Just inside the entrance, Steve began to lecture and I went off on my run. A large green lizard was on the back of one of those much photographed marble lions, and when he looked up at me it seemed he could be thinking, "What the hell are you doing here at this hour?" I had the island to myself as I made my way up a narrow trail to the top of the hill that overlooked scattered ruins. The morning sea presented white caps as I looked off toward Mykonos, the playboy island of the Aegean. How is it that I got to run alone on the island where nobody in ancient times was allowed to give birth or die? Am I lucky, or am I lucky!

(11) One can feel rather lonely and cut off, running the streets of Hanoi in the dark. I approached the "Hanoi Hilton" remembering those American pilots who had spent years within its yellow walls. This run was in 1993, when Vietnam was just beginning to open up to U.S. travelers in their capital city. I had seen military guards at the entrances to the old Hilton from our van the day before. They were poised with machine guns, a memory which made me cautious about circling the compound by myself and eager to head back to where we were staying. I began this run before breakfast, before our tour group structured my day. Not many hours before, I had seen small caskets covered with American flags on the runway of the Hanoi airport. Body parts were being flown home. And just before landing, I witnessed those large, circular craters in the rice fields, evidence of our B-52 bombs from twenty years before. It was still dark as I ran around a little lake in front of our accommodations, looking down at women on the street heating soup in large pots. I ran through a mini-park named in honor of Lenin, where the Vietnamese were playing badminton and engaging in Tai Chi-type exercises under large light bulbs connected to wires attached

to an unclear source of energy. It was a quick run, but I saw how Hanoi begins a day and avoided the sea of bicycles that would soon weave gracefully in great numbers through the streets.

(12) A guard at a barrier would not let me go down the road to see the most admired profile on our planet. The famous Sphinx resides below the Great Pyramid in Egypt. When the guard became occupied with other travelers, I slipped by and jogged down to make contact with this king with a lion's body. The sun was just disappearing below the western horizon, offering a crimson red backdrop to the 4500-year-old work of art. I thought about how Freud so wanted to come to Egypt. Freud had kept many small Egyptian statues on his desk. As I looked up at the profile, continuing to jog in place, I felt that in a certain way I was seeing the Sphinx for Freud. For decades, psychoanalysis rode on the back of a sphinx: the one in Thebes, Greece; the play, *Oedipus Rex*; the controversial theory. Just as I began to run back up the ramp to the Great Pyramid, I noticed that I was wearing a T-shirt that depicted Freud smoking a cigar. How ironic; I did bring him to the Sphinx. My stride was fed with enormous energy as I ignored the Great Pyramid and ran back to tell Patricia of my thrilling run.

(13) Three tall black African women carrying baskets filled with greens on their heads laughed when they noticed me jogging up a hill below them. Each was long of stride, with uncompromising rhythm. White teeth flashed teasing smiles. How silly I must have looked to them in my shorts. We were on the Sahara, in the village of Timimoun in southwest Algeria. I had just run past a beautiful oasis with water running quietly through petite canals when the three Africans and I encountered one another. When I had first passed the oasis on at the start of this brief run, the great sun to the west absorbed me into its brilliant deep reds and oranges. I have never witnessed such a powerful sunset. The desert sand beyond the oasis was as smooth as glass. It was the desert a traveler wishes to see. After a shower I went to have a beer while Trish took some time for herself before dinner. At the bar in an old French fort I learned from two Algerian journalists that the

military government in Algiers had just cancelled the democratic elections because the fundamentalists had won too many seats in the parliament. This led within weeks to a civil war that murdered over one hundred thousand Algerians. The oasis, sunset, smooth desert sand, three tall women from a deeper Africa, the journalists at the bar in an old French fort; remain brilliant, lasting, vivid memories. I cannot think of a better reward for travel.

Eleven Personal Track Memories

World record in 1953 — 1:49.2
USC school record in 1953 — 1:52.2
American junior college record — 1:53.7
American high school record — 1:53.9

(1) On April 7th, 1954, two great Cal half milers, Spurrier and Wilson, came into the meet with the second and fifth fastest 880 times in the nation. Captain Spurrier was desperate to finally defeat a USC team. Cal took an early lead, scoring points in the javelin, going one-two in the mile, and winning the high hurdles in an upset. The Berkeley crowd was buzzing with excitement. I reacted to a slow pace in the 880 and took an unfamiliar lead after the first lap. Two blue uniforms appeared by my side as we faced a very long finishing stretch some 200 yards later. I kept them peripherally in view, staying relaxed, but gradually applying pressure by increasing the speed. Then there was only one blue uniform. A string was stretched out across the finish line. Did I touch it before Spurrier? An official walked up to me and said, "You won." My USC immortality was delivered in those words, because with my victory over Spurrier and Wilson, Cal lost any chance of defeating USC that afternoon.

(2) When I was in junior high school, I attended the famous Coliseum Relays, identifying with USC runners. At age 19 in 1953, I was on the track myself, anchoring my junior college sprint medley team in

the famous Coliseum Relays before a crowd of 40,000 people. I heard the stadium announcer say, "Here comes Taylor!" The world record for the half mile was 1:49.2. I ran it in 1:52:7, over six seconds faster than my fastest official half-mile time—it was a gift from the gods. Suddenly I was nationally ranked as a half miler. The next Monday, my coach, Jim Slosson, informed me that USC, the national championship team, had called to offer me a full track scholarship

(3) The 1952 junior college state finals took place on a cold, windy Saturday evening in Santa Rosa. Before we left the San Fernando Valley for the long drive north, I wasn't considered likely to place. I was only a year out of high school; only twelve months before, I had finished last in my L. A. City high school half-mile heat. Coming down the finishing stretch a year later I passed all but one runner, placing second in the final. The winner, Ed Wilson of Sacramento City College, finished only two-tenths of a second ahead of me.

(4) A very hot afternoon in Riverside turned into ideal half-mile weather for the twilight meet. Dave Casper, "the Ghost," was my junior college rival. That evening he set such a fast pace that we both came close to breaking the national junior college record. This was the night before the Coliseum Relays sprint medley race. I closed and closed on Casper—at the finish I was only two-tenths of a second behind him. Our times, 1:54.5 and 1:54.7, approached the existing junior college national half-mile record of 1:53.7 set by Olympian-to-be Jerome Walters, when he ran for Compton Junior College several years before.

(5) In 1956, My Quantico teammate, Wes Santee, the most famous track athlete in the country at the time, told me before the All-Marine 800-meter final that he was going to run the first lap of the two-lap race very, very fast—in "fifty flat." He told me to hold back, and to let him destroy a former Dartmouth star who would foolishly go out with him on the swift pace. This tactic actually left me in position to close on both of them. The former Ivy League runner was a wet noodle by the time I flew around him on the final turn. Then I closed on my

Olympian teammate, Santee. My time of 1:52.2 was a gift from Wes. Now that I look back, I see that it actually closed out my serious running life, for I would never train for a full track season again.

(6) Tonsillitis struck me down, ending my USC dream of winning or placing in the nationals. But only ten or so days before that happened, I reached my finest moment as a collegiate half miler. On my half-mile relay leg in the opening meet of the 1955 season at Westwood I was given the baton behind a UCLA runner. I flew past him on the backstretch of the second lap and opened up a lead of perhaps fifty yards. This was crucial because UCLA was anchored by Bobby Seaman, the one person at the time who people were forecasting could replace Santee as America's best miler. Teammates told me after that relay leg that they had never seen me run with such fluidity. The next week, Los Angleles sports writers nominated me, along with two Olympians-to-be—Rafer Johnson and Max Truex—as Track Athletes of the Week for the Southern California area. Not many days later tonsillitis struck and I never returned to this form.

(7) On a relay leg the year before, I became part of a USC school record distance medley team. At the 1954 Modesto Relays, I took us into first place on my half-mile stint with a 1:52.7 clocking. Later that night, due to a leg strain in one of our outstanding mile relay runners, I ran on a foursome that recorded a top national mark. Jimmy Lea of USC out-leaned two-time Olympic 800-meter champion Mal Whitfield at the tape. I ran my leg in 48.4; our team's dirt track clocking was 3:12.6, one of the better times in the country that season.

(8) Dave Casper and I were the lead junior college track and field story in the Los Angeles newspapers going into the 1953 California state final because we had approached the national record at Riverside. We both won our respective trial heats easily. In the final, Casper took it out quickly once again. I went after him on the backstretch of the second lap, closing the gap, but this time he waited for me. His coach, Hilmer Lodge, had instructed him to rest a bit before the final 100

yards. I came up within two or so yards, but could close no further. Thus, for the second year in a row, I missed winning the state by two-tenths of a second. Dave and I were both under the California junior college record.

(9) I received the baton well back in the pack in a distance medley at the 1954 Fresno Relays and, by the baton exchange, brought USC up into second. A record-setting Oklahoma A&M team was out in front. Nonetheless, my time was the fastest half-mile clocking of the field that night. This was later confirmed in *Track and Field News*, the authoritative "Bible" of the sport. Yet again, my USC dream of being a significant runner was affirmed. My excitement was encouraged when two former classmates at Valley Junior College raced over to me by the relay zone when I finished and were clearly ecstatic about my place in the track world.

(10) I had just finished a steak at the Santa Barbara Relays in 1953 when Coach Slosson rushed into the restaurant and said that the event schedule had been changed and I would be running in a few minutes. I was given the baton behind my arch rival, Dave Casper. When I came up on him going into the last turn I noticed that his left leg stepped off the track. "The Ghost" was struggling. One could hear the waves of the Pacific Ocean pounding across the sandy beach that separates the track from the waters. When we reached the finishing stretch I was able to easily go by him, recording the fastest time in the state for junior college half milers.

(11) The 1954 Pacific Coast Conference meet was held in Seattle where I was born. On the flight north, I had a bad cold. Fortunately there were no trial heats for the half mile. There was a drizzle, the track was heavy, and Spurrier made a foolish mistake by going out too quickly, hence bucking a very stiff wind coming off the lake. When we charged after the man who would break the world half-mile record the next season, he came back to us nicely. A veteran Washington State runner won, a two-time Canadian Olympian running for Oregon was

second, and I thought I had edged Spurrier for third. Even though I was only six-tenths of a second out of first place, my official finish was fourth. I am now very proud of this effort. You virtually could have spread a blanket over the four of us. But in Seattle that afternoon, feeling ill, I was terribly disappointed. Behind me by some distance was Ed Wilson of Cal, the victor two years before at the junior college state final in Santa Rosa. When Coach Mortensen of USC sent word that he needed me for the mile relay, I sent word back that I was too sick to run. I had to be really ill to pass up a gold medal in the Pacific Coast Conference final. The half-mile effort, while of courage, basically ended my junior year at USC. My legs did not come back over the next few weeks.

Map of Toluca Lake

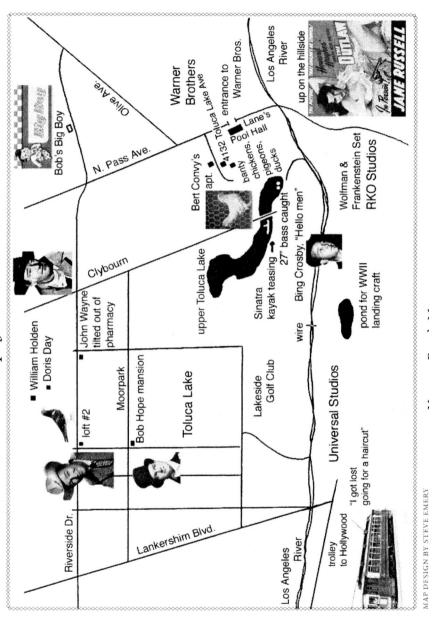

YOUNG BILL'S NEIGHBORHOOD